WHAT TO DO WITH

YOUR ENGLISH OR

COMMUNICATIONS

DEGREE

By Rachel Klein and Lisa Vollmer
and The Staff of The Princeton Review

PrincetonReview.com

What to Do with Your English or Communications Degree

By Rachel Klein and Lisa Vollmer
and The Staff of The Princeton Review

Random House, Inc.
New York

The Princeton Review, Inc.

2315 Broadway

New York, NY 10024

E-mail: bookeditor@review.com

ISBN 978-0-375-76624-4

Publisher: Robert Franek

Editors: Adrinda Kelly, Michael V. Palumbo

Designer and Production Manager: Scott Harris

Production Editor: Christine LaRubio

Printed in the United States of America.

9 8 7 6 5 4 3 2 1

2008 Edition

ABOUT THE AUTHORS

Rachel Klein, MS, NCC, is a career counselor at the University of California—Berkeley. A former English major and consummate word enthusiast, she has sought out practical and sometimes unusual applications for her love of rhetoric, and enthusiastically encourages others to do the same. You can visit her on the Web at: RightLivelihoods.blogspot.com.

Lisa Vollmer is a freelance writer and editor specializing in business, finance, and career-management topics. Drawing on her previous work experience in both investment banking and management consulting, she authored numerous career guides for San Francisco–based publisher WetFeet Press, including *Job Hunting in San Francisco* and *Beat the Street II: An Investment Banking Interview Practice Guide*. More recently, she has worked as a freelance journalist for the Stanford University Graduate School of Business and as a research editor at *Sunset* magazine in Menlo Park, California. She is a graduate of the University of Virginia.

ACKNOWLEDGMENTS

I am humbled by . . .

Elisabeth and Bob, whose words inform and encourage; Dr. Robert Chope, B. T., R. H. and J. C., Maestro, and the many friends and family whose words have provided both shelter and inspiration; Jennifer, whose words save lives.

—Rachel Klein

This book would not have been possible without the contributions of several members of the Book Publishing team here at The Princeton Review. Our wonderful publisher, Robert Franek, lent his support and expertise to the development of this book; our production dynamos, Christine LaRubio and Scott Harris, transformed the raw manuscript into the finished product now in your hands; and finally, Mike Palumbo, my talented co-editor, merits special thanks for the valuable input he provided along the way.

—Adrinda Kelly, Editor

CONTENTS

CHAPTER 1

What Will You Do with that Liberal Arts Degree in English or Communications?

INTRODUCTION

Have you ever been asked, "What are you going to do with your major?" Most college students find that this question is a standard conversation starter for everyone from your parents to landlords to the chatty person sitting next to you on the bus. Angst-provoking though such an inquiry may be for any student, liberal arts majors face a different kind of dilemma. With so many career pathways that are appropriate for you, how can you possibly know the one for which you're best suited?

English and communications are two of the most popular majors on any college campus, yet in response to the question of what they're going to do with their majors most students are liable to answer: "I don't know." Not knowing because you are still in the process of actively exploring different career options is one thing; not knowing because you are uncertain about what your skills are and where you can apply them is another. That's where we come in. This book is meant to do the following:

- Help you understand the market value of the skills you've developed as an English or communications major.

- Offer you tips for maximizing the value of your degree through experiential learning opportunities.

- Provide you with an overview of some of the careers and graduate school programs that make excellent use of your skills.

- Give you insider tips on how to deal with everything from fellowship applications to resumes to better networking strategies and advice on negotiating job offers.

English and communications degrees emphasize one of the most positive advantages of a postsecondary education: highly developed and adaptable communication skills. Like all liberal arts degrees, these programs teach students how to think analytically about the world around them. The study of each can contribute to professional success in a variety of fields, including some, which on the surface, may seem to have little to do with either discipline. It is this book's intention, however, to discuss options that would make *best* use of your degree in English or communications.

This book should help you come up with better answers to the ubiquitous question of "What are you going to do with your major?" and many others. Be sure to take the time to complete any chapter exercises and read the sidebars, where you're likely to find some of the most useful tips that each section has to offer.

Let's jump right in.

ENGLISH: MORE THAN JUST G.U.M.S. AND SIMILES

Anthropologists use the word "tribe" to describe a group of people bound together by common dialect, culture, and kinship. There are qualities which distinguish one tribe from another. Some of these qualities are superficially apparent (choice of clothing, cars, and iPod playlists), but there are many others that aren't as easily definable. If one were confronted with the challenge of identifying the typical college English major, what kinds of qualities would distinguish him or her from the masses?

The typical English major is imaginative and inquisitive. He or she is the student in class who isn't afraid to challenge the instructor with a new and interesting perspective on age-old "chicken or the egg"–style arguments. He or she can breezily draw sophisticated parallels between Shakespeare's lesser-known political plays and last night's episode of *The Sopranos*. English majors are also identifiable by their energetic participation in all manner of academic and social activities; these are the students flocking to cutting-edge classes or campus clubs. English majors tend to be visionaries who readily embrace new and provocative ideas. Psychologically attuned and verbally astute, typical English majors can make even outlandish proclamations appear not only logical but, in fact, brilliant and revolutionary!

The student with his or her face buried in a book between classes, after classes, and well into the wee hours of the morning is often an English major. True lovers of words in every form, English majors are fans of Scrabble and make vicious opponents. Better listeners than talkers, members of this tribe stand out because of their sensitivity, insightfulness, and keen ability to remain open and receptive to new ideas.

Famous English Major: Toni Morrison

Poet, playwright, and author, Toni Morrison won the Pulitzer Prize for her book *Beloved,* which was hailed by the *New York Times* as the best novel written in 25 years. She also received the 1993 Nobel Prize for her collected works. Born into a working-class family during the Great Depression, Toni read constantly and was an eager audience for her father, who told her folktales of the black community. Morrison earned a bachelor's degree in English from Howard University, then a master's degree from Cornell. It was during her tenure as a professor at Howard University that Morrison published her first book *The Bluest Eye* to somewhat lukewarm reviews. She was 39 years old, and the single mother of two children. With each successive novel, critics grew more fervent in their praise of Morrison's obvious talent. On the topic of writing, Morrison once said, "The ability of writers to imagine what is not the self, to familiarize the strange and mystify the familiar, is the test of their power."

WHAT YOU LEARNED AS AN ENGLISH MAJOR AND WHY IT MATTERS

You understand the social relevance of the Boxhill picnic episode in *Emma* and received praise from your professor for a shrewd analysis of how modern-day horror flicks constantly play on man's confrontation with his Jungian "shadow." Your vocabulary is already extensive and is becoming steadily more so. The carpet in your room is worn from the constant stream of friends and acquaintances who have learned that you know how to identify dangling modifiers and sentence fragments, and continually pop up in hopes that you'll have time to take a "quick look" at their papers. Clearly you possess some formidable skills. But what exactly are they? How can you translate these skills into resume-friendly terms, or describe your talents to a prospective employer?

Many of the skills you've developed as an English major are what are known in recruiting circles as "soft skills." Although this terminology often evokes unpleasant limp-noodle imagery, soft skills are often more sought after than "hard skills," which typify very specific types of knowledge (for example, familiarity with Adobe Photoshop). While the lack of a particular hard skill can bar you from getting a job, it's the soft skills that usually help you beat the competition, keep your position, and receive steady promotions. This is because hard skills can usually be taught with ease, while the most marketable soft skills, such as razor-sharp critical-thinking abilities, take years to hone. Here are some of the relevant skills you've developed as an English major and some of the easiest ways to market them.

Expert in the mechanics of language

You are able to identify pronouns, prepositions, and dangling participles, and if you aren't, you still probably have an excellent instinct about what "sounds wrong," and how to make it better. You also understand that if politicians don't use enough qualifiers in speeches, their arguments are going to seem weak, and that if they use too many, they'll come across as disingenuous. Understanding how to break a sentence down into microscopic components or how to better phrase a thesis statement is the net result of intense reading, analysis, and writing. English majors have a corner on this market, having been drilled mercilessly on everything from Neruda's poetry to Beckett's plays. Esoteric knowledge about authors and literary genres can certainly come in handy, but what you are really peddling is pure brain power. Let's say that you've been employed by a nonprofit organization as a grant-writer. You have to successfully persuade a private foundation to part with large sums of money to support your cause. Your expertise in the mechanics of language clues you into the fact that certain buzzwords are going to resonate more with foundation members, and that a clever use of imagery and metaphor may make your particular request stand out among countless others. Additionally, a well-crafted grant proposal with impeccable grammar and sentence structure is bound to convince a wary audience that your organization employs intelligent and competent people, worthy of being entrusted with the big bucks.

Famous English Major: Conan O'Brien

Late-night television show host Conan O'Brien says, "When life gives you lemons, make some kind of fruity juice." If fruity juice was the fuel that helped ignite O'Brien's career, then we should all be growing lemon trees. A former Emmy-award winning writer for *Saturday Night Live*, and producer for *The Simpsons*, O'Brien has been laughing his way to the top ever since his debut as a student writer for the *Harvard Lampoon*. It was at Harvard that O'Brien chose to major in English and history and has clearly continued to put his skills to test. As David Letterman's replacement on the cult-status late-night talk and variety show, O'Brien had to live up to some lofty expectations. After a few years of fumbling, *Late Night with Conan O'Brien* gained tremendous popularity. He and the *Late Night* staff have also been six-time recipients of the Writer's Guild Award.

Develop this skill! Taking your language skills out of the classroom

A high GPA and an honor's thesis in English may speak volumes about your command of the English language, but most employers would prefer to see how you used this skill in a non-academic setting. The following are some suggested low-key volunteer, internship, and work activities that will allow talented language architects to flex their chops:

- Offer to write, edit, and distribute promotional materials for a student organization. *Any* student organization. Keep track of how membership enrollment/event attendance/faculty sponsorship increases based on your efforts.

- Tutor English at your college's student learning center, or for a private household. Retain positive evaluations and make a note of any other "before-and-after" success stories that are particularly impressive.

- Nonprofits are always looking for smart, articulate folks to help them get the word out about their organization's mission and/or services. Visit Idealist.org or your campus career center's job listing site for volunteer or internship opportunities.

- Know a small business owner? Offer to develop written content for their website on a pro-bono or low-wage basis. If they're happy with the result, ask them to recommend you to other business owners for a reasonable fee.

- Volunteer or intern for a local music promotion company writing bios for their artists.

- Create your own blog or website where you can showcase articles that you've written (humor, interesting events in your community, reviews of movies or music). Make a note of how much traffic your website receives. Blogger.com or social networking sites like MySpace offer easy templates for technophobes.

What does this look like on a resume?

Let's say you ignore the advice to seek out experiential learning opportunities, and you are relying on academic experience alone to convince a potential employer that you are a language engineer par excellence. If you've been wise enough to hold onto papers and projects that would garner praise out of even the stodgiest academic, then you're in luck. Here's a sample of how you could present solely academic experience on a resumé:

Relevant Projects

"Poe's 'Ligeia' and the Birth of Glam Gothic" Term Paper English 216 Fall 2005

- Presented an analysis of how themes of perversion and romance set a precedent for the work of twentieth-century authors, notably Jorge Luis Borges.
- Researched Gothic short stories from the turn of the century to the present-day, and cited sources using standard ALA format.
- Received an "A" and the following praise from my professor: "This is the most well-crafted paper of its kind that I've seen in this class. Refreshingly free of grammatical errors."

An honor's thesis is always an impressive resume-builder, and, as in the example above, can be treated like a project for which you performed research, composed drafts, and edited a final copy (which was hopefully well received!). Again, remember to keep copies of your most prized papers; these belong in your portfolio and may come in handy if an employer wants to see an example of scholarly writing.

For those who have transported this skill out of the academic laboratory and into the work setting, here are some examples of the different ways in which you could present language skills on your resume:

Relevant Experience

Sales and Marketing Assistant Campus Repertory Theater Fall 2005–present

- Independently managed between 25 and 75 phone inquiries per day regarding ticket sales, current shows, and special membership programs.
- Wrote and edited promotional fliers intended to increase student interest in upcoming shows; saw a 15 percent increase in ticket sales to students while fliers were circulating.

Note: *Quantifiable evidence that your ability to write clearly and persuasively had a positive impact on a target audience is priceless.*

If you have managed to parlay your writing skills into several positions, you may consider presenting this information in a "Summary of Qualifications" or "Profile" section at the top of your resume:

Summary of Qualifications

- Well-developed writing and editing skills. Three years of experience editing student papers, writing a weekly opinion column, and creating brochures for student organizations.
- Fluent in spoken and written Spanish.

"Liberal arts students bring a variety of skills and experience that we find useful. Through delving into their area of interest, they demonstrate a high degree of intellectual curiosity, a trait which is crucial in learning the world of finance. Frequently they have a demonstrated ability to tackle an abstract question, take a position, and defend that position with rigorous reasoning and examples. Many liberal arts students have excellent communication and public speaking skills which we find valuable in both internal and client communication."

Jill Hitchcock, Recruiter and Group Vice President, Fisher Investments

Holistic thinking skills: How to identify synergies and make connections

The interpretation of literature requires a shrewd and sensitive intellect. Looking beyond the surface value of events, whether fictional or not, and understanding their historical and psychological significance is one of the skills that English majors develop. Holistic thinking abilities are sought after in every imaginable work setting. Consider the role of the physician: He or she must listen to a patient's analysis of their problem (sore throat), investigate all possible culprits (diet, exposure to an allergen or virus) and connect the dots to eliminate the symptom and address its underlying causes. One psychologist said that a major in English is the best preparation for therapists-in-training because each school of psychological thought and each patient's history is like the work of an author which must be translated properly.

Holistic thinking also teaches us that the whole is greater than the sum of its parts. In the workplace, this can translate into great leadership/managerial ability. English majors are particularly adept at identifying people's individual talents and assembling effective teams.

"In my opinion the most desirable quality for a new hire is the right attitude (after intelligence, good ethics, and an appealing or interesting personality, of course). The right attitude is equal parts enthusiasm, adaptability to changing circumstance, drive and ambition, maturity, and professional behavior (including decent manners), and, finally, creative abstract thinking."

Ember Martin, Financial Planner

Develop this skill! Taking your holistic thinking skills out of the classroom

The academic environment is probably the best training ground for deconstructors. Professors and doctoral students spend the better part of their career chipping away at the works of Camus, Proust, and Goethe (among others), and as a student you followed suit. Although the ability to identify coherent themes is useful in the work setting, heed the advice of one recruiter and former English major: "Liberal arts majors are great at analysis, but I really don't care if you can deconstruct a book in 15 different ways; I want to know what you can create!" The following are some activities that should help you make connections and synthesize information in a constructive (rather than deconstructive) way:

- Volunteer or intern as a research assistant for a writer or professor. These positions are usually abundant on student job-listing sites and will give you experience sifting through piles of online and print material in order to find information relevant to the project. Make sure to discuss any research outcomes on your resume.

- Work in peer-counseling or advising positions where you must listen to your client, analyze their problem, provide relevant facts and materials, and devise unique solutions.

- Act as a campus or community liaison for a student organization. For example, the community liaison for an English undergraduate association would be responsible for inviting local writers or professors as guest speakers, or developing a mentorship program.
- Coach a high school debate team.
- Teach an adult how to read. Volunteer literacy tutors must instruct their tutees on how to make connections and synthesize information, which in turn fortifies their own skills.

What does this look like on a resume?

Because the classroom is an ideal laboratory for making connections and synthesizing, academic experience is fairly easy to present. Here's an example:

Student Lectures   English 150, Senior Seminar   Fall 2005
- Researched and presented lectures on Alfred Edward Houseman and Lord Byron, describing their significance in Tom Stoppard's *The Invention of Love* and *Arcadia*.
- Received the highest grade in the class for a two-hour lecture on female characters in Tom Stoppard plays, notably his alignment with young Thomasina Coverly in *Arcadia*.

The level of preparation and insight required to present a well-received lecture to your peers is convincing proof of your ability to draw connections and identify synergies. When presenting these skills in a non-academic setting, be sure to focus on results. Below is an example:

Research Assistant
Undergraduate Research Apprenticeship Program   Fall 2006–Spring 2007
- Gathered data, read and reported information for a one-year research project on Chinese-American literary history.
- Produced and presented three individual reports on research findings that *helped my professor/supervisor define subfields within Chinese-American literature.*

The italicized portion above is a good example of a specific result. While research rarely yields such straightforward and satisfying conclusions, you can always describe the aim of the research study, and the gains in knowledge, however small.

Successful collaborations are the result of understanding that one community can enhance another, creating synergy. One of the best ways to demonstrate your ability to think holistically is by identifying and forging such relationships.

How to clarify complex material and synthesize information for the use of others

You didn't read piles of novels—and piles of criticism on those novels—for nothing. The ability to penetrate inscrutable themes and distill information so that even the most confused reader or listener can understand its significance is useful in any field, and particularly for would-be teachers, journalists, or attorneys. Talented educators know that their lectures will be received with less resistance when they are able to guide their students towards major themes and therefore the *significance* of a lecture topic; likewise, journalists can only succeed if they are able to present current events knowing that Joe Bloggs Public doesn't necessarily share their historical, cultural, and political knowledge.

English majors are natural interpreters. This may just be the *most* marketable skill that you possess, necessary in nearly every field, yet so rare. Lack of ability to communicate clearly is the demise of many employees, especially those who are required to give presentations or write for the public. When any employer says that they are looking for "communications skills" (the number-one soft skill that employers seek) what they mean is that they are looking for your ability to break industry mumbo-jumbo into digestible, but no less accurate, sound bytes for fellow employees or the public.

Develop this skill! Taking your interpretative skills out of the classroom

You've participated in numerous class discussions and secretly felt like a genius when your comments shed new light on a tired topic. Why not teach somebody else how to think critically and argue a point? Many internships and jobs for students involve some type of instruction; what better way to try your hand at translating complex information (and helping to teach others to do so)? Consider some of the following options for honing your interpretation skills:

- Interested in politics? Try a speech-writing internship or one with the state legislature, analyzing bills. By the time you're through, you'll be an expert at distinguishing jargon from substance.

- Technical writing/editing internships are comparable to translating text from a foreign language into English. Educational publishing houses often hire interns to edit textbooks in order to ensure that the information is clear and accurate.

- Volunteer for a program such as one of the Literacy Works projects, which place college students in local high schools to tutor students one-on-one to develop their critical thinking and writing abilities.

- Try an internship in public relations. Drafting press materials, media alerts, and pitch letters allows you to practice translating a company's products and services into consumer-friendly verbiage.

Famous English Major: Carol Browner

In 1997 Carole Browner, former head of the Environmental Protection Agency, received the "Mother of the Year" award administered by the National Mother's Day Committee. Although she is the mother of one son, she received the award because of her dedication to all children, through her many efforts to ensure that the food and water we eat and drink is clean and safe, and that our land is protected. Appointed by President Clinton, Browner had a long history of activism—dating back to her stint working with the now-defunct Citizen Action, a grassroots environmental and consumer organization. Born and raised in Florida, Browner attended a Dade County community college and completed her bachelor's degree in English at the University of Florida, where she also earned her law degree. Praised for her ability to deal with difficult issues such as wetlands protection and hazardous waste disposal, Browner enjoyed the longest tenure of any administrator for the Environmental Protection Agency.

What does this look like on a resume?

Try to get some hands-on experience with clarifying complex material. Although you are relying on this skill in the classroom everyday, there are ample opportunities for you to develop your communication abilities outside of the classroom, and employers would much prefer to read about your hands-on experiences. Here are some examples of how you can display this information on your resume:

Experience

Writing Project Tutor   Street Stories, SF   Aug 2005–May 2006

- Helped SFUSD middle school children conceptualize and write autobiographical stories.

- *Edited over 50 student stories, and guided students in improving the clarity and content of their stories in preparation for the yearly anthology.*

Young people's writing is imaginative, expansive, and often in need of focus— assisting students in finding their voice and improving their overall writing skills is one of the best ways to show that you can impose clarity on chaos. Here's a good rule of thumb for resumes: Try to quantify your work, whenever possible. The example above is strengthened by the student's assertion that he or she worked with over 50 student stories—a pretty impressive total. The example below demonstrates how this skill can be exhibited in a multitude of ways in one single position:

Development Intern   Homeless Action Center   Fall 2005–currently

- *Cowrote and edited grant applications,* soliciting local businesses, drafted brochures, and updated website.

- *Compiled research data on local homeless population into a two-page brief which was utilized in promotional materials.*

- *Wrote and presented a concise overview of HAC's services and internship program to a local university during their service learning orientation.*

This student's experience included research, oral presentations, and writing, all of which effectively demonstrate a keen ability to taper vast amounts of information down to a manageable size, without eclipsing core meaning or the organization's mission. This student's ability to properly represent and promote the organization is a skill that most employers are looking for. Excellent interpreters are often sought after to be the "faces and voices" of their employer. Try to seek out at least one experiential learning activity that requires you to present complex material regularly to small or large groups, as in the following example:

Not every college offers a program like De-Cal, which allows students to teach for-credit courses, but nearly every school's service learning center can set you up with opportunities to teach in your community. Contrary to the myth that teaching experience only prepares you for teaching careers, the ability to research, prepare, and effectively deliver lectures is a boon to almost any position. If you would prefer to instruct in a less conventional classroom environment, consider working as a public health intern, or joining your on-campus student leadership organization. Oftentimes, these settings allow you to give lectures or lead discussions on a broader array of topics.

On Joining a Student Organization: Interview with Lisa Caravello, Senior English Major, UC—Berkeley

Many students do not take advantage of the many student organizations on campus, which can be wonderful sources of information and great networking opportunities, but can also provide the opportunity to take on leadership roles which might otherwise be unavailable to them as a student.

Why did you decide to join the English Undergraduate Association at UCB, and how did you snag your current position?

When I heard an announcement about the EUA in one of my classes, I was glad that an active group of English majors was on campus. I also learned that all declared undergraduate English majors are automatically members. I wanted to meet other English majors so I started to attend the EUA weekly meetings. The meetings provided a fun and casual environment to meet other English students who could talk about books, classes, professors, and events going on in Berkeley. After a semester of participation in the group, I applied for an officer position and became the publicity officer and website editor for the 2004–2005 school year.

How has being an officer for EUA altered your perspective as an English major?

Being an officer for the EUA has allowed me to work with English majors, grad students, professors, and departmental staff. This has helped me stay current on departmental functions and events. I feel more connected to the department as an EUA officer.

What rewards have you reaped from this position?

My officer position has been very rewarding. I have met many fellow English majors whom I would not have met otherwise. I learned how to create and maintain a website for the group. I have also had first- and second-year English students come to me with questions about the major, and it is very rewarding to know that I helped them make decisions about their academic careers.

Do you have any advice for fellow English majors?

Join a club. Whether the group is academic or recreational, you will probably be glad you participated. At a large university like Berkeley (especially in the highly populated majors like English), it is really helpful to belong to a group.

Helicopter Parents: How to Deal

It's a bird! It's a plane! It's mom and dad, perennially hovering over your life and passive-aggressively attempting to control your every move. No matter where you go to seek refuge from your parents' anxious attention, they always seem to find a way to heap their unsolicited advice or demands on you. This can be especially frustrating when it comes to choosing a major and a future career path. Students who are pursuing careers or majors that may seem risky in terms of financial outlook are particularly vulnerable to tidal waves of parental neuroses. This phenomenon may sometimes manifest itself in the form of gentle or not-so-gentle directives ranging from "We're not sure that being an English major is the best choice for you" to "If you major in English, we'll stop paying tuition." The helicopter school of parenting has always existed, but has recently experienced a renaissance. Why? Students have never faced such difficult odds of being accepted to a top-tier school, and parents have grown accustomed to carting their children from soccer practice to capoeira lessons, academic decathlons to dance recitals, all in the name of being offered a coveted position at one of the world's greatest universities and securing a great job after graduation. Needless to say, your parents' handholding habit is a hard one to break. Not to mention the fact that most students are financially dependent on their parents, and with ever-increasing tuition fees, seeing Joe Jr. make the best use of his college education has become a major financial investment. Don't despair: There are some tried-and-true techniques for assuaging parental anxieties while happily pursuing your vocational dreams.

1. **Acknowledge that your parents have your best interests in mind.**

   Most parents are surprised by the notion that their well-intentioned comments have an adverse effect on your mental health. Before presenting any other arguments to them, make sure that you preface your statements with, "I realize that you care very much for me" or "I know that you want what's best for me." This sets a nice tone for any discussion; it'll appear that you care about being collaborative, and that you are also giving them the benefit of the doubt.

2. **Avoid getting emotional.**

   Nothing will sabotage a well-constructed speech faster than an emotional outburst. Whether this takes the form of door-slamming and stomping, tears and pleading, or silly proclamations such as "I am *too* the boss of me," any display that is driven more by pathos than logos will likely convince your parents that you are, in fact, too young and immature to make decisions for yourself. The more well prepared you are to present your argument, the less likely you are to lose your cool.

3. **Stick with the facts.**

   Because parents are most often concerned about the practicality of your choices, take the initiative by presenting them with facts and figures that support your point. For example, if you plan to major in English and pursue a career in broadcasting, check your college career center's website for any statistics about graduating students or alumni in that major. If there are several students who are employed in broadcasting, cite those examples. Visit trade websites and print out information on internship opportunities and entry-level positions. If your parents aren't aware of the ins and outs of a particular profession, such literature can help keep doubts and concerns at bay. Remember to choose facts that don't backfire on you! Salary range information can be particularly alarming, as most entry-level positions in nearly any industry aren't terribly impressive.

4. **Offer them a road map.**

   Sure, you don't know exactly what you'll be doing in a month, let alone two semesters from now. But by committing some goals to paper you'll be able to show your parents that you have considered the various options available to you, and that you are making their money count for more than just the academic side of your college experience. Additionally, your map will show them how your future goals build on immediate goals, eventually bringing you to a satisfying outcome. It is likely that your map will undergo a facelift more than once during your college experience, but the exercise of setting short- and long-term goals is positive both for you and the well-intentioned parental units who love and worry about you.

5. **Invite them to participate.**

   If your parents never attended college, or find themselves worrying excessively about the ramifications of your choices, invite them to join you during a visit to your college career center. Nearly every career counselor is open to family appointments, and this gesture will show them that you not only appreciate their input, but that you welcome their active participation in your life. Career counselors can be particularly helpful at mediating parent/caretaker/student disputes about major and career choice, especially when it comes to generating alternative options that will satisfy all parties.

COMMUNICATIONS: TRAILBLAZERS AND TRANSFORMERS

Considering that communications is one of the top ten most popular college majors, defining the "typical" communications major is a challenge. Although this population of students is as diverse as the major itself, there are some qualities that bond these gifted gabbers together. Not surprisingly, communications majors are fascinated with all forms of media—they are the students sitting in your 8:00 A.M. class who already know the breaking news, and actually own subscriptions to a national newspaper. Exceptionally personable, communications majors are also great conversationalists and are likely to trade banter with just about anyone, and because they're also usually attractive and energetic personalities, most people are happy to engage. Communications majors enjoy staying connected to others and sharing their views, and many have personal web pages. Driven by their insatiable curiosity, they also ask a lot of questions. Perhaps it's a consequence of being so aware of what is going on in the world around them, but communications majors are very accustomed to thinking outside of the box, and openly reject the status quo. Not surprisingly, they often prefer MACs to PCs, and are the first to buy all of the latest technical gadgets—any tool that helps them access and share information faster.

What you learned as a communications major and why it matters

You have an uncanny ability to predict future trends in everything from sports to architecture to technology, and you have yet to meet a person with whom you couldn't develop near-instantaneous rapport; in fact, you have yet to find yourself at a loss for topics to discuss ad infinitum. Your website gets more visitors than the Eiffel Tower, and you're thinking about hiring somebody to manage your social calendar. Nobody wants to watch *Jeopardy* with you because you know something about everything. Even without the word "information" tattooed neatly across your forehead, everybody else seems to know that you're in the know. But how do you define your skills and present them to employers?

Famous Communications Majors: James Gandolfini

Best known for his role as Tony Soprano on the HBO series *The Sopranos*, James Gandolfini has garnered critical praise for his acting skill, including three Emmy Awards. Gandolfini attended Rutgers University where he chose to major in communications before pursuing acting roles on Broadway. He also purportedly worked as a bouncer and DJ at a New Jersey club, before pursuing a career in acting at the urging of one of his close friends.

Expert understanding of all media forms

The presence of the media is pervasive, and its influence on our lives is undeniable. Driving to and from work we listen to talk radio, and when we arrive at work we often grab a copy of the local newspaper or tinker around on the web while drinking our morning coffee. When we return home, most of us drop our bags and reach for the remote. What we buy, what we eat, the movies we watch, and the political views we subscribe to are often directly linked to the ubiquitous media. As a communications major, you've learned how to analyze and think critically about different forms of media and are keenly aware of the underlying messages therein. You also know exactly how the various forms of media are used to reach different audiences to inspire, persuade, repel, or stun. Given that we live in the information age and are always in dire need of ethical, well-informed media navigators, expertise in this area is a tremendously marketable skill.

Develop this skill! Taking your media savvy out of the classroom

There are so many ways for you to develop an understanding of the media outside of the classroom that your only problem will be deciding on the form of media that most intrigues you. Be warned, however: Students across the board have tremendous interest in communications internships (especially those offering appealing on-air types of opportunities) so the competition can be fierce.

Here are some suggestions for possible extracurricular activities that can complement what you've learned in the classroom:

- **Seek an internship at your local network television station.** Most internships will be focused on areas of promotions and marketing, community affairs, design, or sports. Expect to spend your time researching topics, booking guests, producing scripts, or writing and editing highlight tapes.

- **Check out the internship opportunities at your college radio station.** If you want to be an on-air presence in the future, college radio gives you the chance to (occasionally or regularly) host your own show, play the music you like, and interview the guests you invite on air.

- **Work for your college newspaper.** This is the perfect environment for you to get your start in copyediting, reporting, or layout and design of print media. These positions seriously boost your chances of snagging an internship at a local or national paper later on.

- **Seek out on-campus media relations internships and jobs,** especially with non-academic departments or offices such as Resident Life, the Student Learning Center, or the Career Center. Many of these offices hire student interns or work-study students to help with marketing efforts.

- **Lead marketing initiatives for the extracurricular organizations you belong to.** There would be no student attendance at meetings, and no campus liaisons for student organizations without the efforts of at least one member who is in charge of promoting the group. If your organization doesn't have a marketing or promotions officer, elect yourself to this position. Depending on your skill set, you could become a webmaster for your organization's website or talk your way into an advertising spot on the campus radio station. Make sure that you carefully record the tangible outcomes of your efforts, whether that means spikes in club membership, increased attendance at sponsored events, or more visibility for your group on and off campus.

- **Land a job as a campus representative for a media company.** Companies like Apple or Vault hire campus representatives. These positions are paid, and provide you with an introduction to direct and indirect marketing strategies, from mass mailings to career-fair tabling.

What does this look like on a resume?

If you are relying solely on your academic experience to display your understanding of media, consider a few possible methods:

Objective

Assistant marketing coordinator, Iris Independent Films

Relevant Course work

Integrated Marketing Communication; Ethnographic Film, Race and American Film; Political Sociology; Chicano/Latino Film; Movie Criticism and its Cultural Context.

This student is applying for an entry-level position with a small (and, for the purpose of this exercise, fictitious) film production company that mostly produces films about race relations in America. Although the student has no film industry experience, by displaying her relevant course work this student has shown that she understands the kinds of films the company produces, and has demonstrated that she has at least a theoretical knowledge of film criticism, politics and the media, representations of race in film, and marketing communications.

Or, try this approach:

Media Projects: **Mass Communications 220**   **Fall 2006**

Conducted an experiment to see if brand influence matched brand recognition among diet soda consumers. Major brand diet soda was preferred even during a blind taste test. Authentic flavor was deemed to be the leading reason.

This student's academic project involved research, analysis, and a savvy understanding of media influence, and even discusses the project outcomes.

Here's a straightforward example of how to display media savvy in a non-academic context:

Student Representative   Campus Health Center   Fall 2005–present

- Acted as the student spokesperson for the Campus Health Center during freshman welcome week, addressing an audience of over 800 students and their families.

- Promoted campus health center services through mass mailings, flyer campaigns, and promotional advertisements in the campus newspaper. Increased health workshops attendance by 35 percent in a single semester.

- Fielded questions, suggestions, and complaints through the health center website and telephone hotline. Made improvements based on feedback. Supervisor called the resulting changes to the website "invaluable."

Again, this student focused on demonstrating the *results* of her efforts as a student rep for a campus department. Showing that you understand how to reach a target audience and how to generate interest in your product or services is excellent fodder for your resume.

Accomplishment stories: Giving employers evidence

Think of an experience that you feel proud of. It can be anything—it doesn't need to be related to jobs or careers. Scan your work as a volunteer, a friend, or a member of a team. Sometimes the best accomplishment stories start out as your worst nightmares. (Like that time the student club treasurer quit right before the big fund-raiser dinner and you were left holding the bag in the middle of midterms.) Jot down some thoughts in response to these questions. You'll be well on your way to crafting your own accomplishment stories.

1. Describe the experience.

2. What led up to it?

3. What did you do?

4. Why did you undertake this experience?

5. Why did you select it as one of your accomplishments?

6. Why did it give you satisfaction?

How to do Page Layout, Page Design, and Web Building

The Alphabet of Manliness, a book by George Ouzounian, a satirist better known by his fans as "Maddox," recently hit the *New York Times* bestseller list. George isn't a writer for a well-known periodical—he's famous for his website, "The Best Page in the Universe." Personal web pages have become a powerful vehicle whereby ordinary people can express their views, showcase their writing or other creative endeavors, and (let's be honest) exert their influence over the eager masses. Browsing MySpace and Facebook has become a regular practice for employers who are seeking more intimate information about potential employees.

Communications majors are already aware that the internet may just be the most accessible form of media to date, and usually have a basic knowledge of web page design. The market value of this skill is obvious. The ability to create a website compelling enough to attract numerous visitors means that people may just be listening to whatever it is you have to say; this is the main goal of any successful media campaign. It's also a means to interact with people with whom contact was previously impossible. Anyone who has the skills to dissolve the boundaries between service providers and potential consumers will be of interest to any employer.

Famous Communication Majors: Spike Lee

Those who aren't familiar with Spike Lee's critically acclaimed films *Do the Right Thing, Mo Better Blues, Malcolm X,* and others, are probably familiar with the controversy that his name arouses. Outspoken about race relations in America (a theme which informs most of his film plots) Lee has been a pioneer in challenging the status quo by attempting to ensure that Americans don't just turn a blind eye to injustice. His comments about the government's lethargic response to the Hurricane Katrina crisis unveiled some unsavory facts about racial discrepancy, government conspiracies, and plain old-fashioned ignorance. Born in Atlanta and raised in Brooklyn, Lee decided to attend his family's alma mater, Morehouse College, where he chose to major in mass communications. During a talk at a San Francisco conference in 1996, Lee cited the all-encompassing nature of mass communications as his reason for choosing the major. Although his primary medium of expression has been film, Lee has stepped out from behind the camera frequently to address the masses on talk shows and as a popular keynote speaker. He has also produced shows and segments for TV, and recently completed an HBO documentary entitled *When the Levees Broke,* about Hurricane Katrina.

Develop this skill! Taking your web design skills out of the classroom

Outside of taking courses in web design or critiquing online media, this skill isn't easy to present in an academic context. If you haven't already created a personal web page, you've probably thought about doing so, and developing a presence on the web is probably the best tool you can use to attract potential employers (so long as you carefully manage the content of your website.)

Here are some other examples of ways in which you can develop your web design and layout skills:

- **Become a webmaster for a campus organization.** The student organizations with the most attractive websites receive more visits, and therefore gain more recognition, sponsors, members, etc.

- **Create your own blog** on a website such as eBlogger.com, and write your daily, weekly, or monthly journal entries on topics relevant to your major. Point potential employers towards your blog to read samples of your writing, and to get a sense of your ability to think critically.

- **Volunteer your web design services.** Know somebody whose business could benefit from a new or improved web page? Offer to get their site started. If business picks up, give yourself some of the credit on your resume (and be sure to collect a glowing reference letter).

What does this look like on a resume?

If your experience with web design or layout is limited to a college course in Adobe Photoshop, Quark, or Dreamweaver, then display this information under the "skills" portion of your resume, like so:

Skills

Advanced course work in Quark, Adobe Photoshop, Dreamweaver, Microsoft Office, and Filemaker Pro.

Consider how much better this example would be if it was accompanied by an example of how the student actually used their web design skills. The example below is an expanded version of the student's resume, including extracurricular experience:

By quantifying the number of visits a website receives per year or the number of people the listserv reaches, the student has proven that his efforts (at least in part) have contributed to the success of their organization. In other words, their media campaign has been effective.

Before including a personal website or blog on your resume, use common sense about what information you want employers to see. Obviously, vulgar pictures or bawdy jokes, while appealing to some viewers, are going to give most prospective bosses the impression that you're immature and that you lack discretion. Here is a list of acceptable content for any website you intend to cite:

- An updated copy of your resume.
- A list of your publications (online, academic, print, etc.) The website could also include a copy of a research project of which you are particularly proud that was never published.
- Articles and reviews about relevant industry topics (less relevant information can be included, of course, as long as nothing would be considered truly defamatory).
- Links to other websites that you've helped develop, or consider relevant and interesting.
- Pictures of yourself that you could comfortably show your grandma, or images of any sort of creative work that you've done.

Here's the same student's resume including information about their personal website:

Objective

Media Planning Assistant, Ace Marketing

Skills

- Advanced course work in Quark, Adobe Photoshop, Dreamweaver, Microsoft Office, and Filemaker Pro.
- Fluent in spoken and written Spanish.
- Honor's thesis received second highest grade in class.

Personal Website: www.johansmythe.com

- Developed and designed personal website that receives over 2,000 hits per month.
- Publish weekly blog on interactive media; mediate a live monthly forum for marketing students.
- Nominee for "best personal blog" by Top Blogs.

Relevant Experience

Webmaster   Undergraduate Marketing Association   Fall 2004–present

- Develop content for UMA's website, including layout, graphics, and links. The website receives more than 2,000 visits a semester, the second-highest number for a student organization.
- Update website on a weekly basis, including links to relevant campus events. Developed a mailing list which reaches 839 students every two weeks (a 25 percent increase year over year since becoming webmaster).

Now potential employers know a few things about this student. His websites get traffic, people like hearing what he has to say, and his efforts at gaining a broader audience yield results.

Public speaking and persuasion skills

Thousands of people flock to therapists every year and crowd the self-help aisles of their local bookstore in hopes of finding a cure for their phobia of public speaking. Sweaty palms, tremors, panic, pregnant pauses, and dry mouth are some of the physical and psychological symptoms associated with what many experts claim to be the number-one phobia in America. Whether you have to nail a panel interview, pitch a concept to your boss or coworkers, or deliver a keynote speech, strong public speaking skills are integral to your success. This means that the courses you've taken as a communications major in the fundamentals of speech may have given you an edge in an area which inspires feelings of terror in the majority of the population. You understand that research, practice, the effective use of visual aids, and knowledge of group dynamics can mean the difference between facing a room full of thumb-twiddlers or a room full of eager listeners. Because you've also studied ethical and socially responsible methods of persuasion, you may even be able to help mold the views of your audience and inspire them to think critically.

Top 10 Characteristics Employers Seek in Job Candidates

1. Communication Skills
2. Honesty/Integrity
3. Interpersonal Skills
4. Strong Work Ethic
5. Teamwork Skills
6. Analytical Skills
7. Motivation/Initiative
8. Flexibility/Adaptability
9. Computer Skills
10. Organizational Skills

Source: National Association of Colleges and Employers Job Outlook 2005 Survey

Develop this skill! Taking your public speaking skills out of the classroom

The spontaneous speech-making we see in films (the kind that is usually followed by slow claps that turn into standing ovations) may be inspirational, but rarely occur in the real world. As a communications major, you know that speechmaking is a carefully honed skill that requires patience and practice. So much practice, in fact, that speechwriting is a profession in and of itself. Sadly, you cannot cite that masterpiece of a monologue you performed for your professor about why your C paper deserves an A upgrade, Oscar-worthy though it may have been. Here are some activities that can help warm up your windpipes outside of the classroom:

- **Join your college forensics/speech and debate team.** The opportunity to compete in national debates about political, cultural, or technological issues is an ideal way to hone your oratory talent.

- **Lend your voice to minority student organizations.** Feel strongly about the issues facing LGBTQ or other underrepresented student populations? Your on-campus multicultural, LGBTQ, or women's center is almost always looking for outreach volunteers and interns. These positions often require you to represent the organization at campus functions or in classrooms. Your passion about an issue can make for some excellent oral presentations.

- **Become a peer tutor.** Tutoring or instruction of any kind, not surprisingly, is one of the best ways to develop your oral communications skills. Programs such as AmeriCorps offer plenty of opportunities for students.

- **Join a student leadership program.** Student leadership programs—usually found through your community learning center—offer many positions for those who want to learn to speak persuasively about an issue on campus.

- **Volunteer to host a social/fund-raising/community service event for a student organization.** This, of course, requires that you are a member of said organization.

Famous Communications Majors: Walter Cronkite

Famous as much for his career as a trusted and popular anchor for the CBS evening news as for his parting line of "And that's the way it is," Walter Cronkite's ability to deliver the breaking news in a fast, factually accurate, and interesting way earned him more supporters than any television anchorperson in the history of the profession. His coverage of the NASA space program earned him an "Ambassador of Space Exploration" award, an honor previously reserved for NASA scientists. He is most famous for his coverage of President Kennedy's assassination, the Apollo 11 moon landing, and the Cuban Missile Crisis. Cronkite attended the University of Texas in the 1930s, and although he never completed his bachelor's degree in communications (like a typical student of communications, he challenged the status quo) Cronkite taught for many years and chaired the communications department of his alma mater.

What does this look like on a resume?

Classes in speech, persuasion, communication for leaders, or similar subjects are an excellent way to become acquainted with the fundamentals of oral communication, and unlike other skill areas, can often stand on their own when it comes to resumes. The following is one example:

Oral Communication

Relevant Courses:

Communications 210, Fundamentals of Speech   **Fall 2006**

- In-depth study of communication strategies, research, group dynamics, and multimedia presentation techniques. Delivered two 20-minute speeches on sex education in elementary schools and on first-year attrition rates among Chicano/Latino students in community college.

Business 190, Communication for Leaders (elective)   **Spring 2007**

- Participated in numerous group activities and cultivated oral communication skills targeted for organizational settings. Presented multiple speeches on such topics as conflict resolution and motivation.

This student decided to take supplemental courses in speech, which indicates her abiding interest in developing her oral communication skills. Although general-education courses provide you with fundamental knowledge, elective classes are often smaller and therefore provide a friendlier environment for constructive feedback. Also, courses such as the one above are often taught by instructors who hold jobs outside of academia, making them well qualified to evaluate how your skills will be received in a non-academic setting.

Here's the same student resume showing relevant non-academic experience:

Relevant Experience:

Fund-raising Chair, Students for Ethical Communication
      Spring 2005-Present

- Coordinate and host two yearly fund-raising events, attended by over 150 students. Introduce guest speakers, and give presentations on SEC's "semester in review."
- Represent SEC by visiting freshman seminars and introducing SEC's mission; recruit 25–55 new members per semester.

Peer Advisor, Transfer and Outreach Center   **Spring 2007**

- Provide group and one-on-one advising services to students at local community colleges who plan to transfer to Acme U.
- Facilitate several Welcome Week "Welcome Transfers!" orientations, each attended by over 100 students. Present overview of TOC services and campus resources.

This student's resume tells her prospective employer(s) that she is capable of:

- Making presentations in front of individuals and both small and large groups.

- Adapting her style of delivery depending on whether she is lecturing or instructing.

- Communicating with different audiences (transfer students, fellow communications majors, corporations, or community organization leaders).

- Seeking out additional learning experiences that will further enrich her knowledge about speechmaking.

Analyzing qualitative and quantitative research

Focus groups, interviews, surveys, polling, statistical analysis . . . without research data, the marketing team can't identify its target audience, voters can't scrutinize a candidate's record, and reporters would have to rely solely on hearsay. Your knowledge of various social science research methods can be applied in a variety of contexts. Few majors require a foundational knowledge of research methods, and should you choose to pursue an academic career, you will find that your understanding of how research informs practice is an invaluable tool. Industry professionals, especially news analysts, those working in marketing and public relations, and political pundits also rely on their ability to collect and interpret data.

Develop this skill! Taking your research skills out of the classroom

The best way to enhance your own ability as a researcher is to snag an undergraduate research assistantship. These programs (found on nearly every college campus) allow you to join forces with a faculty member whose research interests align with your own. The research, for funding reasons, has to be performed on campus, but there is no easier way to benefit from the resources, expertise, and support available to you as a student while performing legitimate research for which you will be able to earn credit. Here are a few other ways to develop this skill:

- **Participate in focus groups.** There's no better way to learn about this ever-popular market research method than by being on the other side of the one-way mirror. You'll also earn some cash for your time. Websites such as Craigslist.org usually post plenty of local focus group opportunities.

- **Seek an internship with a consulting firm.** Many companies hire consultants to do market research and analysis to help them meet their business objectives, and they aren't just interested in business and economics majors—they're looking for brainy students who understand how to crunch numbers and translate their findings in layperson's terms.

- **Complete an independent research project.** Interested in studying intercultural communications in Japan, India, Germany, or another country? Try taking a semester abroad through the School for International Training (WorldLearning.org), where you'll be able to pursue independent research projects and field study opportunities in communications.

What does this look like on a resume?

This student's resume includes academic and relevant work experiences that display her research skills:

Objective
News Analyst internship

Relevant Qualifications:
- Campus research assistant for one year.
- Completed honor's thesis exploring how accurately breaking news is recounted on two popular internet news hubs.

Education:
- BA Communications, San Francisco State University. Expected date of graduation: May 2007.
- United States International University, Kenya, Media Studies and Communications, Summer 2006.

Research Experience:
Research Assistant, Communications Department, SFSU Fall 05–Spring 06
- Gathered and compiled data for research project on how social protests have been broadcast from the 1960s through the 1990s.
- Offered another research position for next year by faculty advisor, Dr. Polly Medea.

You do not need all of this experience to demonstrate your abilities as a researcher. Employers will be equally impressed with purely academic research experience (i.e., honor's thesis or class projects) as long as you present them with panache. Provide details! What was the nature of the project? How did you choose a research design? Did your research give rise to any new questions about the research topic?

COMMON GROUND

Curriculum aside, English and communications degrees help students develop some very similar skills. Although English majors aren't trained to be quite as tech-savvy, and communications majors aren't trained to write on cue, both are prepared for careers that involve a lot of research, analysis, and historical perspective. Below is a chart showing the skills that are specifically acquired in each major, as well as common skill areas:

Figure 1.1

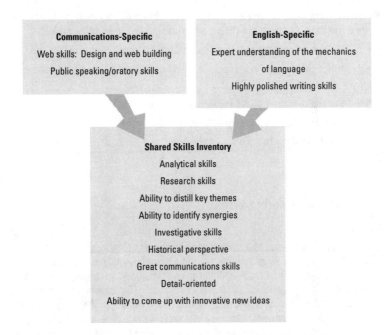

Communications-Specific
Web skills: Design and web building
Public speaking/oratory skills

English-Specific
Expert understanding of the mechanics of language
Highly polished writing skills

Shared Skills Inventory
Analytical skills
Research skills
Ability to distill key themes
Ability to identify synergies
Investigative skills
Historical perspective
Great communications skills
Detail-oriented
Ability to come up with innovative new ideas

Who cares?

Because you are competing for many of the same positions, it's important to understand which unique skills you've developed in your major, and which ones you have in common. By no means do communications majors have writing skills inferior to those of every English major, and many English majors are just as capable of developing a flashy website as their communication-major counterparts. But if you are hoping to snatch a position based solely on the skills you've developed in school, most employers are going to perceive you according to the textbook definitions of those majors—that those studying communications are interested in all kinds of media, and are chatty, and that English majors are shyer, more bookish, and mostly interested in writing. Is this yet another shameless attempt to urge you to find internships, volunteer positions, and jobs? Perhaps. Whether or not stereotypes of majors are justified, they persist, and internship and extracurricular experience can certainly make you appear more multidimensional.

Hopefully this chapter has helped you define some of the skills you've developed in your major, and you have a better understanding of how they can be further developed and marketed. Now you are ready for the two-minute sound bite. What on earth are we talking about? Once you understand your particular value in the job market, you can articulate your abilities to friends, relatives, total strangers, and, most importantly, the people who may want to hire you—most of whom will decide whether or not to do so in 2 minutes or less.

Rather than standing around and clearing your throat at your next job interview or college career fair, consider practicing a two-minute sound bite that covers

- Why you are interested in that particular employer and job.
- Why you chose your major, and what skills you've developed in that major.
- Any special awards or honors you've received.
- A brief overview of relevant work experience.
- Other exciting facts about you.

Anatomy of a sound bite:

English major

"I was excited to see that your organization was going to be at this career fair—I've been reading about your latest community outreach efforts, and I was really impressed that in addition to the resources you already provide, you're also giving something back to the community. **[Explains why she is interested in this company, and demonstrates her knowledge of the company.]** That's particularly important to me because I've been doing fund-raising for the Young Writer's club here on campus, and helped launch our school outreach program. **[Discloses something about her relevant experience, and aligns herself with the employer.]** Part of the reason I chose to be an English major was to learn how to write very clearly and persuasively, and with all the research projects I've worked on as well as my honor's thesis, I've really learned how to research topics and distill a lot of information and present it clearly, which is part of the reason I want to write reviews for you." **[Explains what specific skills she's developed, why she chose her major, mentions her honor's student status, and why she wants the job.]**

Communications major

"I first became interested in doing brand management for your company because of your logo. I think that it represents your products perfectly, because it is simple but also very sophisticated and contemporary. So are your products, and your clientele. **[Explains why he is interested in the job, the company, and demonstrates his knowledge of the company's products.]** As a communications major, I'm very accustomed to researching and analyzing different media, and how to present products and services so that the right audiences will find out about them. **[Seamlessly adds a comment about his major and the skills he developed that are most relevant to the position.]** This is what inspired me to take my last internship as a marketing assistant at a greeting card company. I loved being able to participate in various campaigns to find new markets for the cards. In fact, I helped the company create partnerships with local businesses, and the new line of humor cards really took off as a result. **[Mentions relevant hands-on experience, and the outcome of his efforts.]** Your location here is terrific—it's not too far from where I used to teach kids jazz dance. **[Adds an interesting fact about himself, a potential conversation starter.]**

Don't practice your two-minute sound bite so often that it sounds rehearsed; recruiters can tell, and they'd rather meet the real you. Take five minutes to jot down some of your greatest accomplishments, some (ideally) unique reasons for choosing your major, and the main reasons why you're interested in the company.

The Case of the Blank Resume: Hands-on Experience *Required*

Heather's Story

Heather is a senior in college majoring in English with a minor in psychology. She's an excellent student who makes the dean's list every semester. After she graduates she plans to land an exciting entry-level position in publishing or broadcast journalism, although she doesn't know much about either field. In fact, Heather doesn't know much about any career fields, since she hasn't volunteered, interned, or held a job since high school. Heather's friends are beginning to seek out positions in their respective areas of interest, so Heather decides she'd better start applying to jobs as well, when she keeps running into a problem; her resume is staring back at her, utterly devoid of new material. After expanding on her academic achievements (dean's list, honor's thesis) Heather realizes that she can't cite high school work experiences (too dated). Whenever Heather submits a resume, it is met with stony silence by employers, although the occasional "Dear Heather" note graces her inbox. Heather is beginning to figure out that employers are more interested in hiring some of Heather's classmates, the ones who have complemented their academic experiences with experiential learning. Discouraged, Heather decides that she must need another degree to get a decent job, so she starts looking into PhD programs.

Julia's Story

Julia is a sophomore in college, majoring in English. Having realized that she doesn't know much about the career options that will be available to her after graduation, Julia decides to join a student organization for undergraduate English majors. Every month, the organization invites guest speakers to describe their various career paths. Through her participation in these events, Julia quietly eliminates certain career options (editor, reporter, literature professor) and discovers an interest in corporate communications. Shortly thereafter, Julia visits her college career center's website and logs in to browse internship and volunteer activities. She finds a summer internship in marketing for an office supply company. She applies (citing her recent high school experience as an editor for her school newspaper) and lands the internship. Within her first few weeks on the job, Julia realizes that she isn't terribly interested in corporate marketing, and finds the office supply industry in particular to be dismally boring. She does gain some valuable skills in creating marketing materials and targeting specific audiences, and pitches some interesting ideas to her team, which results in a very strong letter of recommendation from Julia's boss.

Julia needs to earn some money, so she takes a part-time position as a receptionist for the campus student health center. After sitting in on an excellent but poorly attended lunchtime seminar on stress management, Julia offers to publicize the seminars to her fellow students. Through flyers, listservs, and a college radio station spot, Julia's efforts result in a tenfold attendance at the next seminar series. The student health center hires Julia as a health intern in charge of public relations for the center. By senior year, Julia has learned that she wants to pursue a position in public relations in the nonprofit setting, and her resume looks impressive to employers. She receives multiple job offers.

Moral of the Story....

1. No matter what your major, employers want to see your skills in action. Even business or applied mathematics majors are going to struggle to find positions if they haven't completed internships, jobs, or volunteer positions. Unless a certain major is a requirement for the job, most recruiters spend a grand total of three seconds looking at your major. What they really want to see is how you apply the skills you've learned.

2. Employers rarely place higher value on paid positions. The meatiest, most interesting opportunities available to students are usually unpaid, and employers understand this fact. Don't pass over an opportunity because it is labeled as "volunteer" or "unpaid internship."

3. Get started early. If you wait until your senior year to seek out hands-on experience, you will find that the competition is much greater. Even a two-hour-per-week volunteer position can be a great resume builder and can open up doors.

4. Your internship/volunteer position/job does *not* have to be directly related to your projected future career goals. As long as you are able to capitalize on the skills you've developed and translate them into your next position, you aren't wasting your time.

5. Speaking of future career goals, the fastest way to determine whether or not a particular pathway is a good fit for you is to immerse yourself in that work environment. If you arbitrarily decided to go into forensics, then realized the job was more *Office Space* than *CSI*, you'd be in for a huge shock.

CHAPTER 2

Advanced Degrees and Fellowships

IS AN ADVANCED DEGREE FOR ME?

Perhaps the most critical decision you will make in your career is whether or not to pursue a graduate degree. The benefits of acquiring additional degrees may, at first, seem limitless: more job opportunities, or at least more opportunities for advancement; approval from others for being such a tenacious scholar; and, let's face it, the ability to remain comfortably ensconced in "student mode." While there are a myriad of reasons (some more compelling than others) for you to stay in school, if you choose a program for the right reasons and understand the likely outcomes, you will reap the rewards of a graduate education. A poorly conceived decision can land you in debt and draw you even further away from a satisfying career. Nothing is more discouraging than finding yourself halfway through a doctoral program and asking the question "Why am I here?" This scenario is woefully common, but also avoidable.

A happy graduate student is an informed graduate student. Weighing key factors such as time and financial commitment as well as the content and objectives of each program will help you avoid most pitfalls. A number of students who are intelligent and motivated make the decision to apply based on such faulty logic as "My friend told me that if I don't major in business or science, I'd need to get a graduate degree to earn money." On the other hand, many students engage in very thoughtful decision-making when considering graduate programs and may benefit phenomenally from those programs as a result. This chapter will give you an overview of the most important factors to weigh when considering an advanced degree, as well as information on the most common graduate degrees for English and communications majors.

GETTING STARTED

According to a recent study by the Council of Graduate Schools, more than 1.5 million people enrolled in its member institutions in the fall of 2005. Education and business programs enrolled the largest numbers of students—about one-fifth of the grad school population pursued advanced degrees in education and approximately 14 percent studied business. Humanities disciplines (including English, history, and others) accounted for about 7 percent of graduate students, and social sciences (a category that includes both sociology and psychology) accounted for slightly more than 7 percent of the total.[1]

If you've enjoyed yourself as an undergraduate student, the notion of returning to the safe cocoon of campus life might seem appealing. We should point out, however, that even if you pursue an advanced degree in the same subject that you majored in at college (and many people study something different), graduate school will hardly seem like a continuation of your undergraduate education—the purposes of the two

---

1 Council of Graduate Schools. *Graduate Enrollment and Degrees Report: 1986 to 2005.* September 13, 2006. 3–5. www.cgsnet.org.

degrees are very, very different. Even though you specialized in college to some degree simply by declaring a major, the real purpose of your liberal arts studies was to obtain a body of knowledge in a wide range of fields. The purpose of graduate school, on the other hand, is to explore the body of knowledge in a particular field.[2] The two most common types of advanced-degree programs—master's programs and doctoral programs—are explained below:

The master's program

As a master's candidate, you'll spend about two years at graduate school. The purpose of this program, in the university's eyes, is to give you a solid education in a specialized field of scholarship. At many universities, you may be able to study part-time while working to support yourself. You'll receive less financial help than declared doctoral candidates do (in fact, it's possible you won't receive any financial assistance at all). In a typical two-year master's program, your academic experience will look something like this:

- **Your First Year:** You'll take courses much as you did in college, fulfilling the course work requirements of your degree. The workload is heavier, the course topics are more specific, and much more is expected than was in college. You'll either be assigned or choose an advisor at the beginning of your program. With your advisor's help, you'll begin to develop an academic focus. A number of professors will supervise the work you do.

- **Your Second Year:** You may take further courses to complete your degree requirements. Deciding on your research focus, you'll direct more and more energy toward your concentration. Taking one semester or an entire year, depending on the program, you complete your master's thesis. The purpose of this thesis is to demonstrate mastery in your field. If you show promise, you may be encouraged to continue toward the doctorate.

The doctoral program

The doctoral candidate spends five or six years at graduate school. From the university's perspective, the purpose of the program is threefold: to give the candidate extensive knowledge of the field; to train him or her to do original and meaningful research; and to prepare him or her to function as a member of a teaching faculty.

In a typical six-year doctoral program, your academic experience will look something like this:

- **Your First Three Years:** You'll take courses to satisfy your degree requirements and gain a broad knowledge of the field. If you're fortunate, you'll gain valuable experience by snagging a research or teaching assistantship. (Most appointments are filled with

2 John A. Goldsmith, John Komlos, and Penny Schine Gold. *The Chicago Guide to Your Academic Career.* Chicago: University of Chicago Press, 2001. 20.

fourth- to sixth-year grad students.) You'll gradually focus your research interests, working with an advisor who is usually appointed at the beginning of the program, and you'll develop your working relationships with professors prominent in your areas of interest. At the end of your second or third year, you'll complete a thesis or take comprehensive exams, or both. The thesis or exams will help demonstrate your qualification to continue with doctoral work.

- **The Last Three Years:** Course work becomes a much smaller part of your academic work, and may end altogether as you work at conceptualizing your doctoral dissertation. Your dissertation must constitute a new and meaningful contribution to knowledge in your field. You'll teach more and more classes, and may even teach a course of your own design. You'll collaborate increasingly with faculty members, who may rely on you for research and who will inform you of their own work. You will probably become closely associated with a single professor who will become your dissertation director. You'll devote more and more energy to your own research. Your program culminates in the completion of your dissertation, which may include an oral defense of your work before a faculty committee.

Why me? Reasons to go

The decision to attend graduate school isn't one that should be made lightly. "Over the years, I've come to realize that many, if not most [graduate students] seriously underestimate the enormous investment of time and money that graduate school will require," says Tom Thuerer, Dean of Students in the Humanities at the University of Chicago.[3] If you decide to go to graduate school, you don't want to fall into this camp. As with any investment, consider your goals and objectives well in advance to ensure you get the best possible return.

We'll discuss the financial realities of attending graduate school later in this chapter, but suffice to say, it can be an expensive proposition. Pursuing an advanced degree also requires significant personal and professional sacrifice—at least in the short-term. While you may have been encouraged to explore several different academic paths as an undergraduate—trying on various majors to see if they fit with your skills and interests—graduate school doesn't offer the same level of flexibility. In graduate school, the stakes are higher—and the cost of changing your mind is much, much higher. True, just because you've started working toward your degree doesn't mean you're obligated to finish it, but investing the time and money in a program and not having a degree to show for it is a scenario you'd like to avoid.

3 John A. Goldsmith, John Komlos, and Penny Schine Gold. *The Chicago Guide to Your Academic Career.* Chicago: University of Chicago Press, 2001. 30.

To ensure you get as much as possible out of the investment—and the experience itself—be sure to give serious thought to whether grad school is the right choice for you. Pursuing an advanced degree can influence your personal and professional life in a big way, so your decision to attend should involve some honest self-assessment and good, old-fashioned soul searching. Grad school isn't the right choice for everyone. Sure, you could probably get through it (you wouldn't be offered admission if you couldn't do the work), but do you really want to white-knuckle your way through a program that's not only expensive and time-consuming, but one that's supposed to be intellectually stimulating and enriching? There are numerous reasons people go to grad school; if you're like most people, these are the ones most likely to apply to you:

Because you have to go

In many fields, graduate-level studies are part of the drill if you want to obtain the licenses and certifications necessary to work in your chosen profession. Medicine and law are two obvious examples of this—if you want to be a doctor, there's no way around medical school (which is a good thing for everyone), and if you want to be a lawyer, law school is in your future. Teaching often requires a graduate degree, though the educational requirements will vary depending on the subject and grade level you hope to teach, you'll probably need to complete some level of postgraduate work, whether it's a required teacher-training program, or (if it's a tenure-track college professor career you're thinking of) a master's degree or PhD.

Career advancement

In some industries and organizations, graduate studies are required—either officially or unofficially—for upper-level or management positions. Even if it's possible to get in the door of an organization without an advanced degree, you many find that you can only move so far up without one. In some cases, an advanced degree is actually a prerequisite for a step-up in seniority; in others, it's more of an unwritten rule. Either way, think of an advanced degree as a type of currency—depending on where you work (or where you'd like to work), you might just have more purchasing power when it comes to getting promoted. And it's not necessarily because the skills or knowledge you picked up in grad school are directly applicable to the everyday responsibilities of your job. "I enjoyed my master's program immensely," says Mary, a 28-year-old analyst with the U.S. government who obtained her master's degree in public policy. "But I wouldn't necessarily say I'm using what I learned in my job every day. Even so, I probably wouldn't have this position if I hadn't gone to grad school. The department that I work for is pretty stringent about its master's degree requirement." The good news is that if you're considering grad school as a possible way to move up within your current organization, there's a good chance your employer will foot at least part of the bill. Many companies offer generous tuition reimbursement programs.

Because you're switching careers

You probably already know that people switch jobs more frequently today than they ever have before—and not just across organizations or functions, either. In fact, not only are job changes becoming more frequent, they're becoming more dramatic, too. It's not uncommon to see dancers and artists become journalists or doctors, bankers become small-business owners, teachers become therapists, or investment analysts become CIA operatives. As we've said before, careers don't always evolve in a linear fashion. Sometimes, the position that we once considered our "dream job" becomes less satisfying over time. Other times, our personal priorities or circumstances change, making the career path we're currently on seem less appealing. For some folks, taking a class, attending a lecture, or getting a part-time job class transforms a one-time hobby or interest into the focus of their professional aspirations. The reasons behind peoples' career changes are as varied as the occupations that they move in and out of. In many cases, pursuing an advanced degree provides a bridge between two disparate careers. Graduate school provides much more than just expertise when it comes to establishing your credibility with future employers; the very fact that you took the time to pursue an advanced degree proves you're committed to building a career in the field.

For the love of money

When it comes to graduate school, there's no money-back guarantee. In fact, the only thing that earning an advanced degree guarantees is a few extra letters at the end of your name. And while U.S. Census Bureau data supports the notion that earnings increase with higher educational levels, there's no question that some letters are worth more than others—at least when it comes to salaries. According to Census Bureau research, people with professional degrees (MD, JD, DDS, and DVM) earn higher salaries on average than any other segment of the U.S. workforce. For the rest of the working world, progressively higher education levels correspond to higher earnings, all other things being equal. These salary trends make sense; like any other market, the labor market is driven by supply and demand. Higher demand for your skills—and/or a scarcity of supply when it comes to your particular skill set—will drive up the "price" that employers will pay for your efforts (in other words, your salary). In general, the higher your level of educational attainment, the higher your level of specialization—and the more scarce your skills, knowledge, and experience generally becomes.

However, depending on the specific graduate degree you're pursuing, the dollar increase in your new salary might not be enough to offset the cost of obtaining the degree in the first place. With the cost of higher education increasing each year, students are carrying more debt upon completion of their undergraduate degrees than they ever have before. Tack on the cost of funding a graduate degree, and you'll quickly find that all of this learning comes at a steep price. If your interest in graduate school springs primarily from the promise of a fatter paycheck, proceed with caution: You'll need to conduct a thorough cost-benefit analysis to figure out whether the enhanced earning potential justifies the substantial costs. The Bureau of Labor Statistics' website, BLS.gov, includes hiring projections in addition to salary ranges for various occupations; by reviewing resources such as this one, you'll learn what factors influence the job market in your field— and what the landscape might look like by the time you graduate.

Network connections

As we'll discuss in detail in Chapter 5, networking will be an important part of your job search whether you have an advanced degree or not. The connections forged in grad school could potentially give you a leg up when it comes to learning about job opportunities in your field. Even if they can't hook you up with a full-time job, grad school classmates will often be able to provide you with professional advice that's just as valuable. "Not only did the 23 other people in my MFA program become some of my closest friends, but they've become a powerful network of professional contacts that I continually rely on," says Lisa, currently a senior travel writer with a consumer lifestyle magazine. Lisa, who earned her MFA in fiction writing, recently co-edited a collection of anthologies and is currently working on a book scheduled for publication in the spring of 2007. "The people who were in my writing program were able to put me in touch with agents and publishers who would be able to help me put a book deal together," she says. "I don't know if I would have been able to get that done without them." Connections like these will pay off whether you're intending to stay in academia or not; as always with job-hunting, it pays to know people and to have them know you, too.

You just can't get enough . . .

. . . of school, that is. Many people pursue graduate studies purely because they're absolutely fascinated by their chosen field of study, and they want to develop a highly specialized area of expertise. Whether you eventually want to teach at the college level, or you just want to breathe, eat, and sleep your academic passion for a while, graduate school will enable you to fan your intellectual flames. Those who go all the way with their studies and earn their PhD are a unique breed—a species of intellectual omnivore that enjoys learning for its own sake. Such individuals are visibly charged by scholarly debate and discussion and have the patience and single-minded focus to endure a half-dozen years or more in an academic environment.

Because it's the path of least resistance

Just because there are many perfectly legitimate reasons to go to grad school doesn't mean there aren't a few bad ones, too. Pursuing an advanced degree as a default option (i.e., you still haven't decided what you want to do and are hoping to postpone the inevitable transition into the real world) isn't a great idea. And if you're simply frustrated with the way your job search is going, or hoping to use graduate school to wait out a downturn in the economy, think again. Graduate school is hardly a quick fix for a broken job search, and the economy may very well pick up long before you've even made a dent in your student loans.

So how can you tell if you're using grad school as a stall tactic? Well, only you know for sure, but if you find yourself contemplating graduate school but haven't really narrowed in on a field of study, that's definitely a warning sign. It's possible that the relative security of being a student—and not necessarily a commitment to a particular field—has captured your interest. That doesn't mean that you shouldn't explore grad school as an option, but you should consider your other alternatives, too, to be sure that fear isn't the only factor motivating your decision. Trust us, there are other ways to bide your time—and most of them require far less time, energy, and money than graduate school. For the grad school experience to be worthwhile for you, it should make sense as part of some larger plan for your career.

Do you have what it takes?

When deciding whether grad school is something you'd like to do, it helps to consider the skills and attributes successful grad students consistently demonstrate—not just the attributes that make them capable of doing the work grad school requires, but the personal qualities that make them gush with enthusiasm when they describe the experience ten years down the road. Across disciplines and institutions, graduate students who both succeed in their programs and seem to genuinely enjoy them typically have these four things in common:

Compound interest

Far and away, experts say a genuine passion for the subject matter is the single most important factor determining which grad students thrive and which become frustrated and disappointed with their decision. A genuine passion is very different from a peripheral interest—in other words, pursuing a master's degree in linguistics because you took a single English literature class probably doesn't represent the most well-informed choice. In order to make the most out of your graduate school experience, you need to have a deep, enduring interest in the subject, the profession, and its literature. When you apply to programs, admissions staff will examine your transcript and resume not just for evidence of academic achievement (though the importance of solid grades and test scores can't be overstated), but for classes and extracurricular activities that demonstrate an interest in— and a commitment to—the field.

Not-so-idle curiosity

In addition to an inveterate desire to study the field you've chosen, it helps if you're an intellectually curious person in general. In other words, do you enjoy exploring concepts and ideas, whether or not they specifically relate to your chosen field of specialization? Do you enjoy the process of pulling things apart—literally or metaphorically—to understand how they work? Are you intrigued by the challenge of understanding—and expressing— two or more seemingly contradictory perspectives on the same issue? Is your pursuit of knowledge driven largely by your interest in the question more than the practical application of its answer? Whether you're pursuing a two-year master's program, a six-year PhD program, or a full-fledged career in higher education, you'll enjoy your time in academia a lot more if you're excited by the *process* of learning—not just the degree you'll have in hand when you graduate.

Perfect timing

Well-honed time-management skills are another prerequisite for graduate school success. If you're attending school full-time, you'll probably be balancing competing academic priorities within the classroom walls and possibly the demands of extracurricular involvements, a part-time job (whether it's related to funding your studies or not), a family, and some semblance of a social life. Samantha, who completed a master's degree in English, juggled a couple of different jobs in order to finance her graduate education. As part of the fellowship she was awarded during her first year, she participated in a program known as "Artists in the Schools," where she taught writing to elementary, middle, and high school students throughout the state. "I also worked as a reporter for the university press office," she says. "And I did freelance work for the daily paper, doing book reviews. And I also worked part-time at a café serving lattes. Thinking about it now, it's no wonder I didn't produce as much writing as I would've liked." If you're pursuing your degree on a part-time basis, the demands of a full-time job are most likely in the mix. Either way, you're likely to have a lot on your plate, so understanding how to prioritize is key if you want to finish your program with your sanity intact.

Eyes on the prize

Somewhat paradoxically, the ability to work on a single task for an extended period of time—whether it's a dissertation, thesis, or any long-term research project—is just as important as the ability to juggle multiple tasks at once. The research and writing required in graduate school is highly focused—much more so than in undergraduate studies—so grad students devote a seemingly inordinate amount of time exploring a highly specialized area of interest within their field of study. By its very nature, work like this requires a great deal of autonomy—not to mention a better-than-average attention span. Successful degree candidates are therefore highly motivated, unusually self-disciplined, and comfortable working independently. A good dose of patience doesn't hurt, either—even the most exciting and ground-breaking research projects usually involve some fairly monotonous tasks. In general, the road to completing an advanced degree and seeing it pay off is long and arduous. If instant gratification is important to you when it comes to your academic pursuits, a professional degree might be a more suitable choice than an advanced degree in the liberal arts.

Ask and it shall be answered

We know what you're probably thinking: "Of *course* I have all of those skills and attributes! I am literally bursting with excitement about my field of study, I can handle multiple competing priorities, I love monotony, and I have the self-discipline and patience of a saint!" If you have a killer transcript, a resume full of related extracurricular activities, and work experience to boot, then it's time to sign you up. All you need to know is where to send the check, right?

Not so fast. We said that considering graduate school required a great deal of introspection and honest self-assessment, but we didn't say that was all that was required before you jumped on board. In Chapter 5, we'll stress the importance of networking and conducting informational interviews to make informed decisions about your career—and just because you're thinking of applying your talents to academia for awhile doesn't mean you're off the hook where this type of legwork is concerned. You need to ask questions before you decide to apply to school—not only will this type of research make your applications more compelling, but, more importantly, you're far more likely to choose the right program—and the right field of study, for that matter—if you've taken the time to look before you leap. In the *Chicago Guide to Your Academic Career*, the book's three authors (all distinguished professors and scholars themselves) emphasize the importance of seeking advice from as many informed perspectives as possible before you apply. Here are some specific questions they suggest you ask as you begin to gather information:

- **To professors (past or current) who know your work well:** Do you think graduate school, in this particular field, would be a good choice, given my level and kinds of talents? Do you think I would have a contribution to make?

- **To professors in your field who have completed graduate school within the last five years or so:** What are the current issues in the field? Where do you see the field going? What is graduate school like these days?

- **To graduates of your own college or university who are now in graduate school in a field close to yours or who have recently obtained jobs (your undergraduate teachers, the Career/Placement Center, and/or the Alumni Office should be able to provide you with names and contact information):** How have you found the graduate school experience? Were you well prepared for the program you entered? Is there any advice you wish you'd received before entering graduate school?[4]

Two words: Manage expectations

Even if you've determined that you'd probably succeed in graduate school—meaning you'd not only do well academically, but you'd probably really enjoy it—you may not be entirely convinced you should go. If you're trying to decide whether the investment would be worthwhile for you, you're not alone. Formulating realistic expectations—in terms of the graduate school experience itself and its expected payoff in the long run—is one of the best ways to assess whether attaining an advanced degree is the best possible next step. If you take the time to speak with current grad students, recent alumni, professors, and other prospective grad students (like yourself), you'll probably find that people's objections to graduate school fall into two categories: the practical and the personal.

Practical Concerns

The practical reasons all relate to two things: the cost of school and the likelihood of getting a job afterward. Together, these two factors will determine whether graduate school makes sound practical sense for you. It's possible to land a job easily after earning an advanced degree and still struggle to pay back your loans. It's also possible to complete a graduate program with no debt and still have trouble finding work. Many people would find each of these scenarios unacceptable. To avoid any nasty surprises, spend some time researching the probable cost of your graduate program and study the state of the job market in your field. The

---

4 John A. Goldsmith, John Komlos, and Penny Schine Gold. *The Chicago Guide to Your Academic Career*. Chicago: University of Chicago Press, 2001. 22.

most important aspects of the job market are the availability of positions and the salary range. Together, these pieces of information give you some idea of what your professional future (and loan-paying power) might look like. The more information you dig up, the better you'll be able to appraise the practical obstacles to graduate education.

Personal Concerns

The personal pitfalls of graduate school are a little more complicated. They depend on your likes, dislikes, and powers of endurance. Many people begin graduate programs and never complete them. This is especially true for those pursuing doctorates: Some of these people quit for financial reasons, but many leave because they find that the life they're living is unacceptable. Beginning a graduate program you never finish is the worst-case scenario. Investigating graduate programs should involve not only research into the broad academic outlines, but also research into what your daily life as a graduate student will be like. In an informal survey of hundreds of graduate students, these are the top five lifestyle complaints students made:

- It's hard to make ends meet financially.
- There is little or no free time.
- There is not enough socializing in the department/school.
- There is nothing to do in the university community or surrounding area.
- Fellow graduate students are neurotically competitive.

When making your decision, be sure to consider these aspects of graduate life as well as anything else that could have a substantial effect on your quality of life. Once you can clearly articulate why you want to go to graduate school, you'll be able to make an informed decision as to whether the advantages of an advanced degree outweigh the sacrifices you'll need to make in order to get one.

Timing is everything: When to go

When you started thinking about college, you probably knew when you were going to be attending—about three months after you graduated from high school, most likely. With graduate school, there's a little more variation in this regard. Some unusually focused college grads pursue their advanced degree immediately after obtaining their bachelor's degree (which means, of course, they're going through the application process while they're still in school). Most graduate students, however, have taken at least one year off between their undergraduate and graduate programs—usually to work, sometimes to travel or volunteer, occasionally just to take a break. In fact, more often than not, practical experience—particularly as it relates to the advanced degree you're hoping to pursue—makes you a more desirable applicant than one who has little to no work experience to speak of.

So when should you go to grad school? Well, the short answer is: it depends. On one hand, many people find the years between college and graduate school to be an extremely valuable time for exploring professional options—and for doing some important self-exploration, too. Because you've had a few years in the workplace, you'll probably bring a more informed perspective to bear on your academic pursuits. You might also have saved a little bit of money during your working years—or at least been able to pay down some of your undergraduate debt, if you had any. But more important than any nest egg is the greater sense of clarity and purpose you'll have since you've had some time to consider what you really want to do—and what's especially important to you in your career. No matter how much you enjoyed college or how much you excelled there, perhaps there wasn't ever really a question you would go. When you enroll in graduate school—particularly after you've taken a few years off to work—you're usually there because you want to be there. And if the pure love of learning isn't enough, the fact that you've taken out loans or depleted all of your savings to finance your higher education will probably motivate you to squeeze every last drop of value out of the experience.

On the other hand, taking time to work in between your degrees means you'll have to adjust to life as a student again, which can be difficult for some folks who have been out of an academic routine for several years. If you've been earning a regular paycheck, you might find it difficult to give up that income and learn to live as a modest graduate student. The longer you wait, the more likely it is that personal commitments—a spouse, a significant other's job, children, or mortgage—may complicate your decision of what program to attend (or whether to go at all).

There's no magic formula when it comes to deciding whether to take time off between your undergraduate and graduate studies, or (if you decide to work for a few years) how many years you should work (or travel, or do whatever it is that you're doing between degrees) before you go back. The only absolute guideline is that you should go to graduate school when you're absolutely certain it's what you want or need to do. As we've belabored in the preceding pages, pursuing an advanced degree isn't something you should take lightly, so you shouldn't apply until you're sure it's right for you. The option to go to grad school will always be there and spending time in the "real world" can actually make you more interesting to graduate schools once you decide what you want to do and are ready to apply. The richness of your life experiences will cause the most difficult part of the application—the personal statement—to write itself. You will have cultivated a sincere interest in a particular degree that you need in order to advance your career or gain more influence in a particular field. Your enthusiasm and ability to convey how the degree fits into your long-term goals will leave Admissions Committees inspired and ready to offer you a spot in their next class.

That said, finding out what's typical for other students in the programs you're considering doesn't hurt. Most of the time, graduate programs will post statistical information about their current students on their websites, and oftentimes, the average age of entering students is listed. Again, you shouldn't feel discouraged to apply if you're a few years off the mark (these numbers are averages, after all), but they can help to shape your expectations of how your experience will be different. Kurt, who recently began a MFA program in writing after working as a teacher for 9 years, was surprised how old he felt on the first day of school. "Not only have I been working for a while, but I've been married for 3 years, and my wife and I are expecting our first baby. A lot of my classmates are 23 or 24. I feel so old!" Conversely, if you're attending grad school right after college, you may find that you're the only 22-year old single person in your class. Again, the extent to which you do or don't fit into the prevailing demographics is only one data point, but it's one that will definitely shape your experience in and out of the classroom.

A law school insider's observation: Waiting might have been a better option

Bill Hoye, Associate Dean of Admissions with Duke University School of Law, shared his observations about the advantages of waiting a few years to apply to law school: "Plenty of law school students have gone directly from college into their legal education. Many do just fine, and have no regrets. Others wistfully wish that they had taken some time off to travel the world, serve the community, campaign for candidates, or read for pleasure. For the train really picks up speed as it pulls away from the law school. Commencement stage—first stop is preparation for the bar exam, and then many years of long hours in the office before there is time and opportunity to pursue other interests. Still others may find themselves unhappy in law school or in law practice and wish that they had taken some time to explore other possible paths before taking the jump into law school. Finally, taking some time off before heading to law school may make one a stronger candidate by virtue of the experience gathered and maturity gained."

What to consider when deciding where to apply—and where to go

Like deciding whether or not to go to graduate school, selecting target schools is more complex than it first seems. Filling out applications is a huge demand on your time and energy, and whether you're taking undergraduate exams or holding down a job, you probably can't afford to spend weeks dealing with a large pile of applications.

Applications are a financial drain as well: Grad school application fees range from $20 to $90, and average about $50. These high fees are no accident. Many universities, with Admissions Committees swamped by record numbers of applications, have raised their fees in order to prevent less-motivated applicants from applying and reduce the number of incoming applications. Given today's fees, you can expect 10 applications to cost you about $500—and that's before you figure in postage, transcript handling fees, photocopying, and so on. It can really add up.

Economically speaking, you can see the saturation-bombing technique that a lot of people use to apply to college isn't very practical for grad school. It pays—in time and money—to narrow your field down to four or five good target schools. To figure out which institutions make the cut, you'll probably want to consider the following six factors:

- **Academic fit**

   In selecting schools, the most important aspect of any school is its academic fit—that is, how well suited the school is to the research you want to do. If you're a prospective grad student in, say, philosophy, then it's certainly a good idea to find out where the leading philosophy departments are; but to have a really good graduate school experience, you need more than just a respected department. You need individuals on the faculty who share your research interests, and who will become involved in your work and involve you in their own.

   The importance of finding professors to work with varies according to your degree ambitions. If you're looking for a master's degree to round out your education or give you that professional edge, then the overall quality of the faculty may be more important to you than finding the ideal mentor. Because your grad school experience will probably involve more course work than research, you'll want to make sure the classes offered are relevant to your interests and will give you some background for your research. If you are decided on doctoral work and an academic career, however, the specific research interests of professors become much more important. If you already have an area of academic specialization in mind, you need to find out whether that subspecialty is well represented in the departments you're considering. In any case, graduate work will always be more profitable and enjoyable if there are professors in your program who will take a personal interest in what you're doing.

   As you gather information about your prospective professors, remember that the most brilliant scholars in the world are not always the best teachers. No matter how celebrated the scholars are that you'll work with, it won't really matter if teaching isn't their scene—or if they're rarely accessible to students. Make no mistake about it: The quality of teaching can make or break your experience. "I was surprised by the lack of professionalism exhibited by some of my well-paid teachers," laments one recent master's grad. "Overall, I'd give the experience a 6 out of 10. I wish I had gotten an MBA." To avoid any nasty surprises, talk to other students to gauge their level of satisfaction with the teaching. Also, try to schedule interviews with the faculty members you are most interested in working with.

- **Reputation**

  To a greater extent than our undergraduate education, graduate schools represent an affiliation with a specific department, just as much (if not more than) an affiliation with a specific university. Keep this in mind as you consider which programs you'll apply to. When it comes to reputation, the excellence of a particular program doesn't always correspond to the institution's overall reputation—or the strength of its undergraduate programs. Harvard, Princeton, and M.I.T. might vie for the top spots of the various undergraduate rankings each year, but, when it comes to department-specific rankings, there's a lot more variety.

  Most of the people we spoke to relied—at least to some extent—on department rankings, which are published annually for graduate programs in much the same way they are for undergraduate institutions. (Keep in mind, though, that rankings aren't available for every advanced-degree program you might consider). While rankings can provide some useful information as you make your choice, remember that they represent just one data point. Be sure to read the fine print about research methodology as you interpret ranking information. Consider the following excerpt from the 2007 edition of *U.S. News & World Report's America's Best Graduate Schools*: "Rankings of doctoral programs in the social sciences are based solely on the results of peer assessment surveys sent to academics in each discipline."[5] There's nothing inherently wrong with this approach, but you should be aware that that these particular rankings do not incorporate the quality of teaching (mentioned above) or the availability of job-placement resources (mentioned below). If that information is relevant to you, you'll need to obtain it through additional research.

  Irene, who completed a one-year master's program in journalism, considered the overall reputation of the school more important than the reputation of the program. "I wasn't sure I was necessarily going to stay in journalism forever," she explains, "so I wanted to go to a school where the overall reputation of the university would mean something to employers outside of journalism. There were probably better journalism programs out there, but, when I decided where to go, I placed a lot of importance on the overall quality of the school—not the quality of the program alone."

5 "Social Sciences & Humanities: PhD Programs Ranked Best by Department Chairs and Senior Faculty." *U.S. News & World Report: America's Best Graduate Schools.* 2006. 65.

- **Job placement**

  When you're considering which programs to which to apply—and, eventually, when you're deciding which school to attend—be sure to visit the career center and ask what resources are available to graduate students. While some universities have excellent, program-specific career-planning resources devoted to their graduate students exclusively, others do not. Talk to students currently enrolled in the programs you're considering and ask if they've found the resources available to them to be satisfactory. Many students enroll in programs assuming job placement—or at least career counseling—is part of the deal, and they're unpleasantly surprised to find out how few resources actually exist. Regardless of whether you're hoping to snag a position in private industry or make a career in academia, ask questions. Find out whether employers visit the campus to recruit graduate students in your program. If you're going the academic route, ask whether recent grads have gotten academic positions, how long their searches took, and where they're working. In the end, you may not lean on the resources your program provides—in fact, you may not use them all. As we've said before, though, it's important to develop realistic expectations before you sign up.

- **Students**

  To really figure out whether a particular program might be a good fit, you need to talk to the students currently enrolled in it. As you make your final decision among programs, you'll ideally visit each campus and talk to current graduate students. Ask them about the faculty's level of commitment to the graduate program, whether they enjoy working with their professors, and whether they feel they've been given enough guidance and opportunity to develop their own research. Ask them to describe the good points and the bad points of the department and the school. If you can, schedule time to speak with a graduate advisor; ask how well the program is organized, and what the ratio of graduating students to entering students is. If you take the time to gather qualitative and quantitative information like this, you'll make a much more informed decision than you would if you relied on rankings alone.

  While you're on campus, be sure to ask students about their quality of life, too. Your lifestyle will not necessarily resemble the one you enjoyed as an undergraduate student. ("Grad school is mostly devoid of the cultural and social atmosphere that is so intoxicating about undergrad life," says Scott, who recently completed a two-year master's program in urban planning. "And the football was worse in grad school, too.") Still, you want to enjoy your experience as much as possible, and that means taking the time to consider what your life will be like outside of the classroom as well as in it. Ask whether there are opportunities to socialize, and whether there's a strong sense of community among graduate students. As you talk to people who are attending the programs you're considering, give some thought to whether you can see yourself fitting in at each place. Not only are you going to grad school to advance your formal education, but you're going to be building a network of friends and supporters too—your fellow students should ideally be people you like and respect. The impressions you get as you visit different campuses are a valuable part of this decision-making process.

- **Geography**

  This one's pretty straightforward: The geographic location of the university should influence your decision to attend. If you have a particular aversion to rain, then you might prefer not to spend the next few years of your life in Seattle; if you're especially claustrophobic, New York City might not be the place for you. But the question of geography isn't just about personal preferences—there are practical implications, too. For example, depending on your field of study, it might be considerably easier to secure part-time jobs (or jobs between academic years) in some parts of the country than in others. If you have your heart set on settling down in a particular region, then you'd probably be best served attending graduate school there (or somewhere close by). If you have a spouse or significant other who's going to accompany you, your partner's career prospects in each of the locales you're considering will also influence your decision.

Making the Most of Your Experience

In 2001, about 32,000 graduate students participated in a survey conducted by the National Association of Graduate-Professional Students (NAGPS). When asked what specific advice they would provide to entering students, getting a head start on career planning was the suggestion that survey respondents offered most frequently. Building a network of personal and professional contacts—by attending professional conferences, joining student organizations, and actively seeking the support of professors and advisors—was another popular recommendation.

Source: Adam Fagen and Kimberly Sudekamp Wells. "A Little Advice from 32,000 Graduate Students," *The Chronicle of Higher Education.* January 14, 2002. http://chronicle.com/jobs/2002/01/2002011401c.htm.

"Rapunzel, Rapunzel": Getting into the ivory tower

While you might think the graduate school application process begins when you start trawling around various schools' websites and committing program rankings to memory, it really begins months earlier—albeit only informally. The process starts when you begin to consciously seek out and nurture relationships with your undergraduate professors and advisors as well as professors or researchers at your target graduate institutions. It continues when you prepare for and then take the GRE, a topic discussed in more detail below (while not a required application element for every program, the GRE is compulsory for admission to most programs). Whether you start thinking about your applications six months or six years before they're due, one thing is certain: With all the pieces that go into a graduate school application, it's definitely not something you can whip up over a weekend or two.

Many universities have a single application form for all their graduate programs and a set of basic application requirements to which individual departments may add. At some schools, individual departments have their own applications. At these schools, you will have to request an application from an individual department rather than a central office.

Once you've accessed and reviewed the admissions materials, it's time to complete the applications to your target schools. Before you dig in, take some time to consider all the application pieces (we discuss these below) and set a schedule with self-imposed deadlines that are possible to meet. The applications themselves typically require a general information form, GRE scores, transcripts, recommendations, and a personal statement. Some programs may have additional requirements, such as an interview or portfolio.

Due to differences in departmental requirements, it is difficult to make generalizations about applications. Still, application processes across institutions and programs usually involve the following:

- **Deadlines.** First things first: Meeting your schools' deadlines is one of the most important details of the application process. You don't want to be rejected from a school for which you might otherwise have qualified simply because you were late in filing your application. Check with each individual department to which you are applying to find out their specific deadlines. Also be aware that there may be separate (usually earlier) deadlines for those students seeking financial aid. Get your applications in as early as possible.

- **Test Scores.** Almost all graduate schools ask applicants for applicable standardized test scores, such as the GRE General Test, a GRE Subject Test, or the Test of English as a Foreign Language (TOEFL). Here again, you must check with individual departments to ensure you meet their specific requirements. Although there are a few programs that don't require the GRE General Test, most do. Only a few programs require a GRE Subject Test.

All foreign students from countries where English is not the native language are required to take the TOEFL.

Preparing for the GRE may require the single biggest investment of time when it comes to applying for graduate school, so get started early. Ryan, who recently completed a two-year master's program, says he prepared for the GRE by completing a single section of a practice test "maybe every other day at work. My boss was very encouraging." (If you are currently working full-time, we should point out that few managers are likely to be as supportive of practicing for the GRE while you're on the clock).

No matter when and where you prepare for the test, however, make sure you've budgeted enough time for it. The weight placed on your GRE score in relation to the other factors Admissions Committees consider (e.g., undergraduate GPA, letters of recommendation, relevant experience in your chosen field, etc.) will vary from school to school and from program to program, but it's never insignificant. The scores from these tests (like SAT scores when you were applying to undergraduate schools) are one of the few objective metrics that help Admissions Committees evaluate candidates with very different academic and professional backgrounds. In addition to influencing admissions decisions, GRE scores are an important factor in the awarding of teaching and research assistantships and merit-based financial aid.

- **Transcripts.** A transcript is a certified, official copy of a student's permanent academic record. All graduate schools require official transcripts of your grades from any colleges you attended. Most schools ask that transcripts be sent directly to them, but some ask that you collect the information and send in a complete application package. Contact the registrar's office (at every undergraduate institution you have attended) to request that your transcript be sent either to you or directly to the school to which you are applying. If your school used an unusual grading scale, you will often need to translate your transcript into the requested format.

- **Application Fee.** Application processing fees range from moderate (around $30–$45) to expensive (over $75). As mentioned earlier, these high fees are no accident—they are designed to discourage less-serious applicants from bombarding busy Admissions Committees. Fee waivers are occasionally offered by a school for applicants who can prove financial need. A good rule of thumb: If you failed to qualify for a fee waiver for the GRE, you are unlikely to qualify for a fee waiver from an institution. Check with the graduate Admissions Office of the schools to which you are applying to find out if you qualify for a fee waiver.

- **Letters of Recommendation.** These letters are one of the most influential aspects of your application to a graduate program. Committee members use them to get a more personal perspective on an applicant. Keep this in mind when choosing your recommenders. Their words will (hopefully) be what set you apart from the other applicants. A borderline student is often pushed into the acceptance pile because of excellent recommendations.

  Some application packets include recommendation forms that ask a recommender to rate your abilities in various categories; such applications generally also provide blank spaces for open-ended comments on an applicant's personality and potential. Other applications simply ask recommenders to write their own letters. Most schools require two or three letters. Try to get three, or even more, in case one is lost or submitted late. Some programs require more recommendations for PhD applicants than they do for master's degree applicants. Others require additional recommendations for students applying for funding. Be sure you know the specific procedure for the department to which you are applying. If there's any doubt in your mind, call the Dean's Office or the admissions contact for that department.

  If you've been out of school for a few years, you might find it difficult to approach professors from your alma mater and ask them for recommendations, and understandably so: Their recollections of your academic performance aren't exactly fresh. Jessica, who applied to master's programs three years after she completed her bachelor's in sociology, asked for a few recommendation letters before she completed her undergraduate course work— even though she wasn't sure exactly which degree programs she'd eventually apply to. If you're still in school, you might consider this approach: This way, even if the specific applications require that your recommenders fill out additional forms, your professors will have some record of all the nice things they said about you when your academic prowess was still fresh in their minds. If it's too late for that, consider drafting a sample letter— or even an outline—that can serve as a map for the person writing your recommendation. In it, you'll want to include the points you'd most like your recommender to cover, including any specific academic achievements—in his class or otherwise—and the topics of any research projects you undertook during the class. Also provide your recommender with a copy of your transcript.

  No matter what your circumstances—and no matter whom you approach—give your recommenders plenty of warning when you ask them for letters! If you ask the week before the letter is due, chances are your professor (or manager or coworker) won't be able to devote enough time to crafting a compelling recommendation.

- **Personal Statement.** While applicants to medical, law, and business school are often asked to submit fairly lengthy essays about their motivations, goals, greatest achievements, character flaws, and/or solutions to hypothetical problems, applicants to other graduate programs are usually asked to submit a personal statement only. The personal statement may be called anything from the Autobiographical Statement to the Letter of Intent. Whatever its name, if you are required to write one, do it well. No matter what type of graduate program you are applying to, Admissions Committee members will evaluate the following: how clearly you think, how well you have conceptualized your plans for graduate school, and how well your interests and strengths mesh with their programs.

- **Interview.** Of major importance for admission to some graduate programs, interviews are not required for entrance to others. However, many schools encourage you to visit the campus and set up appointments to speak with Admissions Officers and individual faculty. It's a good idea for you to check out the places at which you're thinking about spending the next several years. You'll get insight into the school and the programs that you just can't get on paper. If an interview is optional, take advantage of the opportunity to make a personal impression.

Tips from a faculty member for getting letters of recommendation:

- Get to know the professor early on. Get to know the professor early on. Get to know the professor early on.

- Thoughts on how to hold a conversation with your professor in office hours:
  - Tell me that you like the class.
  - Tell me a thought you had about the lecture.
  - Recommend a book I might like.
  - Just show up so I can get an idea of who you are. I need to speak to your personality a bit. Is he energetic? Does she talk in class?

GRE—Section by Section

ANALYTICAL WRITING	• 2 essays
	• 30 minutes for one essay and 45 minutes for the other
QUANTITATIVE	• 28 multiple-choice questions
	• 45-minute section
VERBAL	• 30 multiple-choice questions
	• 30-minute section

For more information, check out the GRE website at GRE.org.

Source: Princetonreview.com

Your unwritten application

As we've said several times now, the application process begins long before you start filling out all of those forms (and paying all of those fees). A large part of your application is never put down on paper. It consists of the contacts you've made with faculty at the programs you're applying to, your conversations with them, and the impressions you've made. Put this "unwritten application" on your checklist right beside "Bother Professor So-and-So for a recommendation" and "Study for the GRE." It's that important.

With all the piles of paper involved in applying to graduate schools, it's easy to conclude that paperwork is what it's all about. You spend weeks poring through faculty listings, course offerings, and graduate bulletins to choose your schools, and then you start filling out application forms, requesting transcripts, and writing essays. Of course, all of these documents are important. But in the graduate admissions game, you have a big advantage if you talk to people.

Unlike undergraduate schools, a typical graduate program receives hundreds—not tens of thousands—of applications each year. From this applicant pool, a program might extend offers of admission to a few dozen, expecting some of those admitted to choose other schools. It's a group of applicants small enough that the Admissions Committee can reasonably expect to meet—or at least talk to—a fair number of them. Some graduate programs receive fewer than 100 applications annually, making an individual applicant's chance of making personal contact better still. At the same time, some popular graduate programs do receive several thousand applications each year, and the Admissions Committees in charge of these programs won't necessarily have time to chat. In general, however, there's a lot of room in the graduate admissions process to talk with professors and other members of the department.

To put together the strongest possible application, you've got to be a go-getter—or at least pretend you're one. This means talking to professors in a way that makes your research interests and career intentions clear to them. If you've done some thinking about what you want from a graduate program, professors will sense your clarity and direction and get a better feel for you as a prospective student.

There are two steps to developing personal contacts within a department: first, knowing what program you hope to enter and what field you want to work in, as well as what you want to learn from your conversations with faculty; and second, picking up the phone and making some calls—even if it makes you nervous.

Footing the bill

Okay, now it's time for a pop quiz to see if you've been paying attention: Do you remember what the average starting salary was for a recent graduate with a degree in the liberal arts? In case you don't remember, it's approximately $31,000 per year. According to *U.S. News & World Report*, $31,000 also represents the average cost of attending graduate school for one year.[6] While that figure includes tuition and living expenses, it doesn't include the cost of being out of the workforce if you're attending graduate school full-time (and according to the Council of Graduate Schools, more than half of graduate students—around 55 percent—attend full-time).[7]

When considering the cost of graduate school, you can't ignore the implicit costs as well as the explicit ones: You're not just foregoing a real income, but you're also delaying possible career advancement opportunities. Even if your graduate program is related to the job you left behind—or the job you aspire to get—you're out of the workforce to one degree or another while you're in school. And, depending on your degree program, you may not be getting any on-the-job training that's directly applicable to what you'll be doing once you finish.

The simple truth is this: Whether you're hoping to attend grad school before the ink has dried on your undergrad diploma, or whether you've been out of school for several years and would like to return to school as a way to improve your earning potential or even change careers entirely, grad school is an expensive proposition.

That said, the cost of attending graduate school alone shouldn't deter you from pursuing a graduate degree. The fact is, you have many options for financing your education, and, if an advanced-degree program is where your professional and personal stars align, then the investment will eventually pay off. However, it's important to understand how the investment will influence other decisions in your life: It's not uncommon for graduate students to postpone major milestones—like purchasing a house or starting a family—in order to fulfill their educational aspirations (and the

6 Kristin Davis. "The Hunt for Money." *U.S. News & World Report: America's Best Graduate Schools*. 2006, 13.

7 Council of Graduate Schools. *Graduate Enrollment and Degrees Report: 1986 to 2005*. September 13, 2006. 3. www.cgsnet.org.

ensuing financial obligations). While only you can decide whether choices like these are worth it—or whether they're even necessary, you need to research the implications of attending school so that you're not unpleasantly surprised once you've got your hard-earned degree in hand. To help alleviate some of the financial pressure of graduate school, the primary ways of financing a higher education (other than calling a wealthy relative, of course) are listed below.

- **Earn it.**

  For many graduate students—especially doctoral candidates—fellowships and assistantships go a long way toward paying the graduate school tab. At the graduate level, grants like these are usually awarded based on merit. The most generous award packages not only cover tuition and fees, but also pay a stipend and provide health-insurance coverage. Not all awards represent a totally free ride; while fellowships usually have no work requirement, graduate assistants typically work up to 15 hours a week teaching, grading papers, leading discussion groups, supervising lab courses, or assisting faculty with research. If your financial aid package involves an assistantship, teaching responsibilities will place significant demands on your time. Completing your academic work will already take a major amount of time and energy, so consider whether the academic intensity of the program you choose—not to mention your time-management capabilities—will enable you to get everything done.

  The amount of fellowship and assistantship aid available to you depends on the field of study you're pursuing. In the humanities, for example, only about half of full-time PhD students and 40 percent of full-time master's degree students have assistantships, and the stipends awarded are usually lower than they are in other disciplines, such as engineering, math, and computer science. To make the financial picture even more sobering, keep in mind that high-paying internships between academic years—par for the course in professional degree programs—aren't as commonplace in liberal arts fields.

  The first step toward getting a fellowship or assistantship is to indicate on your admissions application that you want to be considered for all forms of financial aid. The choicest awards are often made by departmental committees on the basis of application materials and sometimes supplemental recommendations. To find other awards or assistantships, check with your school's financial aid office, graduate school office, and fellowship coordinator (if there is one), or seek out faculty members in your department who are directing research funded by outside grants. Several government agencies and private organizations also sponsor outside fellowships that students can apply for on their own.

As part of the process of researching individual schools and programs, ask what percentage of students in the program are funded through fellowships, grants, and assistantships, and ask whether that changes after the first year. Some programs fund only a small percentage of students during the first year and provide funding in subsequent years based on academic performance (it's definitely worthwhile to ask whether the programs you're considering employ this approach, since it inevitably creates competition among students).

- **Borrow it.**

  Most graduate students will borrow money to pay some or all of their graduate school costs. According to the National Center for Education Statistics, 69 percent of full-time master's degree students borrow to cover their expenses; on average, they carry a total of $32,500 of debt (including remaining undergraduate debt) once they finish their master's program. Some degree candidates have no choice but to finance their degrees with savings or loans; for those who earn their degrees part-time while continuing to work full-time, assistantships are impractical, and their income typically disqualifies them from subsidized student loans.

  Of the borrowing options available, subsidized Stafford loans represent the cheapest type of student debt available. Interest rates are currently 5.3 percent, and you can borrow up to $8,500 per year ($65,500 in total). The federal government pays the interest on your loan while you're in school and for six months after you graduate or drop below half-time status. Even if interest rates rise significantly by the time you need to repay, they can't exceed 8.25 percent.

  Students qualify based on financial need, so it's necessary to file the Free Application for Federal Student Aid (FAFSA) to get subsidized loans. If your need is high, you may also be offered a subsidized Perkins loan, with an interest rate of 5 percent. You can borrow an additional $10,000 a year in unsubsidized Stafford loans (and up to $138,500 in Stafford loans overall). Rates are the same as for the subsidized Stafford, and you can defer making payments, but interest begins accruing right away.

  If your school participates in the Federal Direct Student Loan program, you'll borrow directly from the federal government. Otherwise, you can choose your own lender. Rates are usually the same no matter where you go, but some lenders waive upfront fees or offer attractive repayment incentives that make loans even cheaper. Student loan giant Sallie Mae, for instance, rebates 3.3 percent of your loan amount after you make 33 on-time payments.

For students who own a home, a home-equity loan or line of credit is another choice. Many banks were recently offering lines of credit at 6 percent or less, and the interest you pay is generally tax deductible. (So is up to $2,500 a year in student loan interest if you earn less than $50,000 as a single taxpayer and $105,000 if you file a joint return. A lesser amount of interest is deductible if you earn up to $65,000 or $135,000, respectively.)

If loans like these don't entirely meet your needs, keep in mind that you can borrow more money with private lenders than you can with government lenders, whose maximum loan amounts may not provide you with the funding you need to cover all your expenses. For information on connecting with private lenders check out the "Scholarships & Aid" section of the Princeton Review's website—PrincetonReview.com/grad/finance.

However much you borrow, make sure you know exactly how much it will eat into your monthly expenses once you graduate. Several websites—including FinAid.org—provide online calculators that will let you know how much debt you can afford to take on in order to fund your master's or doctoral program.

- **Ask your employer for it.**

  If you're currently working and can make a compelling case that your advanced degree is job-related, it's possible that your employer may be able to foot at least part of the bill. According to *U.S. News & World Report*, approximately 49 percent of private firms offer tuition-reimbursement programs for job-related educational expenses as an employee benefit. About 14 percent will help employees pay for courses that aren't job related. The percentages are significantly higher for professional and technical employees and for employees of large and medium-sized firms. While employer-sponsored funding is more common among business school students financing their MBA, it's often a compelling option for employees of colleges and universities too. Educational institutions often offer significant tuition breaks for employees—so if you're currently working at a college or university (as a research assistant or an administrator, for example), remember that your employer might help fund your advanced degree. Even if you're not pursuing an advanced degree, many schools allow their employees to take a certain number of credit hours—or continuing education classes—for free, which is something to keep in mind. No matter who your employer is, be sure to read the fine print before you tap into this kind of funding, because you typically can't just take the money and run—there are usually restrictions on how long you must stay with the company once you've obtained your degree.

- **Tell Uncle Sam about it.**

  Students paying out of pocket for tuition and fees can take advantage of the federal Lifetime Learning tax credit, worth up to $2,000. The credit equals 20 percent of the first $10,000 you spend in tuition and fees each year. If you file a single return, you're eligible for the full tax credit if your income is $45,000 or less and for a partial credit with income up to $55,000. For married couples filing jointly, the tax credit is fully available with income up to $90,000 and partially available with income up to $110,000. You can use the credit even if you don't itemize deductions, and it reduces your tax bill dollar for dollar.[8]

Academic vs. professional degrees

A traditional "academic" graduate school program focuses on work that will generate original research in a particular discipline. You may believe that a PhD is a "stronger" degree than a master's but it really depends on your individual career objectives. A master's curriculum focuses on applied topics while the theoretical and technical topics at the heart of a doctoral education train scholars for careers in academia and in high-level positions within research institutions. Some master's degrees are designed to lead to a doctorate degree while others are the "terminal" degree for a profession (e.g., Master of Library Science; Master of Business Administration).

A "professional" degree program, on the other hand, is designed to provide relevant skills and knowledge to future professionals in a particular field. Professional schools provide a quick foundation of academic course work relevant to the field coupled with a specialization. The curriculum includes academic course work, exposure to advanced analytical tools, and fieldwork.

Many academic and professional advanced degree programs adopt an interdisciplinary approach to focus on a particular problem or interest area. You can combine disciplines within one degree program—for example, a master's in law and literature or a master's in English and creative writing. Even if you are committed to one degree— let's say law school—you are often able to take graduate courses in other departments on campus—for example, environmental science or public health—to enhance your legal education training. And of course there are the official joint-degree programs—the graduate level version of a double major—where you can leave a university with two degrees under your belt.

Although English and communications majors can certainly pursue advanced degrees in anything from anthropology to social welfare, the following programs are popular choices for the communication savvy, and make excellent use of the skills you've already developed.

8 Kristin Davis. "The Hunt for Money." *U.S. News & World Report: America's Best Graduate Schools.* 2006. 13–15.

CREATIVE WRITING: THE MFA OPTION

Many English and communications majors dream of becoming novelists, poets, and playwrights. Aspiring authors need not apply to Master's of Fine Arts (MFA) or MA programs to realize their dreams of being published, but graduate study in creative writing can certainly have its advantages. For one thing, the structure that graduate programs impose can help prevent writers from becoming derailed by other distractions. Also, those who have been writing in isolation will have the opportunity to share their work with a community of talented writers and receive critical feedback. Unlike other graduate programs, most students in MFA and MA creative writing programs also work full-time and therefore programs are generally very flexible, with less rigid expectations in terms of a timeline for completing the degree. Some students finish in two years, others in three or four. There are always exceptions; the sought-after creative writing MFA at the University of Iowa is a two-year residency program.

Creative writing programs seek applicants with a tremendous amount of talent and potential as writers; this means that they are far less likely to penalize applicants for an unimpressive GPA or lackluster recommendations. When it comes to creative writing, the proof is in the pudding, and the pudding is the work you've already been crafting long before you actually apply to the MFA or MA program. Although there is no particular major associated with successful entry into graduate-level programs, the majority of students do have a background in English, communications, or the social sciences. Ultimately, those with a voracious appetite for books are the most likely to be strong writers (and therefore strong candidates for acceptance), though programs accept all kinds of applicants, from accountants to plumbers.

Although some prolific and illustrious authors make millions of dollars a year writing books, most writers can't support themselves solely by writing, and must rely on other positions to supplement their income. Teaching is a popular option, whether at community colleges, university extension programs, or full-time tenured positions at colleges and universities (although these positions are scarce). Most schools offer both an MA in English with a focus in creative writing, or an MFA in creative writing. The English/creative writing combo is focused on developing knowledge of various forms of literature in addition to developing one's own work. This track can be advantageous for those who plan to teach, given the dearth of creative writing positions in comparison to the number of teaching positions available in composition or literature. Gaining experience as a teacher's assistant in your MFA program or interning at local schools or universities can give you a boost in the right direction if you are interested in teaching. Because many applicants are already professionals, they have no intention of giving up their full-time job; they just want to improve their writing skills and join a close-knit community of like-minded people.

Interview with Maxine Chernoff, Dean of the Department of Creative Writing at San Francisco State University

What distinguishes an excellent applicant from the average applicant for your program?

What distinguishes an excellent applicant for our fiction writing program from the average applicant is an outstanding manuscript. Our students are a broad mix of ages; most are in their mid-to-late thirties, and their writing style reflects their life experience and the fact that they've had more time to write. We've also admitted plenty of undergraduate applicants whose writing style is already well-developed, interesting, and mature. Where you went to school, what recommenders say, or whether or not you've been published carries far less weight than your actual manuscript. We have admitted unpublished authors who are brilliant, and published authors who aren't quite as brilliant as they thought they were.

What kinds of career opportunities does the typical MFA student pursue after graduation?

Our graduates almost always continue writing. We track their publications through a yearly newsletter. Many also pursue teaching positions. A published book is necessary for most tenure-track teaching positions, but with a few publications, students can teach in a part-time capacity. It's usually necessary to cobble together a teaching career in creative writing, literature, and composition courses, though it's more possible with time to find a full-time position in creative writing. Some students are also interested in working in small press distribution, arts organizations, and as editors. We offer internship opportunities in a wide array of organizations, or students can develop their own.

What kinds of surprises do you think students have in store when applying to programs in fiction writing?

One of the pleasant surprises about fiction writing programs is that you are suddenly surrounded by other writers, and that peer group can be such a critical source of support. In an industry where so much is determined by peer evaluation, having lifelong writing friends is an excellent resource. This is also one of the reasons why some of our students stay in the program longer than they expected they would. One of the unpleasant surprises is that *you have to keep writing*. Some students get here and find themselves busier than they thought they'd be. You are learning an awful lot, but you aren't necessarily working on what you imagined you were going to be. Instead, you find interesting "distractions" which end up being creatively motivating and they move you in new directions. You don't always maintain interest in the story you thought you'd be writing . . . many students cross genres. All of a sudden you are writing a play, and you don't know why.

Do you have any specific advice for prospective students?

Send in something that you think is *reliably* your best work. Definitely make sure that you want to do this. Getting an advanced degree in creative writing is much more about your own dedication and love for doing it than the pursuit of big rewards. Surveys by various institutions that track writers show that the average writer in America makes less than 600 bucks a year on writing. Be willing to go to some length and make sacrifices. Often, good things do happen.

Choosing a program: Money and mentors

Acquiring an MFA or MA degree in creative writing isn't about the pursuit of hefty paychecks. Thus, students should contemplate how much money they're willing to spend in order to join a community of writers and further develop their craft. Private schools like Brown University, Syracuse, or Mills College are going to demand higher tuition costs than, say, San Francisco State University, or New Mexico State University. This doesn't mean that one choice is inherently "better" than another, or that the public's perception of a program is dictated by the prestige of the university in which it is housed or its status as public or private; the very highly regarded program at the University of Iowa is, after all, a public school program. Rather, consider the qualities of that particular writing community. For example, is mentorship encouraged? The impact of merit-based funding on the peer community of a program can also be tremendous. Imagine if you were the recipient of full-ride tuition at a program, and found yourself surrounded by students who received no funding, or vice versa. This scenario can certainly cause tension between peers, and inspire an unpleasant kind of competition. Not all schools offer merit-based funding, so if you imagine that you would find it difficult to thrive under circumstances in which you knew some of your peers had received merit awards, take a look at programs with more egalitarian funding options. Also, consider browsing the course schedule for that program; are there specific course offerings at that college that pique your interest or directly speak to your works in progress?

If you are interested in more cutting-edge or experimental forms of writing, and a particular program wants to groom more "traditional" writers, you probably aren't going to fit in. The best way to discern the flavor of a program is to get in touch with current students. If the program's website doesn't provide contact information for current students, get in touch with the program administrator and ask for a list. Students are far more likely to present a view of their program that is refreshingly free of glossy images and platitudes. When you speak to them, don't be afraid to ask specific questions, such as the following:

- Do you feel that this program has encouraged your development as a writer?

- What kinds of extracurricular opportunities are available to students in this program?

- Do you have a program mentor? Is there a built-in mentorship program for students? If not, how easy is it to develop such a relationship?
- How diverse is the program?
- Would you feel comfortable presenting experimental work to your peers?

Do not underestimate the importance of a mentorship. As you read the faculty roster and faculty biographies you should find yourself drawn to the particular type of work that they're doing. If you can't identify a single teacher with whom you would want to develop a mentor/mentee relationship, then you are definitely looking at the wrong program. Fortunately, there is enough variability in programs that there is truly a home for every type of literary aspiration. Again, don't be shy about asking administrators and students what they're looking for. Success in these programs is largely peer-driven. You don't want to find yourself presenting a story with a lot of fantasy elements to a group of hardcore realists or vice versa . . . in these scenarios the feedback you receive will likely be stilted and far from helpful.

The MFA application process

Program requirements vary, although nearly every program requires a substantial sample of your work (check each school's admissions requirements for guidelines on length), a statement of purpose, and two or three letters of recommendation which are generally academic, though they may be industry-related if you happen to know an editor who is willing to rave about your work. Again, realize that these letters rarely make a big difference in terms of whether or not an applicant will be picked. The magazine that published your work obviously thinks you're a class act, but the people you really have to impress are the readers behind the stacks of manuscripts and admissions envelopes. In other words, if they don't think much of your poetry, they aren't going to care that an editor does. Many programs require the GRE general test, although the scores are very rarely a factor in admission; most of the time the scores are required for the graduate division's record-keeping purposes, not for the actual department. Many others also require a resume.

What you'll learn and how long you'll be there

Most creative writing programs offer a two-year curriculum, although the non-resident programs are more likely to be populated by students who are working full- or part-time, and are unlikely to complete their degree in two years. The curriculum for MFA programs in creative writing usually involves a number of fiction and/or poetry workshops (in which you present your work and your peers give you feedback) and elective courses in anything from literature to history, depending on your area(s) of interest, and its relation to your writing project. A titanium ego and unsinkable spirit are necessary tools for survival in the fiction or poetry workshops; criticism is intrinsic to your professional growth, and peer criticism is especially important because published authors are at the mercy of their peers in literary reviews. Many programs require a thesis or master project, in which you will work directly with a faculty member to develop a particularly promising piece of work, be it a novel, play, series of stories, or series of poems.

How much will it cost?

The cost of tuition partially depends on whether or not you'll receive funding from your program. For example, some MFA programs provide funding for students in the form of teaching assistantships, or fellowships for which all incoming students qualify. Other schools offer merit-based funding for particular students, while others offer minimal funding or none at all. Many programs offer specific sources of funding for underrepresented students. One of your criteria for choosing a program should certainly be available funding sources, unless money is truly no object. Nonresident programs tend to provide less funding for students. If you have to rely partially or fully on outside sources for financial support, see Appendix II for an overview of some of the most common types of financial aid. Fortunately, there are many scholarships available for creative writing MFAs. See Appendix II for information on some of the most popular.

GRADUATE PROGRAMS IN PUBLIC RELATIONS, MARKETING, AND ADVERTISING

A graduate education in public relations, marketing, or advertising is almost always the culmination of an already successful career in communications. Most programs award master's degrees which help boost their students into managerial roles within their already established niches. Some offer PhDs, which are intended to prepare students for academic and research careers. If you are hoping to enter the communications field via a graduate degree, you should be looking for volunteer experiences, internships, or other types of training programs that will provide you with hands-on experience before you apply to grad school. If, however, you have held entry to mid-level positions in communications, a graduate degree can certainly groom you for future promotions. The departments in which programs are actually housed varies from school to school. You may have already discovered that some MBA programs offer an emphasis in marketing, while other public relations programs are housed in the communications department. You may also be surprised to find that a number of master's programs in advertising can be found in art academies. Where you decide to pursue your graduate degree will mostly be dictated by the particular role you plan to fulfill. If you are going to create the graphics that appear in an advertisement, you may very well attend a totally different school than the advertising account managers, who work directly with clients and have little to do with the creative side of the process. Following is an overview of the different specializations in graduate communications programs.

Public Relations

Master's level programs are mostly aimed to prepare students to take on managerial roles such as a marketing communications manager or an account executive. Bear in mind that a master's degree is rarely a requirement for such positions; rather, it is viewed as an additional credential that may help distinguish you from your colleagues, and orient you to the more theoretical side of public relations. Oftentimes, the master's degree is a stepping-stone for those students who want to complete their PhD and devote their professional lives to public relations research and instruction. If an academic career is in your future, you must be ready to choose a very specific area of specialization within public relations in which you will conduct research; this can include anything from interpersonal/intercultural communications, to global public relations, to conflict management. Most master's level programs offer a thesis and non-thesis option, the non-thesis option being available only to students who do not plan on completing their PhD. In place of a thesis, there is usually some other type of exit requirement, such as a comprehensive examination.

Marketing

The majority of students who are interested in pursuing a master's degree in marketing are going to find themselves perusing information about business schools. MA programs in marketing aren't nearly as prevalent as the MBA option with an emphasis in marketing, although there are a number of programs (most often in a university's continuing education department) which offer degrees in marketing management, or marketing communications. What is the difference? MBA programs require the student to take the GMAT rather than the GRE, and require general education course work in business administration, whereas communications-based degrees tend to focus more specifically on marketing. Both programs require applicants to have two to three years of industry experience and a desire to move into managerial roles in marketing. PhD candidates almost always have a background in marketing management, and are trying to make the transition into academia. MBA programs do not generally require a thesis or exit exam of any kind, although incoming students should be able to articulate an interest in a particular area(s) of marketing such as brand management, international marketing, or product strategy.

Advertising

Work in advertising encompasses a number of different but interrelated positions for which academic training often differs. If you are artistically inclined and find yourself attracted to the field of advertising because it seems like an excellent means to earn money while flexing your creative muscles, you'll probably be looking for programs in the art and design department of a university or at various art academies. Be warned: Many (but not all) of these programs only offer training at the bachelor's (rather than master's) level. It isn't at all uncommon for advertising design enthusiasts to pursue a second bachelor's degree, although the tuition at art academies can be quite expensive. Such programs can help boost students into the role of creative or art director, or advertising copywriter.

If you intend to work as a media planner, or an account manager, you will most often find appropriate graduate training in the communications department of a university or, less often, the business school. For industry newcomers, there are a number of programs that are friendly to applicants who lack an advertising background; for example, the University of Texas at Austin asks students to take a number of prerequisite courses for their advertising program, but industry and prior academic experience isn't required.

Graduate Degrees in Advertising and PR: What We're Looking For

Dr. Debbie Treise is the Associate Dean of the Division of Graduate Studies and Research, and a professor in the Department of Advertising at the University of Florida, whose communications programs have consistently been ranked among the best in the country. Debbie shares her insights about what makes an excellent candidate for graduate programs in advertising and public relations.

We are looking for students who have a genuine commitment to the profession of public relations. This includes a commitment to developing their own professionalism by gaining academic knowledge and furthering the professionalism of the field by applying the theoretical principles of public relations to research and practice. Prior work experience that is the most impressive would include executive or managerial responsibilities specifically in public relations in either the private or public sector. Positions involving relationship building, reputation management, and organizational social responsibility initiatives would be considered the upper echelon.

Prospective advertising students should have a passion for great ideas, the motivation and leadership to improve the advertising profession—both in the field and in advertising research and scholarship—critical-thinking skills, and a strong work ethic. We're most impressed by the type of work experience that provided applicants with the focus, understanding, background, and motivation for graduate advertising education. The typical career paths for students graduating with a Master's of Advertising degree are: research analyst, marketing manager (including developing and implementing marketing communication plans for various practice areas), account executive, account manager, or communications manager. And, of course, our doctoral students are prepared to teach advertising at the university level.

Choosing a school: Who's hiring?

If your interest in a graduate degree in communications is driven by images of a well-lit corner office complete with doting assistants and an expense account, then choose schools that can help you achieve that goal; if you imagine that you'll be happiest working in a hectic, team-oriented nonprofit environment, then choose schools that can help you achieve *that* goal. In other words, your decision to attend a particular school should largely be driven by the kinds of opportunities that its alumni are able to pursue after graduation successfully. Ask the Admissions Office where alumni are being hired. Better yet, visit the school's website and contact students and/or alumni directly. You may also find a short list of places where alumni have been hired. For example, the Newhouse School of Communications at Syracuse University and the University of Texas at Austin both offer exiting information for their graduate students, so it's easy to see who is working where. Prospective PhD students should also be browsing the faculty roster for teachers whose research interests align with their own.

The application process

You may be applying to an MBA program in marketing, an MFA program in advertising, or an MA/MS program in public relations; these application pathways are going to look very different. While it is up to you to do your homework to find out the specific application requirements for the program in which you are interested (start by visiting PrincetonReview.com), here's a brief overview of what you can expect. If you are applying to MBA programs, be prepared to take the GMAT (Graduate Management Admissions Test). Almost all of the other programs require the GRE, though MFA programs in advertising often do not require the GRE. Instead, your portfolio is more likely to be the focal point of your application. Most programs want two to three letters of recommendation, and these are usually academic or industry references, or both.

What you'll learn and how long you'll be there

- **Public Relations**

    Master's programs can last anywhere from one to three years; PhD programs last between five to seven years. The shorter degrees (and generally more flexible in terms of timeline) tend to be offered through university continuing education classes. Core courses are often in public relations research, writing, and management, as well as media law.

- **Marketing**

    The typical MBA program lasts two years. Marketing master's programs last one to two years, although many students spend more than two years finishing up. PhD programs can last anywhere from four to seven years. Most marketing programs require course work in global marketing, consumer behavior, marketing strategy, business marketing management, and pricing tactics.

- **Advertising**

    Master's programs are typically 2 years long; many of the adver-
    tising design master's programs (MFA) are only one year long. In
    management and media planning, you will likely be taking
    courses in communications theory, advertising media and research,
    advertising management, and some sort of practicum course for
    your field placement. In advertising design, you'll probably be tak-
    ing courses in copywriting, digital graphics, and branding.

How much will it cost?

Due to the practical orientation of most of these programs, students are often able
to work part-time or sometimes even full-time during graduate school (the exception
being those who are enrolled in PhD programs), which can help relieve some of the
financial burden. Otherwise, the cost of tuition varies widely according to the type of
program and institution. Public university tuition can range anywhere from $2,000 to
$8,000 a semester compared to private school tuition which can range from $10,000
to more than $15,000 a semester. Financial aid and private loans can help offset the
cost of tuition. See Appendix II for information on financial aid.

JOURNALISM SCHOOL

Journalism School (or J-school) teaches you how to be a reporter in various communications media: radio, television, print, and online. Although some argue that
good reporters are born, not made, proponents of J-school will tell you that one of the
most critical lessons you'll learn as a graduate student in journalism is how to be an
ethical reporter which, according to the Society of Professional Journalists, is
defined as one who properly represents facts, identifies sources, and supports the
open exchange of views. Because faculty in most programs are former or current
industry professionals, J-school students have access to a broad network of field
contacts, and are often engaged in fieldwork for the duration of the program.

In order to be a competitive applicant, you must be able to demonstrate superior
writing and critical-thinking skills, and be able to impress the Admissions Committee
with published clippings or other writing samples. If you haven't already interned at
your college newspaper or local radio station, choose academic writing samples that
show your ability to form and defend an argument, especially one that revolves
around hotly debated issues.

Journalism schools tend to favor applicants who have several years of work experience behind them. Applicants who are able to demonstrate an abiding interest in
journalism and communications will have an edge over those who lack any exposure
to the field. Prospective students who have years of professional experience in a
niche area that they intend to explore as reporters, (a former museum curator or bal-
lerina who intends become an arts journalist) will also be viewed favorably. It's a

good idea to show that you have a well-rounded liberal arts education by taking a broad range of course work, from English to psychology to world history.

> "Graduate journalism study isn't for every aspiring journalist. There are many ways to establish a journalism career, and most good degree programs are aimed at exceptionally smart, curious people who have had enough experience in the field both to know this work is what they want and to understand what kinds of skills and practice a graduate program can offer them. We look favorably at most kinds of undergraduate degrees, although journalism and mass communication degrees are not regarded as an advantage; we tend to think those are redundant. Strong writing skills and personal statements show us a natural journalist in the making, matter more to us than high grade point averages or GRE scores."
>
> **Cynthia Gorney, associate dean and professor from the UC—Berkeley Graduate School of Journalism**

Choosing a journalism school: It's not the place, it's the people

There are those who will swear up and down that if you rebelliously decide to apply to a middle-ranking J-school, your peers who are hanging up Syracuse, NYU, and Columbia diplomas will squeeze you right out of the job market. There is no denying the market appeal of the top-ranking J-schools, if for no other reason than that they attract excellent and well-connected faculty, which can make or break your J-school experience. Truth be told, there are numerous schools that lack the Pulitzer glow of Columbia, but employ outstanding faculty who can also be very helpful in helping students launch their careers. Before shunning your state school's journalism program, take a look at the faculty roster and see what kind of work the students are engaged in doing. You should also consider the student organizations on campus through which you could develop a strong peer network, which is truly the cornerstone of a successful transition into professional life. This is, perhaps, the best way to determine what a particular J-school can do for you.

The journalism school application process

Although journalism schools often seek the same kinds of applicants, the actual application process varies widely. Many schools require the Graduate Record Examination (GRE) or, for students whose second language is English, the Test of English as a Foreign Language (TOEFL). Some schools require minimum qualifying scores for admissions tests, and some do not require tests at all. Still other schools require interviews. All schools are looking for three letters of recommendation, and a stellar personal statement. Make sure to get in touch with each school, or check their website for specific application instructions.

How long you'll be there, and what you'll learn

Most master's-level programs in journalism last three to four semesters and are designed for full-time students. However, some schools offer more flexible enrollment options for its working professionals; Columbia University offers a part-time program that allows students to complete their degree in two to three years. By the time you're ready to apply to J-school, you should have a strong sense of the media platforms that interest you most, and what niche areas you want to cover. Are you interested in environmental journalism? Photojournalism? Do you want to be a political pundit or a society columnist? J-schools offer courses and fieldwork experience in a variety of areas, and much of your elective course work will be concentrated in your niche. Some schools also offer joint-degrees in which you can earn a master's in biology or French studies concurrently with your master's in journalism; this can be especially useful if you intend to become an international reporter, or you are pursuing a niche that requires an industry-specific vernacular.

The J-school core curriculum usually covers research methods and editing, intermediate and advanced reporting (these are usually practicum courses which require you to study reporting methods intensely in class, then spend 20 or more hours a week pursuing and developing original, publishable stories), and media law and ethics, which focuses on first amendment law and case studies illustrating ethical dilemmas in reporting such as slander and communications theory. Most programs also require students to complete a master's project or master's thesis. Unlike the traditional master's thesis, journalism theses often reflect the diverse media that the students study; video, audio, text, and photos or some combination of these are perfectly acceptable forms for a typical J-school thesis to take.

How much will it cost?

Many of the top journalism schools are private, which means hefty tuition. Be prepared to pay around $32,000 a year in tuition and student fees alone for a top-ranked private school. Those who are less concerned with reputation will find that there are a number of excellent public J-schools as well, with comparatively modest tuition and fees. There are also many scholarships and fellowships available to prospective J-school students. Later in the chapter, we'll describe a few of the most well-known scholarship and fellowship programs; you should use this information as a starting point for your own research into outside funding sources to help finance your education. See Appendix II for information on the most common loan programs.

The great J-school debate

Journalism school skeptics abound. A single Internet search will reveal a slew of opinions about the worthiness of a J-school education. Many skeptics, including some graduates of J-school programs, say that a graduate education in journalism isn't necessary to become a successful reporter, and some go so far as to say that J-school is a waste of money and time. Certainly, the majority of reporters do not boast a graduate degree. A determined fledgling reporter can succeed without a graduate education by starting at a local newspaper or television station, working as a fact-checker or copyeditor, and building his or her way up to a more glamorous position. However, happy J-school grads claim that the exposure to influential people in the industry as well as mandatory fieldwork experience make a J-school education worth every dime. Choosing a program that focuses on reporting news rather than news theory may also help you get a leg up if you plan on being a reporter rather than teaching journalism or communications.

"Journalism school is a safe environment in which to fail"

"Before I entered J-school, I had no real credibility to go into the market. I had been working in investment banking for five years, and almost everybody else in my entering class lacked real reporting experience. I chose a program that had an extraordinarily practical focus, with teachers who were still working in the field. This gave me access to newsrooms, and my work was being published the whole time I was there, for major publications. The contacts that I developed were so worthwhile that I was able to go work at the *New York Times* for a year, a nearly impossible feat if I had attempted to start from scratch. Because you're a student, you also have the chance to make mistakes you'd never be able to make if you were a "legitimate" reporter . . . if you turn in a pile of rubbish, it's just a learning experience. Journalism school is a safe environment in which to fail."

Daniel Levine, Biotechnology Reporter, *San Francisco Business Times* and Author of *Disgruntled: The Darker Side of the World of Work*

LAW SCHOOL

As your typical sharp-witted, verbally dexterous English or communications major, you have undoubtedly been asked whether or not you plan to put your talents to good use as an attorney. Law school is certainly a popular professional choice for lovers of the written word. Attorneys rely heavily on their ability to distill information, extract themes, and formulate impermeable arguments; these are all skills that you've developed as an English or communications major. The actual study and practice of law is often less about courtroom glamour and more about the effective management of paper (and lots of it). Lawyers have to be detail-oriented, objective advocates for their client, whether those clients are corporations, families, or environmental agencies. The most attractive candidates for law school should be able to demonstrate their ability to effectively advocate for others. Many successful applicants have experience as mentors for young people, outspoken student leaders for nonprofit organizations, or government agency interns. Your passionate, exquisitely crafted personal statement should convince the admissions committee that you are not only a natural advocate, but that you are certain law is the best medium for you to continue to help others.

Contrary to popular opinion, an undergraduate degree in legal studies or pre-law is unnecessary. Many schools even prefer that you've had minimal exposure to law, as they'd like to teach you from the ground up. All admissions committees, however, need to see evidence that you are aware of what attorneys do. Any student considering a career in law should first shadow an attorney or take on a volunteer or internship position that will put them in direct contact with attorneys. Many students arbitrarily decide that attending law school will place them securely on the fast track to big pay-checks, and are eager to please mom and dad with their lofty ambitions. First-year attrition rates in law schools are somewhat high for this reason. Law can be an exciting field, but it certainly isn't the best fit for every enthusiastic and intelligent liberal arts student. Not all attorneys earn massive salaries, and those that do often have to work long hours as first- and second-year associates. Moral of the story: Make sure that you know what you're getting into before deciding on a law career.

Interview with Diana DiGennaro, third-year law student at Boalt Law School

What should students expect during their first year of law school?

The first year of law school is a lot of work and it is difficult work. If students want to do all the required reading, they should expect to spend at least four to five hours per day on it. The amount of time spent depends in part on the student's prior familiarity with judicial opinions and the U.S. legal system. If you are not familiar with reading judicial opinions, it takes a long time to read each individual case. For the first month, it may take you two hours to read 10 pages in a casebook. Likewise, if you don't have a strong sense of the structure of the U.S. legal system, it is difficult to understand the big picture behind the legal rules you are learning in the cases. In the second semester, the work becomes more manageable (two hours to read 20–30 pages) as your familiarity with reading cases increases, as does your overall understanding of the framework in which to read them.

The other aspect of the first year of law school is the psychological one. The first semester may be intimidating because of the use of the Socratic Method in class (professors will "cold call" on students at random and ask them moderately difficult questions to test their understanding of a given case or legal issue) and because the other first-year students are likely to act very confident regardless of whatever confusion they may be experiencing. Students should expect this and understand that pretty much everyone is in the same boat when it comes to understanding the first-year curriculum.

How did you know that law school was the most ideal career path for you?

It was essentially a process of elimination. As a double major in literature (concentration in French literature) and psychology, I considered several different career paths before deciding on law school. I initially wanted to be a clinical psychologist but after taking Abnormal Psychology, I realized it was not for me. I then considered doing a PhD in French literature but I was not really interested in teaching. It was at this time (my fourth year of college) that I began to consider law school mainly because it seemed to be a more versatile degree and because I had always been interested in constitutional and international law issues. I did an MA in French language and civilization immediately after undergrad and that experience, while interesting and enjoyable, solidified my interest in going to law school instead of entering a PhD program. My MA was fascinating, but I realized I wanted to do something more practical in sense of having an impact on society or helping people in a practical, immediate way. I went to law school gambling on the presumption that I would either want to be a lawyer or that a JD would open doors to other careers that would interest me.

Did your bachelor's degree in literature come in handy?

Yes. Particularly at a law school where theory and policy (and thus critical thinking) are emphasized, being able to read critically and write well is very helpful. A close textual reading of a case or piece of legislation requires many of the same skills as a critical reading of a literary text. Similarly, although legal writing is structured differently from academic pieces, the same principles apply, and a strong ability to write well is crucial to doing well on exams and papers. In addition, just being comfortable writing in an exam situation (with time pressure) is very helpful. I had many in-class, closed-book essay exams in my literature classes and this was great preparation for law school exams, which are almost exclusively essay questions.

What was the biggest surprise about law school?

The amount of work. It is difficult to exaggerate the massive amount of time law school consumes if you attempt to do the majority of the assigned reading and fulfill your extracurricular obligations. The other surprise was that, if you put in the time to do the work, you are already ahead of most people and it is possible to do very well. This comes as a surprise because when you enter law school, many if not all of the other students will seem very confident and very at ease. It is easy to be intimidated and think you're the only one struggling. But if you are struggling, it is because you are doing the work, and this usually pays off on exams.

What does it take to thrive in law school?

First, actually taking the time to do the work—primarily reading the cases—counts for a lot. Also, modifying but essentially maintaining the study patterns that worked for you in undergrad is helpful. Many people change their whole approach to learning material because it is "law school," but if you have an approach that worked before, stick with it to the extent possible.

Second, use the professors. They are intimidating but ultimately they're there to help you learn and asking questions in class or in office hours when you don't understand something is extremely helpful. Study groups can be helpful if they are small and if the people in the group study the same way (same level of depth, practice problems versus abstract learning, etc.) you do. Third, don't take on too much. Law school is filled with opportunities, many of which seem like amazing, once-in-a-lifetime, or necessary-to-my-career–type opportunities. These include work on law journals, involvement in student groups, doing research for professors, moot court, clinics, and involvement in student government, admissions, and faculty hiring. It is easy to sign up for too many of these extracurriculars such that you no longer have time to do the work for your classes. In the long run, it is far more important to get decent grades and actually learn the material than to stockpile your resume. Law journals and research positions with professors are among the most helpful because they are universally respected (in the private sector, public interest, and government fields) and because they can generate strong references and/or letters of recommendation. However, orient your choices toward the career you are interested in. For example, participation in clinics serving a particular group or population, or addressing a issue (e.g., human rights, environmental law, law and technology) can be very helpful if you already know you want to work in that field.

Now that you're done with the academic portion of your program and you're studying for the bar exam, what advice would you give prospective law students?

Before going to law school, make sure you need a JD to do what you want to do. If you have a career in mind that requires a JD, be certain that career is what you want to do. While it is true that a JD is versatile and law school is an intellectually interesting experience, it requires a lot of loans. This kind of financial debt can limit your career options and loan forgiveness programs are limited.

If you must go to law school, figure out what area of law you are interested in and start law school with some focus on a specific career or specific area of law. This is very, very helpful. Keeping track of the big picture (the rest of the world beyond law school) and the reasons you want a JD will help motivate your studying but also keep you from getting too caught up in law school politics.

Choosing a school

Once you've made the decision to apply to law school, generate a list of prospective schools based on a three-tiered system. Your top-tier choices should be "stretch" schools, those that are competitive and very reputable, perhaps even slightly out of your range based on your LSAT scores and GPA. Then list a number of middle-tier schools where your application is likely to be competitive (schools where your LSAT scores and GPA are within the school's reported ranges). Finally, choose some safety schools as your ace-in-the-holes (your LSAT scores and GPA will be slightly higher than the reported ranges for these schools). The Princeton Review website PrincetonReview.com offers information on law schools accredited by the American Bar Association. The Law School Admissions Council website LSAC.org also offers law school rankings and other information that can help you produce a solid list of target schools. Most students choose to apply to seven to fifteen different schools, depending on their budget for the application process and the strength of their GPA and LSAT scores. Students with lower-than-average LSAT scores may choose to apply to more schools to increase their chances of success. Those students with very strong scores and otherwise competitive applicants may decide to take a gamble solely on top schools. Here are some other factors that are worthy of consideration as you narrow down your list of prospective schools:

- How diverse is the school? Does the faculty reflect the diversity of the student body?

- Where are the graduates working now? What kind of job placement rates is typical for this school and in what kind of practice?

- Are there courses available in your area of interest? If you want to be a human rights attorney but the bulk of elective courses are in intellectual property or corporate law, you probably won't get what you need out of the law school experience at this school.

- At least some of the faculty should have areas of interest and practice that reflect your own.

- Where would you be living, and do you want to live there for three years?

- What kinds of programs are available to supplement your law school application? Could you study abroad? Acquire a joint-degree?

- Also consider the location of the school. If you plan on establishing a practice in a specific state, realize that your school's reputation carries more weight on its own home turf. Of course, if you are accepted into a top-10 law school with a globally recognizable name, you will also have a competitive edge in almost any state where you may wish to practice.

LSAT—Section By Section

READING COMPREHENSION	• About 27 multiple-choice questions
	• 35-minute section
LOGICAL REASONING (Arguments)	• Multiple-choice questions
	• 2 sections, about 25 questions each
	• 35-minute sections
ANALYTICAL REASONING (Games)	• About 25 multiple-choice questions
	• 35-minute section
EXPERIMENTAL	• About 25 multiple-choice questions
	• 35-minute section
ESSAY	• 1 essay
	• 35-minute section

For more information, check out the LSAT website at LSAS.org

Source: PrincetonReview.com

The application process

Assembling your law school application is a fairly straightforward (albeit time-intensive) process. The first and most essential step in the application process is to register for the Law School Admissions Test (LSAT). There is, interestingly, a new score reporting policy for the LSAT. In previous years, scores were averaged; now, only the highest score is reported to schools. Nevertheless, statistics reflect that very few students see a major improvement in their LSAT scores, especially if they take the test again and again within a brief time frame (you're only allowed to take it three times within a one-year period). Sometimes scores even drop. Rater than approaching the LSAT with the mindset that you can always take it again, consider practicing using ItemWise, an online tool that allows you to take practice tests for a one-time fee of $18.00 at LSAC.org. You will also want to register with the Law School Data Assembly Service LSDAS, the central application service that distributes your information to various schools. You can register online at LSAC.org or mail in the form from the latest LSAT or LSDAS registration packet.

At this time, begin planting seeds for letters of recommendation. Most schools are going to ask for two to three academic letters, ideally from faculty, although letters from graduate student instructors can be equally compelling if they are better able to comment on your academic fitness and your personal attributes. Letters written by graduate student instructors and co-signed by professors are very common in larger schools, where class size means that students have limited contact with faculty. It is also absolutely necessary that you take the time to visit your professors and teacher's assistants during office hours, particularly if you attend a large public university where instructors are unlikely to remember your excellent work unless you make yourself known to them on a personal basis. Do not underestimate the importance of recommendation letters; although your GPA and LSAT score are weighed heavily, letters can be the deciding factor for many Admissions Committees. If you are lucky enough to secure an extra letter, hold onto it in case you are wait listed. Sometimes sending a stellar letter while you're on a waitlist can be the factor that propels you onward. A word to the wise: "Personal" letters from family or friends, or letters from political figures or other high profile people in the legal industry will most often be disregarded by Admissions Committees, or may even be detrimental to your candidacy.

Once you've received your LSAT scores (three to four weeks after the test date,) you can begin to think about writing your personal statement. Why should you wait? If you feel that there is a significant discrepancy between your performance on the LSAT and your GPA or vice versa, the personal statement gives you an opportunity to acknowledge and explain that discrepancy in the form of an "addendum." The addendum is a brief paragraph at the end of your statement where you can explain any inconsistencies in your application. Be sure not to abuse the opportunity by veering in the direction of excuse-making. The Admissions Committees will decide for themselves if your reasons are legitimate, and they would much rather see you take responsibility for your mistakes then make excuses for them. Remember, the personal statement is the only sample of writing that Admissions Committees are going to read. Make it count. Although schools have slightly different instructions for the theme of the statement, you should be prepared to cogently express your reasons for pursuing a law career, as well as your reasons for targeting each specific school. The more specific you can be the better. For example, rather than saying "I am passionate about the law because I want to advocate for others," describe the first time that you successfully passed a law in student government, or helped raise funds for the non-profit where you volunteered.

With your completed personal statement, letters of recommendation, LSAT score and official transcripts, you are now ready to request admissions materials from schools and apply. Be sure to check and see if the schools to which you're applying require Dean's Appraisals. This is essentially a letter of good standing which provides information on the conferral of your degree as well as any disciplinary records. The registrar's office at your undergraduate institution is most often responsible for providing this document. Your applications should be completed and sent by late November.

Assembling a letter "kit"

Does the idea of lingering outside your professor's office to ask for a letter of recommendation inspire fear? If so, you certainly aren't alone. Most students would rather eat their honor's thesis and wash it down with a pint of hot glue than ask for help from one of their professors, especially if there has been no prior vis-à-vis contact. Truthfully, the fear of a possible negative response is not unfounded. Professors are very busy, and they will turn down a request if they feel that they don't know a student well enough to write a strong letter. There is, however, something you can do to make a "yes" answer far more likely: Prepare a kit. The kit should include:

- Unofficial copies of your transcripts.

- Any work from the professor's class for which you received a stellar grade.

- A draft of your personal statement, or a brief cover letter describing your interest in pursuing graduate or professional school.

- A resume.

- Information about your school's letter service, including any supplemental forms they may need.

- A list of schools to which you're applying.

The kit will not only provide your potential recommender with exciting new facts about you that may make for a more personal and interesting letter, but it will also make you appear more serious in your endeavor to attend graduate school. Frankly, when presented with a kit, most professors will say "yes" simply because they can't turn down a student who has put so much effort into their proposal. Remember: If a professor does turn down your request, kit or no kit, don't take it to heart. They are sparing you from the fate of a vague and boring letter.

How long you'll be there and what you'll learn

Law schools typically demand three years of full-time study, the first of which is notoriously challenging. Your initial exposure to law comes in the form of torts (or wrongful acts), contracts and civil procedure (or "civ pro"), and property, criminal, and constitutional law and legal methods. This is also the year when students are introduced to an often-dreaded form of instruction called the Socratic Method, which is almost always combined with the Case Method. It works like this: Without warning, students will find themselves being called on to provide a cogent summary of whatever judicial cases that they've been assigned to analyze for that day's class. Although "case study" sounds innocuous enough, these cases are lengthy, complex, and chock full of indecipherable legal jargon. Intended to enhance critical-thinking skills, the Socratic Method involves the instructor asking a barrage of questions without providing much lecture material for students to draw from. Then, the instructor points out any overlooked details, faulty logic, or other inconsistencies in the students' responses.

Aiming for high grades (A's and B's) during your first year boosts your chances of being selected to write for your school's law review. The granddaddy of all law school accomplishments, writing for one of these student-produced and student-run periodicals requires participation in a writing contest, in which the students' anonymous writing (on an actual court case) is evaluated by a panel of professors. Those with stellar grades are often shoo-ins for Law Review, while those who shine in the writing competition but lack academic luster have a slightly lesser chance of getting selected. Some schools are far more democratic than others, and select their law review members purely on the basis of the quality of the student's writing.

Being selected to participate in moot court, a close second to the law review, is another resume-building experience for which first-year students must compete. Tryouts usually consist of a short oral argument and the submission of a written brief. If you are elected, the whole moot court team then produces two appellate briefs in response to a phony legal problem. Moot court teams also attend national competitions.

If your school bears a highly recognizable and respected name, you may also find that internship opportunities at fancy-schmancy firms are available to you after your first year, though the vast majority of students will not snag an internship until their second year.

During the second and third years of law school, there are fewer required courses for students to take, thus the academic focus is mostly on electives in the student's area of interest. Additionally, students must focus on landing an internship, ideally with a prestigious firm. Most students pursue their first internship during the fall of their second year. Excelling in your first internship will increase your chances of landing a summer associate's position between your second and third year of law school, which in turn, should increase your chances of being hired by any law firm (but especially the firm in whose program you've participated).

The final hurdle between you and the title of "juris doctor" is the bar examination. Administered twice a year, in February and July, the exam takes two days to complete, and consists of a number of essay questions, and 200 multiple-choice questions in six different areas of U.S. common law. Although the statistics vary from state to state, the average passing rate for the bar is around 65 percent. This means that many students should be prepared to take the bar more than once.

Preparing for a Legal Degree: Core Skills and Values

- Analytic/Problem-solving skills
- Critical reading
- Writing skills
- Oral communication/Listening abilities
- General research skills
- Task organization/Management skills
- Public service and promotion of justice

Source: Pre-Law Committee of the ABA Section of Legal Education and Admissions to the Bar

How much will it cost?

Make no mistake: A law school education is expensive. Tuition can range from a little over $4,000 a year to over $20,000 a year, excluding living expenses. Most students rely on a combination of grants, scholarships, loans, and federal work study to finance their law school education. The Law School Admissions Council (LSAC.org) offers in-depth information about the various forms of financial aid available to prospective law students and how to initiate the qualifying process. See Appendix II for information on the most common federal aid programs.

Joint-degree programs: Have your tort and eat it too

If one degree is good, then two must be great, right? joint-degree programs are designed for those students who have sagely determined that a juris doctor can be enhanced by almost any other professional degree, from a master's in social work to an MBA. Consider the possibilities: You want to work as a family attorney, but rather than taking on an adversarial role you envision yourself as a mediator and counselor—picking up a degree in marriage and family therapy along with your JD can not only help you meet this goal, but will give you the additional skills you need to carve out a nice little niche for yourself in an otherwise saturated market. Law schools offer joint-degree programs in such areas as:

- Medicine
- Business
- Environmental science
- International studies
- Social work
- Latin American studies
- Sports administration
- Clinical psychology
- History
- Literature
- Public administration
- Urban planning

Be prepared to apply to both the law school and the department that houses your other prospective degree. This may mean taking the GRE or GMAT in addition to the LSAT, and may also mean preparing for a longer stint in grad school in order to complete the requirements for the combo program. For many students, however, the time and financial investment is worth it. A JD-Master's/MBA/MD combo can open up a world of professional possibilities.

MEDICAL SCHOOL

Medical students learn all about the art and science of preventing and treating illness. The highly sought-after title of MD is the end result of four years of intense classroom and clinical learning, and at least three additional years of internship and residency. Medical school is an enormous commitment, not just because others' lives will be in your hands as a practicing physician, but also because the preparation requires tremendous foresight on the part of the applicant. In order to enter medical school directly after finishing your bachelor's degree, it is necessary to complete a challenging series of premed course requirements in biology, chemistry, physics, and mathematics. This sequence is prelude to and preparation for the Medical College Admissions Test (MCAT), which, in addition to a competitive GPA, is the most important qualifying factor for Admissions Committees. Applicants should acquire solid clinical experience prior to applying to medical school in order to prove their readiness to enter the field with their eyes wide open. By working in a clinic, prospective medical students are able to view physicians in action and, under ideal circumstances, interact with patients themselves. Certainly, the road to getting into medical school can be as difficult as medical school itself, and many misinformed students often believe that non-science majors aren't even eligible to apply. The truth is dance, philosophy, and English majors are considered just as desirable as the premed biology set. In fact, Admissions Committees often seek out non-science majors because they appear more well-rounded and often have valuable communications skills that are essential for a successful career in medicine. Patients feel safest in the presence of lucid, mild-mannered physicians who are able to communicate effectively both verbally and in writing, making naturally talented communicators excellent medical practitioners. These "soft skills" are often harder to develop than proficiency in the sciences, and most medical schools will allot a certain number of seats in their incoming class specifically for liberal arts majors.

The most competitive medical school applicants will be able to prove that they are natural leaders as well as gifted educators. Tutoring students at a local elementary school or taking on a leadership role in a student organization are two ways to showcase your leadership/mentoring ability, but there are many ways in which you can demonstrate your ability to take charge and communicate effectively to others. For example, students whose parents do not speak English and who have acted as translators between their parents and the family physician, or students who studied abroad for a semester and had to navigate a new culture, language, and living situation have demonstrated their capacity to be mature, effective leaders.

The cost of a medical school education can be daunting for many students. This is one educational track where the possibility of maintaining even part-time work while in school is nearly implausible. Being a medical student is your full-time, around-the-clock job. Therefore, most students rely heavily on parental support, student loans, and scholarships to sustain themselves.

Despite the challenges, most medical students have no regrets about their career choice. Aside from being a real-life superhero and improving the overall quality of life of your patients, you'll enjoy a very pleasing cache to your title.

Postbaccalaureate Programs

Postbacc programs are an excellent option for "nontraditional" students who discovered their interest in medicine late in the game. These programs are designed to help non-science majors, re-applicants, economically disadvantaged students, underrepresented minorities, and those who need a GPA boost to complete their premed requirements. Some of these programs are even degree or certificate awarding, meaning you can pick up your master's degree on the way to your MD. For example, Georgetown University offers a Special Master's Program (SMP) in which students can complete their premed series and earn a master's degree in physiology and biophysics. There is no easy way to rank postbaccalaureate programs, as each program is designed for a different population. In order to select a postbacc that is right for you, call the school's Admissions Office and ask the following questions:

- What was the acceptance rate to medical school for applicants from this program?
- What level of access will I have to faculty teaching the courses in the postbacc program?
- Would it be possible for you to put me in touch with a former student?
- What will be my official classification, and am I eligible for financial aid?
- Does this program admit out-of-state students?
- What sort of additional services are provided by the program; are any of the following included: MCAT preparation, tutoring, personal statement review, interview practice?
- Does the program have special admissions arrangements with any medical schools?

Although the application process varies, most postbacc programs are looking for two letters of recommendation, transcripts, and a personal statement that describes your reasons for wanting to pursue a medical career. Postbacc programs can range from one to two years in length depending on the curriculum. To search for postbacc programs by state and type of program, visit the American Association of Medical Colleges website: Services.AAMC.org/postbac/.

Choosing schools: Reputation, reputation, reputation; location, location, location

You'll want to apply to an equal number of top-tier, middle-tier, and fall-back schools, although you should bear in mind that the admissions process is competitive across the board. If you are accepted to any school, you should consider this a true accomplishment. The Medical School Admissions Requirements (MSAR) guide available on the AAMC website (AAMC.org) can help you identify the schools that would likely find you an appealing candidate based on your MCAT scores and GPA. How a school is ranked does matter; although any medical school will turn you into a doctor, reputable schools can help you snag more attractive residency opportunities. In addition, you must seriously consider one other seemingly obvious factor in your decision: location. The next four rewarding but stressful years of your life can be markedly less painful if you are able to look out your window and see a landscape that makes you smile, or if you are likely to find stimulating outlets for your very precious free time. Die-hard water sports fanatics are going to suffer immensely if they find themselves on a landlocked campus. Lovers of serene country living may find the transition to urban life jarring. Although a change of scenery is often called for if you want to pursue a professional degree, medical school in particular is more bearable if you are close to creature comforts that are tailor-made for you. Therefore, at least your top choice schools should always be located in areas where you wouldn't mind living for the next four years.

Should You Apply to In- or Out-of-State Schools?

Before you get your heart set on staying in the Golden State, The Show-me State, the Big Apple, or any place in particular, make sure to take a look at the "Applicants and Matriculants" section of the American Association of Medical Colleges website (www.aamc.org). If Yale University School of Medicine is your top choice, you'll see that in the year 2006, the entering class was comprised almost entirely of out-of-state applicants. Mercer University School of Medicine accepted exactly zero out-of-state applicants in 2005. To further complicate matters, some schools have special agreements with neighboring states that don't have centralized medical schools. For example, the University of Washington School of Medicine has a partnership with Wyoming, Montana, Alaska, and Idaho (a program known as WWAMI) to treat their state's applicants as residents. Meet with a premedical advisor at your college to find out more about how applications from students at your alma mater fare at particular schools, and make sure to apply to both in- and out-of-state schools that are likely to be friendly to your residency status.

The medical school application process

If you are planning to apply as an undergraduate, be prepared to meet with a premed advisor as early as your freshman year. As a non-science major, carefully planning your schedule to make room for science and math prerequisites is necessary so that you will be ready to take the MCAT. Remember, medical schools do look at your cumulative GPA, but they also evaluate your science and "other" non-science GPA separately. Therefore, it is imperative that you shine in your science courses. Most students take the MCAT during their junior year, shortly before they submit their primary application, which includes transcripts, biographical information, and a personal statement. Medical schools use a central application service called AMCAS to process your application and distribute your information to schools; the schools that are interested in learning more about you then send you a secondary application. At this point in the process, you will need to submit three letters of recommendation to the schools. Most will be expecting you to submit recommendation letters from professors although some may specify that they want two academic letters and one non-academic letter. The final step is an interview. Spendthrifts beware: Between the AMCAS fees, test prep courses, travel costs for interviews, and ordering transcripts, many students spend as much as $5,000 on the application process. Prepare yourself far in advance to avoid sticker shock and investigate the availability of any fee waivers for which you might be eligible.

MCAT—Section by Section

PHYSICAL SCIENCES	•	52 multiple-choice questions
	•	70 minute section
VERBAL REASONING	•	40 multiple-choice questions
	•	60 minute section
WRITING	•	2 essay questions
	•	60 minute section
BIOLOGICAL SCIENCES	•	52 multiple-choice questions
	•	70 minute section

For more information, check out the MCAT website at MCAT.org.

Source: PrincetonReview.com

How long you'll be there, and what you'll learn

Consider the four years of medical school to be an incubation period in which pre-meds become "baby" doctors. You begin your journey in the classroom, following a rigorous curriculum of medical science courses and applying your newfound knowledge to clinical case studies. Expect these first years to be challenging: "First-year premed" is shorthand for "sleep-deprived formerly happy-go-lucky undergraduate." After your second year in medical school, you'll have to pass the first of three board examinations. The infancy of your career as a physician is born in the third year of medical school, when students become pseudo-clinicians doing rotations in various medical specialties, from surgery to pediatrics. Medical students agree that the transition from classroom to clinic marks the most difficult point in their educational experience. By the fourth year in medical school, you will have chosen a specialty that you plan to pursue in residency, and you must prepare to participate in a gamble known as the residency match, in which you'll interview at various hospitals, rank them, and wait to see if they've ranked you in return. During "match week" you'll find out whether or not you landed one of your top choices. Although you can officially go by the title doctor, you're still considered by your post-residency peers to be a "baby" doctor. Residency, which can last anywhere from three to seven to years, transforms baby doctors into full-grown, shingle-hanging MDs.

How much will it cost?

A medical education is an investment, and the cost of tuition at most medical schools reflects this fact. Being a medical student is full-time job, and students can't easily offset the cost of living expenses with part-time work. Therefore, students must find funding for tuition, student fees, and living expenses from financial aid, scholarships, and family coffers. Whether you attend a public or private medical school, expect to rack up student loan debt anywhere from $70,000 to over $100,000. Though these costs may seem prohibitive, bear in mind that you will probably not feel the pinch; lenders will pro-rate your loans based on salary, so underpaid residents won't have to see their paychecks shrink significantly. See Appendix II for an overview of some common federal financial aid programs.

Naturopathic and Osteopathic Medicine: Exciting Alternatives

In recent years, people in the U.S. have taken a greater interest in more comprehensive forms of medicine than the traditional allopathic variety. A naturopathic doctor is fully trained in the same basic sciences as traditional allopathic medical students, but also receives complementary training in clinical nutrition, counseling, acupuncture, botanical medicines, natural childbirth, and homeopathic treatments. Naturopaths focus more on the prevention of illness, and this comes in the form of individualized plans for each patient designed to promote their personal health and holistic well-being. Given the rising cost of health care, preventative health maintenance is no longer a luxury—it's a necessity. As a result, expect to see the number of students in naturopathic medical schools increase.

More and more states are also granting licensure to NDs, which means that soon health insurance coverage for treatments from NDs will be more common. Although most ND programs are four years long (just like traditional allopathic medical schools) many students find that with the additional curriculum, five years is a more realistic timeline. However, unlike traditional medical schools, ND programs do not require their students to participate in residencies. For more information on naturopathic programs visit AANMC.org.

Osteopaths (or DOs) are licensed to provide all of the same services as an MD but they are trained with a slightly different philosophy; one with a specific focus on the manipulation of the musculoskeletal system in order to alleviate pain and increase ease and range of motion. They also embrace a more holistic outlook on health, with a strong focus on preventative care. Unlike NDs, DOs are essentially licensed physicians (their licensure exams are very similar to the allopathic exams), and after completing four years of medical school, DOs go on to complete residencies in the same hospitals and clinics where MDs work. Although competitive, the requirements for osteopathic medical schools are slightly less stringent than those of allopathic schools; therefore, many premed students opt to apply to both.

There are 23 osteopathic medical colleges in the U.S., and their application deadlines vary; most operate on a rolling admissions basis. Like allopathic medical schools, osteopathic schools use a central application service known as AACOMAS through the American Association of Osteopathic Medical Colleges. To learn more about particular schools and the history of osteopathic medicine, visit AACOM.org.

CAREERS IN ACADEMIA: THE PHD OPTION

In order to complete a doctorate degree, you will need to be able to conduct independent research resulting in the creation of new knowledge. Including the time it takes to write and defend a dissertation, this degree can take anywhere from five to seven years to complete. Progress towards the degree can be slow, and a few major hurdles need to be overcome early—qualifying exams, course work in the first couple years, and the defense of a dissertation idea before a self-selected panel of professors.

If you want to tackle the hard problems in society and have activist instincts, you may want to go elsewhere (like Capitol Hill). Academia may not be the agent for social change it used to be, but you can expect to make a very positive difference on a small segment of the academic community and your students. As one graduate student told us, "I would encourage anybody who is thinking about going to graduate school with the intention of pursuing an academic career to try something else for a while and see if your passion for the subject leads you back to it. If it does, then you are in the right place."

You may have gotten to know the graduate teaching assistants in your English or communications classes. But life as a graduate student involves quite a bit more than teaching undergraduates. Once you enter a PhD program you are not a "student" in the same way you were as an undergraduate. You are part of the academe, and you are treated by professors as a colleague. There is no pressure for grades and you probably won't take tests, but the workload is very demanding. The general absence of hard and fast constraints means that self-discipline is essential for finishing the degree. However, you are still a "student" in some ways, and as such, you'll enjoy all the rich opportunities for culture and fun that are part of campus life. Most graduate students we talked to agreed that, despite the many challenges, the path is vastly rewarding.

Going all the way: An academic career

The traditional employment objective of PhDs is a tenure-track faculty position. While these positions aren't impossible to obtain, landing one is far from a sure thing, and the path toward getting one is arduous. A master's degree may be sufficient to qualify to teach in a two-year college, but a doctoral degree is required to teach in four-year colleges and universities. And while the PhD dissertation is the most important element of the search for a first job as a professor, postdoctoral experience—teaching or research done by PhDs after they've earned their doctorates but before they've landed tenure-track teaching positions—is also crucial. For the coveted tenure-track positions, virtually every successful job candidate now boasts at least one and usually two "postdoc" years, and these are necessary to remain competitive, which means gathering a sufficient backlog of publications and writings in progress. Personal relationships with faculty are also critical in this hunt for a first job, as teaching positions in many areas (particularly the humanities) can be scarce. While approximately 80 percent of college jobs are in four-year institutions, about a third of all college faculty are employed part-time or in non–tenure track positions, and this percentage has risen in recent years as colleges attempt to control costs.

It's worth noting that landing your first job after you've completed your PhD is far from the end of the road. You'll spend at least five or six years as an assistant professor. In your seventh year, you'll be evaluated for a tenure position on the basis of teaching and research (which almost always means published work). Institutions vary in the relative importance they place on these criteria, but it's always some combination of the two. Those who earn tenure are—for the most part—virtually guaranteed job security until they retire. Tenure also effectively separates junior faculty from senior faculty at most institutions. Senior, tenured faculty members have far more discretion when it comes to deciding what to teach as well as when (or whether) to conduct research than do junior faculty.

Folks who are jazzed enough about their studies to go this route aren't necessarily motivated by money or the certainty of getting a job—and that's a good thing. Not only do most doctoral candidates live pretty frugally while they're working toward their degree, but, unlike advanced degrees in business or medicine, there's no guarantee of recouping the financial investment. According to a recent article in *U.S. News & World Report*, roughly 30 percent of PhDs who earned their degrees in 2004 were still seeking employment or planning further studies in 2006, thanks in large part to a perennially tight job market for tenured professors. And according to the same article, PhDs in the humanities and liberal arts face a particularly formidable challenge when it comes to landing a job. Of course, non-academic jobs are an option, too; in fact, approximately 4 out of 10 PhDs go the private-sector route. Still, the relative scarcity of available jobs—especially when compared to the investment of time and money that a PhD requires—leads to a fairly high attrition rate among doctoral candidates. Roughly 40 to 50 percent of matriculating students never earn their PhD.[9] And some master's degree candidates who toy with the idea of pushing forward for a PhD decide against it when they take a hard look at the job prospects. Lisa, who we mentioned earlier, enjoyed her MFA in fiction writing so much that she briefly considered pursuing a PhD in literature. She eventually decided against it. Looking back, she's glad she did. "I'm pretty sure I would have been miserable," she says. "And I would have just finished a few years ago with a mountain of debt and limited and depressing job prospects—with guaranteed low salaries at all of them."

The good news, however, is that the job outlook for future professors is considerably brighter than it was even a few years ago. According to the Bureau of Labor Statistics, employment of postsecondary (i.e., college and university) teachers is expected to grow much faster than the average for all occupations through 2014. And that's good news if you're in for the long haul: The BLS predicts that "PhD recipients seeking jobs as postsecondary teachers will experience favorable job prospects over the next decade."[10]

9 Silla Brush, "Beyond the Ivory Tower." *U.S. News & World Report: America's Best Graduate Schools*. 2006. 54–55.

10 Bureau of Labor Statistics, U.S. Department of Labor. *Occupational Outlook Handbook, 2006–2007 Edition*, Teachers—Postsecondary, on the Internet at http://www.bls.gov/oco/ocos066.htm.

Though job prospects will vary significantly depending on the field you're in, there are a few demographic trends working in your favor if you want to be a professor. First of all, significant numbers of current professors (many of whom were hired in the late 1960s and the 1970s) are expected to retire over the next few years. And not only is the supply of professors expected to shrink, but demand for professors is expected to increase. The BLS predicts higher enrollment numbers at colleges and universities, which stems mainly from the expected increase in the population of 18- to 24-year-olds (who make up the majority of the college-student population).[11]

Even with the decreasing supply and increasing demand for college-level professors, however, it's important to remember that a significant proportion of the resulting job opportunities will be part-time positions. The BLS predicts that while competition will remain tight for tenure-track positions at four-year colleges and universities, there will be a considerable number of part-time or renewable, term appointments at these institutions and positions at community colleges available to them.[12]

And now the good news . . .

While a career in academia isn't the right choice for everyone, it can prove to be an immensely satisfying, rewarding profession for many people. (If there weren't an awful lot to recommend it, why would so many people be clamoring for it?) If you love reading, observing, and figuring things out, then there are few careers that offer greater opportunities for indulging your unique intellectual interests. And as a professor, you're not just developing an area of expertise, a significant portion of your time and energy will usually be devoted to knowledge creation. The profession is therefore best suited for motivated self-starters, and its highest rewards are given to those who can identify and explore original problems in their fields.

You're also paid to teach that material to people who are interested in learning it— and for many professors (including—hopefully—the ones you'll be working with) the opportunity to contribute to other people's learning and growth provides the greatest source of professional fulfillment.

There's also a lot of variety in an academic career: Many full-time faculty engage in outside professional activities. Economists consult with governments and corporations; engineers and academic labs develop products for private industry; humanities professors write articles which appear in newspapers and magazines. Many find this ability to work professionally on terms they define, while remaining in their institutions, to be among the most satisfying aspects of the profession. In addition, the significant administrative positions in colleges and universities are usually filled by former and current professors, and it is not uncommon for careers in university administration to develop from teaching careers.

11 Ibid.

12 Ibid.

Aside from the career satisfaction many professors enjoy, there are other—more practical—perks that come with the job. In addition to the time spent teaching in the classroom (which amounts to as few as three hours a week in graduate schools, up to 12 to 16 hours a week in undergraduate schools), professors spend time meeting with students during designated office hours, sitting on committees, and completing any number of administrative duties associated with teaching a class or running a department. But they can allocate the rest of their time as they see fit. Professors get summers off, too—or they at least get a three-month break from their teaching and administrative responsibilities. In actuality, few professors spend three months on the beach every year; many devote the majority of that time to conducting their own research, catching up on journal reading, and planning the courses that they'll be teaching the following semester. Still, they can complete that work whenever—and wherever—they choose. It's worth pointing out, however, that this degree of flexibility can be a double-edge sword. "Academic work is both flexible and all-consuming," says Penny Gold, a history professor at Knox College in Illinois. "One can read a book or journal article anywhere, and so it's a challenge to keep work from creeping into every available space. Sometimes I think wistfully of a nine-to-five job, where I would come home at the end of the day and be done with it."[13] But despite those occupational hazards, most consider this flexibility—certainly greater than what most non-academic jobs allow—to be one of the real benefits of an academic career.

Job security is another big draw. A tenured-professor gig isn't the guaranteed job for life it once was (post-tenure review is now required at most universities, and those who fall behind on teaching and independent scholarship may not be as secure as they would have been 10 or 20 years ago). Still, once professors earn tenure they have considerably more job security than their counterparts in the private sector. Of course, they typically don't earn the same fat paychecks, either. In 2004–2005, salaries for full-time faculty averaged $68,505. Specifically, the average salary was $91,548 for professors, $65,113 for associate professors, $54,571 for assistant professors, $45,647 for lecturers, $39,899 for instructors. Educators in four-year institutions earned higher salaries, on average, than did those in two-year schools. In fields with high-paying non-academic alternatives—e.g., medicine, law, engineering, business—professors tended to earn higher-than-average salaries, while professors in others fields—e.g., the humanities, education—typically recorded salaries on the lower end of the range.[14]

13 John A. Goldsmith, John Komlos, and Penny Schine Gold. *The Chicago Guide to Your Academic Career.* Chicago: University of Chicago Press, 2001. 9.

14 Bureau of Labor Statistics, U.S. Department of Labor. *Occupational Outlook Handbook, 2006–2007 Edition.* Teachers—Postsecondary, on the Internet at http://www.bls.gov/oco/ocos066.htm.

FELLOWSHIPS: KEEPING THE DREAM ALIVE

Imagine being paid as a student to do research and produce articles on the Arctic National Wildlife Refuge, to present your dissertation at a conference on comparative literature surrounded by intellectual luminaries, or being courted for editorial positions at various well-known newspapers due to a summer spent right in the belly of a newsroom. Ah, the innumerable and diverse joys of a fellowship. A true acknowledgment of your professional potential, fellowships allow you to pursue your research interests and learn directly from some of the most prominent leaders in your field. More importantly, they can help fund your graduate education. Essentially, fellowships are like scholarships that provide undergraduate, graduate, and postgraduate students and professionals with short-term intense learning experiences lasting anywhere from several months to over a year, and specific professional development opportunities that will have a direct impact on the fellow's future career path. Most fellowships are sponsored by the academic department to which you're applying and are intended to provide particularly gifted students with the time and resources to immerse themselves completely in their areas of study. Some of the most prestigious fellowships are privately funded. The following is an overview of some of the different types of fellowships, and a description of a few of the most sought-after and interesting fellowship opportunities for English and communications majors.

Fellowships administered by graduate departments

Mostly based on your academic fitness (translation: research interests), these fellowships may come in the form of a 12-month stipend lasting at least two to three years, but award amounts and durations vary substantially. This kind of supplementary funding allows students to dive into their research without having to moonlight in a minimum-wage food-service position in order to support themselves. In order to qualify, you must create and present a fellowship proposal, a sometimes rigorous process during which you must defend the importance of your prospective research, and explain the unique qualities you possess that would help further the project (knowledge of particular languages, for example). Each department has its own specific guidelines for fellowship proposals, but in general, you must be prepared to provide the fellowship committee with exhaustive details about your research and the particular role it will play in furthering the field. Most fellowship deadlines are during the fall of the year preceding the year when you need funding.

Extramural fellowships

Looking outside of academic departments for funding is a mixed bag. On the upside, more money is often available from deep-pocket foundations, corporations, and even the federal government, resulting in larger stipends, and more exciting fringe benefits. On the downside, the competition is at a national rather than departmental level and is correspondingly difficult. Using searchable databases is probably the easiest way to identify private fellowship opportunities, Check your school's website, as many universities provide their own database for students who are interested in extramural fellowships. There are literally thousands of opportunities available. Here's a breakdown of some of the most prestigious extramural fellowship options:

- **Harry S. Truman Fellowships**

  If you want to devote your life to public service, then the Harry S. Truman foundation may have some money to devote towards your goal. These prestigious merit-based scholarships are awarded to a very small pool of students who plan on attending graduate school in a public service-related field. With only 70–75 spots available and over 600 applicants nationwide, the competition is pretty steep, though the rewards are well worth the grueling application process—ranging from $3,000 to $30,000. Students must be in the top third of their class academically, must be full-time students with junior class standing, and *must* be able to demonstrate an abiding interest in public service through extracurricular activities. Involvement in Greek organizations or other campus-sponsored activities does not qualify as public service experience. Internships, jobs, or volunteer positions with the government, partisan political organizations, or nonprofits are considered top-tier experiences.

  Naturally, there are a number of impressive perks that come along with a fellowship of this tenor. Truman scholars are invited to participate in a variety of programs: the Truman Fellows Program, Truman Leadership Week, and the Summer Institute, to name a few. Fellows are also showered with fringe services such as internship placement, career counseling, and graduate school admissions and professional development. Bragging rights are complementary.

  The application process itself requires a personal statement, an application which includes brief descriptions of your activities and accomplishments, letters of recommendation, and a policy proposal. This is a memo to an actual state or U.S. government official outlining a particular problem or need in society which would concern this official. Be prepared to defend your proposal at the Truman interview, where final candidates are selected. Remember: Schools have their own deadlines for when Truman applications are due, which may be different than the deadlines set by the foundation; be sure to check with your scholarship/ fellowship office. To learn more, download sample applications and policy proposal tips, and read essays by former Truman scholars, visit: Truman.gov/index.htm.

- **Rhodes Scholarships Program**

  Arguably the most well-known prestigious scholarship, the lucky handful who win a Rhodes scholarship are invited to enter the hallowed gates of Oxford University in England for four semesters of study, or potentially longer. Students can pursue a bachelor's, master's, or doctoral degree. During this time, all matriculation expenses, tuition, and laboratory fees are paid by the Rhodes Trustees. Established by Oxford alumni Cecil John Rhodes in 1902, the scholarship was intended to offer bright and motivated young students an opportunity to study at a university campus which Rhodes believed was ideal for promoting intellectual and personal growth and quiet contemplation. Many notable or famous journalists, policymakers, scientists, and future Nobel Prize winners were recipients of the Rhodes Scholarship, and the competition is intense. The four main criteria by which candidates are judged are:

1. Literary and scholastic attainments

2. Energy to use one's talents to the full, as exemplified by fondness for and success in sports

3. Truth, courage, devotion to duty; sympathy for and protection of the weak; kindliness, unselfishness, and fellowship

4. Moral force of character and instincts to lead, and a sincere interest in the welfare of one's fellow beings

Yes, you read correctly—sports. Rhodes scholars are expected to be well-rounded, although involvement in sports is certainly not the most important factor in selection. Thirty-two scholars are selected, and with hundreds of applicants, the ability to distinguish yourself is critical; if you aren't involved in sports, be prepared to demonstrate your energy and zest for life in other ways. Evidence that you are a natural-born leader through your choice of activities, honors, or awards is essential. The application process requires eight letters of recommendation, four from the academic institution where you are pursuing or have already completed your bachelor's degree, a letter of endorsement from your college or university, official transcripts, a personal essay, a list of activities, a photograph, and proof of U.S. citizenship. To read some frequently asked questions, and learn more about the Oxford campus and the lives of Rhodes Scholars visit: RhodesScholar.org.

- **The Macarthur Fellows Program**

  Designed for those who demonstrate extraordinary creativity within their fields, the MacArthur Fellows program offers recipients the generous sum of $500,000 over a 5-year period to pursue endeavors which will promote innovation in their field, whether as artists, scientists, engineers, or business moguls. Dubbed by many as the "genius grant," intellectual prowess alone isn't enough to land one of these hefty awards; demonstrated creativity, an ability to deal with adversity, and other qualities are considered. Unlike some of the other prestigious fellowship programs, MacArthur candidates are selected by official "nominators," people who are usually leaders in their field, experts, former nominees, or even selection committee members. These nominators may endorse as many candidates as they choose. Many recipients are unsung heroes, who are doing groundbreaking work behind the scenes. Twenty to twenty-five candidates are selected each year by a committee of twelve individuals representing many disciplines and industries. Fellows are notified of their acceptance by letter. To read some frequently asked questions, about the history of the MacArthur Fellowship, and browse a list of past and current fellows visit MacFound.org.

ANOTHER OPTION: YEAR OF SERVICE PROGRAMS

There are other ways to spend some time out in the "real world" before applying to graduate school. Below are a couple examples of "year of service" programs. These are often "in the trenches" jobs that involve teaching or working in the community. These programs are very highly regarded by both employers and graduate schools and can give you serious hands-on experiences with which to shape your graduate school and career objectives. Another great benefit of these programs is that participants may be eligible for federal loan forgiveness and/or loan deferment programs.

- **AmeriCorps**

  AmeriCorps is a network of local, state, and national service programs that connects more than 70,000 Americans each year in intensive service to meet our country's critical needs in education, public safety, health, and the environment. AmeriCorps members serve with more than 2,000 nonprofits, public agencies, and faith-based and community organizations. Since 1994, more than 400,000 men and women have provided needed assistance to millions of Americans across the nation through their AmeriCorps service.

  Full-time members who complete their service earn an education award of $4,725 to pay for college, graduate school, or to pay back qualified student loans. Some AmeriCorps members may also receive a modest living allowance during their term of service.

- **Peace Corps**

  Do you think of the Peace Corps and imagine teaching in a one-room schoolhouse or farming in a remote area of the world? While education and agriculture are still an important part of the Peace Corps' many initiatives, today's volunteers are just as likely to be working on HIV/AIDS awareness, helping to establish computer learning centers, or working on small business development.

Peace Corps volunteers work in the following areas: education, youth outreach, and community development; health and HIV/AIDS; agriculture and environment; business development; and information technology. Within these areas, the specific duties and responsibilities of each volunteer can vary widely.

All Peace Corps volunteers commit to 27 months of training and service overseas. The Peace Corps provides volunteers with a living allowance that enables them to live in a manner similar to the local people in their community. The Peace Corps also provides complete medical and dental care and covers the cost of transportation to and from your country of service. When you return from your 27 months of service, you will receive just over $6,000 toward your transition to life back home.

AmeriCorps members address critical needs in communities throughout America, including:

- Tutoring and mentoring disadvantaged youth
- Fighting illiteracy
- Improving health services
- Building affordable housing
- Teaching computer skills
- Cleaning parks and streams
- Managing or operating after-school programs
- Helping communities respond to disasters
- Building organizational capacity

CHAPTER 3:

What's Out There? Popular Jobs for English and Communications Majors

THE BIG PICTURE

Maybe you already know what you want to do and that's great; we hope to provide some good job-search strategies for you in this book. But maybe the big "a-ha!" moment will not arrive by the time you walk across the stage to get your diploma. (For some strange reason, graduation dates rarely coincide with a clear understanding of what you want to do for the rest of your life.) All is not lost, even if you find yourself watching the soaps as the fall semester begins without you.

The professional world is not made up of 15-week semesters, and entering the job market is not the same as arriving on campus and deciding on a major. The fact is there is a lot "out there," so it might be worth having a bit of a direction when you do finally set sail. Sometimes it begins with a bit of looking around. You might ask yourself, "I want to do what that person does—how did she get there?" or "Can I really keep doing research and pay the rent?" Keep looking around. Just a kernel of an idea will release the initiative to get you off the couch.

There's more good news. The first thing you do after graduation is not what you have to do for the rest of your life. At your first job you will meet many different people, and networking can lead to more interesting opportunities. So don't think that what you decide to do now is necessarily going to be what you'll be doing for the rest of your life. For better or for worse, career paths are easily (and frequently) readjusted.

From psychiatrists to dentists, welders to puppeteers, there are a lot of gainfully employed folks out there who majored in English or communications. Given the breadth of soft skills these majors develop and the marketability of those skills, nearly every occupation is populated with at least a handful of communication-savvy individuals like you. That said, most word-wizards are far more interested in entering professions where they are likely to be able to demonstrate their creative chops— reading, writing, and analyzing—on a daily basis. Here are some of the most popular career options for English and communications majors. While the list is hardly exhaustive, it should give you a good idea of the breadth of career paths available to you.

Quick and Dirty Self-Assessment Exercise: The Other Side of the "What's Out There" Equation

There are people who have carved out a place for themselves making a living doing exactly what makes them happy. So what really floats your boat? As crazy as that might sound, it's a practical place to begin. Employers can spot an unfocused "I'll do anything" applicant from a mile away, and they usually aren't interested. They want to see that spark in your eye (i.e., motivation) as proof that you won't run screaming from the office right after they've trained you.

Ask yourself the following questions:

- When was the last time you lost all track of time? What were you doing?
- If you won five million dollars in the lottery what would you do (after buying stuff and sitting on the beach on a tropical island)?
- If you could switch places for one week with anyone, who would it be?
- If you had six months with no obligations or financial constraints what would you do?

Your answers to these questions may reveal important clues about the things that make your eyes light up.

Talk to 10 people about your answers to these questions and the potential for it turning into a job. After that, the question becomes "How do I get there?" which any smart English or communications student can figure out!

JOB PROFILES

Advertising Executive

Number of people in profession	85,000
Average hours per week	50
Average starting salary	$36,300 (for entry-level position)
Average salary after 5 years	$58,800
Average salary after 10–15 years	$88,400

Life on the Job

Advertising professionals combine creativity with sound business sense to market a product based on financial, sociological, and psychological research. To ensure this complicated process works smoothly (and to be prepared when it doesn't happen smoothly), you'll spend a lot of time in the office (a six-day week is not unusual). Most of your time is spent brainstorming, creative blockbusting, and sifting through demographic research; less time is spent meeting with clients or pitching advertising campaigns. Fluidity of daily activity marks the life of the advertising executive who jumps from project to project. But it can't happen at the expense of attention to detail, and it doesn't. It takes a very disciplined person to handle both the creative end and also effectively manage the details. Advertising executives work in teams on projects, so the ability to work with others is crucial; those who are successful have the ability to add to other people's ideas and help them grow. "You can't have an ego in this business," mentioned one executive, "but be aware that everybody has one." The need to be flexible cannot be emphasized enough.

As a number of large players in the industry move toward "computer-based brainstorming,"—a way in which creative ideas are kept in a fluid database without regard to account specificity—computer skills will become even more valuable. Like most project-oriented careers, you can expect periods of intense activity during which you have little, if any, free time. At other times, the workload is light and mundane. In this profession, you'll get recognized when you have a good idea, but failures are also always recognized. The ability to work on a team is one of the most important skills that a successful advertising executive has; however, the opportunity to experience team camaraderie is not why people enter advertising. In this industry, the word "friend" is a four-letter word.

Insider tips

You don't necessarily need advertising internships to get your start in the field; rather, you need to understand advertisements. You should always know which advertisements you like, which ones you don't, and why. Check out agency websites through AdWeek and AdAge. Make sure you know which clients a particular agency is representing, and that you've done enough research on what those clients' needs may be. If you haven't already prepared one yourself, expect to be asked to create a mock-up campaign for a particular client during an interview. Informational interviews do matter in this industry. If you haven't had any luck getting your foot in the door, start calling ad execs just to ask some basic questions about how to break into the field. Stay in touch. If they like you (and they'll certainly appreciate how proactive you are) then they may very well call you when a job opens up.

Attorney

Number of people in profession:	704,000
Average hours per week:	50
Average starting salary:	$72,500
Average salary after 5 years:	$95,000
Average salary after 10–15 years:	$135,000

Life on the job

Lawyers counsel their clients on matters pertaining to the law. Law can be intellectually fascinating, and many take great satisfaction in the daily challenges. Detail mavens and big-picture thinkers alike find a friendly home in the loose definition of attorney. It is impossible to mention attorneys without mentioning the public perception of attorneys. One attorney we spoke with reminds us of the joke: "What's the difference between a run-over snake and a run-over attorney? There are skid marks in front of the snake." Attorneys are blamed for a variety of social ills, from the litigious nature of our society, to hindering new inventions from reaching the marketplace, to getting guilty people off due to technicalities or sloppy police work. While these labels speak to the excesses within the profession, many people apply them to the profession as a whole. "It's hard to work 14-hour days researching a case when you know that even your client thinks you're a bloodsucker," wrote a New York attorney. The work is hard. Attorneys can work 18-hour days and spend up to 3,000 hours per year on cases. "On some level you have to like what you do, because you're doing it all day long," mentioned one attorney. Many lawyers are subordinate to senior associates and partners for the majority of their careers. Attorneys usually work at a number of firms before finding a position perfectly suited to them. Many spend their first few years finding out if they want to focus on transactional work (corporate law or real estate law) or litigation (criminal or civil cases). Some specialized lawyers have restricted areas of responsibility. For example, district attorneys prosecute accused criminals and probate lawyers plan and settle estates. The quality of life is low during the early to middle years, but many find the financial rewards too enticing to abandon. Those considering entering this field should have solid work habits, a curious mind, and the ability to work with—and for—others.

Insider tips

Attorneys must have a law degree from an institution accredited by the American Bar Association. While in law school, students spend their summers working for potential employers, finding out what the working attorney's life is like, and discovering whether or not they want to work in a particular area. Before an attorney can practice in a given state, he must pass a state bar exam, a two-day written examination that tests the prospective attorney's knowledge of the specific laws of that state. Following passage of the written part of the test, many states require "character and fitness" oral examinations to test the ability of a person to practice law in a given state.

In law, the pressure starts early. Law school admissions are extremely competitive—the top 25 schools have an admission rate of about 10 percent. You can get tracked early: The kind of school you attend affects what kind of summer job opportunities you may have; this in turn affects the kind of permanent job you secure. The starting salary and kind of experience you have as a corporate lawyer can vary greatly depending on the size of the firm and geographic location. In a smaller firm, you will have more responsibility and more client contact early on, but the salaries can be tens of thousands of dollars lower than in a large firm. The content of your practice will be different, too: A small-town lawyer may take care of a house closing, drafting a will, and a divorce settlement in a day; big-city lawyers can spend months negotiating a single commercial transaction.

Interview with a Professional

Boalt Law School graduate Andrea Brunetti offers the following insider tips for pre-law hopefuls: "Students interested in becoming lawyers should seriously consider taking time off between college and law school instead of going straight from college. Work experience can provide a lot of perspective which comes in handy in a very stressful, competitive, and demanding law school environment. Students should be certain that they want to go to law school. It is difficult enough, particularly the first year, without having any doubts about whether or not you should even be there." Andrea's own decision to attend law school was driven by hands-on experience: "I always knew I wanted to be a lawyer, but decided to take a break between college and law school. I worked at a law firm and went through a long period where I wanted nothing to do with law school or lawyers. But I ultimately came back around and decided that I definitely wanted to be a lawyer. This break between college and law school, along with my resolve, were key to my success in law school (particularly the first year). What I love about my job is working with clients. I love advising them, working with them, and generally interacting with them. The worst thing about my job is billing my time. I hate it! And I agonize over it."

Book Publishing Professional

Number of people in profession:	175,000
Average hours per week:	45
Average starting salary:	$23,000
Average salary after 5 years:	$28,300
Average salary after 10–15 years:	$44,000

Life on the job

Book publishing is an extraordinarily large business, and those who (successfully) enter the profession have no illusions that what they do is merely artistic in nature. "You've got to keep things on schedule. You've got to make them pay for themselves, or you're out of business," said one publishing professional, adding that "publishing" is a term that can encompass many positions within a publishing house. The most high-profile job is that of editor, who works with authors to produce a quality product. Many other positions are available for those interested in the industry, including managing editors, who control production flow; publicity managers; promotions specialists; subsidiary rights managers; production managers; and salespeople. These occupations are critical to the successful functioning of a publishing house. Those who want to pursue a career in this industry should examine their own skills in light of the variety of opportunities available for ambitious and creative individuals who find the prospect of working with books exciting. Managing editors are the traffic controllers of the publishing industry. They track production schedules and budgets, allocate personnel, and control the flow of material between departments. A large publishing house can have hundreds of projects running simultaneously, and the managing editor needs to be attentive to detail and be able to anticipate problems before they occur. Publicity, promotions, and sales positions reward creative and outgoing personalities. Successful professionals in this industry utilize their interpersonal skills to drum up consumer interest and encourage sales by bookstores. Salespeople spend significant amounts of time on the road meeting with bookstore buyers and managers. Subsidiary rights departments are usually divided into two arms: domestic and international. Subrights people negotiate international publishing deals with foreign houses or contract for copyrighted work to appear in another medium. The most lucrative rights for works of fiction—movie rights—are usually negotiated only by senior personnel experienced in negotiating with production companies. It requires putting in long hours to rise from assistant and administrative positions to positions of responsibility. For all but the highest up, salaries remain relatively low in this profession. People in the publishing industry were quick to note that contacts are crucial. Those who want to advance pursue new opportunities zealously, and any advantage one can gain over other candidates is key. Few described the profession as cutthroat, however; instead, many praised their associates and coworkers. Publishing is a financially tough life, but it's ideal for those who are dedicated to books and who want to spend their days with like-minded people.

Insider tips

Aspiring book-publishing professionals should be persistent and willing to do anything to get started in the field. Editorial or publishing experience in college literary magazines, newspapers, or journals is advantageous for applicants. Those who wish to advance in this profession should understand that work may occasionally take up all of their free time.

Editorial assistants provide administrative support for editors. If you have no prior writing experience but will do whatever it takes to get started, this may be your launching point.

For those who are able to pay great attention to detail, there is also the job of proofreader. Proofreaders check content to detect errors in typesetting or keyboarding and mark them for correction before the final printing of a book, magazine, or newspaper. There are also copyeditor positions; these folks tidy up prose, correct inaccuracies, ensure that proper grammar and usage is employed, and are make sure all cross-references direct readers to the proper places.

The Chicago Manual of Style, a handbook for editorial professionals around the world, is perhaps the most essential reference for anyone who works with words. When the University of Chicago Press first opened in 1891, professors who were planning to publish manuscripts brought their work directly to the compositors at the press; the compositors would then attempt to decipher and consistently typeset the manuscripts before passing on these newer versions to proofreaders. To remedy the problems that this process had the potential to create, the compositors teamed up with a proofreader to make a single list of the most common errors they were coming across. This meeting marked the birth of the manual. The list turned into a pamphlet, which grew into a book; and more than a hundred years later, it's still the reference source that sits on the desks of those whose business revolves around the written word.

Equally influential in the history of editing in America, Maxwell Perkins used connections to get his foot in the door of the *New York Times* in 1907. After covering his share of entry-level emergencies (police reports, fires, and disasters), Perkins applied for a job with Charles Scribner's Sons in 1909 and was granted an interview a year later. Working his way out of advertising, Perkins moved up to the editorial floor and made his first discovery in 1919: a Princeton dropout named F. Scott Fitzgerald. Other breakthrough writers soon followed: Ezra Pound, Ernest Hemingway, Thomas Wolfe, and Marjorie Kinnan Rawlings.

College Administrator

Number of people in profession:	25,000
Average hours per week:	50
Average starting salary:	$30,000
Average salary after 5 years:	$64,640
Average salary after 10–15 years:	$98,500

Life on the job

College administrators make recommendations about admissions; oversee the disbursement of university materials; plan curricula; oversee all budgets from payroll to maintenance of the physical plant; supervise personnel; keep track of university records (everything from student transcripts to library archives); and help students navigate the university bureaucracy for financial aid, housing, job placement, alumni development, and all the other services a college provides. Many administrators eventually specialize in one field, such as financial aid, in which responsibilities include the preparation and maintenance of financial records and student counseling about financial aid. Specialists in information management are responsible for coordinating and producing the majority of university publications. Administrators who specialize in student affairs (sometimes referred to as student services) deal with residence life, student activities, career services, athletic administration, service learning, health education, and counseling. Competition begins with the onset of a specialization. At upper levels, a graduate degree in education, business, student personnel administration, counseling, or information management is required. The hours increase, and administrators spend even more time away from the office at university events or other schools.

Insider tips

While entry-level positions in financial aid offices, registrar's offices, and admissions and academic offices often require only a bachelor's degree, a PhD or an EdD is standard among those who hold influential positions in college administrations. Candidates for administrative positions should have good managerial instincts, strong interpersonal skills, and the ability to work effectively with faculty and students. People involved in the financial aspects of administration, including administering financial aid, should have significant knowledge of statistics and great mathematical skills. Computer proficiency is necessary at all levels.

Depending on the context of your campus job search, a master's degree can be helpful in making you more competitive. Even if an advanced degree isn't a requirement for the position, you should do whatever you can to enhance your marketability, such as completing relevant training courses or getting professional certifications in an area related to the job responsibilities.

Now that the job market is tougher than it was a few years ago, it might be useful to look into administrative assistant positions to get your foot in the door. It can be easier to market yourself and what you have to offer when your name or face is already known on campus.

As for the job search process, take care in writing your objective—clarity is key. And be sure to submit a resume along with a cover letter for jobs you are interested in. If you think of your resume as being like your transcript, then your cover letter is like your personal statement. Both documents are helpful to campus employers in more fully evaluating your fit for the position.

Interview with a Professional

Brian Ellison, Dean of Faculty Tenure at the City College of San Francisco, offers the following tips to those considering careers in college administration:

1. Spend some time (i.e., a minimum of three years) as a faculty member learning how a community college functions. While the basic division of labor is instructional services, student services, and administrative services, there are several permutations under each of these headings and it takes time to fully understand and appreciate the relationships that bind these areas together.

2. Pursue a doctorate in education. These days and into the future a doctorate (EdD or PhD) will be essential for securing an administrative position. This is especially true at the senior management level.

3. Find an administrator who will serve as your mentor. A mentor can provide you with an insider perspective about administrative work that isn't available to rank-and-file faculty. Contrary to the opinions of some, administrative work is different and not simply an extension of the work done by faculty. What administrative work entails (i.e., issues, challenges, and opportunities) can be shared with you by a mentor.

4. Consider external administrative positions. Many prospective administrators cannot think beyond the boundaries of their own college and will only pursue administrative positions at that college. Your frame of reference as a manager is broadened when you have worked at more than one college which, of course, makes you more attractive to potential employers.

5. Network, network, network. I cannot overemphasize the need to network with your colleagues and sustain those relationships. Your network can be a great source of information when you are thinking about applying for an administrative position, especially when applying for positions external to your college. One strategy for developing a network is to join those committees at your college that function at the institutional level. This will give you a broader perspective of your college and allow you to interact with its key leaders. One perk these committees sometimes offer is the opportunity to serve as a liaison between your college and other colleges and educational organizations. If serving as a liaison is a possibility take advantage of this excellent opportunity to build your network.

6. Don't get discouraged. With the appropriate career building in place and good timing of the job market, opportunities should come your way.

In answer to the question of what Brian cherishes the most about his work, and what he likes least, he responds, "The most exciting aspect of administrative work is the ability to impact the college on the institutional level and make a real difference for students, faculty and staff. The least exciting aspect of this type of work is dealing with the many layers of the organization and the amount of time that represents."

Copyeditor

Number of people in profession	N/A
Average hours per week	50
Average starting salary	$27,800
Average salary after 5 years	$45,500
Average salary after 10–15 years	$65,000

Life on the job

Copyeditors are not proofreaders: There's more to their job than replacing commas with semicolons (though copyeditors are certainly expected to know the difference!). Copyeditors are responsible for tidying up prose, correcting inaccuracies, and ensuring that proper grammar and usage are employed. It's also their job to make sure that the redheaded girl who appears on page 67 still has red hair on page 150. They are responsible for ensuring that all cross-references direct readers to the proper places. Depending on the publication, some copyeditors are relied upon to catch potentially libelous stories and to alert editors to pieces that require additional consultation with the author. There is often some rewriting involved; for example, copyeditors who find an inappropriate or awkwardly-worded phrase often make the necessary improvement themselves. In smaller publishing houses, copyeditors may find themselves wearing many hats—that of fact checker, layout artist, headline and caption writer, and monitor of wire services. A good copyeditor needs excellent reading and comprehension skills and must be a first-rate writer. You'll find that most people in this field have their noses in books both on and off the job. Copyeditors must also be very detail-oriented. Copyediting is not a job for the disorganized; with so many people to please, egos to manage, and bosses to impress, copyeditors must be highly organized.

Insider tips

For those who want to specialize in particular areas, such as technical or medical copyediting, experience in the given field proves helpful. Familiarity with electronic publishing software is also a definite plus. A good (and sometimes, the only) way to gain some of the experience that larger employers want to see on your resume is to complete an internship. Community newspapers, literary magazines, and college publications often supply valuable—yet often unpaid—opportunities to perfect your writing skills, and magazines and newspapers offer internships for students. Interns usually write short pieces, conduct research, and perform various clerical duties. Though post-graduation jobs aren't guaranteed for interns, offers for competent candidates are likely, and industry experience and contacts are invaluable assets for securing a position in any sector of the publishing world.

Fund-raiser/Institutional Solicitor

Number of people in profession	300,000
Average hours per week	45
Average starting salary	$40,000
Average salary after 5 years	$50,000
Average salary after 10–15 years	$68,000

Life on the job

People who are successful at fund-raising develop large plans and execute them down to the tiniest details, identify a target audience and tailor a unique appeal to that demographic; have excellent writing skills, a good understanding of how and when to approach people, and an unbelievable sense of organization. Fund-raising on a large scale may entail up to seven different appeals to over 20,000 potential donors; fund-raisers without organizational skills quickly get dragged under by the tide of material that passes through their hands. Planning and attending meetings takes up the majority of the professional fund-raiser's day. Fund-raisers must remain abreast of the concerns of potential donors, be responsive to the changing needs of their institution, and build up a successful system of reaching donors. Fund-raisers spend ample creative energy recreating campaigns to ensure success year after year. While broad-based fund-raising (letter campaigns, high-profile events, and programs) are all important for visibility, publicity, and support, the real work high-level fund-raisers do comes through presentations, education, and targeted solicitation. Meeting skills, educational skills, and a touch of finesse are all critical to the successful fund-raiser. Meetings with patrons, employees, and executives can take place after hours or late in the day. The ability to communicate the value and the need of your employer to others is required in this occupation, and makes the difference between those who succeed and those who fail.

Insider tips

Most fund-raisers start out as development assistants, providing general administrative support and calling donors rather than doing any sort of "real" fund-raising work. Familiarize yourself with fund-raising organizations through the American Association of Fund-raising Counsel (AAFRC.org) and consider pursuing internships and volunteer positions in the nonprofit setting that involve grant writing and fund-raising; Idealist.org has lists and lists of these. It is easy to parlay previous experience in education into fund-raising work. In fact, many former teachers and educational administrators pursue fund-raising positions. Leadership skills, an ability to distill lots of information into digestible terms, and the ability to speak persuasively are all essential to effective fund-raising, and experience as an English or communications major is excellent preparation.

Working in Foundations: Grant-making, the Other Side of the Fund-raising Picture

Foundations often provide technical assistance to applicants, review grant proposals, conduct site visits, and monitor the work of grant recipients, and there are many English and communications graduates working to support those efforts. One graduate working with a foundation providing grants to nonprofits has this to say: "The biggest challenge I face is demystifying the funder-grantee relationship. Historically, philanthropy has been a very inaccessible institution. I am very invested in my work and the communities and nonprofits we serve. They are the leaders doing the work in the community that is making a difference and it is often difficult to build relationships with people who feel they have to always put their 'best foot forward' when trying to get their projects and programs funded."

Journalist

Number of people in profession	70,000
Average hours per week	45
Average starting salary	$28,100
Average salary after 5 years	$44,600
Average salary after 10–15 years	$69,300

Life on the job

There are many types of journalists, from the local beat newspaper reporter to the foreign correspondent, the magazine feature writer to the freelance book reviewer, and so on. It is difficult to pin down the daily routine of an average journalist. Journalists interview sources and review records to assemble, collect, and report information and explore the implications of the facts. Journalism informs, educates, chastises: Do not underestimate the power a journalist holds. (Remember Watergate, when Robert Woodward and Carl Bernstein, two reporters working for the *Washington Post*, discovered and published information that led to the resignation of President Richard Nixon?)

Professionals must be able to report quickly and accurately, and time pressure is one of the most distinguishing features of this job. Journalists must maintain a point of view while remaining objective about their subjects, which can be difficult. Interpersonal skills, excellent writing skills, and a reporter's instinct (the ability to accurately assess the significance of obscure and incomplete information) are essential to success. The uncertainty of the daily routine makes it difficult to incorporate family, hobbies, and any regularly scheduled plans; but those who detest the predictability of nine-to-five jobs are attracted to journalism because no day is a carbon copy of the day before. Long hours and chronic deadline pressure can be significantly negative factors. When an editor calls you in on a breaking story, you have to be prepared to drop everything; when you're on deadline, you can get crazed trying to write a complicated story in half the time you need. This ball and chain to the office leads many to resent, and eventually reject, the reporter's life. Journalists who are protective of their prose rarely last in this profession, since articles are often edited for publication without their consultation. More than 40 million people read newspapers in the United States each day, and more than 50 million people read magazines each week. The opportunity for your writing to reach a large audience is tempting indeed, and many find the initial low pay, uncertain and occasionally dangerous conditions, and chaotic schedule a fair tradeoff to be allowed to do what they do. In fact, many seem drawn by the excitement and challenge of these very conditions.

> Journalism is the first draft of history.
>
> —old adage

Insider tips

More than a few distinguished journalism careers have begun at the school or local magazine or newspaper, before ever progressing on to a large metropolitan publication. Building a collection of clippings (samples of your work cut from the newspapers in which they were published) is key to being able to make this transition successfully.

Bone up on your proofreading skills before applying for any job. Skills required of journalists include: Good grammar and spelling, extensive vocabulary, curiosity, ability to respond well under pressure and meet deadlines, ability to write under duress, and diverse background and life experiences.

If you enjoy research and investigation, starting in the field as a fact checker may be your ticket to working for a large magazine or news organization. Fact checkers verify the accuracy of text written by reporters. They research information and statements of fact through print and internet-based resources in addition to phone interviews. Don't expect much pay when you're first starting out. It's all about the experience you gain and the people you will meet. The big bucks will come later, after you win that Pulitzer.

Interview with a Professional

Harriet Chiang, former legal affairs reporter and reporting instructor at San Francisco State University had this to say about getting a break in journalism: "I would start small, accumulating a set of clips to show newspapers/websites. Most journalism students apply for internships—Hearst Corporation has one, as do many local newspapers. I would also try writing freelance pieces for neighborhood newsletters, as well as local papers and websites—any forum where you can show your writing and reporting skills. I've had students get hired by neighborhood newsletters as well as small newspapers after doing some freelance pieces for them. What I like most about my job is meeting a lot of interesting people and being able to tell their story to others. The worst is the drudge work—knocking on people's doors right after a tragedy and not knowing if anyone will talk to you. As far as the most interesting thing that has happened . . . I can't pick just one. I've certainly had my share of great stories. A few years ago they called on me and a photographer to follow the pursuit of a bald eagle that had escaped from the San Francisco Zoo but was unable to survive in the wild. When the eagle and its trainer were finally reunited it was exciting to stand so close to this beautiful and magnificent creature. On a different note I remember a series of stories I did about a former inmate who had spent 13 years in prison wrongly convicted of murder. A photographer and I accompanied him on a visit back to a prison near Sacramento where he gave an inspirational speech. It was amazing to be milling around with inmates convicted of murder, sexual assault, and other serious crimes."

Librarian

Number of people in profession:	167,000
Average hours per week:	40
Average starting salary:	$33,560
Average salary after 5 years:	$43,090
Average salary after 10–15 years:	$54,250

Life on the job

Librarians are the custodians of our culture's retrievable media—books and audio and visual materials—and other data or physical objects that can be catalogued and stored. The modern librarian is the manager of an enormous warehouse, and people rely on him or her to help them navigate the increasingly voluminous world of data. Research and computer skills are important; therefore, people who are generally less comfortable with computers find the transition to online archives much more difficult. Be prepared to work under real deadlines and significant pressure; individuals with corporate library jobs will find that although the salaries are higher, "if you can't do the job when they really need you, they'll show you the door." Librarians who specialize in medicine or law will find their professions more lucrative than general librarians, but the books won't be the kind you take home and read for a little relaxation. Especially for specialists, graduate studies prove invaluable for a successful transition to working life. A librarian spends more than 60 percent of his or her day working with people, either library patrons or other staffers and back-office workers. Strong interpersonal skills are required for individuals who hope to succeed in this field. "You've got to be polite even when you want to break someone's neck, which happens Monday morning at about 10:00 A.M. and lasts through Saturday at 4:00 P.M.," said one 15-year veteran of the St. Louis public library system. Librarians also work closely with their colleagues; they loan books, advise one another, and discuss daily work issues on a regular basis. "I'm surrounded by books all day, and that's all I've ever wanted," reported one happy librarian. A librarian does far more than sit at the desk and check books in and out of the library. A large part of his or her job is research. The most-cited positive feature about being a librarian is the opportunity for continuous education. Librarians are challenged daily to find creative ways of retrieving different information, and how well they can satisfy these requests determines their success and satisfaction in the profession.

Insider Tips

Librarians are often misunderstood. The latter-day frumpy denizens of the stacks have been replaced with creative, worldly, technological whizzes from all walks of life. If you want to be a competitive applicant for academic library positions, make sure that you choose a specialization (health, law, art, curating, etc.) and be prepared to pursue another master's degree in your niche. Snagging entry-level positions in public library settings will help bolster your chances of getting accepted at a top program, tenfold. Also, a demonstration of knowledge and ability when it comes to web design and research will earn you some extra kudos. Don't forget about corporate and law libraries—some of the highest-paying library positions are in these unlikely settings.

Interview with a Professional

Renata Gibson, a recent graduate of the renowned library sciences program at the University of Texas at Austin encourages those interested in this profession to take some time to explore their options: "Before I even applied for graduate school I decided I should work in a library first to see if I would indeed like working in that environment. I had held a number of other positions in various industries, without much satisfaction. Not only did this solidify and clarify my goals of becoming a librarian, but it also allowed me to make valuable contacts within the library community. The director of the library I was working in as a reference assistant became a sort of mentor for me. She answered questions about the profession, gave advice about what classes I should really take, and has since provided excellent recommendations for me when I have applied for professional positions. Working in a library during graduate school is another great thing because, again, you make great contacts who can provide references and who may even offer you a job! I work at a community college at the reference desk mainly, although I do teach classes as well here in the library. The best parts of my job are the fact that I learn something new every day by helping students with their research papers; I get to interact with people all day long, and I feel like I am really helping people who are working hard towards their degrees. Since it is a public service position, however, there are days when you have to deal with very difficult people, and hours spent answering sometimes redundant questions can be exhausting—both are definite downsides."

Unexpected and surprisingly rewarding opportunities have made Renata's job interesting: "The most interesting thing that has happened has been that I learned that I really enjoy teaching classes. I always knew I liked the one-on-one interaction at the reference desk, but was more hesitant about teaching library skills to an entire classroom. But I have recently started teaching classes weekly and find that I really enjoy the group dynamic. Also, I had never expected to be so technologically savvy! As a graduate student I learned to create my own website and navigate really difficult databases."

Market Researcher

Number of people in profession	72,400
Average hours per week	45
Average starting salary	$38,100
Average salary after 5 years	$59,800
Average salary after 10–15 years	$93,300

Life on the Job

Market researchers prepare studies and surveys, analyze demographic information and purchasing histories, review the factors that affect product demand, and make recommendations to manufacturing and sales forces about the market for their product. This multifaceted job requires financial, statistical, scientific, and aesthetic skills, as well as common sense.

Market researchers work on projects that proceed in stages. At the beginning of a project, a market researcher may spend three weeks with other market researchers designing a survey and testing it on small samples of their intended population. In later stages, they may define demographics, distribute the survey, and collect and assemble data. In the final stages, they may analyze survey responses to uncover consumer preferences or needs that have not yet been identified. Like all scientific experiments, "the assumptions we make are key. If we don't get those clear at the beginning, it's going to affect our entire study," one market researcher told us. Those people who specialize in public opinion surveys are particularly careful about how they phrase their questions, as a single misplaced modifier can dramatically affect the meaning of a question and, likewise, its responses.

Insider tips

Invest in a statistics or research methods course. Work experience that demonstrates a creative intellect and the ability to work on teams is also well regarded. Prospective market researchers should be aware that early jobs in the field entail plenty of menial work—copying, proofreading, inputting data, and the like. Individuals who are willing to carry out these entry-level tasks go on to fill positions of responsibility. Graduate degrees in marketing, business, or statistics are becoming more common among individuals in management positions.

Media Planner

Number of people in profession	7000
Average hours per week	50
Average starting salary	$38,000
Average salary after 5 years	$49,800
Average salary after 10–15 years	$66,900

Life on the job

Ever wonder why you don't see commercials for Depends during Disney's *One Saturday Morning* or commercials for tattoo parlours during *7th Heaven*? It all has to do with demographics. You've got a lot of little kids watching television on Saturday morning. The commercials they'll see are filled with cool toys and sugarcoated chocolate cereals. And *7th Heaven's* relatively conservative audience really wouldn't be too keen on advertisements for body art or piercing. Businesses want to place their products and services in front of audiences they know are watching, listening, or even driving by on the road. How do they know when to do this? They turn to media planners. Media planners work in the media department of most advertising agencies. They are responsible for putting ads in the right place at the right time, to reach the desired audience for the least amount of money.

Media planners gather information on the people's viewing and reading habits. They evaluate editorial content and programming to determine the potential use of media such as newspapers, magazines, radio, television, billboards and electric displays, buses, subways, taxis, airports, bus terminals, or the Internet. Media planners have to know demographics and statistics, and use extensive formulas to chart out the best way a business can spend its money in order to get its product in front of consumers. In addition, media planners have to know their math; they turn their information over to media buyers who track the media space and times available for purchase, negotiate and purchase time and space for ads, and make sure ads appear exactly as scheduled. Most media planning jobs are found in the big cities: New York, Chicago, and Los Angeles. Other top cities include San Francisco, Minneapolis, and Dallas. Media planners may work in small advertising firms that employ fewer than 10 people or big firms that employee dozens. Other media planners may work in-house, meaning they work for a company that produces its own advertisements for its products. No matter where they work, media planners can expect to put in a good 50 or more hours per week, as they strive to put together proposals for clients in a very short amount of time. Advertising is a high stress business, but the monetary reward of seeing your work pay off for the client can be well worth it.

Insider Tips

Beginners in the advertising world usually enter the industry in the account management or media department. Most media planners don't stay in their positions for the duration of their careers, so training in marketing, psychology, accounting, and creative design allow media planners to move to other positions within an agency. Media planners possess good people skills, common sense, creativity, communication skills, and problem-solving abilities. There is also a need for additional training for individuals already employed.

Knowing the newest technology and using it to your customer's advantage are fundamental to success. Media planners must also stay in tune with the culture as it ages and changes. Success in small projects will lead to bigger ones, and success in these endeavors can lead to supervisory positions.

News Analysts

Number of people in profession	66,000
Average hours per week	45–50
Average starting salary	$20,000
Average salary after 5 years	$40,000
Average salary after 10–15 years	$70,000

Life on the job

News analysts collect news reported by various sources, interpret it, and facilitate the broadcast to the public. Their purpose is to distill the enormous quantity of news that happens every day. News analysts are often newscasters, either full-time, behind-the-desk anchors or reporters called on to comment on specific stories. If a reporter delivers a story live from a specific location, the anchor will often carry on a question and answer session with the reporter to establish important facts for the audience. Sometimes the anchors have time to prepare their questions; at other times, they do it on the fly. Some news analysts specialize. Weathercasters and sportscasters, for example, are news analysts. News analysts who specialize in election coverage may be called on in late October to give a report in which they distill polling numbers, campaign speeches, and key issues.

News analysts usually work long and irregular hours. Depending on how important a news item is, they may have to go on air immediately, with little or no preparation, and stay on indefinitely. On a normal news day, analysts will arrive at their offices several hours before the newscast, review wire reports coming in, and write their stories. For television and radio news, this process also entails working with editors to produce the video or audio clips for taped stories. News analysts who work for newspapers typically write features, op-eds, or regular news pieces. Their deadlines vary depending on the sensitivity of a given story.

Insider tips:

This is a tough field to break into directly after college. If you're lucky, you'll land a position at a local radio or television station (like aspiring radio and television producers, you may want to prepare yourself for a temporary move to the 'burbs). Your beat will be more about local council meetings and sporting events than the national economy or the spread of the West Nile virus. Be prepared to stick it out—as you accumulate experience, you may be assigned a particular beat and/or have enough experience to be considered for a reporter's position.

Nonprofit Administrator

Number of people in profession	355,000
Average hours per week	Varies
Average starting salary	$88,000
Average salary after 5 years	Varies
Average salary after 10–15 years	Varies

Life on the job

Whatever the mission of the nonprofit organization, the administrator's job calls for the management skills of a chief executive officer. Writing grant proposals and fundraising take up more and more of the administrator's time as budget cuts flourish. The administrator must be prepared to delicately balance limited budgets with the compassion needed to provide basic care to the clients served and to preserve the general mission of the organization.

The responsibilities of the nonprofit administrator vary depending upon the size of the organization. Executive directors (EDs) are often responsible for entire operations within a small organization, while within large nonprofits specialists run specific departments, such as the accounting, budgeting, human resources, policy analysis, finance, and marketing departments. EDs of both types are highly educated individuals responsible for overall policy directions and overseeing compliance with government agencies and regulations.

Program managers have independent oversight over a particular program area within the nonprofit. Their responsibilities could include initiating new projects and managing their implementation. If the nonprofit relies on membership donations for funding (for example a museum or public broadcasting station), there is a need for a volunteer manager to bring members in and keep them engaged and happy.

Insider tips

Here's some advice from folks working in nonprofits.

- Undergraduates should balance their classroom and volunteer experiences. Longevity of exposure is important—show that you have had an interest in the field you are hoping to work in through exposure that goes beyond one day of volunteering in the very recent past.

- Be willing to take an unpaid internship, even after you graduate. If necessary, couple it with a night job or other part-time job. That commitment you show will make you first in line when the nonprofit gets new funding and can hire new staff.

- Learn how to coordinate and organize things on your own. Coordinating the recycling program in your unit or a one-day event are examples. Be able to show employers how you are different. Take into consideration your background, skills, education and be confident. Have the mindset that they should hire you over anyone else.

- Follow-up and persistence make a candidate stand out. In the interview, employers look for candidates who show "willingness to help out when needed," leadership, and an ability to take initiative.

- A master's degree in public administration or business administration may qualify graduates for entry into the higher levels of nonprofit administration. Graduates with a bachelor's degree often work in the field before starting a master's program. They advance by taking on more responsibilities and moving up and into such positions as associate director or program coordinator.

Interview with Tina Sang, Program Coordinator, Adolescent Health Working Group

What do you do on the job?

Most recently I had been coordinating all the administrative details necessary to put on a large conference to increase the medical community's awareness of adolescents and ADHD. This was attended by primary care providers, mental health care providers, school health providers, school counselors, parents, and youth.

My regular ongoing responsibilities are to research and help write a handbook to serve as a resource to primary care providers when they encounter issues related to mental health and substance use in teens. Our goal is to have primary care physicians ask these kinds of questions during a routine physical exam with a teenager.

What are the rewards and challenges?

It was hard to learn the ropes in the beginning. I read articles in medical journals to glean the important information and summarize it in one-page summaries for the handbook for healthcare providers. It was about a three to four month learning curve for me to become familiar enough with psychology and medical journals to understand what was important.

My job is incredibly rewarding. The nonprofit I work for is really small—an executive director (ED), four full-time staff, and two part-time volunteers. Our ED is a medical doctor who decided to become an activist. I really like the people I work with and the philosophy of the organization.

The downside is the funding situation; private foundations fund our projects year by year and it's the projects that get funded, not the staff. So if new projects are innovative enough and get funded, then my job is good for another year but if not, I'll be out of a job.

But even with having to "chase down the money," I'd like to put in a plug for working for a nonprofit. It's a wonderful place for people to start because, especially in smaller nonprofits, they give you a lot of trust and assignments that researchers with graduate degrees would be doing if they could afford to hire them. Getting that level of responsibility really fosters confidence and I am proud to be a part of an organization that's doing great things.

Professor

Number of people in profession:	900,000
Average hours per week:	60
Average starting salary:	$28,500
Average salary after 5 years:	$53,000
Average salary after 10–15 years:	$73,000

Life on the job

College professors organize and conduct the functions of higher education. They engage in a variety of activities, from running laboratory experiments and supervising graduate student research to conducting large undergraduate lectures and writing textbooks. With the exception of scheduled classes—which can consume as few as three hours a week in graduate universities or up to 12 to 16 hours per week for undergraduates—a professor's time is largely spent on research, preparing class material, and meeting with students. This profession is thus best suited for motivated self-starters, and its highest rewards are given to those who can identify and explore original problems in their fields. Tenured professors have relatively high job security and professional freedom. Once tenured, a professor can largely set his own responsibilities and decide how to divide his time between teaching, writing, researching, and administration. However, tenure no longer means complete immunity; post-tenure review is now mandated at most universities, and those who fall behind on teaching and independent scholarship may not be as secure nowadays. The most difficult years of being a professor are the early ones, when there is great pressure to publish a significant body of work to establish the credentials that lead to tenure. However, the work of junior and senior faculty is quite similar, and the profession offers intellectual stimulation and freedom to all its members.

Insider tips

The path to becoming a tenured college professor is arduous. While a master's degree may be sufficient to qualify to teach in a two-year college or in some cases, as an adjunct, a doctoral degree is required to teach in four-year colleges and universities. PhDs generally take four to seven years to complete; after completing two to three years of course work, the graduate student will usually teach classes and write a dissertation (an original piece of research taking about three years to complete that is the most important element of the search for a first job as a professor). For the coveted tenure-track positions, virtually every successful job candidate now boasts at least one and usually two postdoctorate years, and these years are necessary to remain competitive, which means gathering a sufficient backlog of publications and writings. Personal relationships with faculty are also critical in the hunt for a first job, as teaching positions in many areas (particularly the humanities) can be scarce. While approximately 80 percent of college jobs are in four-year institutions, about a third of all college faculty are employed part-time or in non–tenure-track positions, and this percentage has risen in recent years as colleges attempt to control costs.

Publicist

Number of people in profession	12,000
Average hours per week	45
Average starting salary	$29,400
Average salary after 5 years	$51,000
Average salary after 10–15 years	$69,600

Life on the job

A publicist gets press coverage for his client. The publicist is often the middleman between the high-profile personality and members of the media. He/she usually wants his client to receive positive attention, but many publicists readily cite the old adage that "the only bad publicity is no publicity." Politicians and captains of industry require a little more spin-selling on their press—they want to be seen as forward-looking and confident—but other professions are less picky, as in the case of the rock star who reveals the sordid details of his seamy nightlife to cultivate a rough image. Publicists also perform damage control, attempting to counteract any undesirable press coverage the client receives. This position as "last line of defense" is what distinguishes the adequate publicist from the extraordinary one. Good publicists can turn scandal into opportunity and create valuable name-recognition for their clients. Publicists don't only work for the famous. Sometimes they work for a little-known person or industry and create reasons for them to receive press coverage. In a case where a company desiring publicity is hampered by its esoteric nature or technical jargon, the publicist must translate its positions into easily understandable language. A major part of the publicist's day is spent writing press releases and creating press packets, which have photos and information about the client. Publicists spend a lot of time on the phone. They put in long hours, and most receive little financial reward in return. They operate under hectic conditions and must adhere to strict deadlines which coincide with publicity events, such as the release of a movie or the publishing of a book. They have to ensure that they get the appropriate information to the media in time for the event for which they are generating publicity, such as a record release or automotive sale. They must always be available for comment (even when that comment is "no comment") and remain friendly with the media, juggling the agendas of both their clients and the reporters on whom they depend. But at the end of the day, they go to the hottest parties in town, and rub elbows with all the "fabulous people."

Insider tips

Most publicists recommend interning at a firm before plunging into this job—a low-responsibility position allows them to see the pace of the profession firsthand. Besides, it helps to make as many contacts as possible in this "it's-who-you-know" field. All publicists start at the same entry-level positions and work their way up. Experience is the key to obtaining a good job, especially in the entertainment industry, which is the hardest to break into. While long hours and low pay are the norm (at least initially), by the time a seasoned publicist has made enough contacts and pitched enough good stories, they can relax a bit. Although they are still working long hours, they can begin to enjoy the glamour factor. Many publicists have a lot of influence over the media. Some of the best ones start their own firms or become entertainment television hosts on the small cable networks.

Edward L. Bernays: The Father of Public Relations

When Bernays took on Diaghilev's Ballet Russes American tour in 1915, he wrote, "I was given a job about which I knew nothing. In fact, I was positively uninterested in the dance." He wasn't alone. Americans thought male dancers were deviants and of limited interest.

Bernays began to connect ballet to something people understood and enjoyed. First, as a novelty, a unifying of several art forms; second, its appeal to special groups; third, its direct impact on American life, on design and color in American products; and fourth, its personalities.

Beginning with newspapers, Bernays developed a four-page newsletter for editorial writers, local managers, and others, containing photographs and stories of dancers, costumes, and composers. Articles were targeted to his four themes and audiences. For example, the "women's pages" received articles on costumes, fabric, and fashion design; the Sunday supplements received full-color photos.

Magazine coverage, timed to appear just before the ballet opened, was his next approach. Bernays tailored his stories to his editors. When *Ladies' Home Journal* said that they couldn't show photographs of dancers with skirts above the knees, he had artists retouch photos to bring down the hem. His ability to understand editors' needs resulted in wide coverage on that front.

Bernays created an 81-page, user-friendly publicity guide for advance men to use on the tour. When a national story about the Ballet Russes appeared, advance men could tailor it for local coverage. The guide contained mimeographed pages, bios on the dancers, short notes and fillers, and even a question and answer page that asked, "Are American men ashamed to be graceful?"

He persuaded American manufacturers to make products inspired by the color and design of the sets and costumes, and national stores to advertise them. These styles became so popular that Fifth Avenue stores sold these products without prompting from Bernays. He used overseas media reviews to heighten anticipation for the dancers. When they arrived at the docks in New York, a crowd was waiting. Bernays then took photos of the eager crowds and placed them in Sunday magazines throughout the country. The ballet was sold out before the opening.

The ballet toured American cities; demand had already dictated a second tour and little girls were dreaming of becoming ballerinas. Bernays had remolded biases to get his story told. The American view of ballet and dance was changed forever.

Source: The Museum of Public Relations. "Edward L. Bernays." Prmuseum.com/bernays/bernays_1915.html

Radio Producers

Number of people in profession	N/A
Average hours per week	Varies
Average starting salary	$30,800
Average salary after 5 years	$38,600
Average salary after 10–15 years	$48,300

Life on the job

With the recent opening of the airwaves by the Federal Communications Commission (FCC), more and more individuals will be able to start their own radio stations. For now, though, there are large radio stations that employ a radio producer, someone who is responsible for the on-air programming. Radio producers decide what type of music will be played and supervise on-air personnel. Most radio producers come to the profession after years spent working as a disc jockey. For stations that play music, the ability to tell the difference between the Beatles and Barenaked Ladies is sort of required. Radio producers for stations that do all-news formats are sometimes called upon to edit and write the news stories from information collected by reporters. Radio producers often hire station employees, work with sales associates, and act as a go between for upper management and the on-air talent. In smaller stations, radio producers take on many different roles, including bookkeeper, administrative assistant, and marketing manager. Some radio producers plan, develop and create live or taped productions. A touch of artistic talent is needed when writing scripts, helping sound technicians, and developing other production elements. Radio producers deal with station managers, accountants, the community, and the FCC.

Insider tips

Three words: College radio station. Internships at college or local radio stations are truly the best, and in some cases, the only stepping stones for would-be radio producers. Be prepared to move to a rural area to land your first paid radio management opportunity, although National Public Radio and other major networks hire entry-level production assistants (though your odds are 1 in 100 of being picked). Don't worry; if you must move to a less cosmopolitan area you won't languish for long (unless you prefer the slower pace!). Many rural stations produce soon-to-be high-profile radio producers at well-known networks.

Interview with a Professional

Ben Manilla, founder of Ben Manilla Productions, (www.bmpaudio.com) has extensive experience in radio production, and recommends that radio production hopefuls be ready and willing to do whatever is necessary to catch their break: "Be willing to do anything to get in the door. Most operations will allow team members to contribute. So even if you don't have the dream job, if you're fun to be around, excited about what's happening, and offer ideas at appropriate times—you will be noticed and before long, find your proper niche. Also, read the trades—*Current, Association of Independents in Radio, Radio and Records, All Access*—some of it will be in jargon and may be hard to follow, but if you are up on what's happening people will want to confide in you. The best thing about my job is that radio is an incredibly creative medium. Whenever I'm allowed the freedom to be creative, I get tremendous job satisfaction. On the other hand, the worst aspect is being forced into the position to pay people small amounts of money for large amounts of work. Also having to dun people into paying me for work they've contracted and I've delivered." What's most interesting about Ben's job? "Because I have chosen to be a generalist, I have learned about fascinating things: children's literature, philosophy, Olympic sports, gay travel . . . things I might never have pursued if left to my own devices. Truly, the best thing about my job is the opportunity it offers to meet interesting people, ask them probing questions, and be paid for it."

School Administrator

Number of people in profession	427,000
Average hours per week	45
Average starting, salary	$54,500
Average salary after 5 years	$66,500
Average salary after 10–15 years	$80,900

Life on the job

Administrators, unlike teachers, work a 12-month year. They are fairly busy for most of that time. Whether running a small, private day care center or an overcrowded public high school, an administrator's tasks are numerous and varied, ranging from curriculum development to student discipline. The most familiar school administrator is the principal. Assisting the principal are vice principals, whose duties tend to be more specialized and who have more responsibility for the day-to-day operation of the school than does the principal. In a central administration office, other specialists work with some or all the schools in a given district, overseeing particular programs, such as the evaluation of student academic achievement. Any one of these administrators may be responsible for infrastructure maintenance, the hiring and training of teachers, and student affairs.

School administration is a combination of intellectual work and grunt work. Organizational skills are key, as is the ability to operate within constantly tightening budgetary constraints. Since duties can range from hiring a basketball coach to providing AIDS education, administrators need to be versatile and flexible. An administrator must have a great deal of patience to deal with the enormous bureaucracy often associated with educational institutions. Finally, and perhaps most importantly, since administrators are responsible for the education of young people, a particular dedication to and an understanding of children's needs are essential.

Insider tips

Most beginning administrators have acquired related work experience—usually in teaching or management posts—and, as might be expected in an academic environment, they also have advanced degrees, including doctorates, in education, administration, or a combination of the two. Recently, some schools have begun to require their applicants to have a Master of Business Administration degree. At the university level, deans are expected to bring a rich academic and professional background to their jobs. As with many educational jobs in the United States, school administrators must be certified, with exact requirements usually determined by the state government.

Teacher

Number of people in profession:	3,300,000
Average hours per week:	45
Average starting salary:	$38,000
Average salary after 5 years:	$50,000
Average salary after 10–15 years:	$65,000

Life on the job

The majority of teachers are employed by primary or secondary schools. Their focus is a specific subject or grade level. Before arriving at the classroom, teachers create lesson plans tailored to their students' levels of ability. At school, usually beginning at 8:00 A.M., teachers must begin the difficult task of generating interest in their often sleepy students. A good sense of humor and the ability to think like their students help teachers captivate their students' attention. Teachers have to generate interest in subjects that students often find tedious. Rousing them from their apathy and watching their curiosity grow is a giant reward of teaching. One teacher said her favorite aspects of teaching are the creative challenges and the "iconoclastic opportunities." Teachers must have high expectations of their students and also be able to empathize with their concerns. They must be comfortable dealing with a wide spectrum of personality types and ability levels, and must be capable of treating their students fairly. About a fifth of the teacher's work week is devoted to their least favorite aspect of the profession: paperwork. Teachers have a block of time each day, called a professional period, to work on paper grading; however, all teachers report that this is not enough time.

Teachers also perform administrative duties, such as spending one period assisting in the school library or monitoring students in the cafeteria. Teachers also need to be accessible to parents. Some teachers meet with parents once per term, others send progress reports home each month. Most schools require teachers to participate in extracurricular activities with students. A teacher may be an adviser to the school yearbook, direct the school play, or coach the chess team. Often they receive a stipend for leading the more time-consuming extracurricular activities. Teachers may also be required to act as chaperones at a certain number of after-school functions, such as dances and chorus concerts. All good teachers agree that the main reason for entering this profession should be a desire to impart knowledge. Teachers must want to make a difference in the lives and futures of their students.

Insider tips

Interviews for K–12 teaching positions involve a lot of demonstration. Expect to be asked to present a brief lecture on a prescribed topic within your subject or multiple subjects. Your interviewers will be looking for clear communication skills, an inventive presentation style, and an ability to promote critical thinking skills in students. Other questions usually revolve around your particular teaching philosophy, and how you handle difficult and controversial situations, such as whether or not to integrate developmentally delayed students into regular-track classrooms, or how to handle racial tension within a classroom. One teacher mentioned that she was surprised to find so many interviewees didn't even know much about the discipline they're supposed to be teaching to others! Make sure that you prepare in advance, if possible, and generate a list of examples of how you've dealt with challenging situations. Realize that as a teacher, a big part of your job will be dealing with parents' questions and concerns, and that a lot of misdirected anger can be aimed squarely at you. Some teachers feel that there are greater expectations now from parents that teachers will take care of a host of problems which aren't necessarily related to a student's performance in school. Developing strong boundaries is a must, and expect that as a new teacher, you will feel guilty at times for enforcing necessary rules—one new teacher was very saddened by the fact that she had to fail a high school senior who had been granted early entrance at a prestigious school.

Interview with a Professional

Susan Charlip, an English teacher at a public high school in California has the following insights to offer those who are eager to teach: "The competition for jobs is not exactly like *American Idol*. If you are eager to teach in the public schools, there are plenty of jobs. They are the kind of jobs that just keep giving. As long as families are having children, there will be jobs for teachers. Find out which schools are the best in the region you want to live/work. Research your options before taking a job. Useful websites for such information include GreatSchools.net and JustForTheKids.org. Start out in a good district, or transfer to one before you become entrenched in a bad one and it's too costly for you to switch. Most districts will give you only five years of service credit so if you have twelve years of tenure in District A and want to move to District B, you will leave your seniority and your salary level behind."

Susan says the rewards mostly come in the form of watching one's students develop: "The best part of the job, besides summer break and all the vacation time, is the enormously rewarding experience of working with kids. Comparatively, I cannot think of too many other jobs which inspire such passion, fun, and creative spirit. It is also enormously satisfying spending your life spreading the gospel of great literature to hungry young minds. For English teachers in particular there is no escape from essay grading if you want to be a conscientious teacher. The foundation of effective teaching lies in the relationship that is built between the teacher and the student writer; if you want to see growth in trust with a student, it happens in the papers. Also, while years ago, the state used to be the people who gave you the credentials and then paid you, there is now an increasing load of paperwork associated with the movement towards standards and accountability—yet there are no fewer expectations in the classroom, and teachers are incredibly overburdened with the extra demands from the state. Additionally, the unrealistic pressures parents place on their kids to take AP classes adds to the general insanity of high schools in America today."

Television Producers

Number of people in profession	42,000
Average hours per week	55
Average starting salary	$22.500
Average salary after 5 years	$42,900
Average salary after 10–15 years	$93,900

Life on the job

Television producers make sure that every aspect of a television show runs smoothly, and take responsibility for everything from coordinating writers and performers/correspondents right down to overseeing the fact-checking of credit names and titles. Having complete responsibility for all facets of on-air production can be a very stressful job, and the successful TV producer has to be tightly organized, able to communicate clearly and succinctly with everyone on and off the set—from actors to directors to writers to technical crew—and they must have a gift for thinking on their feet, ready to come up with creative ideas under extraordinary time pressure. Television producers report high excitement and job satisfaction despite the physical toll of the work (all report being tired a lot).

These are innovators and problem-solvers with exceptional project-management skills—they love to see tangible results for their hard work. The public's perception of the television industry is one of high-profile personalities, and while it helps for the TV producer to act as a dynamic, motivating force, nearly everything a producer does is known only to those involved with the show itself. "Only other producers can tell a really well-produced show. You never get any fan mail," said one 15-year veteran producer. Another was quick to add, "It's not as glamorous as it seems on television," saying that even the smallest detail must be checked and rechecked before a show goes on the air. A good producer should have enough of an ego to make important decisions and defend them, but should not be afraid of drudge work. Even writing script may be a part of the TV producer's last-minute job. Most producers rise in the ranks from production assistant positions, so they know what it takes to get a show made from concept to broadcast. Producers ultimately take credit for a successful broadcast but also have to take the blame for anything that goes wrong on their watch. Between fellow producers, there is respect but little camaraderie. Fierce competition—even "backstabbing" behavior—is not only common but virtually expected in the industry. For those who can master it, television production is an exciting, difficult job that can be quite financially rewarding.

Insider tips

Be prepared to work hard for little or no dough when you first start out. "Coffee fetcher" or "general office girl/boy" are common titles for newcomers. Production assistants often do a variety of odd jobs, from reading scripts to standing in line at Starbucks, to babysitting the producer's dog. Many people wait tables or work at a late-night copy store to make ends meet. If you haven't gained experience and contacts through a college internship, consider working for a community (cable) television station. This is a way to produce your own material (albeit pro bono) and get some producing credits. Local event coverage or interviews with local celebrities are good program ideas that will usually be embraced by cable networks that are required to air a certain amount of community-related material. Be willing to show how much you're willing to sacrifice to make your dream happen. This means working very long hours, and graciously taking on assignments that may seem unrelated to your job description—within reason, of course!

Interview with a Professional

Daniela Ryan, producer at Basra Entertainment, acknowledges that there is no "easy" way to break into production. "It is not an easy field to get into at any level by anyone. Even Stephen Spielberg, in the studio that he created, gets 'nos'. Here is the first thing: If you can possibly think of anything else you would like to do then go do that. At *most* levels in the entertainment industry there is not very much money, glamour, or appreciation in it. It can be long hours, tedious work, and many, many highly talented and creative people have gone years without a shred of success. My best advice is to get your emotional self in order as soon and as thoroughly as possible before you step foot in Hollywood or New York. You will be rejected often in small and large ways. Once that is done try to hone in on what aspect of the business you think you'd like to be in. If you are not sure take the first job in the industry you are offered—no one will bat an eye if you quit in six months and move on to something better. Be persistent. A 'no' sucks, it can hurt, it can send you reeling (no pun intended) but, as a very wise and talented producer once said to me, it only takes one 'yes'. Then get yourself ready to deliver the most brilliant work you can muster . . . and then start the process all over again."

What's worse than a world of no's? Daniela feels it's the excruciatingly slow pace of production. "The worst part of the job is not the many 'no's' as one would immediately think, but how glacial the whole process of getting a movie made is. If you are producing for a local television station or a show, where they are in constant need of shows to fill their schedule, you get your marching orders, you produce the show and you may or may not like it. But if you are an independent producer—which every one of them is until they have a show on the air and then once it's off they are independent again—it can take years to get a film off the ground. If you are producing TV shows then you can come up with your best idea ever, all your friends at dinner *love* it, you can shop it to all the networks and cable channels and they can all say 'no', and it is effectively dead, without possibility of resurrection. Then next year, the exact same idea can be the season's biggest hit. . . . Sometimes the reasons are just not ascertainable. The best part of my job is that it is extremely fun when you are working on a production. Long hours, lots of work, but if you are a creative person and you like problem-solving it can be exciting and rewarding. There is nothing like seeing your first credit roll by. The most interesting thing that has happened to me is meeting people, other creative people, and having that meeting come around to be mutually beneficial in work. It is a small world and you just never know who will have the next great show or if your turn is next. If you want predictable, this is not the business for you. It is the constant possibility dangling in front of you that makes the business fascinating."

Web Editor

Number of people in profession:	340,805
Average hours per week:	50
Average starting salary:	$45,000
Average salary after 5 years:	$80,000
Average salary after 10–15 years:	N/A

Life on the job

A web editor develops the content or editorial plan of a website, working with a team that may include a creative director, writer, designer, and information architect. web editors at different types of companies have varying responsibilities. Someone at iVillage.com, for instance, deals with major amounts of content and updates it on a daily basis. An editor at an online magazine could be brought in to match the site's particular style or to provide an original voice. But if you work for a web developer that produces original content for different companies, your work will be more project-oriented. You will develop material for a range of clients, as well as ensure that the information is accurate and conveys the true voice and tone for the site. The editor's work encompasses a broad spectrum of writing and can run the gamut from writing a short article or product description copy to creating a script. Copyediting and proofreading may also be part of an editor's job. An editor in the web world has a very different job than one in a traditional print position. The online world is one of interactivity, which may involve creating single-loop feedbacks, such as real-time polls, or developing community-oriented content—information that is taken from people responding to a site. While print media is geared toward the masses, interactive content relies on an understanding of the one-to-one nature of the Web. "In most traditional media, once you've written a piece, it's done," notes writer Amy Gahran. However, many online writing projects are never really finished, especially when it comes to website content. "Expect to update, revise, expand, or tweak existing written materials not just occasionally, but continuously," said one web editor. "Editing and project-management skills are helpful for any writer, but having a background as an editor or managing editor can prove especially lucrative. Many online publishing venues lack experienced editorial talent. Being an editor as well as a writer is likely to open more doors for you in online media than it would in print media," observes Gahran.

Insider tips

As a web editor, it's important to familiarize yourself with HTML and a variety of page design programs. A web editor should have an understanding of certain back-end technologies; for instance, if you are writing copy for an e-commerce site, it's helpful to understand the functionality of how an online store works and how it operates before you actually write material for it. Gaining some HTML knowledge will help you understand the possibilities and limitations of online media much better than someone who only writes, and you can easily teach yourself basic HTML and basic web design from a good book.

Web editors require a combination of editorial common sense and good writing skills. They must also embrace the technology. "If someone is out to write his novel and wants to pick up some interesting work on the side, this is a harder road," cautions one web editor. "People who really have a curiosity about the medium and are jazzed by learning about it tend to flourish more."

Interview with a Professional

According to William Morris, a web editor and PR specialist at San Francisco State University, "The technology side of marketing/PR can always be learned. Much more important is to have good writing and communication skills, very good analytical skills, and excellent judgment. English and communications majors should already have such skills and judgment. In order to break into the field, the best thing students and recent graduates can do is: acquire the technology skills (information architecture, content management, web publishing, etc.) in the most professional setting you can—whether that's building a personal website that's professional (i.e. not a MySpace page—do something that not only looks good, but also requires some information architecture and has a decent amount of content in it) or finding a nonprofit group or small business that needs help building a website or other e-communications program, or getting an internship, temporary, or entry-level job in the area. The exact technical skills you need will vary. I suggest looking at the skill requirements for job listings for the areas and organizations that you are interested in and then start working on acquiring them. The beauty of web-related skills is that they can be self-taught; there are plenty of online tutorials, resources, and communities to help, and there are also workshops and classes you can sign up for that aren't incredibly expensive. Anybody can learn HTML or CSS or Java."

"Second: Find a way to convince potential employers of your communication, analytical, and good judgment skills—whether that's re-writing your resume, lining up references who can vouch for this, putting together a portfolio, or finding any sort of work or volunteer experience that will put you in the position to exercise these qualities. Third: You need to demonstrate that you can produce, edit, and publish content. Fourth: If all else fails, get a copyediting job somewhere."

"The best aspect of the job is working with varied content and deciding how to best deliver it to the audience we want to reach. Because of the relatively low-cost barriers for delivery and design in the electronic world, there is a lot of flexibility in how you approach things —from e-mail newsletters to blogs. I also enjoy being able to work on both the content creation and content delivery side of things. And being able to write means that I can bring that point of view to design and information architecture. The worst aspect of the job is that everybody thinks they can write and design and so often the people who provide content don't understand quite the effort it takes to package and deliver it as well as the best practices for doing so. Yes, content should be well-written and copyedited. No, we probably shouldn't use blinking pink type. Yes, the design should be well thought out and clean. No, the design should not include five different fonts and a ton of graphics. Yes, we should send out an e-mail newsletter. No, the newsletter shouldn't go out five times to the same list with the same exact content. You get the picture."

Writer

Number of people in profession	319,000
Average hours per week	40
Average starting salary	$29,150
Average salary after 5 years	$42,790
Average salary after 10–15 years	$58,930

Life on the Job

Writers come in all shapes and sizes—film critics, novelists, editorial columnists, screenwriters, technical writers, and advertising copywriters. Many spend the beginnings of their careers practicing their skills as they await a big break. While all writers prefer to write on subjects of personal interest, most professionals are assigned topics by an editor. Writers may work at home, in an office, or in a hectic newsroom, but wherever they set up their office, writers generally spend upwards of 40 hours a week hard at work—even if only a fraction of that time is spent actually tapping the keys of a word processor. Writers begin by asking questions and researching a subject. The process of "writing" may involve conducting interviews, reading up on a subject at the library, traveling to a far-off location, or even surfing the Internet for clues. A writer must be open to the possibility that new information will change the original angle of a piece. As she gathers the necessary information, the writer gradually develops a working outline from which she is then able to create a draft. Then it may be time for an editor to review the material and suggest changes. A writer may wait and send a completed draft manuscript to an editor, while others may prefer to send the manuscript in "partials" (sections or chapters) in order to give the editor a chance to see the work in progress from an earlier stage. The editing process continues until editor and writer judge the material ready for publication.

Writers collaborate with the other professionals involved in media, such as photographers, graphic designers, and advertisers. Screenwriters and playwrights write original pieces or adapt existing books or stories for the stage or screen. Usually they attend readings or rehearsals to make revisions because problems may appear when the piece is performed that they had not anticipated when they wrote it. Copywriters generally work for advertising agencies, researching market trends to determine the best way to sell their clients' products. Technical writers take esoteric subjects and write about them in simpler terms so that readers can easily grasp ideas and information.

Insider tips

Freelance writers should have a personal website and an online portfolio so that potential clients can easily view their clips. Check out sites such as WritersMarket.com to connect with editors, and make sure that you understand the needs of a particular readership. *Rifle* magazine isn't going to be looking for inspirational stories about women overcoming obesity. When you're starting out, choose topics that you know something about. If you're an indie-music aficionado, let your natural love of the subject guide you towards prospective stories/editors. Watch talk and morning shows to discover good story ideas when you don't have any of your own—just approach the original material from a slightly different angle. Don't cold call editors! Try consulting the ASJA guide to freelance writing at ASJA.org for some general information about writing queries, developing a niche, and targeting editors.

Interview with a Professional

Bill Hinchberger, founder and chief editor of the highly praised "Hip Gringo's Guide to Brazil" offers aspiring writers the following suggestions: Get a specialty (business, health, etc, or a geographic focus if you want to work abroad), and mine your personal contacts to find sympathetic editors. When you know the editor, or are referred by a trusted friend or colleague, everything goes more smoothly. Otherwise your queries usually end up in the slush pile. You must be self-motivated, thick-skinned, and able to not take rejection personally. Most of your proposals will be rejected, no matter how good you are and how great your ideas are."

As for the best and worst aspects of freelancing, according to Bill, the answer is people, people, people. "People pay me to learn, experience things, and explain them to others. I've done and seen some amazing things. Worst: Responses from editors like this one I got today: 'This is a fantastic story. Sadly, we are not allowed to buy any freelance the rest of the year.' Despite falling payment rates, increasingly obnoxious contracts and working with overburdened editors who are often inexperienced, many interesting things have happened to me on the job. I've ridden through the streets of Salvador atop a 'trio elétrico' (the sound trucks that Carnival bands use to roll through the streets), and I've danced in the winning Samba School of Rio's

Carnival parade. I've slugged through Amazonian mud and crouched in canoes with native fishermen after the pirarucu, the world's largest freshwater fish. I've chased down the last remaining speakers of dying Amazon languages. I've toured the mega-dam Itaipú with company officials and flown over nearby Iguaçu Falls in a military plane. I've ridden on horseback through the plains of Rio Grande do Sul. I've witnessed the São João midwinter extravaganza in Caruaru and the post-Christmas Wise Men Festival in Minas Gerais. I've surfed the primo waves of Santa Catarina. I've hung out in the shantytowns of São Paulo, Rio de Janeiro, and Salvador. I've flown over São Paulo in a helicopter courtesy of a bank executive. I've interviewed everyone from the late author Jorge Amado to President Lula. Not only that, but I practice the Brazilian martial art capoeira twice a week."

Interview with a Professional

Barbara Moss, author of *Little Edens* says, "The standard advice for aspiring writers is: Don't write unless you have to, but if you have to, do it with your whole heart. This is a difficult and uncertain profession, and success rarely comes right away. Be prepared to write through dry patches and inevitable rejection, always with the goal of perfecting your work, of bringing the words on the page closer to the vision in your head. No matter how crowded your schedule, try to carve out time to write each day. And when you're not writing, read. The writers you admire will be your best teachers. Read first to absorb the story, and then to analyze how the writer achieved the effects that drew you in. Don't worry about being overly influenced. If your talent is real, you will find your own voice."

Camaraderie, according to Barbara is also very important for writers: "Because writing is a solitary profession, it's important to seek out others to share your work with and to give you honest feedback: a friend, a teacher, a writers' group, a class. The ideal reader will have some receptivity to your writing, but will also be able to view it with cool objectivity. In return, be open to what is offered, and learn to evaluate it, to sift through both praise and criticism for the gold nuggets that will enrich your work. Eventually you may want to consider an extended workshop or a postgraduate MFA program; these are competitive and costly, but they provide a community of serious writers and a wide network of contacts. Nonwriters sometimes think that producing fiction is a simple process akin to automatic writing: Get an idea, record it, and voila! A book.

"They have no idea of the skill and effort and time it takes to create something that lives on the page. For most writers, revision is a constant process. There's some truth to the writer's cliché, 'It's all a draft till you die.' And often this work is done with no promise of remuneration: You won't be getting a stipend while you go through the long labor of mastering your art. Another misconception is that publication guarantees instant fame and fortune. The literary journals that publish most emerging writers' stories have small circulations and smaller budgets; many don't pay at all, and even the most established don't pay much. Of course, the exposure is valuable in itself: when your work is in the world, things can happen. Occasionally a literary novel will reap both critical acclaim and popular success, but in this culture, that combination is a rarity. Very few writers of literary fiction expect that their work will make them rich. Money, when it comes, is an unexpected gift.

"The best aspect of writing fiction is the sheer exhilaration of creating a world out of your imagination. The characters take on a life that seems to be independent of you, and yet you've made them. Things float up out of your subconscious that you had no idea were there. And the shaping process is very exciting—taking this raw material and rendering it in words. It's the ultimate high, and I never let myself forget what a privilege it is to do this work. The worst aspects are the isolation and the constant self-editing and self-criticism—the vision of perfection and the falling short. In this precarious profession there are very few plateaus. Each new project, each day's work, is a challenge, but the moments of triumph are sweeter because of that.

"And then, once the book comes out, there's the marketing process—a whole other subject. These days, writers have to work hard to publicize their own work. The transition from producing the work in private, in this most introverted of professions, to hawking it in public can be a difficult one."

CHAPTER 4

Choosing a Path: Identifying the Jobs that are Right for You

WHERE HAVE I HEARD *THAT* BEFORE?

You've tried to be good-natured about it for a long time, but admit it—you're getting a little tired of having the same conversation over and over again. You know, the one in which a distant relative or long-lost friend congratulates you on your recent graduation and asks what you studied. You tell them you majored in English or communications, and they immediately want to know what on earth you're going to do with your degree. You can detect a bit of cynicism in their tone—as though they don't quite believe you'll be able to be a fully functioning, self-supporting, tax-paying member of society just because you didn't major in accounting or "pre"-something. Sure, the cynicism is wrapped in good intentions and support, but it's still there. And if you say you don't have a job lined up just yet, they try to buoy your spirits by saying something like, "Well, I guess you could always *teach* or something."

If teaching actually *is* among the options you're considering, then a comment such as this probably won't bother you. But if you have a different path in mind, or you haven't fully explored your choices yet, the implication—however subtle—that your career options are limited can be annoying. What's worse, it can be contagious—if you have this conversation frequently enough, anxiety can creep in no matter how passionately you believed in your academic choices.

You'll need to dismiss the notion that it will be harder to find a job with a degree in English or communications than it would be with any other field of study under your belt. Sure, you won't necessarily be pursuing the same types of positions as your more vocationally minded classmates, but that doesn't mean you're any less marketable or qualified for the jobs that interest you—once you've determined what those are.

But maybe you already know that you have literally thousands of career options to choose from (at the very least, you know about the ones we've described in Chapter 3). Perhaps your anxiety stems from not knowing which of these options you should pursue. Maybe all you know at this stage is that you'd like to secure a solid, respectable job—one that will make the best use of the skills and passions that you've cultivated in school, one that will convince mom and dad that paying your tuition was a worthwhile investment, one that doesn't require you to wear a hairnet or break the law. But of the jobs that fit those criteria, how on earth are you going to choose the one that's right for you? Don't worry—that's what this chapter is all about.

First things first: Distinguishing jobs from careers

Before we go any further we should define both "career" and "job," because the two terms are not interchangeable. Most people who are just getting started tend to think of themselves as ensconced in a career only when they have a steady, full-time job with an ample paycheck and a respectable title in an organization, or at least in an industry or field, in which they intend to stay for the foreseeable future. But that's not necessarily the case; you can still work toward your professional goals even if you know the position you're currently in, or the one you're about to take, won't last indefinitely.

What's more, you can still build a career even if the job that pays your bills isn't the one from which you derive the most professional satisfaction, or the one that provides the most opportunities for advancement. A career encompasses a lot more than any one full- or part-time job; rather, a career is *all* the things you're doing at any given point to advance your professional goals. You might work as a waiter while doing internships or volunteer work related to your long-term career aspirations. In other words, your career *includes* your current job, but that's not all it includes.

Taking that idea one step further, we should point out that you as a person are defined by much more than your job or your career. Your hobbies, personal interests, involvement in the community, relationships with friends and family—all of these things are just as important as your vocation when it comes to defining who you are. Obviously, satisfying and meaningful work that makes full use of your skills, abilities and interests is important (otherwise, we wouldn't be writing a book about it), but any specific job- or career-related decision only makes sense if it's consistent with all of the other areas of your life that are important to you.

Granted, it's hard to avoid being identified by the job you do or the occupational field you're a part of. Whether you're applying for a credit card, renewing a passport, or making small talk at a cocktail party, everybody wants to know what you do. We obviously do a lot of things in life, but what most people care about is what we do for a living.

This cultural norm can be a real pain for people who get their intrinsic rewards from pursuits other than the activity that brings them their paycheck. We all know the type—wannabe actors schlepping trays of food, cab drivers writing the next Great American Novel between fares, and personal assistants who get their kicks from the hobbies they pursue on the weekends.

Add to this list those whose jobs are just stepping stones to long-term career goals—e.g., recent grads in the mailroom on the slow road to CEO, aspiring attorneys copyediting while in law school. The jobs recent grads hold don't always hold their full interest or attention. Education usually pays off down the road, but, initially, you may find yourself with a job title and job duties you'd rather not be identified with.

Even if it doesn't exactly fulfill all of your professional goals, however, your first job shouldn't trigger a massive identity crisis—nor should your second or third job, for that matter. Most career experts agree that careers evolve over time, and they rarely progress in a linear way. Few people experience a professional epiphany at the age of 18 or 22 or 26, figuring out exactly what they want to do and sticking to it for the rest of their lives. Most people end up trying several different jobs—often in a number of different fields—before they decide what fits, and that's okay. At this stage, you are gathering information, investigating various options, and gradually refining your career goals as you find out more.

Over time, you'll start building on the themes and patterns you might already see emerging—a commitment to social service, a love of learning, an entrepreneurial streak. Your professional priorities and values might change, and your personal circumstances might change as well. When you move from one job to another to accommodate these changes, you carve out a career for yourself. You may decide to move after you've worked in a particular position for some time. Maybe you'll decide that you need to be closer to your family, or maybe you'll want to start one of your own. Perhaps you'll decide to return to school, and your graduate studies will spark an entirely new realm of intellectual and professional interests. Whatever the reason for the change in your personal circumstances, it's not uncommon for jobs to change along with them. And no matter what's driving the change, your experience from your past job (or jobs) will probably influence what you do next. Let's say you loved the intellectual challenges your first job provided, but wished the work had been more team-driven. Chances are, when you look for your second job, you'll be looking for positions that are decidedly more collaborative. Your second job will tell you even more about yourself and the specific things that float your professional boat, and you'll apply that knowledge and experience when looking for job number three. This process—the process of continually revising your goals, priorities, and values—is what allows your career to evolve over time.

So while you probably won't be able to map out the exact progression of your entire career right now, the good news is that you don't have to. Instead, you can focus on specific experiences that in one way or another weave together your interests, skills, and values.

Narrowing the field of options

Now that we've finished our pep talk, it's time to start thinking about what specific jobs make the most sense for you. As you may already know, there are countless personality tests and skills inventory tests out there intended to help you determine what type of work you're best suited for. But, at the end of the day, deciding what career you're going to pursue all boils down to something far less scientific and formulaic and far more instinctive: What do you like? What do you do well? And what do you care about? The answers to these questions correspond to the categories "interests, skills, and values," which are often seen as the ABCs of career choice. By contemplating these questions, you're also addressing the question: "Who am I and in which environments will I thrive?" The key to finding a job you like is figuring out a way to balance your skills, interests, and values in a satisfactory way.

- Your **interests** are those things you enjoy doing, discussing, or daydreaming about. They include hobbies, sports, academic subjects, work activities, topics you read about, and anything else you like. They might be lifelong passions or just passing fancies. Your job is to decide which interests need to be part of your work life. You might major in art history but then work as a banker, reserving your art appreciation for museum visits on the weekends. Or you might have an interest so strong it must be a part of your daily work life.

- The category of **skills** encompasses three main areas: learned skills (tangible things we've learned how to do, such as using a computer or writing a newspaper article); innate skills (aptitudes or talents); and personality skills (such as being hardworking, detail-oriented, or creative). Deciding which skills you enjoy using is important in defining a career focus and in finding a job you enjoy; as you'll read in Chapter 5, your resume, cover letter, and interviews are all opportunities to tell a prospective employer what specific skills and abilities make you a perfect fit for a job. If you trumpet skills you don't particularly enjoy using, it's entirely possible you'll land in a position you don't like very much.

- **Values** are things that are important to you. You probably already have a good idea of what personal values—e.g., honesty, integrity, loyalty, self-reliance—you hold most dear. For the purposes of this guide, however, we're referring to *professional* values specifically. Identifying your professional values helps you answer the question of what's really important to you in a particular position or work environment. The more closely your job—and your work environment—is aligned with your professional values, the greater the chances you'll be fully engaged and invested in your career at any given time. So what are examples of professional values? Here's a list—by no means exhaustive—to get you started:

  o Advancement opportunities

  o Autonomy

  o Availability of training/development programs

  o "Brand equity" (will people immediately recognize the name of the employer that I'm working for?)

  o Compensation package (base salary, benefits)

  o Contribution to society

  o Creativity

  o Direct contact with customers and clients

  o Diversity of daily tasks/responsibilities

  o Intellectual stimulation

  o Job security

  o Meritocracy (i.e., are the right people promoted? Does exceptional performance get rewarded?)

  o Quality of colleagues (e.g., colleagues that are friendly, supportive, and social)

  o Quality of direct manager

  o Quality of formal/informal mentoring

  o Prestige of the organization/occupation

  o Predictability (in terms of hours, required travel, etc.)

- ○ Relatively low stress level
- ○ Work/life balance

What's your MVV (most valuable value)?

The relative importance we place on each of the values above tends to change over time, reflecting not only changing professional priorities, but changes in our personal circumstances as well. There might be times in your career when making money is your top priority; as your career progresses, things like intellectual engagement or a sense of working toward the greater good might become more important to you. And what's more, if you're still in college or have only recently graduated, you might not really know what relative value you place on the factors listed above; in most cases, it takes actually working in positions that represent different sets of pros and cons before you really have a sense of what's important to you. You may accept your first job out of college thinking that a better-than-average base salary and ample advancement opportunities are the most important things to you, only to discover that intellectual stimulation and colleagues that you can relate to are far more important, even if attaining these things means earning a lower salary.

Figuring out how you assign importance to these factors is a highly personal process—and you probably won't assess individual jobs or careers in the same way (or using the same criteria) that friends or peers would. For example, imagine what would happen if you printed out the list of values we provided above and distributed it to 20 of your closest friends and acquaintances. Let's say you asked each person to go through the list and assign a number between 1 and 10 to each value, where 1 meant that they assigned little importance to that factor, and 10 meant that it was a professional "deal-breaker." Chances are good that even among 20 people—a relatively small sample size—no two people would submit identical assessments. And if you asked the same 20 people to complete the same exercise even two years later, their responses probably wouldn't be identical the second time around.

Lauren, who double-majored in history and French at a New England liberal arts college, accepted a job with a small corporate research firm after graduation. Three years later, she went back to school to earn her MBA. After her first year of business school, when her family and friends asked her what career she was likely to pursue after graduation, she admitted that she still wasn't sure. "All I know is that I have to work for a company whose name people will recognize," she said. "When people asked me where I worked before business school and I told them, I always had to explain what kind of company it was. I'm tired of that. It's important to me that the next company I work for has instant name recognition." Not everyone assigns the same level of importance to brand equity—in fact, some people might consider Lauren's perspective a little bit shallow. But values aren't normative—in other words, there are no right or wrong answers when it comes to deciding what's important to you in a job. But you do need to give some thought to what's important to you in order to find a job in which you'll thrive.

At the end of the day, jobs (even the best, most desirable jobs) represent a set of trade-offs. Especially in the early days of your career, it may be difficult to get everything on your personal and professional wish list. Even so, the process of assessing (and continually reassessing) your priorities will enable you to figure out which trade-offs you're willing to make and which things are too important to give up.

Major breakthrough

If you're getting stuck when it comes to figuring out your skills, interests, and values, spend some time thinking about what you've studied. Your major can tell you a great deal about the type of work you're likely to enjoy. Think of it this way: Many career experts say that the first step in determining your professional destiny is asking yourself what kind of work you'd do for free. In other words, if money weren't an issue, how would you spend your time? The rationale, of course, is that if you're truly passionate about the work you're doing, then you're far more likely to excel and advance in your career.

In a way, your major *does* represent the type of work you'd do for free. Not only were you not paid to study what you did, but chances are you actually paid (in one way or another) for the privilege of studying it. And if you're lucky, you had the freedom to decide what you wanted to study without spending too much energy on the myriad practical considerations that come with choosing a job. You didn't have to factor in compensation or benefits or promotion potential or the part of the country in which you wanted to live: You probably chose a major that you liked—or at least one that you thought you might like when you chose it.

Take some time to revisit the reasons you chose your major: What attracted you to your field of study, and what made it compelling enough to stick with? What made it rewarding for you? What made you glad you did it? What specific aspect of your major did you connect with the most? For example, did you enjoy the fact that it was research-intensive? Or that it involved a lot of writing? Did you appreciate that most of the work you did was independent versus collaborative (or was it the other way around)? Did your classes inspire intellectual debate and discussion that kept you engaged in the material? What specific classes did you find the most rewarding, and what about those classes floated your intellectual boat? How has your major—and the specific skills you developed while you studied it—contributed to success in other arenas? If you switched majors somewhere along the line (and many, many people do) think about what prompted you to switch gears.

Getting to the heart of what drew you to a specific major can tell you a lot about the type of work you'd find satisfying, and, conversely, the type of work that'd be a round hole to your square peg. Consider the specific jobs we outlined in the previous section: A reporter, a copyeditor, and a publicist might all have undergraduate English degrees in common, but it's very likely each one would have a different answer when asked what made their course of study so appealing and so valuable.

Balancing priorities

Once you've identified your interests, skills, and values, you need to weigh your priorities. It isn't always easy; sometimes two or more of these things seem to work against each other. Let's say you took an oil painting class as an elective while you were an undergraduate. The class was completely unrelated to your major, but it inspired a genuine interest in oil painting—and in the arts more generally. You've decided oil painting is something you want to pursue one way or another. However, when you look at the list of work-related values outlined above, you realize that job security and making a lot of money are important to you. The starving-artist route is probably not for you, then, so you'll need to land a job that's more stable and more lucrative—maybe something on the business side of an arts-related organization. Or you may decide to keep your art interest "pure" by painting in your spare time and working a job unrelated to the arts in order to make money. (As we said at the outset of this chapter, the job that pays your rent doesn't have to satisfy all of your interest, skills, and values on its own). However you go about it, you'll need to decide what your priorities are before you can pursue a job that meets your needs. Here are some typical priorities of entry-level job-seekers:

- A foot in the door in an industry or sector in which I have a focused interest.

- Any old job I have the ability to do and at least a basic interest in that will provide some professional experience and allow me to establish a work routine.

- A job that will reasonably fit my interests, skills, and values but will more importantly allow me to live where I want and give me the amount of money I need to gain financial independence.

- A job that bridges the gap to a new career field.

These are all perfectly legitimate ways to frame your short-term career goals so that you can conduct a targeted, focused job search. In fact, they can be especially useful when looking for your first job, as many recent grads haven't figured out their long-term goals yet and need a framework to figure out which jobs to pursue. The key, however, is to continually ask yourself whether the jobs you're applying for are consistent with your priorities—and to ask questions that will enable you to determine if your expectations about the job are realistic.

"Foot-in-door disease"

Many smart and talented folks with liberal arts degrees convince themselves to take jobs they don't really want because they want to get a foot in the door at an organization or in an industry in which they are particularly interested. There's nothing inherently wrong with this approach—as long as it's well informed and realistic.

Imagine, for example, your dream is to write for *Rolling Stone* magazine. Also imagine you are the most astute proofreader in the Western hemisphere—you can spot a wayward semicolon a mile away. Unfortunately, you enjoy proofreading about as much as you enjoy listening to chalk screech on a blackboard.

By stressing your exceptional proofreading skills on your resume, you could probably land a job at one magazine or another—as a proofreader. "That's OK," you say to yourself, "I'll have my foot in the door and eventually prove myself to be the great feature writer I know I am." Who could argue with the logic of this approach? By and large, organizations prefer to hire from within, so doesn't it stand to reason that you'll be able to work your way up fairly easily once people have gotten to know you and like you?

Well, maybe—but maybe not. First of all, you've got to ask yourself how long you can stare at columns of text looking for bad kerns and misplaced modifiers before you want to drive a number-two pencil into your skull. What toll will all the dreaded proofreading take on your mind, body, and spirit? And do proofreaders at *Rolling Stone* have even the slimmest chance of being promoted? Only you can answer these questions, but, in general, it's probably a bad idea to take a job you loathe because you suspect it might evolve into something else down the line. It might very well blossom into something better, but it also might not.

Employees in virtually every industry can get typecast in the same way that actors and actresses do. You might very well be *Rolling Stone*'s next great features writer—heck, you might already be able to write better stories than the person who currently inhabits that role—but if your boss sees you as a proofreader and nothing else, your chances for advancement could be slim. In fact, your proficiency in a role (even one you don't like) might paradoxically keep you from moving up. Your manager might decide that you are such a great proofreader he couldn't bear to hire someone else to replace you if you were promoted to features writer. That's why it's so important to talk to industry insiders in order to make informed choices about your career. During your informational interviews (which we'll cover in Chapter 5), be sure to ask about career advancement opportunities, promotion potential for specific roles, and the organization's philosophy and approach when it comes to developing its existing staff. After all of your conversations, you may very well decide that the foot-in-door approach makes the most sense, and that's okay. But you don't want to get your foot in the door only to find out that the rest of you will not be allowed in, nor do you want to get your foot in a door that you should have left closed to begin with.

GETTING FOCUSED

As we suggested at the beginning of this chapter, landing a job doesn't mean you've got your entire career mapped out. It also doesn't mean that you don't have to be focused during your job search; in fact, one of the easiest ways to sabotage your search is to come across as unfocused. These concepts aren't as contradictory as they may seem. You can be crystal clear that a job you're applying for is right on target for you at the present time, even if you're a little fuzzy on your long-range goals. Your cover letters, interviews, and follow-up correspondence—basically every moment of contact with prospective employers—must convey that you have a focus and have arrived at that area of focus in a careful, thoughtful way. (We'll talk more about how to package your qualifications and career goals in the following chapter). But before you can convince anyone else that you should be hired, you have to figure out for yourself why any given job would be right for you and why you should be hired.

It helps to have a framework for thinking about the universe of job opportunities available to you. Every position you will consider can be defined on three distinct levels: the industry or field (e.g., publishing, finance, education, government), the function or role you'd be fulfilling (e.g., writer, editor, account manager, analyst), and the particular company or organization you'd be working for. The function represents the core of what you do; the industry you're working in and the company you're working for provide context. For example, you could be an editor in any number of organizations representing a range of industries. But the same function (editing) would be an entirely different experience at a *Fortune* 500 company that makes semiconductors than it would be at a consumer magazine. A role that's fascinating and rewarding in one industry might be utterly unbearable in another one.

While the same function can be very different depending on the industry you're working in, the reverse is also true: the same industry (e.g., advertising, government) can offer wildly different experiences depending on the function you have. Every field is highly complex and encompasses a variety of subfields and job titles. Each of these, in turn, requires different skills, credentials, and personality traits. In advertising, for example, there is a world of difference between the work an account executive does and the work a copywriter does. They are two different animals who happen to inhabit the same zoo. If you've identified the career field that interests you most, you've made a good start. And if you know the function you'd like to fulfill at your job (e.g., network administration), even if you don't yet know the industry or field you'd like to target in your search, you've also made some progress. But to make a compelling case to potential employers, you'll need to do legwork to fill in the missing piece. By "legwork," we mean research—checking out all available resources, online and otherwise—that will provide more information on specific fields and functions.

Chapter 3 of this book is a great place to start your research. And the Bureau of Labor Statistics—part of the U.S. Department of Labor—offers excellent career profiles of thousands of specific occupations. Whether you want more information on being a pathologist or a poultry farmer (seriously), the Occupational Outlook Handbook available on the Bureau's website (BLS.gov) will tell you about the training and education needed, average salaries, expected job prospects, job responsibilities, and other job-related details. You can also check out the websites of professional and industry associations (a simple internet search will turn up a lot of them). And when it comes to research, there's really no substitute for good old-fashioned informational interviewing (a process that we'll describe in detail in the next chapter). If you need help, enlist the help of the career-planning office—their resources should be available to you whether you're a current student or an alum.

Practical matters

Balancing your interests, skills, and values is definitely an important part of the job-search process. It's an important part of life, for that matter—and it requires an enormous amount of introspection and emotional energy (if it didn't, networks like the WB wouldn't have any programming). There are also, however, significant practical implications you shouldn't disregard as you evaluate specific jobs. We've outlined a few of them below:

How much do I need to be paid?

A lot of people would like to think that, if given the choice, they'd rather make less money and do something they really care about than earn more money to do something they despise. Then many of these people go to law school, move to Manhattan, or take on a mortgage. The truth is, we'd all like to think that the most important factor determining our choice of profession is the ability to pursue our life's passion—to do work that's consistent with the very core of our being, that makes a difference in the world, or that makes the best possible use of our unique talents. However, unless you happen to be Oprah Winfrey, it can be difficult to balance these needs with the more immediate need to keep a roof over our heads, eat, pay off student debt, and eventually pay for Junior's college education.

The truth can be a bitter pill to swallow. On average, graduates with undergraduate liberal arts degrees do indeed earn lower salaries right out of the gate than their counterparts in other disciplines. According to the National Association of Colleges and Employers (NACE), the average starting salary for class of 2006 graduates with liberal arts degrees is just under $31,000 a year. (By way of comparison, starting salaries for accounting undergraduates start at about $46,200, while finance/economics majors earn about $45,200 their first year out).[1] Gulp.

We're not going to lie to you: Living on $31,000 a year will mean living pretty modestly, especially if you have your heart set on living in a notoriously expensive metropolitan area (depending on the industry you choose, you may find you have to live in such an area in order to pursue the most attractive opportunities). Every year, Mercer Human Resource Consulting ranks cities across the globe according to their cost of living. In 2006, New York City, Los Angeles, San Francisco, Chicago, and Miami ranked as the most expensive cities in the United States.[2] If you're unsure how big-city living might affect your pocketbook, online tools such as Salary.com's Cost-of-Living Wizard enable you to figure out what

---

1 National Association of Colleges and Employers. "High Starting Salaries Show Competition Heating Up for New Grads." April 6, 2006.
www.naceweb.org/press/display.asp?year=2006&prid=233.

2 Mercer Human Resource Consulting. "Worldwide Cost of Living Survey 2006—City Rankings." June 26, 2006.
www.mercerhr.com/pressrelease/details.jhtml/dynamic/idContent/1142150.

you'd need to earn in one city to maintain the same standard of living you would in another.

Salary.com, along with SalaryExpert.com and the U.S. Department of Labor website (BLS.gov), also provides salary information across various industries, functions, and geographic areas. Keep in mind that the salary ranges these sites provide are necessarily quite broad; You'll need to supplement this information with your own research. Occasionally, you'll be able to glean at least some salary information by browsing the postings on job websites, but, more often, you'll need to rely on insiders to give you a meaningful and realistic range. (You'll learn how to ask for salary information tactfully in Chapter 5, under informational interviewing).

Of course, all of the salary information in the world won't do you any good unless you know how much money you really need to keep you going. Though financial planners use slightly different formulae to help people devise their monthly budgets the following guidelines will give you a rough idea of how to allocate your net monthly income:

- 35 percent toward housing. This means your rent or mortgage, utilities, and the costs of any home repairs or improvements.

- 15 percent toward repaying debt. This includes debt of both the student and credit-card variety.

- 15 percent toward transportation. These costs include car payments, car insurance, parking, fuel, and cab, train, or subway fares.

- 10 percent toward savings and investments. You are saving something, aren't you?

- 25 percent toward everything else. This means you've got one-quarter of your take-home pay to cover everything else: vacations, food, dry cleaning, clothing, recreation. Anything that you spend money on that doesn't fall into one of the aforementioned categories has to be accounted for here.

Once you've crunched the numbers, ask yourself if they paint a realistic picture: As we've said before, your salary won't go quite as far if you live in a famously expensive city such as New York or San Francisco, and you'll have even less wiggle room if you're staring down the barrel of substantial debt incurred during college or grad school. Keep in mind, though, that starting salaries are just that—starting salaries. Through job research, you'll (hopefully) find out how quickly and how often you can expect your salary to bump up, either through performance-based pay increases, annual bonus eligibility, or an annual inflation-based adjustment.

There's location, location, location . . .

It's an age-old dilemma (or at least it's been a sub-plot of many sitcoms and motion pictures): Is it worth moving to a new city—perhaps one you've never wanted to visit, let alone live in—for the job opportunity of a lifetime? Though you're unlikely to face such a dramatic decision in the early stages of your career, giving some serious thought to where you'd like to live is important nonetheless. As you consider your options, be sure to ask yourself if the jobs/careers you're considering are available in that locale. Some industries have high concentrations of jobs in particular geographic areas. Finance jobs, for example, are predominantly in New York, Chicago, and San Francisco; technology jobs are clustered in Boston, Seattle, and Silicon Valley; publishing jobs are chiefly in New York; most entertainment jobs are in Los Angeles; and numerous government jobs are in Washington, DC.

There are other factors to consider when deciding where you'll hang your hat: Are the job opportunities in your field of interest on the rise or at least stable for now? Are there interesting, varied places to hang out, like coffee houses, art galleries or museums, and movie theaters? Are there places you could take classes, such as colleges or universities, learning centers, or public libraries? Do there seem to be people you can relate to on an intellectual, artistic, recreational, spiritual, or other level that is important to you? What's the housing like? Is it plentiful, desirable, and affordable? How about the public transportation system? Do you need a car? Can you park a car if you need or want one? Do friends and family live there (or at least close by)? Is that important to you? How about your significant other? Speaking of significant others, if you don't have one but want one, does the city have a vibrant singles scene? Or is it a popular place for families to settle down and plant their roots? Consider these and any other questions that might be relevant to your situation: The extent to which you like where you're living plays a much bigger role in determining your overall happiness than you might think—it might be as important (if not more important) than the work you're doing.

. . . And there's relocation

So you've considered the list above and you've found a city that meets all your criteria. Congratulations! You've figured out exactly where you'd like to live—that's a huge weight lifted off your shoulders. Now, do you want to live there forever? Or just the next few years? It helps to have at least an idea of how you'd answer that question, because your response might help you determine how attractive a particular job opportunity is for you. Just as professional priorities often change over the course of a career, so to do geographic priorities. Some careers can be pursued in just about any area of the country. If you're thinking about a career in social work, health care, elementary education, or family counseling (just to name a few), then you probably have more flexibility when it comes to geographic location than you would if you wanted to pursue a career in magazine publishing or the federal government—sectors in which job opportunities are highly concentrated in discrete geographic areas.

As an example, let's say that you've zeroed in on magazine publishing as a career field you might like to pursue. You know there are literally hundreds of magazines whose editorial offices reside in the New York metropolitan area, which is good news, as the city's energy and diversity—along with the sheer number of cultural and recreational opportunities it offers—have always seemed appealing to you. But while you'd love to live in the Big Apple for a few years, you sense it's not a place where you'd like to settle long-term. Maybe you don't want to rent for the next 10 years. Maybe you can't stand the thought of choosing between a long commute and a tiny living space. Or maybe the West Coast has always held a special place in your heart because that's where most of your family and friends reside. If you decide to move to another part of the country can you parlay the skills you've developed in magazine publishing into another position in an unrelated field? While there are opportunities in magazine publishing on the West Coast, there are considerably fewer of them than there are in New York. If you do find a great editorial job with a West Coast magazine, what will happen if the company downsizes in three years, forcing you to look for other opportunities? Or what if you decide—for whatever reason—that the job or the company no longer satisfies your personal or professional goals? Are you comfortable knowing that there are considerably fewer places to approach for jobs if you decide to jump ship?

Keep in mind that even if your industry isn't highly concentrated in a specific geographic area, the organization that you're considering might offer more opportunities in a specific location (usually its headquarters city) than it does elsewhere. Let's say you've identified a great opportunity in the New York office of a Cincinnati-based consumer products company. If staying in Manhattan for the foreseeable future is among your top priorities, be sure to ask whether career advancement is likely to require a tour of duty at company headquarters before you sign on the dotted line.

Leaving on a jet plane . . . don't know when I'll be back again

If you ask people whether or not they like to travel, most would probably say yes. (We haven't done any scientific research to corroborate this point, mind you, but we think it's a pretty safe assumption to make). Most people think they like to travel, just as most people think they have a good sense of humor: It's rare you'll find somebody who admits to being either a homebody or a drip. If you like to travel and are looking for jobs that will enable you to hop around the globe (or at least the country), at least keep this in mind: Business travel and personal travel are two entirely different animals. Think about the last flight you took: Were there long security lines, interminable flight delays, hours spent in the middle seat directly in front of a screaming baby? Without a vacation on the other side of these annoyances, they can sap your strength—it takes a person with unique energy and stamina to excel at a job that requires frequent travel. If you think a jet-setting professional life means you'll get to see lots of interesting places and rack up hundreds of thousands of frequent-flyer miles, remember these things too: If you're traveling for business, chances are you'll visit lots of interesting cities, but you'll probably only see the insides of those cities' hotels and conference rooms (along with whatever scenery happens to reside between the airport and your hotel). If it's the frequent flyer miles you're after, remember it's pretty hard to redeem those these days anyway. You can always buy a plane ticket and visit interesting places on your own time.

Making the most of your job, once you've gotten it

It's comforting to know no career decision is ever final, and that it's perfectly acceptable (even expected) for personal and professional priorities to change, and for jobs to change along with them. This knowledge, however, can lead to a chronic case of "What's next?" disease. Even if you haven't experienced this yourself yet, you might have heard other people express this type of mindset. They tell you they've gotten a new job, and the first thing they mention is how great their new role will look on their resume. Wouldn't it be nice if you could just take a breather and relax for a minute?

Well, the truth of the matter is it's never a bad idea to be thinking ahead to the next position or company or rung on the career ladder—in fact, it's often what keeps your battery charged in your current role so you remain interested, engaged, and productive. While it's never advisable to announce to the world you've got one foot out the door, it's absolutely advisable to pave the way to future career opportunities by distinguishing yourself in whatever job you've got at the moment. Here are a few specific ways to make the most of your current job:

Find a mentor.

Regardless of the industry, organization, or functional area you're currently in, identifying and enlisting the help of a mentor is one of the single best ways to make the most of your current job. Mentors are a valuable resource no matter how high up the organizational ladder you are, but they're especially valuable early in your career, when the learning curve is the steepest.

A good mentor plays multiple roles when it comes to your career development. First of all, she's a sounding board—someone who will listen to your specific challenges, goals, or aspirations and provide an informed, objective perspective. She's also a valuable insider—someone who can give you the inside scoop on who the real decision-makers are in your department, what it's like to work with (or for) certain people, and what it takes to succeed in your current position, ace your performance review, make a lateral or geographic transfer within your company, or get a raise. In certain situations, your mentor can become your strongest and most vocal advocate—someone who will speak up on your behalf when your performance is being evaluated (formally or informally), or when you're being considered for a promotion or important assignment. Your mentor can also assume the role of professional matchmaker, introducing you to the other people at the company whom you need to know—either because they're in a position to help you achieve your career goals, or because they share your personal and professional interests. Finally, your mentor can be the best kind of critic—one who's honest, direct, and willing to give you constructive feedback and advice with only your best interests in mind. In short, she's indispensable.

Many organizations have formal mentoring programs in place, where senior-level employees are paired with more junior-level employees to help integrate young professionals into the company and provide them with ongoing career guidance and feedback. Whether your employer offers a formal program like this or not, take the time to identify a mentor—and solicit this person's advice and assistance from the outset. (We talk about networking in the following chapter and one of its key tenets applies here, too: By and large, people like to share their experiences and wisdom for the benefit of people who value their advice, so don't be shy when it comes to asking for help). You needn't formalize the relationship with matching t-shirts, monthly lunches, or even an official "mentor" designation. The important thing is to identify someone you trust—and someone who's professional achievement you'd like to emulate—who's willing to share their expertise with you over an occasional lunch, coffee, or happy-hour cocktail.

Remember, too, that your mentoring relationship doesn't have to be an exclusive one. In fact, there may be multiple people from whom you would like to seek advice and guidance and who you think will be of assistance in your career; when it comes to mentoring, the more the merrier. Long-distance relationships work, too; while at least one of your mentors should be someone you see in the office every day, your personal advisory board might also include people outside your office, organization, or industry. As long as someone has valuable advice to share and is willing to share it with you, you owe it to yourself to bring them on board.

Kick it up a notch.

David Bach, a former financial planner who became a speaker and best-selling author, says that in order to get more out of your job, you've simply got to put more into it. Bach offers the following picture of a typical day at the office for many people: "Get into the office around 9:00 A.M. (never early). Have coffee, check in with friends, talk about last night's episode of *Survivor*. Around 10:00 A.M., start to answer voicemail and e-mail. Fiddle around until 11:00 A.M. Work hard for a half hour because it's lunchtime. Get ready for lunch. Go to lunch. Get back at 1:00 P.M., tired from the big meal. Return some calls, maybe go to a few useless meetings, answer some e-mails. Around 4:00 P.M., start winding down and prepare for another busy day tomorrow." Most people achieve the highest levels of productivity, he says, right before they go on vacation—when they realize they have a lot to do in a very short period of time. In "pre-vacation mode," people show up early, make to-do lists, work quickly and efficiently, and then—with everything done and dusted—leave.[3] This general idea could just as easily be dubbed "pre-finals mode" or "pre-term-paper mode": The point is, you tend to get a lot more done during crunch-time than you do when things aren't quite as urgent.

Bach's advice for consistently achieving this level of productivity is simple: Start working every day as though it's the day before you go on vacation. Get to the office early, work hard, get your work done, and then get out of there. Chances are, your efforts will get noticed—in a very positive way. You'll build a reputation as the "go-to" guy (or girl): The person who can be relied upon to show up on time and get things done in a professional, organized, and efficient way. Whether you plan to stay in your current job for the foreseeable future or not, that's a good reputation to have.[4]

3 David Bach. *Smart Women Finish Rich*. New York: Broadway Books, 1999. 271–72.
4 Ibid.

Remember that attitude is everything.

We know where you're coming from: A few months ago, you were listening to a series of commencement speakers who implored you to take your hard-earned diploma and use it to make the world a better place. They got you all hyped up to go out and be wildly successful—either by earning buckets of money, building homeless shelters in your neighborhood, or curing one of the world's major communicable diseases. Those speeches may seem kind of remote if you just spent the last half hour at the Xerox machine mastering the fine art of double-sided, collated copying. But no matter how much you achieved during your academic career, you need to be careful not to fall into a familiar trap: becoming bored and disenchanted with your job, growing increasingly resentful about it, and eventually becoming an underachiever.

The truth of the matter is this: Even though you worked hard in school (and just as hard to get a job), early jobs can be a little bit anticlimactic. If you end up feeling this way about your first job, know that you're not alone—surgeons, lawyers, investment bankers, and countless other highly educated people also start out at the bottom of their respective totem poles, doing mundane things they weren't necessarily dreaming about as they slogged through all those extra years of school.

If you're bored or otherwise dissatisfied with an early job, consider channeling all of your energy—perhaps that intellectual energy your current job doesn't require—toward expanding the scope of your job, or pursuing on-the-job training that will keep you engaged. Remember, you're not going to get promoted into a more rewarding role unless you excel at your current one, so it may be in your best interest to grin and bear it—at least for six to twelve months (according to many career counselors, that's the amount of time it takes to give a job a fair shake). If your dissatisfaction comes from not having enough to do, there is an up side: Less-than-challenging jobs usually leave plenty of time for other pursuits, both during the work day and outside of office hours. So whether you take an evening class at a local university or attend networking events sponsored by industry or professional associations, make sure to spend your extra time wisely. Distinguish yourself in your current role by adopting a positive attitude and looking for processes to overhaul or improve.

For some people, having enough to do isn't the issue; instead, the work they're doing—while more than enough to fill the day—just isn't as fulfilling or as satisfying as they'd hoped. In situations such as these, focusing on an element of the work that is in some way rewarding—even if the position's responsibilities are mundane—

is crucial. If there's another position within the organization that seems to be more aligned with your interests and goals, find out whether it's a position you could be working toward while still fulfilling your current responsibilities. It may mean adding an extra project to an already full plate, but the extra hours you put in might (paradoxically) re-energize you if you're consciously working toward a goal. The same is true for job-related training: If your company offers internal training programs (or tuition reimbursement for job-related courses at local colleges and universities), consider taking one. If you already feel maxed out, taking on extra commitments may not initially seem to make much sense, but trust us: If side projects or courses keep you engaged and invested in your career, you'll have a much better shot at landing a more fulfilling and interesting job down the line—whether it's within your current organization or outside of it.

Along those lines, if you work at a larger company there may be opportunities to serve on a cross-functional team or committee; by getting yourself onto one, you'll have the opportunity to meet people in other departments. From there, you can learn more about your employer, establish a professional network, and build a cadre of mentors (who might eventually be in a position to help you land a job elsewhere in the company later on). Actively seek opportunities to create demand for yourself—if you set a goal to become the person everyone wants on his team, you'll have a better shot at actually getting onto someone else's team.

No matter how much or how little work your current position requires, go out of your way to ask for constructive feedback. Your organization may offer formal performance reviews already (if it does offer such assessments, ask for informal feedback in between reviews). If it doesn't, make it a point to ask what you're doing well and what aspects of your work performance could use improvement.

Know when it's time to move on.

As we said at the outset of this chapter, first jobs often mean taking on responsibilities—and job titles—you'd rather not be associated with or don't make full use of your skills, talents, or education. So if you find yourself in an entry-level job you dislike, how do you know whether it's just part of the inevitable dues-paying process, or whether your dissatisfaction stems from a more fundamental mismatch between you and the career, organization, or position? A recent article on CareerJournal.com (the *Wall Street Journal*'s career-planning website) offers the following advice: Take a look at the responsibilities of more senior colleagues at the organization. Do their jobs seem appealing to you? If so, enduring your current position for a little while might enable you to land a more rewarding role down the line. But if the senior jobs also seem awful—or if they seem palatable, but hardly worth tolerating a job (or series of jobs) you don't like in the interim, that's a sure sign you may want to consider other options. After all, there's nothing to be gained from paying your dues if getting promoted only means another job you'd despise. And speaking of promotion, remember our earlier advice: consider whether entry-level personnel are typically promoted at your current organization—and, if so, how long it takes—before you stick it out in hopes of advancement down the line.[5]

5 Erin White. "First-Job Blues: Adjust or Move On?" *Wall Street Journal* Online. July 26, 2006. www.collegejournal.com/columnists/thejungle/20060726-jungle.html.

CHAPTER 5

Landing the Job: Networking, Resumes, and Interviews

NETWORKING

No man is an island—especially if he's looking for a job

Without question, the universe of liberal arts majors includes its fair share of unassuming, introverted folk. You probably already know whether or not you fall into this camp: You'd rather have dinner with one or two close friends than go to a party and face a room full of strangers (and if you're persuaded to go to a party, you'll spend the next day on the couch, recovering—alone). On an airplane, you fasten your iPod before your seatbelt—just so the person next to you knows you don't want to chat. If a college professor ever gave you the choice between an individual paper and a group presentation, you didn't think twice about going solo. When people tell you that you need to network to land a job, they might as well be telling you that you have to stand on a street corner wearing a cow costume and a sandwich board, pointing passersby to the sale at Lou's Land of Leather. It just seems too vulnerable, too desperate to even consider.

But even if you're not a card-carrying member of the introvert society, the notion that you'll have to network as part of your job search might not sound that appealing—or maybe you just don't know exactly how to go about it. Either way, you shouldn't worry: For all of the negative connotations associated with the term, networking doesn't require you to interact with people in a way that's contrived or insincere. And it doesn't just take place on golf courses and at cocktail parties—or in nondescript hotel ballrooms during designated networking events. It's not a process that's only effective for job-seekers aggressive enough to approach virtual strangers, give a 30-second summary of their professional accomplishments and aspirations, and ask for help finding a job. And the people you'll approach as you build your own network will not—contrary to popular belief—assume you're a pathetic freak motivated solely by self-interest or desperation.

For the networking-phobic, it often helps if you think of networking as research, rather than as a job-hunting tactic. It's a process that allows you to leverage the richest source of information at your disposal: other people. At its most powerful, networking actually helps you decide which careers, industries, and organizations are interesting to you (and on the flip side, it can help you weed out the ones that aren't as appealing). It can also help you figure out what you'll need to do to get started, and eventually help to frame your candidacy once you've gotten your foot in the door for a specific position.

In the following pages, we'll explain what effective networking is—and what it isn't. We'll tell you how to use the contacts you already have to begin building an extensive and powerful network that will give you a leg up when it's time to apply for the job you want. We'll tell you about the various ways you can network—from the casual power brunch to more structured informational interviews, and we'll provide guidance on the types of questions you can ask to make sure you get the most out of your conversations. Finally, we'll give you a list of do's and don'ts for networking so your experiences put you in the best possible position to land the job you want.

Hide and go seek: The hidden job market

If you hang around career counselors for any amount of time, you'll probably hear them emphasize the importance of the so-called "hidden job market"—the one you'll need to tap into to land the perfect job. The term itself implies a little more mystery and intrigue than it probably should; in reality, the "hidden job market" simply refers to the universe of available jobs that are not formally advertised. When it comes to quantifying the size of this market, different experts cite wildly disparate percentages: some say the hidden job market represents about 60 percent of all available jobs, while other sources estimate it's closer to 95 percent. Whatever the actual percentage is, it's too big a number to ignore. If you want your job search to be successful—and by successful we mean that you not only land a great job, but that it doesn't take you longer to find it than it took to complete your degree in the first place—you cannot rely on job boards and company websites alone. You have to find out about jobs before the rest of the world does.

The hidden job market doesn't exist solely to make your life—and the lives of millions of job-seekers like you—more difficult. It arises because positions are often filled before they're ever advertised formally. Once a company identifies a staffing need, it can be weeks—even months—before the position is formally announced. It's not as though Willy Wonka just woke up one morning and decided that he needed a successor to his chocolate throne, posted an ad on Monster.com later that afternoon, and then had Charlie and the other four candidates at the factory for interviews the next day. It was a much more time-intensive ordeal than that: He was probably mulling on it for some time, realizing he wasn't getting any younger and that he couldn't run the factory himself for much longer. Once he decided he needed to hire someone, he had to orchestrate the whole Golden Ticket process—and you can bet he had to get all those Oompa Loompas to approve of it. If someone would have told Willy about a good candidate before he kicked off the Golden Ticket campaign, you can bet he would have orchestrated his series of tests for *that person* first.

The real-life hiring process is also fairly slow-moving. Once a hiring manager decides he needs to create a new role—or find a new person for an existing role—he usually has to obtain approval from the higher-ups first. All along, he's thinking of potential candidates he already knows who might fill the position: people who already work at the company full-time, as well as any freelance, contract, or part-time workers who have expressed an interest in a full-time position. Once he gets approval, he may have to post the job internally first to comply with company policy. While the job is posted internally, the hiring manager is probably asking current employees if they know of anyone who'd be a good fit for the role. (This is where networking comes in—you need to be one of the people at the top of current employees' minds when they hear about the position!) If the well of internal candidates and employee referrals runs dry, then the position is usually posted externally—on the company's website, and/or on job websites like Monster, Hotjobs, and Craigslist.

If the job does end up seeing the light of day, you've got another obstacle to confront: Setting yourself apart from the literally hundreds of other candidates who have also seen the very same job posting and are furiously updating resumes and crafting cover letters at the same time you are. Even if you did nothing all day but hit "refresh" on your internet browser to be sure that you're the very first one to submit your application for any new job that strikes your fancy, you'd still be one in a crowd of hundreds of applicants. Some hiring managers confess they simply just can't weed through the volume of applications the more popular job boards generate: If they get 200 resumes for a single position, they might look at the first 20 that come in, and then pick the best five to invite in for an interview.

All of this might seem miserably unfair to you; after all, if you have all of the experience and education the job posting outlines and you just happen to be the twenty-first person in line, why should you be out of contention? Unfortunately, the job-search process—like life—often falls short of a pure meritocracy. Hiring managers aren't lazy, but they are often overworked and eager to bring in a qualified candidate who will fit into the organization's culture as quickly as possible. In many cases, they know any number of people could do the job—even if they don't have all of the requisite experience when they walk in the door. Still, the more time hiring managers spend reviewing resumes, and the more time they spend interviewing candidates, the less time they spend on their core responsibilities, and the harder their existing teams must work because they're short-staffed.

When you build a network of contacts that can tell you about openings (and potential openings) before they hit the company's website or external job boards, you will have far more success than you would if you went it alone. This is true for two reasons: first, you'll be competing with a far smaller number of applicants if you express your interest before the job is even posted externally. Why would you want to compete against 200 other candidates when you can compete against a handful—or none at all? Secondly, people in a position to hire prefer to bring in candidates who have been referred to them by existing employees—always. When you think about it, this makes perfect sense. Existing employees know what a firm's culture is really like better than anyone else, and they usually have a good sense of what people are likely to fit in—and thrive—in that environment. If you approach an organization through an existing employee, you've essentially made it through the first stage of the screening process. If you're basically qualified, generally likeable, and hardworking, the hiring manager would far rather hire you—or at least interview you—than sit down with a pile of 200 resumes. Wouldn't you?

Think of it this way: When you need a book to read on the beach during your summer vacation, do you go to Barnes & Noble and read the synopsis on the back of every book in the store before you made your selection? Or do you ask friends and family if they've read any good books lately and choose among those based on what sounds the most interesting? Chances are, you do the latter, and it's not because you think there aren't any other books out there that would make a great beach-read. You do it because considering every possible option out there wouldn't be a good investment of your time, so you rely on other people to help you narrow your options down. It's the same with hiring decisions, and it's why networking is so critical to a successful job search.

Networking "Yes, buts"

To help you overcome any anxiety you might have about networking, we've outlined the most common misconceptions about the process. We call these networking urban myths the "yes, buts," and they're usually invoked by job-seekers who are reluctant to network. When we tell these folks how important networking is to the success of their search, they usually begin their objections by saying "Yes, but . . . ." The most pernicious "yes, buts" keep some people from networking effectively, and they prevent other people from networking at all. To help you separate networking fact from fiction, we've outlined the nine most common "yes, buts" below, along with an explanation of why each one should be banished from your internal job-hunting dialogue—forever.

"Yes, but networking seems like a forced and unnatural way to deal with people."

Networking is essentially talking with other people and getting their opinions in order to make an informed decision about something. Chances are, you've done this already—have you ever asked someone else what they thought of a particular book or movie, or if they knew of a good dentist or tailor? Did that seem unnatural? Did people seem annoyed that you asked for their advice? Remember, these scenarios aren't that different from asking for career advice. You're probably better at it than you think, and people will probably be much more eager to give it than you ever expected.

"Yes, but I've never been very good at schmoozing—networking is just a more sophisticated term for schmoozing, right?"

Wrong. Networking sometimes involves schmoozing, but the two aren't synonymous. Think of schmoozing as the art of small talk: Without question, establishing a relationship with someone new requires some degree of small talk. But networking is more than working the room at a cocktail party. No matter how casual or informal the setting, networking has two very specific purposes: learning as much as possible about appealing career options, and telling other people what you're looking for so they can point you in the right direction.

"Yes, but networking feels insincere and manipulative to me. People won't want to help me if they feel like I'm using them to get something."

By and large, people like to be helpful by sharing their experiences and expertise. Unless you give people the impression you don't value their perspectives or respect their time, chances are they will be happy to help you if they can. In his essay, "Life Without Principle," Henry David Thoreau said: "The greatest compliment that was ever paid me was when one asked me what I thought and attended to my answer." This probably rings true for you too. Think back to the last time someone asked what you thought about a class or a professor: did you feel used? Or were you flattered someone valued your opinion enough to ask?

"Yes, but I hate asking for favors. What could I possibly offer them in return?"

There's nothing inherently wrong with asking for help. And what's more, enlisting the help of others during your job search effectively makes other people stakeholders in your success. Once someone provides you with guidance in your job search, they're personally invested in you and therefore want to see you do well. And often times, this investment isn't just metaphorical: Many organizations use referral programs to encourage existing employees to bring in talent from the outside. In these situations, your contacts have more than just the warm fuzzies to gain if all goes well and you're hired.

"Yes, but what if I don't know that many people? I'd have to approach complete strangers and ask them to talk to me."

Networking does not involve approaching strangers in the vain hope that they, one day, may be able to help you land a job. In fact, it actually starts with the people who know you best: your family, close friends, professors and teachers, and current and former colleagues. Consider these—and anyone else you interact with on a regular basis—your own personal A-listers. The people your A-listers know are your secondary contacts. You might know some of them—if only tangentially—but you probably won't know most of them. It's often your secondary contacts who can put you in touch with people close to decision-makers. It doesn't really matter if you've got legions of close friends and professional contacts who know you well; all that matters is whether someone on your A-list knows one or two people who can help you set things in motion. While you're getting word out to your A-list about your job search, don't forget to ask them what's new in their professional lives too: Talking to people you already know (e.g., family, friends, classmates) about what they do can be an incredibly valuable tool—one most people don't use enough.

"Yes, but networking means that I'll have to ask people that I barely know for jobs—and then 'sell them' on my skills and abilities."

If you're approaching it the right way, you won't be doing either of these things during a networking conversation. Networking is not about asking for a job—it's about getting advice from people who are in a position to provide it. Asking the right questions— and actively listening to the answers—is more important at this stage than selling your skills and abilities. A wise woman (advice guru Dr. Joyce Brothers) once said that "listening, not imitation, may be the sincerest form of flattery." Author Dale Carnegie—who literally wrote the book on winning friends and influencing people—once said you'll make more friends in two months by becoming interested in other people than you will in two years trying to get other people interested in you. Their advice rings true when it comes to networking: Your focus should be learning and listening, not talking and selling. And who knows? Maybe you'll make a friend or two along the way.

"Yes, but I'm an introvert. Only extroverted people are effective networkers."

This "yes, but" is a corollary to the previous one, so our response will sound familiar if you've been paying attention. But we'll risk being repetitive in order to make this point clear: The ability to listen to (and remember) what people say is critical to building relationships. At its core, that's all networking is: building relationships. If anything, introverts might have a slight edge over extroverts when it comes to networking conversations and informational interviews, because introverts are often better listeners than more gregarious folk. As we said before, asking someone for their opinion and making it clear you value what they have to say is critical to getting them on your side. Finally, if you really pay attention to what they have to say—and manage to retain it—you'll reap benefits during the interview stage. As you'll read in Chapter 5, the ability to demonstrate a solid understanding of a given job, and a sincere interest in the organization it's with, often distinguishes a successful candidate from the rest of the pack.

"Yes, but I'm very qualified for the positions I'm applying for. My credentials and past performance will speak for themselves and distinguish me from the crowd. I don't need no *stinking* networking."

We hate to be the ones to break it to you, but the real world—and this includes the job market—is far from a pure meritocracy. As a student, you're generally rewarded for what you know and how well you do your work. Sadly, there aren't many jobs where you can succeed by the sweat of your brow and the ingenuity of your ideas alone: With few exceptions, attaining professional success requires you to develop meaningful connections with other people. The importance of personal relationships applies to the job search as well. Remember that old cliché, "It's not what you know, it's whom you know"? Well, it's partly true—in reality, it's what you know and whom you know. As we mentioned earlier in the chapter, an impeccable academic record and stellar professional achievements won't mean anything if your resume never gets read.

"Yes, but networking involves being aggressive and pushy. I'm neither of those things."

Contrary to popular belief, networking is actually more effective if you're not aggressive or pushy. In fact, one of the most common mistakes gung-ho networkers make is advancing their own career agendas too early in the process, which doesn't win them many friends or professional allies. Again, it's important to keep the bigger picture in mind and keep your expectations realistic. Think of networking as groundwork for a job search that will yield results later down the line. No matter how badly you want someone to pass along your resume or act as an internal reference for that dream job you've learned about, you will get much more from your conversations if you really, genuinely approach them as opportunities to learn. Your contacts aren't a means to an end; they're more like a personal "board of directors" whose experiences and perspectives you value. If this type of thinking governs your interactions with other people, you won't be aggressive or pushy—and you won't be perceived that way, either.

Start spreading the news . . .

When it comes to true love, people often say it only finds you when you're not looking for it. Does this maxim apply to finding the perfect job as well as the perfect mate? Sadly, no—not for most people. But that's not to say you can't end up finding out about a great job in the course of a conversation that was never intended to have anything to do with your job search. That was the case with Alison, a 24-year-old consultant who ended up unintentionally networking when she just wanted to hear a familiar voice. "I had just moved to London from New York, and not only was I having a hard time with my job search, but I was incredibly homesick," she explains. "So I called a friend of mine back home, and I was just telling him how cold and rainy it was in London. He mentioned that a friend of his had worked in London for a few years and had experienced a similar thing. Anyway, I found out that the company his friend had worked for when he was overseas was one that I had interviewed with when I was a senior in college. I didn't know that the company even had an office in the U.K., but it turned out that my friend sent my resume to his friend, who in turn forwarded it to my current manager. I got an informational interview at first, then a job interview, and eventually the job."

The moral of the story? Jobs won't usually find you when you're least expecting them to, but romance and job-searching are similar in a different way: You're probably not going to get very far in either endeavor if you never leave your house, or if you never let people know you're in the market. In fact, one of the most obvious mistakes people make when they're networking is focusing on the people they don't know and completely overlooking the people they do.

Spreading the word involves talking to the people on your A-list: family members, close friends, current and former colleagues, classmates, teammates, professors, teachers—anyone who knows you well and interacts with you regularly. (As a general rule, anyone who couldn't pick you out of a police lineup does not belong on your A-list.) Not only should you make sure these folks know you're looking for a job, but you should let them know—with as much specificity as possible—what you're looking for. If you don't know exactly what you want to do, don't worry: the important thing is you've let people know you're in the market. Unless they know you're actively looking, even your close family and friends won't be able to help you. Remember: Your job search might very well be at the top of your priority list, but it's not necessarily on anyone else's radar screen. We're not suggesting you send out a formal press release to inform your friends and loved ones you're looking for a job, but it's important to get the word out. That way, when an A-lister or secondary contact gets wind of a great opportunity, you'll be among the first to hear about it.

Don't look a gift networking contact in the mouth

You've been there, we've been there: You talk about your career aspirations during Thanksgiving dinner. The next thing you know, you're getting regular phone calls from your mother, who's suddenly playing the role of Yenta the Matchmaker in the off-Broadway musical, *Your Job Search.* You said you wanted to be a writer? Well, your cousin MaryBeth is a medical journalist who made six figures last year interviewing doctors and publishing articles on public health issues. She says you can call her and she'd be happy to talk to you. Fast-forward to a few weeks later: Have you called your cousin MaryBeth yet? She's expecting your call.

While it's tempting to roll your eyes and move on to other things, it's probably not a bad idea to call your cousin MaryBeth, even if you're not entirely sure medical journalism is your calling. At the end of the day, effective networkers leverage the resources and the contacts they're given. If someone else is willing to make an introduction or otherwise break the ice for you, then what are you waiting for? Yes, it might seem awkward at first, but chances are you'll be glad you talked to her. Maybe she has some interesting things to say about pursuing writing as a livelihood. Or maybe she has some tips for becoming a great interviewer. You just never know. Motivating yourself to network when you have the opportunity is a lot like motivating yourself to go to the gym: You may dread it with every fiber of your being, but, once you do it, you feel so much better about yourself and the world in general. Networking releases the same sort of endorphins. Will a single conversation with your cousin land you a job? Probably not (in much the same way that 20 minutes on the treadmill probably won't reshape your body), but at least you're doing something, right?

It's a marathon, not a sprint

Keeping with our physical fitness metaphor, we should point out that networking muscles are built over time, not overnight. Some hard-core networking books will tell you to aim for five new networking contacts per day—only you will know whether that's a realistic target for you or not. If you try to do too much too soon, you probably won't stick with it. Networking really is the job-search equivalent of a long-term fitness plan: Unless you can really make it part of your lifestyle, it's not going to do you any good. So don't start out with Atkins when you know South Beach will probably work better in the long run. Don't start by going to impersonal networking events or job fairs. Send an e-mail to one person—just one—who you've been thinking about but haven't contacted recently. Don't ask for anything. Don't tell him you're looking for a job. Just check in, see how he's doing, and ask what's going on in his life. Take the time to acknowledge people's birthdays and anniversaries, and send an e-mail congratulating them when they graduate from school, get engaged, or reach other milestones. If the reason networking makes you uneasy is because you feel like you're getting in touch with people only when you need something, there are really only two ways to avoid that problem: Not asking for help when you need it, or being in touch more consistently so that asking for help is just a natural extension of the relationship you already have. Guess which strategy we endorse?

'Tis the season . . . for continued networking

Of course, going the extra mile to keep in touch with your A-listers is one thing, but what about the folks you know less well—the ones that you've met through referrals, informational interviews, and networking events? You can't possibly be expected to remember and acknowledge their birthdays and anniversaries (unless you want people to think that you're stalking them), right? That's right, but you can take a moment to give them a shout during the holidays—it's a thoughtful, proactive gesture that will keep these relationships current without giving anyone the impression they might need a restraining order down the line. And taking the time to maintain professional relationships means you won't have to feel awkward when you have to call a contact out of the blue about a job opportunity or ask for a reference.

To get started, dig up all those business cards you collected over the course of interviews, summer internships, job fairs, and—if you've already done some structured networking at this stage—power brunches and lunches, formal networking events, and informational interviews. Buy a pack of generic holiday cards and write short notes to your contacts wishing them a happy holiday season and offering a brief update on your professional status. Keep your tone positive, genuine, and subtle. For example, if you're still in the market for a job, your card might look something like this:

> *Dear Carrie,*
>
> *It was great meeting you earlier this year at the Women in the Arts luncheon. Since then, I've had the opportunity to meet with some great folks about my interest in becoming a columnist with a daily newspaper, and while I'm still looking for the right opportunity, I feel excited about the many prospects. I hope all is well and that you're enjoying a wonderful holiday season. I hope to speak with you again soon.*
>
> *All the best,*
>
> *Joanna Jones*

Or, if you're employed but want to keep your list of contacts current, something like this would work:

Dear Samantha,

I know it's been awhile since we last spoke, but I wanted to send a quick note to wish you and your family a wonderful holiday season. Things are going well for me at Smith Public Relations, and I've had the opportunity to work on some exciting new projects. I hope all is going well with you, and that the new year brings you continued success. Let's stay in touch.

All the best,

Robert Yule

While the holidays are one obvious opportunity to send cards or notes like the ones above, keeping in touch doesn't have to take place between Thanksgiving and New Year's Day. The important thing is not the specific holiday or the time of year, but the fact you're reaching out and keeping yourself visible. In fact, if there's one drawback to sending cards around the holiday season, it's that people receive so many cards yours may not stand out as much as it otherwise would. You can send out Thanksgiving cards, which makes it fairly likely yours will be the first holiday card your contacts will receive. Some people even send out networking cards around the Easter holiday (if you go this route, be sure each recipient observes the holiday). Even if there's not a bona-fide Hallmark holiday on the calendar for months, there are other good reasons to stay in touch—if you see an article or news clipping you think would be of interest to someone in your circle, send it to them and let them know you're thinking of them. No matter what occasion you choose, be sure to enclose a business card with your correspondence, or write your e-mail address and contact phone number beneath your signature.

INFORMATIONAL INTERVIEWS

So what exactly do you do once you've tapped your network and identified individuals who might be able to help you with your search? In a nutshell, you ask them to share their experiences, perspectives, career advice, and professional wisdom with you—regardless of whether they have the faintest idea who you are. Officially, this is called informational interviewing, and it's the best way to glean valuable job advice from the people you've met through your networking efforts.

An informational interview is any conversation where the primary objective is finding out about a particular field, company, or job opportunity. Informational interviews are not job interviews (and you shouldn't approach them with the expectation they'll lead to one). Instead, informational interviews are targeted conversations with people who currently work in the industry or field that you're interested in. Targeted doesn't necessarily mean formal: Oftentimes, you'll be able to glean just as much information over a casual brunch with someone you already know as you would during a more structured meeting in an office setting with someone you've never met. But no matter how formal or casual, all informational interviews are the perfect forum for:

Learning about a particular organization—how the company distinguishes itself from its competitors in the industry and how it distinguishes itself among other employers in the same field; its hiring process; its values and culture.

Learning about a specific job/position—what educational background or work experience is required; which personality traits or working styles are particularly well-suited for the role; what the day-to-day responsibilities are; how the role fits into the organization's broader mission; what challenges and rewards are inherent to the job; what career development opportunities are typically available.

Getting advice on your job search—how your background and credentials might be viewed by hiring personnel in a particular industry or at a specific company; what factors interviewers are most likely to focus on during the recruiting process; what "barriers to entry" might exist that you didn't know about before (skills tests, writing samples, background checks, etc.); what successful candidates at a specific company have in common; which other individuals might be willing to speak with you.

Learning about potential job opportunities—how a particular company fills job openings; whether there are industry-specific job boards or websites employers rely on when they have openings to fill; whether there are any industry-wide trends or company-specific developments that might affect hiring (mergers, acquisitions, restructurings, lateral movement, etc.); the most effective ways to find out about positions that have not yet been publicized.

On the approach

In order to snag informational interviews with the people who are best suited to give you advice, the way you ask is everything: Your request should be polite, concise, honest, and unintrusive. While there are definitely situations where it's more appropriate to lob in a telephone call, asking for an informational interview is one task best accomplished over e-mail. You can rest assured you won't catch your contact just as she's rushing into a meeting or out the door for a dentist appointment, and you've left the ball in her court without making her feel awkward about it if she can't accommodate your request. Over e-mail, you can take the time necessary to make sure the tone of your request is appropriate: assertive yet respectful, specific yet flexible, complimentary but never cloying. You provide all of the nitty-gritty details (who you are, how you know who she is, and what you want from her) in a single, seamless paragraph. Here's an example of an e-mail requesting an informational interview:

Dear Ms. Walker,

My name is Karen McCarthy, and I'm a recent graduate of New York University here in Manhattan. I was referred to you by a friend of mine, Scott Davis, who worked with you last summer at the Village Voice. *I am currently considering a career in newspaper journalism, and part of my research process involves speaking to people currently working in the field who are willing to share their perspectives and experiences with me. Scott mentioned that you have a very interesting professional background, and that you would certainly have some unique insights into the skills and experiences I should be building in order to launch a successful career in the industry. If you have a half-hour to spare in the next week or two, I would love to meet with you in person. If an in-person meeting isn't possible, maybe we could schedule a brief telephone conversation at a time that makes sense for you; I'm obviously happy to work around your schedule.*

Thanks so much for your help in advance, and I hope to hear from you soon!

Kind regards,

Karen McCarthy

Take what you can get

There will be times when a networking contact lets you know right off the bat that he can't meet with you in person or (for whatever reason) can't help you along in the hiring process. But if your contact is willing to share advice over e-mail or over the phone, don't discount the value of a dialogue just because it's not what you initially asked for. You can still learn a lot from these "virtual" meetings—and saying "thank you," by the way, is still in order.

The "Power Brunch"

You may have heard of a "power lunch" before, but the term "power brunch" might be an unfamiliar concept. A "power brunch" is the most casual version of an informational interview, and—especially if you're a novice networker—it's a great way to start getting the word out about your interest in a particular industry and getting advice about packaging yourself for maximum success. And if you're a reluctant networker, the power brunch is the perfect way to start out; after a few weekend meals over omelets and cappuccinos, you'll definitely be more comfortable with the idea of asking for help when it comes to finding the perfect job.

Not only does the power brunch enable you to practice your informational interview skills, but you'll probably learn a lot more than you would in a more structured setting. To a greater extent than e-mail, telephone calls, or even office visits, power brunches create a relaxed environment that promotes candor; after all, you're presenting yourself as a trusted confidante rather than a job-seeker on the prowl for insider information. While the focus of a power lunch is selling yourself, there's no such pressure when it comes to the power brunch: Here, the focus isn't on you, but on the person you've invited. Your brunch guest might give you valuable information on breaking into the industry you want (including referrals to other contacts in your target industry), general advice on pursuing opportunities in a specific field, or insider tips on positions that haven't yet been advertised. Compared to weekday lunches—which can often be hurried and seem formal—power brunches are just more fun. You can show up in jeans and linger over a mimosa if the conversation takes off or if you just want to catch up after you've talked shop.

The people you'll most likely invite to a power brunch are actually the people you already know best: the "A-list" we described earlier in this chapter. As we've said before, many people focus all their networking efforts on people they don't yet know, while they overlook the valuable perspectives and advice of the people they already know. After a few power brunches, you'll see there's good reason not to let this group go unnoticed. Remember, your A-list includes friends, family members, roommates, neighbors, teachers, professors, advisors, colleagues past and present—anyone you already interact with on a regular basis. To set up a power brunch, you needn't send a formal, polished e-mail like the one you'd send to someone who didn't know you from Adam: Simply call a friend or family member whom you haven't talked to in a while who's doing something cool.

The "Power Lunch"

With a few power brunches under your belt, you'll graduate to the power lunch—many times, a power lunch will involve someone a brunch date referred you to. The power lunch gives you the advantages of an in-person meeting: You get to observe the other person's body language (which will help you gauge how comfortable they are giving you the inside scoop), and develop the type of rapport only a face-to-face meeting can establish. However, because most power lunches involve contacts you don't know quite as well—and contacts slightly closer to the hiring process—the power lunch isn't quite as candid or relaxed. Though you still aren't expected to treat it as a job interview, you are expected to be professional—that means showing up on time, making sure your lunch sticks to the time you've allotted for it, and thanking your lunch partner profusely for taking time out of his busy schedule to meet with you.

Don't sweat the small talk: Specific questions to ask during informational interviews

Whether an informational interview takes place over the phone or happy-hour cocktails, you should prepare for it by developing a specific idea of what you hope to learn. Of course, the types of questions you'll ask will depend on what stage of the job-research process you're at. If you're just trying to get a sense of what a career in academia might entail versus a career in the private sector, you won't ask the same questions as someone who wants to find out what it's like to work as a research assistant for a specific university professor. The research you've done up until this point (whether online, at your career-planning office, or through other informational interviews) should also help you decide which questions to pose. Have one or two primary objectives in mind at the beginning of the conversation (whether it's finding out about a specific company's culture or figuring out what technical skills a particular job requires) and let that shape the direction the interview takes. If you get stuck, here are a few topics you might want to cover during your conversations, along with a few sample questions in each category:

- **Educational background:** I was wondering if you could tell me a little bit about your background—what did you study in college? Did you go to graduate school? Is your educational background typical of someone in your position? Are there aspects of the job that make particularly good use of the skills you developed as an English/communications major?

- **Job-search tactics:** As you prepared for your interviews, how did you go about conducting research on specific organizations? What strategies did you find most helpful? Looking back at your interviews with this organization, were there specific things about your background and experience that your interviewers were especially interested in discussing? What surprised you (if anything) about the hiring process at your company? Is it fairly common for employers in the industry to give any job-specific tests or assessments to evaluate your suitability for the position?

- **Career path:** How did you decide to go into this particular field? What other industries were you considering (if any), why did you choose your specific organization? How did you arrive in the specific area/department you're currently working in? How do you see your career at Company XYZ evolving? What types of advancement opportunities are available to you? Are lateral moves—either within the company or from one company to another—fairly common? Is it realistic to expect that if I start out in an entry-level role, I'll be able to move up within the organization? How does your organization approach developing its staff and promoting from within?

- **Day-to-day responsibilities:** What do you do on a daily basis? Can you describe what a typical day/week is like? Could you describe for me some recent projects you've worked on and your specific role in those projects? How do your specific responsibilities fit into the bigger picture of what your department does? How does your department fit into the larger organization?

- **Fit with the job:** What do you think it takes for someone to be good at this job, and what do you think it takes for someone to really enjoy it? What have you found to be the most frustrating and the most rewarding aspects of the job? What do you wish you had known about the job before you started it? Does the job frequently require travel, relocation, or long hours? Are people in these positions supervised closely, or are they expected to work independently, with little managerial oversight? Would you describe the job as highly collaborative or not?

- **Fit with the organization/industry:** Now that you're at Company XYZ, what has surprised you about working there? About the industry in general? How would you describe your firm's culture? What do you think is different/better about working there than anywhere else? Are there any factors specific to your experience that might influence your answer? What do you think your firm takes particular pride in?

- **Advice for you:** In general, what advice would you give someone hoping to break into this field? Based on your experience, what advice would you give someone looking to explore career opportunities at your firm? Are there specific areas of the company that seem particularly well suited for someone with my education, experience, and background? Can you recommend other people—either inside or outside of Company XYZ—who might also be willing to share their perspectives of working in the industry? Are there any industry-specific resources (websites, trade journals) that might be helpful to someone researching the industry? Which professional associations are linked to the field and what types of activities do they sponsor? Are there any with which I can be involved right away?

Unless your contact answers your questions with monosyllabic, one-word answers, you probably won't be able to get through all of these questions in a single informational interview, so keep your one or two primary goals in mind throughout the conversation. Regardless of how many or how few questions you ask, you should definitely be conscious of your contact's time; these individuals are not your personal career consultants, nor should you feel as though you can enlist them to support your case with recruiters. Never ask for more than a half-hour of your contact's time; if she's willing to give you 45 minutes, that's great—but be careful not to overstay your welcome. No matter what, be sure to acknowledge that your contact has sacrificed precious free time to speak to you, and always thank her profusely for helping you out.

Compare apples to apples

If possible, speak with contacts whose backgrounds are similar to yours in some way, whether it's their educational background, previous work or internship experience, specific professional interests, geographic location, or even outside interests or hobbies. This is helpful for a couple of reasons: The more you have in common with a person, the more relevant their job-hunting experiences are likely to be to you. Also, if you're interviewing someone you haven't met before, you'll both feel more comfortable if you can find some common ground to get the conversation started—and keep it going. It's human nature, really: As a general rule, we're more comfortable with people who are like us. The more your contact can relate to you, the more comfortable—and therefore candid—they'll be when it comes to sharing the secrets of their success. Tap into your school's alumni directory and extend an introduction to alums who work in the fields that interest you. If you're a member of any social or networking clubs, ask around to see if anyone knows of a butcher, baker, candlestick-maker, or anyone who fits the career profile you're hoping to build for yourself. If there are websites or resources you regularly consult as you're doing research on your target fields, keep an eye out for specific articles that capture your interest, and contact the authors to see if they're willing to speak with you further about the topic.

Practice makes perfect

Like any other skill you're just starting to learn, informational interviewing requires time and practice if you want to become particularly good at it. The more people you talk to, the more natural the process will seem, and the less you'll feel like a 7th-grader working on a research project for your social-studies class. And while conversations with people you've never met might initially make you nervous, you'll eventually find you look forward to them (yes, we promise). But no matter how adept you become at informational interviewing, keep the following rules of the road in mind so your conversations continue to be productive:

Take the road less traveled.

Your conversations with people who aren't directly involved with recruiting might prove the most valuable. If you keep your informational interviews separate from any formal application process, you can be reasonably sure the questions you ask won't have a direct influence on a subsequent hiring decision. You'll be more comfortable asking questions you wouldn't necessarily bring up in an evaluative setting, and you'll probably get more valuable answers than you would get from a recruiter or HR contact; these folks are generally too close to the recruiting process to give you an objective perspective, and, because they're generalists, they won't necessarily be able to provide a lot of detailed information about what it's like to work in any one specific position.

Asking contacts outside the regular recruiting process for the real scoop, however, doesn't mean you can say or do anything unprofessional—just because the details of your conversation won't necessarily get back to decision-makers doesn't mean it's outside the realm of possibility. No matter how informal the setting, you should still approach your informational interviews with professionalism.

Avoid the resume "balk".

Unless your contact has specifically asked you for a copy of your resume, don't fork one over during an informational interview. If someone has agreed to speak with you on a purely informational basis and you hand her your resume, you're essentially changing the direction of the conversation with little or no warning. In other words, you're committing the job-hunting equivalent of a "balk" in baseball (if you're unfamiliar with the term, here's the 411: in baseball, a pitcher must come to a full stop before he pitches, and, once he starts, he's got to follow through or it doesn't count. A violation of this rule is called a "balk"). You owe it to the people who've granted you informational interviews to give them fair warning, too. If you've told someone that you want to speak with them to learn more about a specific industry or job, you can't switch the rules halfway through the game by asking someone to submit your resume on your behalf. At best, your contact might not know quite how to react or what to do with it. At worst, she might question your sincerity and credibility. Of course, you are welcome to submit your resume if your contact asks for it in advance of your conversation—or during it. Have a few copies ready just in case, but don't go until you've gotten the green light.

The favor of your reply is requested.

Whenever someone takes time out to help you with your job search without any expectation of getting something in return, a formal thank-you is in order. Not only is it good manners, but leaving someone with a favorable impression of you makes good business sense, too. A thoughtful e-mail is sufficient, but a handwritten note makes a bigger impact—and not just because it takes a little more time and effort. "I send hand-written thank-you notes because my contacts won't wonder whether they're expected to respond," explains Carrie, a 26-year old assistant editor. "An e-mailed thank-you note might leave the recipient wondering, 'should I send a response to say good luck? Or should I offer to keep them posted on job opportunities?' A hand-written, mailed thank-you note lets you just say 'thank you' without giving the impression that you might expect something else down the line." We think Emily Post—and your mom—would probably agree.

Mind your manners when it comes to money.

When you bring up the issue of money, you always run the risk of getting someone's knickers in a twist over it, and it's no different when it comes to researching jobs and careers. We all know that it's considered impolite to talk about money in virtually any situation, but shouldn't it be fair game as you investigate which career options make the most sense for you? It should, but it isn't. Most people (including us!) will tell you that in the context of a formal job interview, you shouldn't talk about compensation until you're offered a job. But in order to negotiate effectively, you need to have a realistic salary range for comparable positions in mind. Salary surveys and databases are a start, but because the ranges they provide are broad, it's best to have a firsthand source to help you manage your expectations.

But how do you ask about money so early in the process? Very carefully. Perhaps more than any other topic of conversation you'll navigate during the informational interview, the money discussion is a little bit of a dance; the way it unfolds depends entirely on how well you read your partner.

Some people—God bless them—will come right out and tell you how much they make in their current position, or how much they made when they started out in their profession. In that case, they've opened the Pandora's Box of compensation issues for you, and it's reasonable to ask whether or not the figure they've cited is realistic for the type of position you're considering. Unfortunately, most people you'll speak with probably won't volunteer this level of detail. If this is the case, you'll have to gauge how the conversation is going and how receptive your contact is likely to be if asked to provide salary information. If you save the money talk for last (and we recommend that you do), you'll have time to figure this out. If the person is reticent when it comes to discussing his company's interview philosophy, then chances are he's not going to be eager to show you a copy of his W-2. Rely on your intuition and common sense when deciding whether to broach the topic.

If you decide to ask, keep in mind that the less direct your questions, the less threatening they're likely to be. You can always cite the salary ranges your initial research has revealed and see if you get a nibble: Your contact might advise you whether your expectations should lean toward the high or low end of the range. If you haven't been able to pin down any sort of range for the job, you can see if they'll be willing to provide one. Again, the way you ask the question is critical: saying "I'm in the beginning of my job search, and I have no idea what sort of salary range is realistic for entry-level jobs in this field" is very different from asking "Do you mind if I ask you what you make?" Asking open-ended questions that leave room for discretion are preferable to questions that require a single numerical answer. Such questions give your contact an escape route if he or she feels uncomfortable.

While we're on the subject of discomfort, we should emphasize the importance of recognizing it during the interview. If you sense your contact is starting to bristle when the subject of money comes up, there's absolutely nothing to be gained by being persistent—and there's an awful lot to lose.

If your informational interview ends and you're no further along when it comes to salary information, remember you can consult other sources besides the salary databases we mentioned earlier: professional associations, staffing companies, temp agencies, and headhunters can often provide salary data. Scour online job postings for similar positions and look for ones that specify salary. If you're still in school, remember that your career-planning office will probably be able to help you hone in on a reasonable range—even if they don't have firsthand knowledge of the position or industry, they're generally more adept at tapping into other resources, including alumni and recruiters who interview on campus.

Know when to say "when"

We can't overemphasize the importance of not becoming "that guy" or "that girl" in the eyes of your networking contacts: The one who won't stop calling or e-mailing to check on the status of available jobs. Wake up and smell the hummus, folks: Your networking contacts are not your personal career gurus. Nine times out of ten, they don't know about every current job opening their organization has posted, and they surely don't know about all of the ones that are still in the pipeline. Usually, they have little to no influence over hiring decisions. Even if they did, they can't work miracles if you don't have the requisite skills, training, or experience for a given job. If they barely know you, you shouldn't expect that they'll be eager to provide a personal endorsement of your candidacy, so don't ask them to do it. Regardless of whether they're eligible for a referral bonus if you end up getting hired, they're not on your payroll: They have their own jobs, too.

Not only can dogged persistence backfire when it comes to your own job search, but it has the potential to create bad networking karma all around. "When I first graduated from college, I designated myself as a career mentor on my university's alumni database, which meant that current students and other alumni were welcome to contact me for career advice," says Matthew, a 28-year-old analyst at a government agency. "But I got so many e-mails and calls from people who didn't really want advice; they just wanted me to help them get a job. A lot of them just wouldn't quit, even if I told them that my involvement in the process was limited. Eventually, it got old and I took myself off of the list."

Unfortunately, many job-seekers end up misusing and abusing the opportunities that informational interviews provide. While people generally enjoy lending their advice and expertise, even the most generous, well-intentioned person will start to lose patience with someone who takes advantage of his time or just won't back off. Think about it this way: Did you ever like a song the first time you heard it on the radio, but come to despise it after awhile because all the stations played it ad nauseam? When it comes to your networking contacts, know when to pipe down.

Don't be a one-trick pony.

As with any single component of the job-hunting process, you can't rely on networking prowess alone to get the job you want. We said that the most impressive resume wouldn't do any good if no one ever read it, and we meant it. But the inverse is also true: No matter how savvy a networker you are (or eventually become), you won't get the job if you can't convince the person or people in a position to hire you that you'd be good at it. However, information is power: Networking allows you to figure out what you want to do in the first place, what opportunities might be available that fit your criteria, and what you need to know about a specific organization before you interview there. You can use what you've learned by networking to make your resumes, cover letters, and other application materials more targeted and effective. So while networking is an important piece of the puzzle, it's just that: one piece. You have to make sure everything else fits into place, too.

RESUMES, COVER LETTERS, AND INTERVIEWS

What have I done to deserve this?

Now that your job search is underway, you may find a lot of unsolicited (but well-intentioned) advice coming your way. All of a sudden, it seems as though everyone is an expert when it comes to searching for—and getting—the perfect job. If you haven't already heard every job-hunting cliché in the book, just give it time. Chances are good someone will tell you "it's not what you know but who you know," "it's all about eye contact and a firm handshake," and "getting your foot in the door is what really matters—after all, you can always work your way up." With all of the unsolicited guidance coming your way, it can be difficult to distinguish tried-and-true job-hunting advice from old wives' tales perpetuated solely to put anxious minds like yours at ease.

In the following pages, we'll help you separate myth from fact when it comes to landing the job you want. If there's one thing we hope you'll learn from this chapter, it's that hiring processes at most organizations are much more an art than a science. When you're in the market for a job, you'd like to think employers' decision-making processes are—if not completely scientific—at least rational, predictable, and based predominantly on candidates' relative merits. But as a candidate for a given position, you're essentially marketing a product (that product is you, of course), and human beings aren't always rational and predictable when it comes to deciding what to buy. It's not enough to develop the product (by completing your degree, gaining work experience, joining professional associations, volunteering in the community, and so on)—you have to pay attention to the packaging, too. In the context of a job search, cover letters, resumes, and interviews are all part of the packaging: Once you've taken the time to figure out exactly what you have to offer a potential employer, you've got to present your qualifications in a compelling, convincing way. This section will teach you how to do just that.

It had to be you: What employers look for

Before you can figure out how to present yourself—your achievements, qualifications, and experience—to a prospective employer, you need to know which specific attributes organizations will be looking for as they evaluate your candidacy. It stands to reason that every industry (and every company, and every function or group within that company, for that matter) uses its own unique set of criteria to inform its recruiting process and hiring decisions. Nonetheless, employers across industries mention the same qualities over and over again. According to a recent study by the National Association of Colleges and Employers (NACE), an organization that publishes research on recruiting and employment issues for college graduates, employers consider the following skills and personal attributes most important to their evaluation of a job candidate:

Communication skills	4.7
Honesty/integrity	4.7
Teamwork skills	4.6
Strong work ethic	4.5
Analytical skills	4.4
Flexibility/adaptability	4.4
Interpersonal skills	4.4
Motivation/initiative	4.4
Computer skills	4.3

Attention to detail	4.1
Organizational skills	4.1
Leadership skills	4.0
Self-confidence	4.0

(5-point scale where 1=Not at all important and 5=Extremely important)[1]

If the list of attributes above seems like a lot to remember, take heart. We're not suggesting you commit it to memory or that you convince a prospective employer you possess every single one of these traits. Instead, the list is intended to reassure you that the skills you developed as you worked toward your degree are highly relevant in the job market. In fact, many of the skills that were most critical to your success as a student are the ones employers prize most highly. Consider the list above a starting point for taking inventory of your own capabilities and strengths.

In the following pages, we'll help you turn the skills you've developed pursuing your degree into a compelling, marketable package you'll present to prospective employers during your search. And though we address the resume, cover letter, and interview separately, keep in mind that each of these is part of a single process—a process that offers numerous opportunities to demonstrate exactly what you have to offer.

RESUMES AND COVER LETTERS

If it hasn't happened to you already, it will probably happen to you soon: You've successfully landed a "Power Brunch" with a friend of a friend who has the job of your dreams. The two of you have hit it off, and after a few cappuccinos she's giving you the inside scoop on what it's like to work in the industry: what it takes to be successful, what recruiters look for when they're scouting new talent, and how she landed her job in the first place. The more detail she gives you about her work, the more convinced you are you've found your professional Holy Grail. And it gets better . . . there's an opening in her department that would be perfect for you! And she's offered to pass along your resume! Just e-mail it to her, she says, and she'll deliver it to the right person, along with a personal endorsement of your candidacy.

You think about it for a moment: You know you must have a resume somewhere. You can remember writing one, but it's been awhile since you've updated it. You're eager to strike while the iron is hot, though; if your new best brunch buddy has offered to hand-deliver your resume to the recruiting contact at her company, you'd better fire one off to her as soon as possible, right?

---

1 National Association of Colleges and Employers. "Employers rate the importance of candidate qualities/skills," *Job Outlook 2006*. www.naceweb.org.

Well, yes—as long as it's error-free, easy to understand, tailored (to one extent or another) to the job for which you are applying, and accompanied by a concise, well-written cover letter. If it's lacking in any of these areas, it will be worth taking the extra time to get it in tip-top shape before hitting the "send" button and setting your application in motion.

How resumes and cover letters are used

In virtually every industry and organization, employers use resumes as a way to assess which candidates should be considered for an available position. There is no way around it: You absolutely must have one; without it you will not pass "Go," you will not collect $200, and—until someone comes up with a more reliable, efficient way to screen applicants—you will not get a job. When it comes to effective resumes, there's no single magic formula that guarantees success in every circumstance. However, the best resumes have a few things in common: they are concise, results-oriented, and clearly presented. Most importantly, good resumes convince hiring personnel to interview well-qualified candidates. *The primary purpose of a resume is getting an interview. A resume alone will not land you a job offer.*

Once you've been invited to interview, your resume will shape your subsequent conversations with recruiters, hiring managers, and other employees at the company. Every person you speak with during the interview process will likely have a copy of your resume, and each person will probably look for gaps, weaknesses, and inconsistencies that they'll expect you to address during your conversation. Once you've left the office, your resume helps your interviewer (or interviewers) remember you and serves as the basis for the discussion of your candidacy.

Cover letters, can play a less significant role. In general, they aren't read with the same level of scrutiny resumes are; sometimes they're read, more often they're skimmed, and, occasionally, they aren't reviewed at all. Nonetheless, you can't take any chances with your cover letter. There are many recruiters and hiring managers who will look to the cover letters when faced with several applicants that have similar resumes. You'll need to craft a cover letter that effectively introduces your resume, explains your interest in the specific position and the company, and highlights exactly what you can contribute to the role. Don't write one cover letter for several different jobs; make sure every cover letter you send out is job specific.

Together, your resume and cover letter introduce your qualifications to recruiters and hiring managers. Remember the list of attributes we mentioned at the beginning of the chapter? The person reviewing your resume and cover letter will have these qualities in mind and will be actively looking for evidence you've demonstrated them in the past. To give you an idea of how this works, we've listed a few of the key success factors below, along with the questions recruiters will most likely be asking themselves as they review your application materials.

- **Communication skills.** Is your resume well written? Is your cover letter (or cover message) thoughtfully prepared, tactfully worded, and customized to the position for which you are applying? Does your correspondence strike the appropriate balance between confidence and deference? Are your resume and cover letter both flawless, or are they riddled with typos and grammatical errors?

- **Teamwork, interpersonal, and leadership skills.** Have your prior work experiences, academic pursuits, and extracurricular activities required you to work in teams? Do your extracurricular activities and outside interests require a high degree of interpersonal interaction? Does your resume include evidence of your leadership ability? Do any of your credentials suggest you are adept at motivating and persuading others?

- **Strong work ethic, motivation, and initiative.** Does your resume show you've successfully juggled multiple priorities? Are you actively involved in extracurricular activities (or, if you've already graduated, do you consistently pursue interests outside of work)? Does your resume list achievements that suggest you're both self-motivated and committed to excellence? Have you demonstrated that you consistently provide a high-quality service or work product to classmates, colleagues, and managers?

The resume: Getting started

If you've attended a resume-writing workshop or picked up a reference book on the topic, you probably already know that people who receive resumes don't spend a whole lot of time reviewing each one—at least not in the initial screening process. The exact amount of time and energy devoted to reviewing your credentials obviously varies depending on the person who's reading your resume, but a seasoned recruiter probably spends less than 30 seconds deciding your fate.

It might strike you as miserably unfair that you must spend so much time writing, revising, and perfecting your resume while the person who receives it spends less than 30 seconds looking at it—and may not even read it at all. The good news is that a thoughtfully written resume can convey an image of who you are, what you're capable of, and how you have used your capabilities to accomplish results—all in 30 seconds or less.

If this seems like a lot to accomplish, remember that there are ample resources available to get you started. If you're a student, take advantage of the services your on-campus career placement office provides. Many of them compile binders of resumes from current and former students, which you can consult to get ideas. Once you've been inspired to write your own, you can schedule a resume consultation or attend the resume- and cover-letter-writing workshops offered by many campus career centers. Discussing your experiences and qualifications with an expert—

particularly if you've never drafted a resume before—can help you figure out what information to include and how to package it in an effective way. Even if you already have a working copy of your resume, it never hurts to have a second (and more objective) pair of eyes on your work.

Whether you're a student or not, it's worth asking family and friends—especially those who are already working in the industry you hope to break into—for guidance. They may even be willing to send you the resumes they used to land their current positions. At the very least, they'll be able to give you an honest assessment of whether your resume is well written, error-free, and easy to understand. As a rule, successful job-seekers take all of the help they can get when it comes to "packaging" themselves for prospective employers, so don't be afraid to ask for help!

Resume content

An effective resume has—at most—three sections: "education," "experience," and (sometimes) a third section for relevant information that doesn't fit into either of the other two categories. The optional third section goes a few by different names: "activities," "additional information," "interests," "other," or "personal," depending on what you've included in the section. The order in which the sections appear usually depends on how much work experience you have; if you are still in school or if you are a recent graduate, the education section should come first unless your professional experience is uniquely relevant and warrants emphasis (for example, you were a summer intern at the firm to which you're applying). If you're more than a few years out of school, the "experience" section should come first. The longer you've been out of school, the less resume space your education section should occupy. After a few years, you'll need to include only the basic information (institution, degrees conferred, honors awarded, and year graduated). Information on your grades, extracurricular activities, and research projects will eventually get bumped off the page in favor of a beefier experience section. If you include an "other" section, it should always appear last.

Some resume books—and career planning offices at some colleges and universities—suggest that candidates include an objective, overview, or summary at the top of the resume, immediately after the candidate's name and contact information. However well-intentioned the advice, we suggest you leave it out; your resume should already be a concise snapshot of your professional and academic experience to date, so it's redundant to summarize it even further. A career objective doesn't need to take up valuable real estate on your resume, either. If you're not applying for a particular job but are sending your resume to indicate your interest in an organization, it's virtually impossible to write an objective with the appropriate level of specificity. Resume objectives that are too broad not only end up sounding silly ("To be gainfully employed by a respectable firm so that I can afford to live in the city of my choice while avoiding incarceration and simultaneously utilizing my interpersonal, analytical, and leadership skills as well as my corporate wardrobe"), but they don't really tell the reader anything useful. At the other end of the spectrum, including an objective that is too specific introduces the risk you'll be knocked out of consideration if there are no available openings that meet your criteria. If you are responding to an advertised job posting, it should be fairly obvious your objective is getting that job—otherwise, why would you be applying for it? Your interest in a particular firm or your intention to apply for a specific job can instead be outlined in your cover letter.

The optional third section

The question of whether to include a third section ("activities," "interests," "other," or "personal") is one over which reasonable people can disagree. If you're still in school or have graduated within the past year, you're probably fairly safe including a section on the extracurricular activities you've pursued in college. Otherwise, stick to information that's relevant to the position for which you're applying or that distinguishes you in some way from other candidates (professional associations or memberships, for example, or proficiency in one or more foreign languages). The issue of whether to include personal interests or hobbies is another gray area; as a general rule, those that are fairly common (cooking, travel, jogging, and reading, for example) probably won't win you any points because they appear in resumes so frequently. Lines like "traveled extensively through Europe" almost never achieve their desired effect for the same reason. They won't disqualify you from consideration by any means, but they're unlikely to advance your candidacy either. If you're trying to choose which items to include in this section, include the ones most likely to pique the genuine interest of the recruiter.

Resume format

Now that you've figured out the type of information you'll include in your resume, you'll need to package it in a clean, easy-to-read, and error-free way. Keep in mind that conformity is a good thing when it comes to resume formatting: Anyone who picks up your resume should immediately be able to identify the two main sections (education and experience), and, within each of those sections, it should be easy for the reader to understand your achievements and qualifications. Adding too many stylistic bells and whistles—or packing your resume too tightly—just makes it more difficult for the recruiter to identify your credentials. To make your resume easy on the eyes, keep the following resume format basics in mind:

- Keep it to one page. Writing a resume requires careful consideration of which achievements warrant mention, which can be described more concisely, and which should be scrapped altogether.

- Stick to a single, easy-to-read font (Times New Roman and Helvetica are safe choices) in a legible font size (10 to 12 points).

- Use one-inch margins on all sides; don't try to "buy" more space by shrinking the margins.

- Label major sections (education, experience, and other) clearly and leave line spaces between them.

- Write in bullets, not paragraphs. Recruiters won't take the time to weed through densely packed prose. Use the active voice rather than the passive voice, leave out first-person pronouns, use qualifying adjectives and adverbs sparingly, and keep dependent clauses to a minimum—it will help keep your writing focused, action-oriented, and concise.

- Use boldface type, italics, or small caps sparingly. Overusing these features defeats the purpose of calling attention to critical information.

- Within each of the major sections, use a reverse chronological listing. Either the name of the organization or the dates worked should appear on the left (your approach should be consistent throughout the resume).

- For hard copies of your resume (these are a dying breed, but you still need to take a few copies with you when you interview), use high-quality bond paper in white or off-white.

The Magic Bullet

Make no mistake about it: Writing a resume is not the same as writing one of those family newsletters you stuff into holiday cards at the end of the year (and if you don't send these, chances are you know someone who does). You know the letters we're talking about: the ones that typically feature self-indulgent use of the third-person perspective and lots of unnecessary exclamation points. Your resume is a far more objective, achievement-driven, results-oriented summary of your qualifications in which the bullet point—not the sentence or the paragraph—is the primary component. To help you make sure your bullets hit their targets, we've consulted career-management expert and author Douglas B. Richardson, who offers the following tips for making your resume stand out from the crowd:

- **Don't overdo qualifying adjectives.** Descriptions of "major contributions," "dynamic programs" and "significant improvements" aren't objective reality. They're the writer's opinion and are discounted as such. Use high-action adverbs sparingly, too—words like "aggressively," "proactively," "progressively."

- **Avoid the use of "wimpy" verbs.** Use verbs to communicate action and achievement: Manage. Execute. Analyze. Create. Organize. Let the other drip be the one who "aided," "participated in" or "helped bring about."

- **Emphasize your past achievements by using titles, numbers, and names.** Titles show that someone else had enough faith in you to invest you with responsibility. That proves something, and yet many people leave it out.

- **Quantify your achievements wherever you can.** Numbers serve two functions. First, they show magnitude of achievement. The person who "increased plant output 156 percent in seven months" is more impressive than the one who merely "increased productivity." And "managed technical-design staff of 350" is better proof of your skills than "headed engineering group." Second, numbers offer concrete evidence that's rarely questioned.

- **Names carry clout the same way numbers do.** IBM isn't a "major data processing firm." It's IBM. Working there isn't the same as working at Marty's Software Heaven. Imagine if George Washington's resume simply stated: "Played significant role in planning and implementation of major country."

- **But if you can't rely on name alone, provide a description.** Descriptions such as "*Fortune* 100 Company" or "world's largest shoelace maker" can make an enormous difference in how you—and the quality of your achievements—are perceived.[2]

One size does *not* fit all

If you are job hunting in more than one field, or considering different types of positions within the same field, you will need to have more than one version of your resume. For example, let's assume you are applying for two jobs: one as an account representative at an advertising agency and one as an editorial assistant at a publishing house. For each position, you need to emphasize different skills. For the account rep job, you'll need to emphasize your interpersonal, communication, sales, and marketing skills. For the editorial assistant slot, you'll need to stress your attention to detail, ability to work under deadline pressure, and skills as a proofreader. Naturally, there will be some overlap between the two resumes, but the thrust of each should be very different. You should also have a more generic version of your resume available, which you can use for networking purposes. This will come in handy when you meet a contact who wants to know more about your background, but isn't necessarily offering you any kind of employment opportunity.

Electronic resumes

Once you've crafted the perfect resume, you'll need to save three electronic versions of it. That way, you'll be ready to send off your resume regardless of whether it needs to be e-mailed as an attachment, in plain text in the body of an e-mail, or uploaded onto an online database:

2 Douglas B. Richardson. "Skeptical Resume Reader Tells How He Really Thinks." *CareerJournal* . July 30, 2001. www.careerjournal.com.

- **Microsoft Word (or other word-processing software) document.** This is the version of your resume that you'll e-mail to hiring personnel when you're instructed to send it as an attachment. It's also the one you'll print out and take with you on interviews. Though the days of sending a hard copy of your resume by FedEx are all but over, this is the version you'll use if need to send a paper copy for any reason.

- **ASCII format with line breaks:** ASCII (American Standard Code of Interchange) allows databases and data-recognition software to read your resume without the confusion caused by formatting. The "with line breaks" option is critical for e-mailed resumes because there is no standard e-mail program that everyone uses; if the recipient's e-mail program doesn't automatically wrap line breaks, your resume could appear as a single line of horizontal text on the receiving end. By clicking the "insert line breaks" option, you'll avoid this potential problem. Your word-processing software will force line breaks so that no single line will exceed 65 characters of text. In Microsoft Word, use the "save as" tab, save your resume (name it differently from the first version), and save the file as plain text. When the dialogue box appears, choose "other encoding" and select US-ASCII. Also click the "insert line breaks" checkbox.

- **ASCII format without line breaks:** Use this format when you're instructed to upload your resume to an online database and to cut and paste into preset fields. Unlike the version you'll paste into the body of an e-mail, the version for web-based forms should not have forced line breaks (the text should wrap instead). Why is this? Because if you copy and paste a plain-text resume to an online application form and it has line breaks manually inserted, the end result will be a jagged effect. Each webmaster has a different default setting for how many characters constitute a single line of text, so if your resume exceeds this limit, your resume will look terrible. If you create an ASCII resume without line breaks, the text will instead "wrap," which means you won't have to manually reformat your resume once you've pasted it in the appropriate box. In order to save a version of your resume suitable for online application forms, follow the directions for "ASCII format with line breaks" above, but skip the last step.

Joanna C. Bloggs

Present address
903 Laurel Drive, Apt. #5C
Princeton, NJ 08648
609-555-7124
E-mail address: joanna@bloggs.net

Permanent address
1234 Hollyhock Lane
West Chester, PA 19382
610-555-7089

EDUCATION

Princeton University   Princeton, NJ • GPA: 3.9
- BA expected June 2005. Double major in history and English. Extensive course work (approximately 15 credits each) in Business/Management and Public Policy departments.
- Secretary of Class of 2005. Elected by peers to plan activities that promote class spirit and unity among 1200 undergraduates. Head publicity committee to promote major class events.

Henderson High School   West Chester, PA • GPA:4.0
Graduated May 2001. Class valedictorian. National Merit Scholar. Completed advanced-placement courses in English, calculus, physics, and Spanish.

WORK EXPERIENCE

Crane Communications   New York, NY
Public Relations Intern
Summer 2004
- Worked with senior account executives to manage relationships with clients in emerging high technology and health care industries.
- Assisted with the writing, editing, production, and distribution of press materials, including press releases and fact sheets.
- Conducted account-related research and compiled findings into complete coverage reports.
- Developed and maintained media lists and editorial calendars.
- Collaborated with office staff to devise publicity strategy and coordinate publicity logistics for major client events.

Chester County Community Center   West Chester, PA
Director of Youth Programs
Summer 2003
- Led the start-up and development of a youth volunteer program that connects 50 high schools with community organizations in need of volunteers.
- Conducted extensive research to identify participating community organizations, interview organizations' leadership, and determine their most immediate volunteer needs.
- Created a comprehensive database of area schools that enabled program to effectively match student volunteers and community groups.

Princeton University Library   **Princeton, NJ**
Library Staff
September 2001–May 2002
- Managed front desk and circulation records.
- Worked part-time while completing first year of college. Worked an average of 10–15 hours per week while maintaining a full course load.

PERSONAL
- High degree of competency in written and spoken Spanish (founded high school Spanish club; received first place honors at State Declamation Foreign Language Championships, 2000).
- Demonstrated interest in community service initiatives (president of high school volunteer organization; honored at 15th Annual Volunteer Awards of Chester County).

After you've spent hours tinkering with your resume to make it a visual master-piece, you might cringe at the thought of saving it—and sending it, for that matter—in an ASCII format. Don't despair: you can minimize the damage by taking the following steps:

- Replace bullets with asterisks (*).

- Offset category headings with a row of tildes (~), a row of equal signs (=), or capital letters.

- Change your margin settings to 2 inches; 60 characters (including spaces) is the maximum line length. Setting a wider margin allows you to control where the line breaks occur.

- Select a fixed-width typeface like Courier and use a 12-point font size.

- Add white space for readability.

- Do a test run. Send a copy to a friend—or yourself—over e-mail to see how it looks.

JOANNA C. BLOGGS

Present address:
903 Laurel Drive, Apt. #5C
Princeton, NJ 08648
609-555-7124
E-mail address: joanna@bloggs.net

Permanent address:
1234 Hollyhock Lane
West Chester, PA 19382
610-555-7089

EDUCATION

Princeton University
Princeton, NJ
- BA expected June 2005.
- Double major in history and English.
- Extensive course work (approximately 15 credits each) in Business/ Management and Public Policy departments.
- Secretary of Class of 2005. Elected by peers to plan activities that promote class spirit and unity among 1200 undergraduates. Head publicity committee to promote major class events.
- GPA: 3.9.

Henderson High School
West Chester, PA
- Graduated May 2001.
- Class valedictorian. National Merit Scholar. Completed advanced-placement courses in English, calculus, physics, and Spanish.
- GPA: 4.0.

WORK EXPERIENCE

Crane Communications
New York, NY
Public Relations Intern
Summer 2004
- Worked with senior account executives to manage relationships with clients in emerging high technology and health care industries.
- Assisted with the writing, editing, production, and distribution of press materials, including press releases and fact sheets.
- Conducted account-related research and compiled findings into complete coverage reports.
- Developed and maintained media lists and editorial calendars.
- Collaborated with office staff to devise publicity strategy and coordinate publicity logistics for major client events.

Chester County Community Center
West Chester, PA
Director of Youth Programs
Summer of 2002
- Led the start-up and development of a youth volunteer program that connects 50 high schools with community organizations in need of volunteers.
- Conducted extensive research to identify participating community organizations, interview organizations' leadership, and determine their most immediate volunteer needs.
- Created a comprehensive database of area schools that enabled program to effectively match student volunteers and community groups.

Princeton University Library
Princeton, NJ
Library Staff
September 2001–May 2002
- Managed front desk and circulation records.
- Worked part-time while completing first year of college. Worked an average of 10–15 hours per week while maintaining a full course load.

PERSONAL
- High degree of competency in written and spoken Spanish (founded high school Spanish club; received first place honors at State Declamation Foreign Language Championships, 2000).
- Demonstrated interest in community service initiatives (president of high school volunteer organization; honored at 15th Annual Volunteer Awards of Chester County).

Cover letters

If you were to conduct a survey of recruiters and hiring managers, you'd probably be hard-pressed to find one who could remember a truly exceptional cover letter (or an exceptionally good cover letter, anyway). The truth of the matter is cover letters are rarely read closely. As we mentioned earlier, they're more frequently skimmed. In fact, a cover letter is a little bit like a passport photo: Having a really good one is nice, but it isn't going to get you anywhere unless your other paperwork is in order. You can't get very far if you don't have one at all, though, and having a bad one is just plain embarrassing. In short, it's worth taking the time to make sure yours is great.

Your cover letter doesn't need to be a literary masterpiece, but it does need to be concise, well written, polite, at least somewhat personalized, and error-free. "We get so many applications from people claiming to be great writers and editors," says Diane, an HR professional at a magazine publishing company. "I'm always shocked at how many of them include poorly written cover letters with multiple typos." Not only should your resume be flawless, but it should include all the required information: the position to which you're applying, the primary reason for your interest, and a brief overview of the one or two qualifications that make you a compelling candidate. At the end of the letter, you should (politely, never presumptuously) suggest a possible next step—usually a brief telephone conversation or an in-person meeting.

By the time you've covered each of these points, you'll probably have reached the desired cover-letter length: no more than one page in hard copy, and no more than one screen shot if you're sending your resume via e-mail. The following guidelines will help you ensure that your cover letter gets the job done:

- **Address it to a particular person by name.** Be sure to indicate how you obtained that person's contact information. If you were referred by someone who already works at the company, mention that person's name early on; when a recruiter scans a cover letter or e-mail, he's more likely to take the time to review your credentials if he recognizes a colleague's name in the text.

- **Keep it brief.** Remember that the purpose of the cover letter is to set the stage for your resume, not to explain anything on it— or worse, repeat it. The longer your cover letter, the more likely the recruiter is to skim it (which effectively defeats the purpose of including more detail). This is not the forum to explain the genesis of every academic or professional decision you've made to date, nor is it the place to regurgitate your resume in clunky, densely-packed prose.

- **While we're on the topic of regurgitating,** we should point out that the cover letter isn't the place to spit content from the company's website—or, even worse, the posted job description— back at the recruiter. While we absolutely recommend that you conduct background research on the company before making contact about a job, paraphrasing information that's readily available on the company's website isn't enough to establish that your interest is sincere. On the other hand, if you've taken the time to speak with current employees or attend an on-campus information session at your college, you can—and absolutely should—describe what in particular sparked your interest.

- **Show you're a giver, not just a taker.** No matter how brief, the cover letter shouldn't be lopsided. While you should mention one or two specific things that have attracted you to the company, you should balance your approach by describing why the company should be attracted to you. Your cover letter should imply that hiring you would be a mutually beneficial decision. Don't just talk about what the company can do for you: Explain what skills and qualifications would enable you to make a positive contribution to the company.

- **Watch your tone, missy.** We know we just told you that your cover letter should describe your potential contributions to the company, but it should do so politely. Scott, who works in the publications office of a major university, recalls an interview in which the hiring manager commended him on the polite cover letter he had sent her by e-mail. "I was surprised that it had made such an impression," he explains. "But she told me I'd be shocked at how many e-mailed cover letters she received that weren't polite or respectful." While you shouldn't be shy about mentioning your achievements and qualifications, you should never assume a presumptuous or self-aggrandizing tone. There's definitely a fine line separating confident and obnoxious—if you're having trouble deciding whether you've navigated it successfully, ask a friend for an objective, third-party assessment.

- **Take the thyme two proofread.** Because hiring managers often don't read cover letters with the same scrutiny they read resumes, you may be tempted to relax a little bit when it comes to editing yours. Believe us: It's worth the few extra minutes it will take to make sure that your cover letter is error-free. Use the spell-check function, but don't rely on software alone. Spell-check is famous for letting things like misused contractions (you're vs. your, it's vs. its, etc.) fall through the cracks, and it certainly won't let you know if you've misspelled the name of the company or recruiter (and believe us, a missing comma or hyphen in the company or recruiter's name might just tip the scales against you). Spell-check also won't protect you against the famous "mismerge" that has sealed many a candidate's fate (you've described how your fastidious attention to detail will make you a valuable asset to Random House—in your cover letter to Scholastic).

Sending your resume and cover letter via e-mail

In a relatively short period of time, the prevalence of e-mail has completely transformed the way job candidates communicate with prospective employers. It's easier and faster than ever to send resumes and cover letters, but ensuring that your correspondence is flawless—and that it ends up in the right hands—is no less important. The ease and informality of e-mail can (and often does) trip up job-seekers who forget that the way they communicate—even electronically—creates a first impression that will affect how hiring managers view their candidacy. Don't let this happen to you: Put the same care into e-mailed cover letters and follow-up e-mails that you would into any other type of formal correspondence. Because e-mails are transmitted almost instantaneously—and because there's no way to control how quickly or widely they're forwarded—it's virtually impossible to contain the damage the smallest error or impropriety can cause. To play it safe, complete the "To:" field last if you're communicating with a potential employer over e-mail. This way, you're covered if you accidentally click "Send" before your message is ready. Remember, there are no "do-overs" when it comes to e-mails: "Ignore last message!" and "Oops!" e-mails are ineffective and can damage your credibility.

Avoiding the recycle bin

Thanks to the havoc wreaked by both spam and computer viruses, there's no guarantee your message will reach its intended recipient. Many companies use sophisticated spam filters to guard inboxes from suspicious e-mails. Typically, these filters delete suspected spam or divert it into folders that automatically trash e-mails that go unchecked for a certain period of time. In an effort to minimize the serious threat of computer viruses, some companies restrict employees from opening e-mail attachments (including resumes) from external sources. In some cases, their servers may even delete attachments automatically as a precaution.

Overzealous spam filters and stringent external e-mail policies can definitely work against you, so it's critical that you follow the directions when responding to a job posting. If you've been instructed to e-mail your resume as an attachment, use Microsoft Word (or a comparable basic software package). Unless specifically instructed to do so, don't send it as a compressed file or as a PDF. Trust us: If the recipient can't open your file successfully the first time around, she's not going to chase you down to request another one. Make sure to include your name (at least your last name) in the name of the file (e.g., Jane_Doe_resume.doc). Many recruiters and hiring managers save all the resumes they receive for a given position in a specific folder; many also forward resumes to other colleagues or hiring personnel at their organization. A descriptive file name that includes your name ensures that your resume can be easily located and identified regardless of where it lands.

If a company has explicitly instructed applicants not to send e-mail attachments, don't do it. Not only do you run the risk that your message will end up in the recycle bin unopened, but blatantly disregarding the instructions immediately gives the recruiter a reason to eliminate you from consideration (trust us: he's already looking for ways to whittle down that inbox, so there's no need to tempt him with another one). If you can't send it as an attachment, you'll need to send it in the body of your e-mail in plain-text format. It's true that plain-text resumes sent via e-mail aren't the most attractive ones out there, but what they lack in beauty they make up for in reliability. When you don't have specific instructions, sending your resume this way is the safest course of action.

If you're e-mailing your resume, the cover message that introduces it should be in plain text, too. (When you send it in HTML format, there's a slight risk the person on the receiving end won't have an e-mail program that can properly read the HTML formatting—which means they won't be able to read what you've sent. The more significant risk, though, is the spam filter: HTML messages are more likely to trip up spam filters than plain-text messages). Here's how to double-check if you're in plain-text format: If you're writing an e-mail in which you can alter the appearance of text—i.e., you can italicize, underline, or change the font—you're not in plain-text format. Some e-mail providers only allow users to write in plain text; if you're still unsure and you're using Microsoft Outlook, click on "format" in your new message window and be sure that "plain text" is the selected format.

Don't forget about the "Subject" field when sending your application materials. If you're sending your resume in response to an online job posting, you'll often be told exactly what to include in this field. If left to your own devices, remember this: The less your e-mail looks like a spam message, the less likely it will be diverted. With this in mind, never leave this field blank. Instead, include a subject line that is short and descriptive and immediately identifies you as an applicant. If you can, include the job title or requisition number in the subject line (remember that the recruiter receiving your message may be responsible for filling multiple positions). Otherwise, include only your name and the position applied for (e.g., "Zach Glass, Case Manager"). Leave punctuation marks—especially exclamation marks—out of the subject line, and don't use all capital letters in an attempt to grab the recipient's attention.

Finally, you should avoid using words in the subject line—or even in your cover message—that will convince the company's spam-filter technology that your resume belongs in the trash bin, along with e-mails promising enlarged body parts or cheap prescription drugs. You probably have a pretty good idea of what key words we have in mind (if you need a refresher course, take a break from reading this and log in to one of your web-based e-mail accounts). You're unlikely to use most of them in your cover letter or resume (if you need to, you've probably picked up the wrong guide). Still, remember that words like "free," "hard," "offer," "increase," etc. are often used by spammers, so keep them out of your correspondence if you can. If your e-mail address has several numbers to the left of the @ symbol, consider changing it: the numbers could represent something as innocuous as your birthday, anniversary, or the year you graduated from college, but, to a spam filter, they look like the type of tracking code that many spammers use.

As an added safety measure, you may want to ask any personal contact you have within the organization to forward your resume to the appropriate contact. Not only does this increase the odds you'll defeat the spam filter, but internal referrals typically boost your overall credibility as a candidate. If you don't have an internal point person who can forward your resume on your behalf, be sure to run every version of it through a few different spam filters before sending it off; send it to a few friends and family members—and include your own e-mail address or addresses in the CC field—to figure out whether it's going through. This might sound like a lot of trouble, and it is. There is an upside, though, to the omnivorous spam filter: You have a perfectly legitimate reason to follow up with the company and make sure your application materials were received.

"Power Jargon": Learning to talk the talk

Whenever you enter a new industry or company, you'll quickly find that each one has its own unique vernacular you must understand—and eventually adopt. Paying attention to the language insiders use to describe their industry and their specific roles should be part of your job-search preparation. If used subtly and judiciously, incorporating "power jargon" into your resume, cover letter, and interview can help influence the decision-maker in your favor; if you speak someone's language, they'll probably—perhaps subconsciously—consider you one of their own.

Interestingly, the purpose of power jargon is slightly different depending on the stage of the job-search process you're in when you use it. In the context of a resume, the purpose of industry jargon is getting your resume noticed—either by the human being who has the unenviable task of screening through thousands of resumes and deciding which ones make the first cut, or by the nonhuman resume scanner whose job it is to do basically the same thing by identifying and counting specific key words in resumes. In the context of a cover letter or an interview, the purpose is less to get noticed than, ironically enough, to blend in. And once you arrive for your first day of work, the purpose of power jargon is knowing what the heck you're supposed to be doing.

To illustrate the importance of understanding jargon before your first day on the job, consider the experience endured by Monica—now a 30-year-old associate editor—on her first day of freelance proofreading at a food and wine magazine. "I had no idea that in the magazine biz, the term 'hot' means that something is extremely urgent," she says. "So someone came up to my desk and asked me if I'd finished proofreading a particular story. When I said that I hadn't, she politely reminded me that it was 'pretty hot.' Not knowing what she meant—that I needed to get it done ASAP—I thought to myself, 'What's she making such a big deal about? The story's about *coleslaw* for God's sake—what's so trendy about that?'" This is why it's important to do your homework early on in the process—preferably before you make contact with a company about a job.

Understanding the importance of key words, however, doesn't give you license to use them recklessly. Power jargon can be, and often is, overused in resumes, obscuring the very credentials the candidate was hoping to highlight in the first place. And if you use jargon without understanding what it means, you may use it in the wrong context and sound uninformed when you intended to sound savvy. Our advice for avoiding potential power-jargon pitfalls? Have someone who's in the know take a look at your resume and cover letter to alert you to any egregious misuses of industry or company terminology. And in the interview, play it safe—your goal is to use power jargon to blend in, not stand out. Overusing jargon (or using it in a forced, contrived way) won't win you any points, especially with hiring managers who've logged countless hours interviewing candidates. Not only will experienced interviewers see right through your attempt to sound like an expert, but they'll often go to great lengths to put you back in your place. "That happened to me once," says Thomas, an assistant editor for an academic journal. "I was interviewing for my first editorial job, and I mentioned that I was familiar with the *Chicago Manual of Style.* My interviewer said, 'Oh really? Which edition do you normally use?' I was completely stumped. I had no idea which edition it was—I had to look at my copy when I got home (it was the eleventh, incidentally). Even though I had to admit that I didn't know, I got the job anyway. After a few months in the office, I eventually found out that none of the copyeditors knew exactly which version they were using, either. The interviewer had just been doing that to rattle my cage, I guess, and figure out whether I was bluffing."

Even though this story has a happy ending, it still offers a valuable lesson: Don't use terminology you don't understand, and if you are asked a question you don't know the answer to, just say that you don't know. If your interviewer calls your bluff, you've not only lost face, but you've potentially lost a job. It's not worth the risk.

What's the magic word?

In the 1991 remake of the film *Father of the Bride,* Steve Martin's character, George, snoops through the home of his future son-in-law's parents, only to be confronted by a pair of growling, snarling Rottweilers who seem poised to eat him alive. He knows there's a one-word command that will make them go away, but he can't quite remember what it is—only that it begins with "re." He tries a few: "Relent. Recoil. . . Reverse," but they only make the dogs angrier. (The word he was looking for was "release.") As George found out with the attack dogs, using correct keywords is important. For him, it meant he wouldn't get devoured; for you, it means your resume won't get discarded because you appear not to have experience relevant to a particular job.

Keywords are almost always nouns or short phrases. They name the characteristics, skills, tools, training, and experience of a successful candidate for a particular job. As you may already know, many organizations use resume-scanning software to identify qualified candidates among a sea of online applications; by scanning resumes for certain words and phrases, scanning software is intended to streamline the resume review process for time-starved recruiters, who may receive literally thousands of applications for a single job posting. If your target company uses this type of software as a preliminary screening tool, you'll want to be sure your resume includes the relevant key words. The number of "hits" (times the key words appear in any given resume) will often determine which resumes are actually read by a human being.

How do you know which keywords to include? Well, writing a resume in a scanner-friendly way is definitely more an art than a science—and it requires common sense, good judgment, and a little bit of research. Before you submit a resume online, visit the company's website and pay attention to the language used to describe what the company does, what it's looking for in potential employees, and the job requirements it lists for specific positions; the job description and the list of qualifications associated with the position are also great resources when tailoring and tweaking the version of the resume you use.

As is the case with any job-search advice we provide in this guide, it's best to temper your enthusiasm for power jargon with a healthy dose of good judgment. Particularly if you're applying for a position through an on-campus recruiting process or through an internal referral that forwards your correspondence directly to the hiring manager, your resume may be initially reviewed by a human being—not a scanner.

A rose by any other name . . . might be something else entirely

To make matters even more complicated, there are a couple of different levels of jargon you'll need to weed through to use it effectively. There's both industry jargon and company-specific jargon. At the industry level, seemingly identical processes or functions will be described differently depending on the industry in question. For example, book publishing uses different terminology than magazine publishing, and academic and financial publishing each use a different lexicon entirely. If you looked at a "blueline" (the last version of a publication editors have a chance to review before it goes to print) at a magazine publisher, you'd be looking at the "blues," but if you looked at one at an investment bank, you'd probably be looking at a "red." And if you say "blackline" instead of "blueline" because you worked at a law firm one summer and you're still in the habit of saying it, you're going to look pretty silly in your magazine-publishing interview.

At the organizational level, power jargon might include something as seemingly insignificant as the use of acronyms and abbreviations (and it seems the larger the organization, the more acronyms there are to remember). The names of groups, functions, even job titles may be abbreviated so widely within an organization that you'll stand out if you don't use them when you communicate with your potential employer.

Is your head spinning yet? Don't worry. When it comes to power jargon, there are plenty of ways to pick it up so you're at least conversational by the time you apply for a job. When you speak with industry insiders in the context of networking or conducting informational interviews, pay attention to the terminology they use to describe what they do and where they work. (In fact, the ability to pick up on power jargon is one of the many good reasons you should be focused on listening rather than talking when it comes to informational interviews). If your industry insider uses a term you're not familiar with, don't just nod as though you are—ask what it means! Remember, you're not being evaluated during your informational interviews or networking conversations; you're there to learn and ask questions. And if stopping to ask what something means during one of these conversations means you actually know what it means when it comes up later in a job interview, then asking was a worthwhile investment. In addition to one-on-one conversations with insiders, you can pick up power jargon by paying attention to the lingo used in trade publications, on industry-specific websites, and in job listings for similar positions at other companies in the industry.

When it comes time to interview with a specific company, your understanding of that organization's terminology is just as important as your fluency in industry lingo. Before you walk out the door to meet with your prospective employer, you should understand the jargon the company uses in the following contexts:

- **Its name**—Know when a company goes by its initials and when it's abbreviated some other way when its own employees refer to it. We'll illustrate our point using an example from the financial services world: If you were working on Wall Street, you would never call Goldman Sachs or Merrill Lynch "GS" or "ML." If you were an employee—or an industry insider—you'd refer to them as "Goldman" and "Merrill," respectively. However, you would refer to Credit Suisse First Boston as "CSFB."

- **Its job titles**—If everyone at a particular firm always says "RA" instead of "Research Associate," it will ever so subtly work in your favor if you refer to the job that way too (even though it still might mean "Resident Advisor" to you). The same goes for support roles—sometimes, assistants are just that: assistants. At other organizations, they're called "admins" or "PAs" If you're applying for one of those jobs, know what you'll be called (how else will you know when someone's talking to you?)

- **Its organizational structure and hierarchy**—It sounds almost silly, but pay attention to how employees and insiders refer to the specific department with which you're interviewing. Is the custom publishing department referred to as "custom pub?" Is the book publishing division referred to as "BPD" or simply "books"? Even more importantly, how are roles and job titles described? At some companies, "analyst" is a more senior role than "associate," for example, while at others, the exact opposite is true. Know which level and job title would apply to you; if you don't, your ignorance might be misinterpreted as an inflated ego.

INTERVIEWING

If the primary purpose of a great resume is to get an interview (which it is), then it seems as though the point of the interview would be to land the job. But, in reality, that's only half right. One of your goals during the interview process is to tell a compelling story—to present your life (educational, extracurricular, and otherwise) as an entirely logical series of decisions in which this particular job is the obvious next step. The other (equally, if not more important) objective is to learn as much as possible about the position you're applying for, the culture of the organization you're interviewing with, and the extent to which the job fits with your personal and professional goals.

Because you're working hard to present yourself in the best possible light, it's easy to forget that interviews aren't entirely unilateral. When you're being grilled about your resume, your motivations, and your choices, it will undoubtedly seem as though your prospective employer is the one calling the shots. But the interview is also a chance for you to learn about the organization and the position for which you're applying. It's the best opportunity you have, prior to your first day on the job, to fill in any gaps between the pieces of info you gleaned through networking and informational interviews. It's your chance to ask questions, to get a sense of whether or not the organization's culture is one in which you'll fit, and to figure out whether the specific position is one in which you'll be challenged and rewarded for your efforts.

In this section, we'll give you suggestions for making the most out of your interviews. We'll tell you what interviewers will be looking for during your conversations, and we'll describe the types of interview questions they're most likely to ask as they evaluate you. We'll also tell to you how to prepare for interviews—how to anticipate the topics (and questions) you're most likely to confront and how to craft compelling responses. Along the way, we'll give you practical advice—guidance on everything from arriving on time to wearing the right shoes—so you can truly put your best foot forward.

What are interviewers looking for?

Earlier in this section, we listed the personal characteristics organizations value most in potential employees. As we said earlier, the list is intended to be a starting point for your interview preparation; it stands to reason that the relative importance assigned to each of these attributes will vary significantly depending on the industry, the company, and the specific job for which you're interviewing. You may even find, when you interview with multiple people for a single position, that each interviewer emphasizes slightly different things. Across the board, however, the people who interview you are basically trying to answer three questions as they evaluate your candidacy:

- Are you capable of doing the work?
- Do you really want to do the work?
- Would they enjoy working with you?

As a general rule, the less directly applicable your past experience is to the job you're hoping to get, the more emphasis your interviewer is likely to place on the first question. If you've more or less proven your ability to do the work through similar professional, academic, or extracurricular activities, your interviewer is more likely to probe the second two.

Recruiters will be on the lookout for certain intangible qualities throughout the entire interview, too: qualities like confidence, conviction, enthusiasm, poise, presence, and sincerity. For example, do your eyes light up when you talk about your educational background, your professional experience, or (most importantly) the role for which you are interviewing? Do your answers sound heartfelt and impassioned, or is it obvious you've rehearsed them so many times you could recite them in your sleep? Are you comfortable and self-assured talking about your background and accomplishments, or does self-confidence quickly disintegrate into self-consciousness as soon as you step into the interview room? Interviewers don't necessarily measure these intangibles through specific questions, but rather through their well-honed intuition.

Preparing for your interview

Whether you realize it or not, you can predict the vast majority of the questions you will hear during an interview—provided, of course, you've done your homework on the industry, the organization, and the position you've got your eye on. Some questions (e.g., "Why are you interested in this job?") arise so frequently in one form or another you'd be foolish not to take the time to outline your responses well in advance. Though no amount of preparation will enable you to predict the questions verbatim, you can predict the themes the interview is likely to cover. Nine times out of ten, you're going to be asked to discuss the following:

- Why you are interested in this type of work, and why you want to work with this organization specifically.

- How your academic, extracurricular, and/or professional background relates to the job for which you're applying.

- The extent to which you've developed realistic expectations about the job you're considering, and whether or not you know enough about the company to make an informed decision about joining it.

- Whether certain gaps or inconsistencies on your resume are likely to turn into vulnerabilities on the job.

Know Your Achilles Heel

So how do you know which part of your application is likely to be perceived as a gap or inconsistency? It really depends on the nature and level of the job for which you're applying; hopefully, your informational interviews will have shed some light on the gaps that might exist between the ideal set of credentials and your own (if not, the job posting and/or description will certainly provide some clues). But across industries and jobs, there are a few common red flags that might raise questions about your ability and desire to do the work. If any of these apply to you, give some thought to how you might address them in your interview:

Disparity between professional/academic background and desired job

This is the most obvious—and perhaps the most prevalent—of all the instant red flags. If the position for which you're applying bears little or no resemblance to the work you've done in the past—or to the work you're currently doing—then your prospective employer will probably ask a few questions. They'll go something like this: If you really want to do this type of work and are so well suited to do it, then why haven't you done it already? Or, at the very least, why haven't you studied it? And, to be completely honest, these are perfectly legitimate questions.

Time gaps

Keep in mind that the person reviewing your resume might check to see if you've taken off between school years or jobs. Time off is not necessarily a bad thing. Recruiters know that while you're building a career, life can pull you in other directions: people start families, spouses get relocated, family members get sick, and professionals take time off to consider a career change or simply recharge their batteries. Still, you need to be prepared to explain any lapses. You needn't feel compelled to offer a lot of personal detail, but you should be honest, direct, and prepared if questions about time gaps arise. In your response, focus on what you accomplished during that time—not the ground you lost by taking a break.

Inconsistent or poor academic performance

This includes a lower-than-average GPA, test scores, or grades in specific classes. If your accomplishments appear strong in one area but weak in another, you should expect questions about the disparity. The interviewer will want to know the reason behind any low grades (did you work part-time during school?) or a discrepancy between your GPA and standardized-test scores. Be prepared to explain any circumstances that affected your performance, but avoid undue personal detail.

Job- (or major-) "hopping"

If your resume includes seemingly disparate work experiences, or if you've been at several companies in just a few years, you risk being perceived as a job-hopper. This is unlikely to be much of an issue if you're still in school, but keep in mind that switching majors multiple times might be viewed with comparable skepticism. Frequent course changes (of either the professional or academic variety) sometimes give the impression that a person has difficulty sticking with a situation, working through problems, or committing to a job. And if you're applying for a job when you've only been at your current one for a short period of time, prospective employers might wonder if you're likely to jump ship if they hire you, too. If your jobs to date have been short-term by nature (because they've been summer jobs or internships), make sure you've stated that clearly somewhere on your application.

Geographic concerns

If you've spent most of your academic and professional life in one place, you may be questioned about your interest in a job that's somewhere else. Not only will a company probably question whether you're serious about relocating if you're offered the job, but they have practical and logistical issues to consider when it comes to interviewing you in person. A firm that must fly you out for an interview will probably quiz you over the phone to gauge your level of commitment before extending an invitation. Firms also know there's a good chance you may decide not to relocate even if you get the offer—and if you do, it'll probably take some time before you can physically move yourself to your new city and get settled in. All in all, an out-of-town candidate is generally considered a riskier—and potentially costlier—prospect than an applicant close to home.

You'll probably find that thinking of your interview as a conversation intended to address these themes is more effective than thinking of it as a series of questions for which scripted and rehearsed answers are expected. You'll be able to adapt quickly to different interviewing styles and formats, and you won't be thrown off when asked a question you didn't expect.

In the following pages, we'll give you a number of sample questions that tend to arise across industries and companies. Don't let the number of questions overwhelm you—you're not expected to prepare a scripted answer to every possible question, or to memorize the list of interview do's and don'ts. In fact, if you take away only one thing from the following pages, it should be this: *Knowing the job for which you are applying—and knowing exactly how your experiences and achievements relate to that position—is the single most important thing you can do to prepare for job interviews.*

Types of interview questions

Even though most interviewers will be trying to gather the same kind of information, the format of the questions will vary significantly depending on the job, the interviewing philosophy of the organization, and the person sitting across the desk from you. We've outlined the three most common types of interview questions below:

Resume-based questions

No surprises here: Resume-based questions focus on the one-page life summary that landed you the interview. It goes without saying, but we'll say it anyway: You must know your resume inside and out, and you should be ready to talk intelligently and confidently about anything and everything on it. Arrive at your interview with two or three talking points about each line item on your resume. If there's something particularly unusual on it (e.g., you wrote a novel while you were an undergraduate student, you speak seven languages), you can be sure it will come up again and again. Consider the points you'd most like to convey, and make sure you know them cold. If you're asked to summarize your resume, stick to just that: a summary. Use your response as an opportunity to connect the dots (especially if the story wouldn't be obvious to someone reviewing your resume for the first time), not as an invitation to cram in all of the information you couldn't fit onto one page.

Behavioral questions

Other questions require you to cite experiences—professional, academic, and personal—in which you've actively demonstrated specific attributes. This approach is called behavioral interviewing, and it's based on the premise that patterns of past behavior most accurately predict future performance. Advocates of behavioral interviewing report that the technique enables interviewers to most accurately assess whether a candidate possesses the requisite skills and personality for on-the-job success. The logic is appealing: Anyone can rattle off a list of attributes commonly sought by employers in their field, but successful candidates can readily substantiate these claims with examples of competency in a given area. A behavioral prompt would be: "Tell me about a time that you took on a responsibility that perhaps wasn't part of your official job description." In response, you could choose to point out that, at your previous job, you designed a comprehensive training program for new employees, organized guest speakers, and gathered feedback when the program was over to gauge how effective its participants thought it was. Or you might choose to highlight your involvement in a freshman-year economics study group, in which you took up the flag for an ailing team member and wrote a presentation that technically fell outside the scope of your assigned duties. Either example works, as long as it shows that you've taken initiative in the past.

With this in mind, don't simply compartmentalize your achievements into "work experiences," "educational background," "extracurricular activities," and "personal interests" as you prepare for interviews. Instead, think about each of your endeavors in terms of the skills, abilities, and attributes it enables you to demonstrate. For example, which ones helped you develop a strong team-player mentality? How about exceptional leadership skills? Which ones demonstrate your quantitative aptitude and your facility with numbers? Which ones show that you can learn from your mistakes? We've said it before, but we'll say it again: You should know your resume inside and out, and have a ready arsenal of experiences that can prove you're a rock star in any number of areas.

Case interview questions

For years, management consulting firms have used case interview questions as part of their recruiting processes. Designed to gauge candidates' problem-solving skills and general business acumen, these questions are a more highly evolved version of the word problems you were introduced to in third-grade math class. But even if you're not interviewing for jobs in management consulting, you're not necessarily off the hook where these types of questions are concerned. For better or worse, companies in many industries serve up their own version of the case interview question, hoping to approximate the demands of the job to whatever extent possible in an interview setting. If it's a research job you're interviewing for, you may be asked to walk your interviewer through a hypothetical research project, explaining the steps you would take to complete the assigned task. If the position requires a great deal of public speaking, you shouldn't be caught off guard if you're asked to make an impromptu presentation on a given topic. Not surprisingly, writing, editing, and proofreading tests are often administered as part of the interview process for publishing jobs. Part of your research process should involve figuring out what those tests are likely to be.

Tips for winning interviews

In the following pages, we provide hypothetical interview questions covering a range of topics and themes. There are a few interview best practices, however, that transcend boundaries of interview question category, context, and scope. Keep the following guidelines in mind regardless of the particular questions interviewers lob your way:

Honesty is the best policy.

This little nugget is definitely one to remember during interviews. As your mother probably told you shortly after you learned to speak: When you tell one lie, you have to tell five more lies to cover up the first one. For each of those lies, you have to tell five more, and so on. Mom was right about this one; interviews are stressful enough when you're telling the truth, so don't make it harder on yourself by coloring the edges of your resume with fictional experiences, skills, or interests. The truth almost always prevails in the end, so don't tempt fate by bending it—even a little.

Be honest, but emphasize the positive.

Being honest about your screw-ups and weaknesses doesn't mean that you can't spin them in a positive direction. If you're asked about a perceived weakness or mistake, you can be candid while emphasizing what you've learned from each experience. You can use the infamous "What's your biggest weakness?" question, for example, to prove that you're constantly working to overcome your Achilles heel (or, better yet, you could provide a specific example of an instance in which you overcame it).

Remember the three C's.

No matter how much you've prepared for your interviews, make sure your responses are conversational, casual, and concise. While we can't overemphasize the importance of researching the industry, organization, and position before you arrive—and anticipating the interview questions you're most likely to confront—you shouldn't give the impression you're reading your interview responses off of cue cards. In fact, if you sound too rehearsed your interviewer may suspect you've got something to hide. Remember: "Canned" is not one of the three C's.

Answer the question you've been asked.

We know it sounds obvious, but it's easier said than done (particularly if you're a rambler). If you're immersed in a full-time job search, chances are you'll have more interviews than you'd care to remember. Some candidates get so accustomed to fielding certain questions that they become robotic: They hear a few key words, and they're off on their unintentionally well-rehearsed pitch. Interviews will indeed begin to sound the same, but don't forget to listen to the question!

Keep it short and sweet.

On a related note, keep it brief. If you ramble, you're considerably more likely to lose your way—and more likely to exhaust your interviewer in the process! Remember, it's easier for an interviewer to ask a follow-up question than it is for her to rein you back in after you've gone off on a tangent.

Pay attention to your interviewer's style.

A one-size-fits-all approach doesn't work especially well during the interview process; even within the same company, interviewers adopt substantially different styles to figure out whether you're a good candidate for the job. Some are more intense, while others treat the interview as a more relaxed, get-to-know-you session. The more promptly you can pick up on your interviewer's particular style, the better off you'll be—so pay attention.

Don't be critical of previous employers or colleagues.

In fact, you should be wary of sounding even the slightest bit sour on your previous work experiences. Not only would doing so suggest that you're generally negative and cynical, but if you use the interview as an opportunity to vent about a previous employer, your interviewer will wonder how you'll talk about his company when given the opportunity.

Keep track of the questions you're asked.

If a question comes up in one interview, it's quite likely it will come up in another. Particularly if you feel you haven't answered a question effectively, take a minute or two after the interview to jot down the question and outline what you would say if given a second chance. You'll be glad you did when you hear the same question again in subsequent rounds.

Keep your audience in mind.

This is an interview, not a confessional. Don't delve into anything you wouldn't (or at least shouldn't) discuss on a first date: your political views, religious beliefs, or anything else known to spark controversy. Along these lines, remember to temper your honesty with a healthy dose of good judgment when addressing your strengths and weaknesses—try to steer clear of anything so incompatible with the job description it'll make your interviewer head for the hills.

Give off a positive vibe.

We know interviews are inherently stressful, but interviewers simply won't rally behind a candidate who seems uncontrollably nervous or just plain miserable. Keep reminding yourself that interviews are fun—when else do you have the opportunity do talk about yourself for 30 minutes straight?

Popular interview questions

As we said earlier in the chapter, it helps to remember that your interview is nothing more than a conversation with a specific purpose: Your interviewer is trying to figure out whether you can do the work, whether you want to do the work, and whether your prospective colleagues would enjoy working with you. In addition, they may ask questions designed to gauge your honesty, integrity, and ability to learn from your mistakes. And they may throw in a few miscellaneous questions to lighten the mood.

Interviewers can ask any number of specific questions in order to decide whether you're a compelling candidate: The sample questions we provide are not meant to be an exhaustive list, but they'll give you a head start in your pre-interview research process. We've grouped the questions according to the qualities they're usually used to gauge. (Talking to insiders in advance of your interviews will help you figure out which specific areas your interview is likely to emphasize.) You'll have a huge leg up on other candidates if you've taken the time to research and prepare answers to the most frequently asked questions.

APTITUDE QUESTIONS (CAN YOU DO THE WORK?)

Aside from allowing interviewers to gain insight into your initiative, motivation to succeed, and your work ethic in general, questions in this category seek to answer the question, "Can you do the work?" As we mentioned earlier in the chapter, the relevance of your past work experience and academic studies typically is inversely related to the emphasis your interviewer will place on answering these questions. In other words, the less directly applicable your past experience is to the job in question, the harder you'll have to work to prove you can excel at it.

Unless you're applying for a job that's directly related to your undergraduate studies (and many first-time job candidates with liberal degrees are not), you should be prepared to convince every prospective employer that your achievements outside of the industry in question will translate to success within it. As we've said before, the interview is your golden opportunity to explain perceived gaps or inconsistencies in your resume so they're viewed in a different (and hopefully more favorable) light.

If your GPA is on the low side, for example, you should be prepared to talk about it (and even if your GPA is stellar, you should be ready to talk about any rogue C's or the absence of course work related to the job you'll be doing). If you don't have extensive work experience, be prepared to explain how other pursuits—extracurricular activities, sports, or independent research projects, for example—might give you an edge on the job. Whatever the chink in your professional armor, it's important to consider it in advance of your interview, rather than weeding your way through it once you've gotten there.

Questions designed to gauge your ability to do the job include the following:

- Tell me about a time when you worked on a highly quantitative or analytical project. Describe the context, the project, and the outcome.

- What is the greatest challenge you've faced to date? How did you overcome it?

- What motivates you?

- Describe a time when you achieved a goal that required significant personal sacrifice. How did you stay motivated to achieve the goal, despite the hardships that it involved?

- What classes did you find the most difficult in college? Why do you think that's the case?

- Describe any classes you've taken in college that were highly quantitative or analytical in nature? How did you do in those classes? Are you comfortable working with numbers?

- Give me an example of a project (either academic or work-related) that required significant attention to detail. Do you consider yourself a detail-oriented person?

Because your interviewers are assessing your fundamental ability to do the work, questions in this category tend to be the most confrontational. Don't be caught off guard by interviewers who ask you to explain why you chose to study Renaissance language and literature or why you spent a summer lounging in the Caribbean. There's nothing inherently wrong with either of those choices, but be sure you're prepared to convince your interviewer that they're not inconsistent with your interest in the job. Remember, no one expects all of your experiences to be directly related to the position. That said, recruiters want to be sure you're really interested in the work and not just dabbling.

Along similar lines, you should be prepared to discuss your choice of major, particularly if you're applying for a job unrelated to your degree. If you sense your interviewer is skeptical about the relevance of your academic background, your response should be respectful, but not apologetic. Stand by your academic and professional decisions, and share your decision-making process with your interviewer. Don't get carried away, though: Many liberal arts undergraduates fall into the trap of saying things like, "The skills required of [whatever the job in question is] aren't that hard to learn. It's not rocket science, and I'll obviously just learn it on the job." Keep in mind that your interviewer may not have been a liberal arts major, and therefore might not agree with your assessment. So rather than dismissing the intellectual rigor required of other disciplines, emphasize that you're eager to learn things you didn't necessarily study during your undergraduate years.

SUITABILITY/COMMITMENT QUESTIONS (DO YOU *WANT* TO DO THE WORK?)

Whereas the aptitude questions described in the previous section are designed to establish that you can do the work, commitment questions are intended to figure out whether you genuinely want to do the work. First and foremost, your interviewer is trying to figure out how serious you are about the job itself, and whether the company's particular culture is on in which you'll fit—and eventually thrive. By far, the most commonly asked commitment question is, "Why do you want to do this job?" followed closely by, "Why do you want to do this job at this specific organization?" Here are a few other favorites in this category.

- Walk me through your resume and tell me how you decided to pursue this job/career track.

- What are you looking for in your next job? If you could create any position for yourself, what would it look like? What do you look for in a potential employer?

- Explain your role in such-and-such job listed on your resume. What did you learn from that experience that would be relevant to you here?

- What other industries/companies/positions are you considering? Are you actively interviewing elsewhere? Are you presently considering offers at any other organizations? If you are considering multiple offers, how will you make your decision?

- Why are you leaving your current job?

- Why should we hire you? Why do you think you'd be good at this?

- What do you think you would like most/least about this job?

- Where do you see yourself in five years?

- Walk me through what you think a typical day at the office would be like if you were hired for this position.

Your ability to provide solid, thoughtful answers to these questions—responses firmly grounded in realistic job expectations—will definitely advance your candidacy. While no one expects you to have known your professional destiny since age 6, or to have made every significant decision over the last two decades with this job—or any job—in your sights, you will be expected to describe your professional and personal endeavors as a rational sequence in which this position at this company is the next logical step. You should be able to articulate exactly what you hope to gain—both personally and professionally—from the experience and to demonstrate your preparedness for its challenges and demands. Keep in mind that the delivery of your message is important here: You have to believe your own story, or no one else will.

There are multiple "right" answers to the question of why you're interested in a specific job, and there are universally bad answers too. Don't even think about suggesting that you consider it a stepping-stone to something else, that you stumbled across it, that you're ready to take just about anything because you've been out of work for so long, or that you generally think the industry is pretty cool. If you're interviewing for positions that represent a broad spectrum of functions and industries, you aren't obligated to tell your interviewer.

If, on the other hand, the job is one you're really excited about, questions like these give you an opportunity to make that clear. Perceived commitment to (and enthusiasm for) a specific company—not just the industry in general—always influences the choice between two (or more) otherwise comparable candidates. Companies love to be loved, and with good reason: they know that if you've done your homework and genuinely want the job, you're more likely to thrive at the organization and less likely to turn around and leave once you get there. You not only present yourself as a low-risk hire, you also reaffirm your interviewer's choice of company and career (and stoking your interviewer's ego is never a bad thing).

To gauge whether you're not only enthusiastic but committed, interviewers will often ask you to describe how you see your career evolving longer-term. Give some serious thought to how you'll attack questions about what you see yourself doing one, five, or ten years from now. While no one expects you to know for certain what you'll be doing several years into the future (the earlier you are in your career, the less sure people expect you to be), you should at least be able to present a credible scenario that includes the job in question. Taking the time to consider where you'd like to be down the road isn't just interview preparation—it's an opportunity for self exploration, too. If you find you're trying a little too hard to convince your interviewer that this is a job you want—or you find it necessary to convince yourself of it—then it's probably time to reassess whether your heart is in it.

TEAMWORKING/ATTITUDE QUESTIONS (DO WE WANT TO WORK WITH YOU?)

Questions in this category are designed to assess your interpersonal skills, and—as the name suggests—your ability to work as part of a team. Through questions like these, your interviewer is trying to figure out whether she would enjoy working with you, and whether your prospective colleagues, managers, and team members are likely to enjoy working with you. The questions themselves focus on your ability to build and maintain relationships, inspire confidence among clients and colleagues, and resolve interpersonal conflict (not to mention your ability to avoid conflict in the first place). Not surprisingly, these questions reveal an emphasis on teamwork—you might be expected to describe your firsthand experience on teams, and you'll often be asked to discuss the characteristics of effective and ineffective work groups. In addition, interviewers may ask you about your interests and achievements to figure out what makes you tick and what makes you an interesting person to get to know. Here are a few common questions in this category:

- What role do you typically assume when you work in a team setting? Describe the last time you worked on a team and the role you assumed.

- Tell me about a situation in which you've had to work with someone that you didn't particularly like or get along with. How did you overcome personal differences to achieve your goal?

- Have you ever worked on a team that wasn't successful meeting its goals? What do you think went wrong?

- Describe an occasion when you persuaded someone to do something they didn't want to do.

- How would you characterize your leadership/management style?

- What achievement are you most proud of?

- What are you passionate about?

Regardless of the specific questions you encounter in your interview, the way in which you respond to the questions is often just as important as the answers themselves. When interviewers assess a candidate's interpersonal effectiveness, the intangibles we mentioned earlier in the chapter (e.g., confidence, enthusiasm, poise, polish) are especially critical. Of course, you should be ready to provide solid examples that establish your comfort and efficacy in a team-based work environment, but your ability to build a rapport with your interviewer will solidify your case. Recruiters will look for signs you're self-assured, professional, and generally pleasant to work with.

A WORD ABOUT TEAMWORK

There are definitely jobs out there that don't require a lot of human interaction, but they are far outnumbered by positions that do. If the job you're considering requires a substantial amount of teamwork, you'll want to draw your interviewer's attention to the team-oriented pursuits on your resume. Keep in mind, though, that it may not be immediately obvious to your interviewer which activities depended on your ability to interact effectively with people. For example, you may feel your experience as a staff writer for the student newspaper is highly relevant because you managed multiple deadlines for a high-maintenance editor and leveraged relationships with key contacts to obtain hard-to-find information, but "staff writer" may not scream "team player" to your interviewer. Be on the lookout for opportunities to highlight relevant experiences, and don't expect your interviewer to read between the lines. At the same time, don't overstate your team contributions or pretend you've never met anyone you didn't get along with famously—your interviewer will conclude that you're not credible.

QUESTIONS ON HONESTY AND INTEGRITY

Interviewers look for more than just teamworking ability and charisma when trying to decide whether you'll fit in. They place a great deal of emphasis on your honesty and integrity, too (as the list of attributes most commonly sought by employers at the beginning of this chapter attests). They'll sometimes ask questions regarding your mistakes and failures to determine whether you're honest and accountable when you screw up (and we all screw up from time to time, so knowing when to admit it—and knowing how to mitigate the damage—is key). Questions like these also examine your ability to learn from past experiences and continuously improve your performance—a skill that's crucial for professional success whether you're part of a team or not. Popular honesty and integrity questions include the following:

- Tell me about a time you made a mistake. How did you handle it?
- Tell me about your biggest failure.
- What is your biggest weakness?
- Describe an ethical dilemma you faced in the past. How did you resolve it?

The way in which you answer these prompts will say a lot, as questions regarding mistakes and failures require diplomacy and tact—two qualities employers value highly. Of course, you should be honest when you answer questions such as these. We all want to present the best possible image of ourselves during job interviews, so it stands to reason that none of us particularly enjoys talking about our faults. Still, if you're asked about your past mistakes or biggest weakness, you have a unique opportunity to distinguish yourself. If you can demonstrate your maturity, humility, and sense of humor about your foibles, your likeability (and credibility) will skyrocket.

Miscellaneous questions

In an ideal world, all organizations would approach their recruiting processes with the same level of thoughtfulness and sophistication we're advising you to bring to your interviews. Sadly, this isn't the case. In fact, we'd be remiss if we didn't point out that some interview questions will have little or no relevance to the job. At best, these questions are intended to put you at ease, to give you a breather in the midst of an otherwise stressful interview, and simply to allow the interviewer to get to know you a little better. At worst, they can reveal your interviewer's inexperience in a recruiting role. Only you will be able to guess which one applies to your interview. Elisabeth, now an alumni-relations officer at a West Coast business school, was asked the following question when she interviewed for an administrative position on campus: "If you were stranded on a desert island and could bring three CDs, subscribe to three periodicals, and order three television channels, which would you choose and why?"

Make no mistake about it: There's very little an interviewer stands to learn about your ability to do the job by asking you a question like that. "I got the impression that she had never interviewed anyone for a job before, and she got a kick out of being on the other side of the desk or something," Elisabeth told us. You may encounter novice interviewers who enjoy throwing curve balls your way. If you do, be a good sport and humor them—at the very least, the questions might spark some interesting conversation at a future cocktail party.

When it's your turn to ask questions

Toward the end of the conversation, your interviewer will probably ask if you have any questions for her. There are a few different schools of thought on how candidates should approach this part of the interview: Some insiders insist that you should always ask a question when offered the opportunity, and that your question should prove to your interviewer how much research you've done on the industry and the specific firm.

Although this advice is well intentioned, it can easily backfire (especially if you come across as a know-it-all trying to challenge your interviewer). If you approach the interview as a learning experience, then it follows that you should stick to those questions you'd genuinely like answered. Make the most of the opportunity to ask the questions that require insider insight. If you really want to know why your interviewers chose to work at the company you're interviewing with, ask away. You're not likely to lose points for asking questions that aren't insightful or penetrating enough, provided your questions don't display blatant ignorance regarding the industry, the company, or the specific position. The list of informational interview questions in the previous chapter includes topics that would be appropriate to explore if you have the opportunity. The following list may also prove helpful:

- I wondered if you could describe your own career path to me. How did you arrive at this organization, and how did you end up in your current role/department?

- What do you think it takes for someone to be good at this job, and what do you think it takes for someone to really enjoy it?

- What are your three most important strategic objectives for this year?

- I want to be sure I have a clear understanding of how this role fits into the organization as a whole. How would the specific responsibilities of this position fit into the bigger picture of what your department does? How does your department fit into the larger organization?

- Can you tell me how job performance is evaluated with regards to this position? How do you assess whether someone is on track and meeting expectations? Do you have a formal review process? Could you describe it to me?

- Is this a new position or would I be replacing someone?

- What is a typical career progression for someone in this particular role?

- Can you outline the organizational structure in this department? Division?

- What are your company's key competitive concerns?

- How would you describe your firm's culture? What do you think is different/better about working here than anywhere else? What things do you think the company's leadership team takes particular pride in?

- Are there a lot of opportunities for training and development here? Are rotations into different functional or geographic areas fairly common?

Danger ahead: Proceed with caution

Even though it's generally safe to ask questions you'd sincerely like answered, there are some you should probably avoid, no matter how badly you'd like them answered. (At the very least, you shouldn't ask them in an evaluative setting such as an interview). Stay away from questions in the following categories:

- **Presumptuous questions,** such as "How quickly will I be eligible for a pay increase?" or "When can I expect to have my own clients?" Questions like these will give your interviewer the impression that you consider the job offer a done deal, which could make her predisposed to prove you wrong.

- **Questions that suggest you have underlying concerns about the job,** such as "I heard that this job involves a lot of late nights and weekend work. Is that true?" You may have legitimate concerns about the position, but it's probably best to ask someone other than the person evaluating your candidacy for the inside scoop.

- **Questions that imply you've already got one foot out the door,** such as "What do people typically do once they leave your firm?" Unless you're interviewing for a contract job or a position that has a specific start and end date, you should probably avoid giving your interviewer the impression you've already got your sights set on bigger and better things.

While crafting questions of your own, keep one last thing in mind: Most of your interviewers will be on a fairly tight schedule, either because they've got other candidates to speak to or because they have their own jobs and schedules to get back to. Learn to read your interviewer: If it's clear she is trying desperately to wrap things up, don't feel pressured to ask your questions simply because you've prepared them. If you sense she's trying to move things along, a diplomatic response might be, "Thanks. I'm sure you're on a tight schedule, so if it would be better to contact you later with any questions, I'd be happy to do that." This way, you've left it up to her— if she's indeed at the end of her interview tether, she'll take you up on your offer. If she's got plenty of time, she'll invite you to ask away (and she'll be impressed that you respect her schedule, which will win you extra points).

Learning from your interview

As we said at the beginning of the chapter, the interview process will usually leave you feeling as though your prospective employer has the upper hand. And, quite honestly, they probably do. But that doesn't mean you shouldn't be evaluating the company just as rigorously as they're evaluating you—you just can't do it as overtly. As the conversation evolves, ask yourself if your interviewer is someone you would like to work with—does it seem like he would make a good mentor, teammate, or manager? As you learn more about what you'd be doing on a daily basis, do you feel yourself getting more or less jazzed about the job? In general, does the company's approach towards the recruiting process seem organized and professional? We spoke with one job-seeker who recalled an interview experience that quickly changed her impression of a particular firm. "I was supposed to meet with three different people during a single office visit," she explains. "But one of my interviewers just never showed up! I was left sitting in a lobby for an hour and 25 minutes until the third person came to meet me. They ended up scheduling a phone interview a week later, but no one ever explained or apologized for the no-show. It didn't leave me with the best impression of the company."

Though such egregious breaches of interview etiquette are pretty rare, you can still learn a lot about an organization by the way it approaches its recruiting efforts. And we know it sounds a little bit *Oprah,* but listen to your inner voice when it comes to your interviews. If your enthusiasm for a job starts to wane as you learn more about it, pay attention to those feelings. As a general rule, people are never quite as enthusiastic about a particular job as they were before they were offered it; if you become less excited about a position as you learn more about it, chances are it won't grow to be more appealing once it actually starts. One of the few downsides of cultivating exceptional interview skills is the risk of talking your way into jobs that don't necessarily match your skills or interests. So, while it absolutely pays to do your research, know your resume, and invest time preparing for each individual interview, it's equally important you trust yourself when all is said and done.

Thanks for the memories

It's true in tennis and golf, and it's true in job interviews too: Once you've taken a swing at the ball, it's essential to follow through. Whether you interviewed in person or over the phone, and whether it was a first-round screening interview with HR or a final-round cross-examination by the senior vice president of Global Widget Marketing, you need to send a thank-you note at the completion of the interview process. Sending a thank-you note isn't just a polite way to recognize the time and courtesy someone's extended to you, but it's a way to reiterate your interest in the position, jog your interviewer's memory of your conversation, and highlight one or two specific things that make you a compelling candidate for the job. Apply the same sensibilities to your thank-you note you would toward your cover letter: think polite, concise, personalized, and absolutely error-free. Make sure your proofreading efforts extend beyond spelling and grammar; after all, you worked hard to establish your credibility and interest during the interview—you don't want to undo it all by making an embarrassing slip-up in a thank-you note. If you were introduced to multiple people during your office visit, make sure you get their names and titles correct. This is important whether you're sending them individual thank-you notes or mentioning them by name in the note you send your primary contact. "I once sent a thank-you note to a hiring manager after a series of interviews with multiple people," says Sarah, a 26-year old research associate at a consulting firm. "One of the people I met with was named Edwin Famous. But I hadn't taken his business card or written down his name immediately after the interview, so, when I sat down to write a thank-you note to my primary contact, the name that stuck out in my head was—for some reason—'Amos,' rather than 'Edwin.' I thanked the hiring manager profusely for not only taking the time to speak with me, but for introducing me to Miriam and Amos as well.

Unbeknownst to me, the entire office—including the person whose name I botched—found out about my error and found it extremely entertaining. It didn't cost me the job or anything—not only did I get an offer, but I accepted it. But from the day I started until the day I left two years later, I was the one who got the name wrong in the thank-you note. I'll never do that again." When you were little, you may have been told that if you couldn't think of something nice to say, then you shouldn't say anything at all. Well, when it comes to writing thank-you notes to interviews, the rule is this: If you can't get all of the names right, then it's better to not to include them at all. Of course, the best approach of all is to collect business cards from every person with whom you meet—and to proofread your thank-you correspondence diligently before sending it.

While your thank-you notes should always be flawless, they don't have to be written by hand and sent via snail mail to be effective. It was once considered gauche to send anything other than a hand-written note on quality stationery, but most hiring professionals these days agree that a prompt, well-written e-mail (sent no more than two business days after the interview) generally gets the job done. We've said it before, but it bears repeating: Don't let the ease and informality of e-mail give you a false sense of security. Like your cover letter or resume, your thank-you note is an opportunity to convey a confident, competent, and professional image to potential employers; don't waste that opportunity by regurgitating the same spiel you used in your cover letter. If anything, your thank-you note can be a more powerful tool for advancing your candidacy because you can use what you've learned in your interview to write a personalized, targeted note. In it you should mention one or two specific topics discussed during the interview that reinforced your interest in the position. If your interviewer described the specific attributes or qualities the position requires, mention one or two achievements that prove you possess them. And, finally, offer to send any additional information the hiring manager might require in order to make a decision. (Chances are they would have asked if they needed anything, but it's nice to offer nonetheless.)

Cultivating a Professional Appearance

You've put a lot of time and energy into preparing for your interview, so wouldn't it be great if you could rely solely on your impressive achievements and your sparkling personality to get you the job of your dreams? Sadly, you can't. Putting your best foot forward means not only proving you have the academic and professional chops for the role, but looking and acting the part, too. According to a recent report by the National Association of Colleges and Employers (NACE), a candidate's professional appearance does influence hiring decisions. "Job candidates need to remember that their overall grooming and choice of interview attire project an image," says Marilyn Mackes, the organization's executive director. "They are marketing themselves to the employer as a potential employee, and part of marketing is the packaging." The two most important appearance-related factors, according to the NACE study, were personal grooming and interview attire.

Grooming—Nearly three-quarters of NACE's survey respondents said that a candidate's personal grooming would strongly influence their hiring decision. The term "grooming" might sound a little Kennel Club, but it means that your hair should be clean, neat, and brushed. The same goes for your teeth—no one should be able to tell that you had a Caesar salad for lunch. If you're concerned about your breath, you can pop a breath mint or chew a piece of gum—but nothing should be in your mouth by the time you meet your interviewer. If you share your house with a furry friend, be sure the evidence isn't all over your suit; invest in a lint-roller and give yourself a once-over before heading out the door. Your nails should be clean, trimmed, and not brightly painted. Be sure your clothes are clean and neat, without any missing buttons, wrinkles, tears, or stains (check under the arms).

Speaking of underarms, remember that decades-old deodorant commercial that advised, "Never let them see you sweat"? That's good advice for your interview too: Gentlemen, wear a short-sleeved white cotton t-shirt under your dress shirt to mitigate any possible sweat effects. For women, a nice sweater shell underneath your suit jacket instead of a button-down dress shirt will achieve the same thing (you won't have to worry about ironing that way, either). Remember that natural fabrics like wool and cotton are generally more breathable than synthetics, so keep that in mind as you select your interview duds.

If you choose to wear perfume or cologne, don't overdo it; your personal fragrance shouldn't arrive at the interview room before you do. And while we're on the topic of odor, don't ever smoke outside before you walk into the office building. One of the many drawbacks of this habit (don't worry, we aren't here to lecture you) is the lingering smell.

The "less is more" guideline applies to makeup, ladies. Candidates of either gender should steer clear of flashy or excessive jewelry.

Interview attire—Approximately half of all employers who responded to the NACE survey indicated that nontraditional interview attire would strongly influence their opinion of a candidate; another 38 percent said it would have a slight influence. For women, traditional interview attire means a well-tailored suit in a neutral color (black, gray, navy, and dark brown are all safe choices) and conservative shoes (no stilettos, open toes, or even peep-toes). For men, it means a suit in a dark, neutral color (black, navy, or dark gray), a white or light blue dress shirt (no flashy stripes or patterns), a silk tie with a conservative pattern, socks that match the trousers (no white!), and conservative, polished dark shoes.

While a suit is definitely a safe choice, keep in mind that relatively few companies observe a business-attire dress policy these days. You shouldn't assume that the rules that will apply once you've gotten the job will pertain to you as you're interviewing for it, but it's entirely possible that the person scheduling your interview may let you know that a suit is not de rigeur for your office visit. If this happens, consider yourself freed of the suit requirement. You should still err on the side of conservatism, though. The personal grooming guidelines still apply, and even a more casual ensemble should be clean, pressed, and well tailored.[3]

Arriving on Time

Whether the setting is an urban jungle or a corporate park in the 'burbs, and whether you're driving or taking public transportation, you'll need to do some planning to make sure you arrive on time for your interview. Try to arrive at least an hour in advance—that way, you've left ample cushion time in case you run into traffic, encounter public transport delays, can't find a parking place, or get lost en route. In the event your journey goes smoothly and you arrive an hour in advance, you can visit the closest coffee shop and use the extra time for focused interview preparation. You can review the company information you've collected and take one last look at the questions you hope to ask during the course of the interview. And—especially if the trip has left you looking a little less pristine than you did when you left home—you can use the time to tidy up your appearance before you walk in the door.

NEGOTIATING THE OFFER: A CHECKLIST

Congratulations! Your thorough preparation and solid credentials have landed you a job offer. Now what? Well, the same truth that applies to marriages applies to job offers: Just because the ring's on the finger doesn't mean things can't still unravel. You still have more preparation and work to do to ensure that you live happily ever after. You may have heard the age-old wisdom that when it comes to negotiating salary, the first one to cite a number loses. There's some truth to this nugget, but negotiating a pay package that's both attractive and fair is a little more complicated. Here are our top tips for making sure your employment offer is a win-win proposition:

3   National Association of Colleges and Employers. "Employers
     Say Appearance Counts for Job Candidates" May 10,
     2006.(www.naceweb.org/press/display.asp?year=2006&prid=236.

Wait your turn. Until you've actually been offered a job, it's not appropriate to initiate a discussion of salary or benefits. If you're asked in preliminary conversations or early-round interviews what salary you're hoping to earn (or what salary you've made in the past), try to keep it vague; mentioning a specific figure too early in the process is a no-win situation. If you name too high a figure, they'll question whether you're likely to accept the job if it's offered to you; if you name too low a figure, you'll leave money on the table. To continue with the poker metaphor, play your cards close to the vest and don't show your hand too early.

Know your worth. When you apply for a job, you're essentially selling services to a prospective employer. You can't possibly negotiate an offer if you don't know the going rate for those services. Take the time to figure out what people in positions comparable to yours are earning. Web-based tools such as Salary.com and SalaryExpert.com make it easier than ever to obtain a baseline figure for a given job title in a specific geographic area. This should only be a starting point, however (as we said before, the ranges these sites provide are necessarily broad). If you can, check with your contacts in the industry—friends, acquaintances, networking groups, professional associations—to hone in on a salary range you can reasonably expect.

Know your bottom line. Base salary is only one component of the total-compensation picture, but (particularly early in your career) it can be the most important piece. If that's the case for you, have a bottom line—in other words, the lowest base salary at which you'd be willing to accept the position—in mind. Other compensation-related factors (performance-based bonuses, paid time off, company-sponsored retirement plans, paid relocation expenses, and employer-paid health insurance, to name a few) can help you evaluate the offer, but give some thought to the relative importance you assign to those factors in advance of your discussions.

Manage your expectations. The strength of your negotiating position is determined by supply and demand. The more specialized your skills—and the higher the demand for those skills—the more leverage you'll have. In general, the more entry-level the position, the larger the pool of qualified candidates the employer can choose from. The sector you're considering plays a role, too. If you're considering jobs in academia or the public sector, there's usually room to negotiate; if the hiring manager must work within established pay-grade levels, he will have less discretion when it comes to deciding how much to pay.

Manage *their* expectations. If you ask for more money and get it, remember that you'll be expected to make a proportionately greater contribution to the organization you're joining. This isn't a necessarily problem—provided you keep up your end of the bargain. If your performance is less than stellar, however, you'll have damaged your credibility—and your subsequent pay increases and advancement opportunities will probably suffer as a result.

Take a long-term view. Whether it's getting the job offer in the first place or negotiating your salary and perks, it's easy for "winning the game" to become your top priority. But know that the best job opportunity isn't always the one with the fattest paycheck—it's the one that offers the best experience. Consider whether the position will enable you to develop skills that will make you more marketable down the line. Consider the position's promotion potential, learning opportunities, and the extent to which it makes good use of your skills and abilities. Your career is an investment; don't give up long-term career opportunities for short-term financial gain.

Keep the big picture in mind. Know, too, that while paying rent is important, compensation is only one piece of the pie when it comes to your job satisfaction (and your overall mental health, for that matter). Other factors—such as work/life balance, job security, and geographic location—should influence your assessment of the job offer, too. Don't forget that the company's culture—and the quality of your managers, mentors, and colleagues—will have a significant impact on your experience. If you can't stand the thought of going to work every day, no amount of money—either now or five years down the line—will make it worthwhile.

Mind your manners. One of the things that makes negotiating a job offer different from negotiating the price on a used car is the need to preserve the relationship with the party you're doing business with (in this case, your future employer). With that in mind, your negotiation approach should never be confrontational—nor should you give the impression you're unreasonable or greedy. Even if the initial offer falls short of your expectations, be polite and gracious about it. Begin any counter-offer discussions by saying you're appreciative of the offer and the opportunity—and mean it.

Play fair. There's no doubt about it—negotiating your compensation is tricky business. Aim too high, and you run the risk of damaging your credibility or pricing yourself out of the market entirely. Settle for too little, and you'll always be playing catch-up (and you'll probably feel under-valued and unappreciated down the line). So, when it's time for negotiations, keep "fair and reasonable" in mind as you evaluate specific terms. It's in your best interest to earn fair compensation and it's in your employer's best interest for you to feel you're compensated fairly for your efforts.

Thanks, but no thanks: Learning from rejection

As a matter of personal and professional pride, we'd all like to get an offer for every job for which we apply. But, in reality, most of us don't. Sometimes, you know exactly where you went wrong: It's usually the point in the interview where the room starts to get really hot, the walls seem to close in around you, and everything starts to happen in slow motion. "I've had interviews where I knew things were going downhill right from the start," says Paul, who recalls an on-campus interview for a research job at a university. "For some reason, I thought my interview was at 10:30 A.M., and I left myself plenty of time to find the building on campus where my interview was taking place. But, when I walked in, my interviewer introduced herself and said, 'You know, we were expecting you at 10:00 A.M. Did you get lost?' It turns out I had gotten the interview time wrong. Five minutes into the interview, my cell phone started ringing because I'd forgotten to turn it off. So within 10 minutes I was completely distracted and flustered, and I felt I couldn't recover. It wasn't entirely surprising that I didn't get the job."

In situations such as these—where you know your interview didn't go exactly as you'd hoped or planned—the best thing you can do is value the experience as an opportunity to learn. It might not be much consolation at the time, but you'll be far less likely to make the same mistakes (in Paul's case, showing up late and leaving his cell phone on) again, and you'll only refine and improve your approach as you go along. The interview process shouldn't be a game you're determined to win: Instead, it's a unique opportunity to learn about yourself, polish your presentation skills, and explore one of the literally thousands of career possibilities available to you.

What do you do when you've been passed over for a job and there's no "smoking gun"—you knocked every question out of the park, got along famously with every person you met, and still didn't get the offer? How do you figure out what went wrong so you can learn as much as possible from the experience?

First, understand that there are times when even the most meticulous research and thorough preparation aren't enough to land an offer with a particular company. It's entirely possible that you did do an outstanding job during the interview process—it might just be that another candidate did it a little bit better. Or maybe the successful applicant went to the same college as two or three of the people who interviewed him. Or maybe you felt there was chemistry between you and your interviewers, but one (or more) of them didn't feel the same way. There are dozens of possible reasons, and it's just not worth the emotional energy to figure out which one it's most likely to be.

However, if you decide to ask for feedback after you've gotten a "no, thank you," do keep a couple of things in mind:

- **Accept that you might not get what you're looking for.** Even if you ask nicely, you might not get constructive feedback. No one likes to be the bearer of bad news—not even HR folks or hiring managers, who have to deliver it on a daily basis. In the overly litigious society we live in, no one wants to get sued, either; so it's really no surprise that employers are typically reticent when it comes to justifying their hiring decisions. You need to be prepared for the stock answer, which is "we were overwhelmed by the number of qualified applicants for the position and have offered the position to the candidate whose experience and background most closely matched our hiring needs."

- **Remember that timing is everything.** The best time to ask for feedback is when the decision-maker (or, in many cases, the messenger) calls you to tell you you're not getting the job offer. Of course, rejection phone calls are more the exception than the rule these days; in many cases, companies will choose a more passive-aggressive route and send you an e-mail or letter, or not get back to you at all. If you get a rejection e-mail, the best time to ask for feedback is immediately after you receive it.

- **Cross-examinations are not appropriate.** You're far more likely to get meaningful feedback if you steer clear of questions such as "Why aren't you hiring me?" which immediately puts the other person on the defensive. Though it might seem as if you're beating around the bush, you're probably best served saying something along the lines of: "Thanks very much for getting back to me and letting me know. Since I'm still in the process of interviewing with other organizations, I was wondering if you could give me any advice or feedback that might help me with future interviews."

- **Don't ever argue—ever.** If your HR contact or recruiter does give you feedback that you disagree with, it's never appropriate to engage them in a debate about the merit of their decision. No matter how watertight your argument might be, it won't change the outcome; it will just protract an inherently awkward and uncomfortable conversation. You want to keep the conversation short, sweet (or at least bittersweet), and polite. Most employers have zero tolerance for confrontation in this scenario.

- **Take a hint.** If you leave a voicemail or send an e-mail message asking for feedback and you don't get a reply, leave it at that. Don't send follow-up messages or phone-stalk your contact trying to get them to speak with you. If they don't want to give you feedback, they don't have to—and you've got nothing to gain by trying to beat it out of them.

It's not you, it's me: Declining an offer

If, on the other hand, you receive an offer from an organization but choose to decline it for any reason, you should be just as gracious turning it down as you would be accepting it—or negotiating its terms. Let your prospective employer know as soon as you've decided it's not the right opportunity; as a candidate, you may already know how frustrating it is not to receive word after you've invested a lot in an application process. While it may be tempting to delay a potentially unpleasant conversation, letting your contact know promptly about your decision is the gracious, professional thing to do, especially since the organization still has a position that needs to be filled. Just as the first step in negotiating an offer is thanking your contact profusely for extending the opportunity, the first step in declining the offer is also expressing your appreciation. Then, offer a brief explanation—in however much detail you feel comfortable—of why you have decided to decline it. As far as personal information is concerned, leave it out if you're at all in doubt. Feel free to stick to the basics—i.e., "It's just not the right opportunity for me at this particular time."

In some instances, the employer may probe you for more specifics, so be prepared to politely say enough but not more than you feel is appropriate or judicious to reveal. Of course, never bad-mouth any organization—or any individual interviewer or employee with whom you met. Again, thank them for the time they spent speaking with you about the position and tell them you very much enjoyed meeting with them and learning about the role and the organization.

Though it's never quite as much fun to decline a job as it is to accept one, remember that it's okay to decline a position that's not right for you. It's also perfectly acceptable to decline an offer if you just want to wait to see what else is out there in your job search—it's better to be out of a job a few extra weeks or months than quit one six weeks after you started because it's just not working out. Trust your gut as well as your evaluation of the job's criteria. If something just doesn't seem right for you, follow your instincts. Even if your friends, parents, and significant other are telling you what a great opportunity it is, you're the one who's got to go to work every day.

CHAPTER 6

Q & A's with Former English and Communications Majors

A FINAL WORD FROM US. . .

By now you should be feeling pretty darn confident about the many opportunities that are available to you as an English or communications major. This book has sought to show you that the skills and knowledge you learned in your studies have market value in the "real world." We have also given you the tools you need to get in the door, whether the next step is advanced study, fellowships, or launching a job search.

But don't take our word for it. We spoke with several former English and communications majors from all walks of life to find out how their degrees have helped and/or hindered their professional career paths. Some of these folks work in business, others in the nonprofit sector, others in media, and still others in education and/or various creative fields. We asked them about their motivation for choosing an English or communications major, what they learned, how those skills have been useful/not useful in the real world; about internships, their first job search, their current job, the best career advice they received, tips for current English or communications majors, and much more. You'll get to hear straight from them about how being an English or communications major has affected their professional growth.

Remember, this is only the beginning. The next several years will be full of exciting ups and downs as your future kicks into high gear. So buckle up, and remember to enjoy the journey.

Good luck!

Q & A WITH FORMER ENGLISH MAJORS

The following professionals dedicated their time to answering our questions:

John Gray is an associate producer on *Deadliest Catch*, a Discovery Channel documentary series.

Lilit Marcus is an editorial assistant for Beliefnet.com.

Maryelien Goodman is an AfterCare Care Manager at Mercy Home for Boys and Girls.

Richard Strattner runs postsecondary advising for a major educational services firm.

Stephanie Durrell is the Director of Mad Science, an international franchise specializing in science "edu-tainment" for elementary-aged children.

Why did you major in English?

John: I always wanted to be a writer, and no matter how obstinately I avoided the call (majoring for brief spells in architecture, economics, and anthropology) in the back of my mind I knew that eventually all roads would lead to an English degree. And after my first creative writing class, I was hooked. It was the only thing that I was good at *and* I enjoyed, and in the end, what more can one ask for?

Lilith: I couldn't imagine doing anything else. Sure, I loved reading and writing, but what I enjoyed most about studying English was the way every single aspect of culture could be represented in a single text, whether it was gender, sexuality, psychology, personal identity, or something else.

Maryelien: I majored in English because I believe that good literature is an excellent way of studying and understanding human nature, because the great writers are able to transcend both time and place to create messages that are universal and timeless. I also believe in the power of language, and my English major was a way of studying the compilation of words for the best effect.

Richard: I entered college with an intended major in economics. I placed out of freshman English, so my initial course was Introduction to Shakespeare. My professor, David Reade, told the class that he was simply going to read aloud for the entire first class. After that one class, I went to the registrar and changed my major. It was magic.

Stephanie: I honestly chose English because I wasn't sure what I wanted to do. I thought it was a well-rounded start that could be changed later as I further developed my aspirations. I fell in love with classes and the materials, and the art of writing. I considered law and professing, which held me to this major, but I mainly stuck with it because the subject matter challenged and excited me.

What skills or information learned in college do you find yourself making the most use of?

John: Every day I write. Whether it's an e-mail, a voiceover, a screenplay, or a note to my wife, I utilize the written word each and every day, without fail. In fact, I communicate just as much with written words as I do with the spoken. College is where I learned how to write clearly and directly and where I learned how to tell stories. Life is all about the stories.

Lilith: Articulation is key. All those papers I had to write helped me to cogently argue points in the "real world." I'm very confident when pitching a story idea because I can provide good arguments for why it would make a good piece on the website.

Maryelien: The ability to communicate is probably the most useful thing I learned from college. Of course, most of the population can speak, and some majority can write. However, there is a difference between that and effective communication, both written and oral, in which every word is measured and chosen for the effect it will have. This is a skill that I find absolutely invaluable.

Richard: The ability to think critically, the ability to communicate effectively, and the ability to act despite a measure of uncertainty are the three skills I learned in college that I apply most frequently today.

Stephanie: Networking and making friends with people from all areas. Sharing my ideas with them and taking their suggestions to heart. It may seem shallow at first, but really it makes complete sense that the most powerful and effective method to achieve an end is through a personal recommendation. Resumes and experience are great, but nothing compares to a person of consequence making themselves accountable for your performance and repute. Also, core classes that at the time seemed silly now come in to use in networking situations often. It is nice to meet someone from a totally different field and be able to relate to them and take interest in their interests, even if it is on a basic level. Writing is another skill I was able to develop. No matter what the subject, knowing how to write coherently and correctly is incredibly valuable. Even the brightest applicant can induce a grimace when they misspell or misuse a word.

What skills or information learned in college do you find yourself not using at all?

John: I took financial accounting twice, and I dropped financial accounting twice. Granted, I never made it all the way through the class, so the information might not be 100 percent "learned," but if there's one thing I have never used, it's financial accounting. Unless you really want to be an accountant, if you need to do some accounting, here's my advice: Hire one.

Lilith: I rarely get the chance to reference Derrida in my daily conversation.

Maryelien: I actually feel very lucky in that I can't think of a skill that I don't use at all. Math is a skill I use frequently in everyday interactions, the biology that I took helps me to explain to the kids with whom I work how their bodies work and why health is so important.

Richard: Computer programming. I took a class in it because I was curious and haven't done a lick of programming since. The world is most certainly better off for my absence in this area.

Stephanie: Some classes I took where professors taught to a test (this is mostly found in 101 classes). I find not only did I learn nothing in the class, I had to backtrack in any following classes to catch up. Many of the research methods and search engines that took quite a bit of time to master in school I no longer use.

Which internships or extracurricular activities that you pursued in college have been most valuable to you personally and professionally? Why?

John: I worked in the kitchen of a restaurant, which took up a lot of my extracurricular time, but learning how to cook has been insanely valuable. I've done some of my best networking (the only real way to get a job in the entertainment industry) during dinner parties. I was also one of the editors on the school's creative writing journal, which helped me learn the ins and outs of creative collaboration (another necessity in the entertainment industry).

Lilith: I spent a summer in college teaching creative nonfiction at the University of Virginia's Young Writers Workshop. Having to teach something made me learn even more, and my students gave me a variety of perspectives that continue to influence me now. I also learned to reconcile the creative aspects of my job with the more administrative and technical.

Maryelien: I tutored educationally at-risk children in grade school throughout my four years in college, which is what made me think of doing a year of volunteer work after graduation. It was this year of volunteering that helped me to decide to pursue social work as a career. Personally, I ran several times a week with my fellow dorm mates, and found running to be a great stress release. When I first went into my volunteer internship I began training for a marathon, and the long runs became the perfect antidote to the stress and frustration of life in the real world.

Richard: Three activities come to mind: I did an internship for a small arts organization that ran on a shoestring. It taught me that no task should ever be below you or too great to take on. I managed the Student Association budget. Knowing one's way around a budget is a valuable asset no matter what you plan on doing in life. I played soccer. I still do. Having an outlet for physical activity is a must.

Stephanie: I did an internship while completing my graduate degree that was incredibly rewarding; however I regret that I never took one on as an undergraduate. I think that a successful internship can be one of the most useful accomplishments as a student, and it is often much easier to find opportunities to enter sought-after fields or organizations as an intern than it may be as a graduate seeking employment. I did teach a dance class at a local middle school that ended up providing me with very useful experience in my current position. It also instilled in me a very strong sense of community and loyalty for the city of New Orleans. I used to live in the city, not just attend school there.

How did you decide which field, either in academia or the real world, to go into?

John: As a creative writer, there's only a couple ways to take home a paycheck. I tried the journalism route for a while, but I found it a little too creatively stifling. I decided to make a go at screenwriting because: a) I love movies; b) I love television; c) I love stories; and d) after living in Los Angeles for six years, I had enough connections to help me get started.

Lilith: I always knew that I wanted to write. Some of my classmates thought that journalism was a bastardization of creative writing, but I think they're two different things. I don't think I'd be a good investigative reporter—it's too hard to keep my emotions out of what I'm doing. Writing about religion and spirituality, something I care a lot about, is ideal for me. Writing during the day keeps me in practice, but when I go home and work on my personal stuff, I tap into a different part of my brain.

Maryelien: I wanted to do a year of volunteer work after graduation, partly because I wanted to "give back" and partly because I didn't know what else to do. Once fully immersed in the volunteer program, I realized that it was actually a field that I was genuinely passionate about and wanted to pursue.

Richard: I had no outside pressures to choose any one field or profession. I spoke with as many people as would speak to me about their jobs. And then I took a look around and determined where I could actually get a job.

Stephanie: My current job managed to find me. It started out as a fun weekend gig to pick up some spare cash, but it pointed out to me how much I did not enjoy my day job. While looking for another full-time job, my four hours a week became 20, then 30, then full-time! None of the jobs I was applying for held a candle to my 'filler' job, and when the opportunity to join in full-time arose, I was thrilled. I was unwilling to give up this job that truly invoked a passion in me for some lesser job merely because it pertained to my degree.

Did you have a mentor when you entered the workforce/graduate school?

John: I didn't have a mentor, which means I had to do it the hard way. I sent out resumes, answered ads, went to parties, and struggled. For years. But the struggle made me hungry, and I never gave up. I think a mentor would have made things easier, but with a mentor I wouldn't have gone through the struggle, and it was the struggle that pushed me to succeed.

Lilith: No. I moved to New York City without any friends or contacts. I was fortunate to start meeting and working with some great people, but I didn't have anyone at the beginning.

Maryelien: I did not really have a mentor when I entered the workforce, but I have been blessed the last two years to be surrounded by extremely inspirational and powerful coworkers who have helped me to carve out my role in this field.

Richard: I didn't have a mentor when I entered the workforce but I cultivated them once I arrived. They can prove to be an invaluable resource.

Stephanie: While I did receive a large amount of support leaving school, I entered graduate school alone in a foreign country. I began my job hunt back in the U.S. a year later. Because of the distance, I was unable to make good use of all the networking and resources and people who helped me in both situations. If I were to re-enter school for another degree, I would make a point to do it physically close to the location I wanted to work in.

What is the number-one bit of advice you wish you were given before you entered the job market?

John: I wish someone had told me that when offered a job, no matter how bad the money is or how low it is on the totem pole, you should only take the job that's in the field you truly want to be involved in. The money will come, the position will come, but the longer you put off following your dreams, the longer it will take to fulfill them.

Lilith: Send out resumes everywhere. Apply for jobs you don't think you're qualified for. Apply for jobs that are only loosely connected to what you want to do. You can always use more practice interviewing, and you should never rule out a possibility. Often, the way a job is described is different from the way the job is actually structured.

Maryelien: The advice that I would have liked to hear pertains not only to the job market but life after college as well. It is simply that nobody graduates from college and immediately knows how to be an adult. Although it would be nice to have a "Being an Adult 101," there is nothing like that, so you learn as you go. And it's okay to still ask questions and it's okay to make mistakes as long as you learn from them.

Richard: Relax. The vast majority of people will hold more than one functional job for more than one company before they retire. Knowing that, take the opportunity to enjoy each job for what it is and for what it may be able to teach you.

Stephanie: Be aggressive. Brag about yourself and be yourself. As an employer, I don't want to know just what you can do, but how you go about doing it. The more enthusiastic you are about getting the job, the more enthusiastic you will be when it comes to doing it!

What were your job-related expectations when you were still in school, and how did they match up with your experience of the "real world?"

John: I thought it was going to be easy, and of course it wasn't. Not only is it hard to find a job that you enjoy, it's just plain hard to find a job.

Lilith: I worked as a receptionist in the campus art museum for three years. I also had a summer internship at the local Arts Council, writing grant applications. Even though these were peripherally connected to my English degree, they taught me a lot about communicating my ideas and interacting with different kinds of people, skills that have benefited me tremendously since then. Being able to understand painting and sculpture helped me to understand literature.

Maryelien: I remember watching my friends go to job fairs and create portfolios starting junior year and wondering why they were stressing, because we still had over a year before we had to deal with the "real world." This is probably not the best way to start a career in the work force, but I honestly don't think I would do anything differently. The only thing I knew about a job was that I did not want to spend 40 hours of my life doing something I wasn't passionate about. And luckily, in the two years that I've been working, I have kept my passion and continue to be stimulated and to love the work that I do.

Richard: When I entered the workplace, I was amazed at how human people were. I thought you weren't "allowed" to show any emotion or wrestle with any issues. The professional and personal worlds are both populated by real people.

Stephanie: I expected to find a job in my field, and I expected to find it right away. My classmates who lived in the same place as the school quickly found jobs out of internships or recommendations, and I was unable to do so. I was forced to take a job that I could get and was good at for monetary reasons, and then I forced myself to leave this job for mental stability reasons!

What was your first job out of college? How did you find that job?

John: My first paying job out of college was working behind the deli counter at the Wild Oats supermarket in Santa Monica, California. I learned how to cut prosciutto very, very thin. I found the job by eating at the deli; the "help wanted" sign was hanging in the deli window.

Lilith: I did French/English translation for an artist who needed help putting together his portfolio. I found it on Craig's List.

Maryelien: My first job was the volunteer year working at Mercy Home for Boys and Girls, a residential treatment facility for teenagers in Chicago. Specifically, I worked with a group of 14 to 16-year-old girls who were living at the agency and lived with a group of 13 other volunteers. I found the job at a service fair at my school, Notre Dame.

Richard: My first job out of college was working in public relations for a small firm. I found that job by going through the phone book, calling every PR agency listed, and agreeing to work for peanuts.

Stephanie: I worked in a customer call center for The Coca-Cola Company. I had a friend who worked there and she set me up with the temp agency that she had had gone through.

If you went straight into the workforce after receiving your bachelor's degree, do you wish you had attended graduate school first? If you went on to grad school, do you wish you had worked first? In either case, why?

John: I didn't go to graduate school, and I don't have plans to attend graduate school anytime soon. In a field like English, in my opinion, the only reason to go to grad school is if you want to be a teacher, and I'm not ready to be a teacher. Yet.

Lilith: I went into the workforce immediately after graduating. I often wished that I had gone to graduate school, because I missed the lifestyle of college—having summers off, for example. Now, though, I feel like going back to school would kill the momentum I've started to pick up in my career. I don't know if I could do both at once.

Maryelien: I did go straight into the workforce, and I'm glad I did so. I am planning to go back to get my master's in social work after finishing my third year at Mercy Home. I have enjoyed the opportunity to explore the field of social work before committing to a school. I can't imagine going to school without the experience and knowledge that I have gained from spending some time in the field. I believe that this experience will be a huge benefit when I start classes because I will have a working knowledge of the concrete issues being discussed.

Richard: I worked for 7 years before attending graduate school and if I were to do it again, I would do it exactly the same way. The range of professional experience, as well as the opportunity to work outside the U.S. for several years, helped me apply a real-world perspective to the academic subjects being covered.

Stephanie: I am glad I went directly to grad school because I knew what degree I wanted to pursue. After grad school, I was not sure where I wanted to go educationally speaking, and I chose to take time off rather than enter a program I was unsure of. Although this is financially frustrating, I know many people who have dropped out of law school or other graduate programs after only a short period, and I did not want to find myself in that position.

What is the best piece of advice you've received from a colleague?

John: "Keep writing." It sounds like a cliché, but it's just about the best advice you could give a writer. All you need is a piece of paper and a pen, and you can do the thing that makes you happiest. For most artistic endeavors, it's not that easy. You need equipment, personnel, money, [and] extensive amounts of time . . . but if you want to be a writer all you need is something to write with, something to write on, a few spare minutes, and a little bit of discipline, and you can make it happen.

Lilith: Be nice to temps.

Maryelien: The best piece of advice I have received is from my current supervisor, who consistently tells his whole team that the only way we will be a capable staff is if we take care of ourselves first. There is no way that I can give 100 percent of my energy and capabilities if my internal resources are being stretched too thin. Now, when I begin to feel my patience and my sense of humor going, I automatically figure out how I can take a break to recenter myself, even if it's just for five minutes.

Richard: Just do your job. So much in the professional world moves around without our ability to control it that worrying about it will drive you nuts.

Stephanie: Set a goal. Tell people about it. Set the steps. Follow through.

What is the smartest move you've made since receiving your bachelor's degree?

John: I wanted to be involved with the entertainment industry, so I moved to Los Angeles. It's essential that you live in the place where your industry exists and thrives, because that's where the opportunities are easier to come by. Not easy by any means, but easier. You wouldn't move to Arizona if you wanted to get a job as an oceanographer, right? There might be a job or two there (emphasis on the "might"), but it makes a whole lot more sense to move to a place where there's some actual ocean.

Lilith: Moving by myself to New York was both the smartest and stupidest decision I made. It was pretty risky to move here without any contacts or any money, but I scored my dream internship and was willing to come here to follow through. I think that in my first six months out of college, I aged three years. Not only was I having to take care of myself and figure out things like finances and health insurance, I had to do it without my family and friends. Now, though, I wouldn't trade that period for anything. It's made me the person I am. Also, I knew that I needed to move to a large city in order to advance my career. As much as I love my hometown in North Carolina, there weren't exactly a lot of major media companies based there. I knew that if I didn't move right after college, I'd never do it.

Maryelien: I don't really know how to answer this question; I guess the only thing I can say is trusting myself to try something new and making sure that I don't become complacent (thus, the reason I'm planning on going to graduate school).

Richard: Getting my wife to say "yes" when I proposed.

Stephanie: The move overseas! Although it has been frustrating, no experience can compare with being surrounded by a different culture and learning not just to think from a different perspective, but to think *above* perspective.

Describe your current job and its major responsibilities.

John: I'm an associate producer on *Deadliest Catch*, a Discovery Channel documentary series about Alaskan king crab fishing on the Bering Sea. My major responsibilities are pretty broad, but essentially I'm one of the people who makes sure the show comes together. This includes pre-production, when we're organizing everything for the shoot; production, when we're actually shooting footage; and post-production, when we're editing the footage down and crafting the individual shows.

Lilith: I work as an editorial assistant for Beliefnet.com, the world's largest multifaith religion and spirituality website. I write articles, fact check/copyedit others' articles, build newsletters, monitor message boards, request permission for reprints and excerpts, and more.

Maryelien: I am currently an AfterCare Care Manager at Mercy Home for Boys and Girls. For the past year my team and I have been providing ongoing support for former residents of Mercy Home. My responsibilities range from planning and implementing monthly social activities for the former residents, or members, to teaching members about budgeting and job searching, to supporting those who find themselves in debilitating crisis situations, such as homelessness or domestic violence. In other words, whatever issues our members have, whatever goals they want to achieve, I work with them to achieve these dreams.

Richard: I run postsecondary advising for a major educational services firm. As such, I am responsible for launching projects, managing development as well as delivery staff, and keeping my eye on the budget.

Stephanie: I am the director of Mad Science, an international franchise specializing in science "edu-tainment" for elementary-aged children. I oversee hiring, scheduling, equipment maintenance, class content modifications, relationships with clients—including schools, organizations, and parents—and forming new relationships. I also manage the computer databases of all contacts, suppliers, and histories.

What experience was required for your current role?

John: I had to have a good deal of basic television production knowledge, a pretty decent grasp of how cameras and film equipment works, and an understanding of how stories are put together on the screen. This experience was gained through three years of working in pretty much all facets of commercial, film, and television production.

Lilith: The job was open to recent graduates, but I'd been out of school a year by the time I interviewed. I had a strong interest in the subject matter and had been interning at a magazine. The editorial experience got me the interview, but my interest in spirituality helped me get the job.

Maryelien: Because I started out as a volunteer, not that much experience was required from me. I had already worked at the agency for a year in a youth care position, which helped. If I hadn't been a volunteer, some experience in youth care work would have been expected, as well as some sort of background in psychology and sociology.

Richard: My experience as a management consultant and then several years working in higher education met the needs of the job.

Stephanie: I began as equipment manager for the company, which required only instructor experience. Through this, I took on assistant roles with the previous director, which led to my appointment when the vacancy appeared.

To what extent has your degree helped you in your current role?

John: My job requires a whole lot of writing (pitches, plans, scripts, vast inboxes of e-mails, etc), and my writing skills were honed in school. My job also requires a lot of storytelling, and my college's creative writing department is where I developed my sense of story, the ability to weed through a big fat amalgam of aural and visual noise, find the seeds of the experience, and plant those seeds into a story that not only makes sense, but is interesting and unique.

Lilith: First of all, I wouldn't have even gotten in the door without a college degree. It's a basic requirement of the field. On a day-to-day basis, I use my degree for everything—proofreading, analyzing others' stories, being able to pick the most important parts of a press release. My English degree is so integrated into my job that I don't even think about it.

Maryelien: To date, I have never taken a psychology or sociology class, unlike my coworkers, who are consistently surprised when I tell them. However, I believe that the English major allowed me to study human nature, albeit in a more creative manner. Reading literature and then analyzing it is really just another way of studying psychology. Furthermore, it teaches effective communication, which has been useful in working with my colleagues as well as our members.

Richard: My undergraduate degree helped me manage complexity. My graduate degree gave me the technical skills to address how we run the business.

Stephanie: Many consider English to be a good background for any teacher, although I feel it helped more in my development as a person than in the specific skill set needed to perform my job.

What do you like most about your current role?

John: I love that I get to immerse myself inside someone else's life and imbed myself inside an entirely foreign environment. The subject matter of our documentary series is the Alaskan crab fisherman, and—let me tell you—the Alaskan crab fisherman is one interesting dude. Since he was 10 years old, he's been doing things that would terrify the average person. And he does it in a place that 99.9 percent of the planet's population will never see or experience, a place of awe-inspiring beauty.

Lilith: I like getting to write on a regular basis. Even though the site has a specific focus, I still write about all kinds of topics. In the past few weeks alone I have worked on stories about prominent atheists in America, a reality show about gay Jehovah's Witnesses, and the Church of Jon Stewart. My job is never boring.

Maryelien: What I like the most about my degree is the fact that it was not specific. I really enjoyed the liberal arts curriculum, because it is learning for the sake of learning and not just to secure a job. For me, (and I realize how fortunate I am to have this luxury) graduate school is the time to become more focused and career oriented, while undergrad taught me how to think critically. What I like the most about my current role is that I am outside of my comfort zone, and always learning something new, whether it be more details about the public aid system, how to best support someone in an abusive relationship, or how I really handle stress. With all that, I am also in constant interaction with different people and always hearing their stories, which I find fascinating.

Richard: I do not work with students directly. However, the knowledge that my job ultimately helps create opportunities for high school students who might not otherwise be aware of them makes even the mundane activities worthwhile.

Stephanie: I love making an impact on the children we work with. Getting them interested in science keeps them involved and interested in school.

What aspect(s) of your current role do you not like?

John: There is no time clock, and no precise written rules, so we're talking long, long hours here. In a lot of ways, you have to make it up as you go along, and at times that can be sincerely frustrating, but at other times it can make life pretty darn exciting.

Lilith: Something I both love and hate about Internet media is its degree of immediacy. That means that we can quickly respond to a breaking news event, but it also means that I never know when I might have to write a story at the last minute. Sometimes, the quick turnaround is more important than me getting to show off my best writing.

Maryelien: Again, in regard to my degree, the only thing that I would change is that it would be nice to have taken some classes, even if not required, on the more practical issues, such as personal finance. In regard to my job, it has been difficult for me to reconcile the sometimes conflicting roles of direct youth care and the business aspects of any agency. The two are definitely related; had I more experience with business I would probably understand both sides and how they work together much better.

Richard: Contending with political agendas.

Stephanie: I aspire to work on a much larger scale, and I would also like to be more involved with nonprofit work.

What skills have you had to acquire that your English degree did not help you cultivate?

John: I had to learn a lot of technical stuff, like how to work cameras, lights, editing equipment, etc. And I also had to learn how to write according to the defined structure of scripts and screenplays, which is a craft I didn't learn in school.

Lilith: No amount of education can replace making good contacts and being in the right place at the right time.

Maryelien: Social work, like any field, requires a specific skill set that I don't believe can be taught in the classroom. I had to learn, and am still learning, to navigate the various systems (political, educational, public aid, etc). I also had to learn my own approach and technique for working with both my colleagues and other agencies, as well as with AfterCare members. That being said, I believe that my background in English has helped me to absorb that knowledge pretty easily.

Richard: Stronger quantitative skills—which is why I went to grad school.

Stephanie: Computer skills—I am learning to work with new systems constantly. Also, working in professional situations.

What suggestions would you have for those still in college? Are there any "optional" elements of the undergraduate experience that you would recommend they explore?

John: My biggest suggestion is to figure out what it is that makes you the happiest, whether that be writing, baseball, economics, engineering, playing the guitar—just go for it. Don't get into something because you think it will get you a job or because you think it's what you should be doing. Get into something because you love it and because without it life feels a little empty. And then be patient. And persistent. The job will come; the money will come. You just have to be patient, and, above all else, you can't give up.

Lilith: Studying abroad should not be optional. Even if you only work 10 hours a week, having a job is a way to remind yourself that a world exists apart from your university. I think too many college students are isolated from non-academic life.

Maryelien: I think that everybody should go abroad: for a summer service project, for a semester, or for a year. It is an amazing, eye-opening experience that will teach so much more than can be learned in a classroom. I spent a year in Angers, France and learned so much about myself and our country in the broader spectrum of the world. It's easy to live in the United States confident in the belief that we are the most powerful country in the world. But it's a big world we live in, and there is so much we can learn and appreciate from other countries and cultures.

Richard: If at all possible, study abroad and take courses unrelated to what you think you will do when you grow up. Everything you do after undergrad will be targeted.

Stephanie: Get an internship! Do a semester or year abroad. Get to know your professors and keep in touch with them—they are people too, not just authority figures.

Do you have any tips for those entering the workforce/graduate school now?

John: Start networking early. Meet some people, make some phone calls, shoot off some e-mails, and get your network going early, because the people you meet are going to help you somewhere down the line, without a doubt.

Lilith: Learn to write a really great resume. Figure out a way to get health insurance while you're looking for a job.

Maryelien: Do what you love and what you're passionate about; be open to going outside of your comfort zone and trying something different, because you never know what career path and passion you may inadvertently stumble upon.

Richard: Know why you are going to graduate school. Many people take a graduate degree as a function of not knowing what to do next. It is an expensive and time-consuming endeavor, and you should not undertake it frivolously.

Stephanie: Get to know the people you are looking to work with, not just the job. Get to know the business, and make sure you are truly interested. If you are, show that interest.

What is the best way to get a job in your field?

John: If you want to get involved in the entertainment industry, you must move to Los Angeles and start at the bottom, and you must do it now. Don't waste any time, just get in your car and do it. Get an internship or a low-level position at a studio or a production company, and be prepared to work your tail off. As you see all the different facets of the industry, figure out what it is that you want to do, and start moving toward it.

Lilith: Not all jobs in media and publishing are advertised. You can send a blind resume to the head of Human Resources at the magazine, website, etc. where you are interested in working. Lots of people I know have found their jobs this way. Although it's a cliché, networking really works. The trick is not to treat networking like an excuse to get something out of people. My most successful "networking" experiences were when I made solid friendships with people I met. Friends are way more likely to help you than some random person you forced your business card on at a cocktail party.

Maryelien: Network—in any field it helps so much to know people and have contacts. Besides that, never turn down opportunities for professional development such as lectures, trainings, etc.

Richard: Talk to as many people as you can, take on jobs that may not meet your ideal requirements, and don't be afraid to ask as many questions as possible.

Stephanie: Networking. Get in touch with the companies; do not just look for vacancies.

What mistake do English grads often make?

John: They worry that no one will take an English degree seriously, which is pure baloney. Unless, the job you're interviewing for is highly specialized, an English degree is just as impressive as any other degree. I have interviewed and hired numerous people, and their presence in the room was always way more important in the hiring decision than what they received their degree in. Every time.

Lilith: I thought that having an English degree meant I could skip being an assistant. It didn't.

Maryelien: Thinking that there are only certain careers available to them because the English major doesn't necessarily teach a specific skill set. In my opinion, having an English degree actually opens more doors because the foundation for critical thinking and analysis is there, and specific skill sets can always be taught in trainings or while on the job. I've been at the same agency for two years now, and I'm still learning as I go.

Richard: Letting people tell you that an English degree is good only if you want to be a teacher. It's a great degree for lots of things.

Stephanie: Being too open about where they are headed. Narrow down what you want, and it will be easier to locate it.

What is something that you think more English grads should do to advance their careers?

John: Offer to write or edit more stuff. Chances are your boss doesn't like writing his or her business plans and reports, and if you can take that off his or her plate, he or she will be a happy camper. You studied writing, right? So use your skills.

Lilith: Marketing is not a dirty word. You can learn about it and not compromise the skills and beliefs you already have. If you're writing for an audience, there's nothing wrong with trying to learn more about your audience and who they are.

Maryelien: Even though it's not required, I think that everyone should take basic computer classes (for databases, spreadsheets, etc) and also trainings on job skills and career advancements. It is something that I never interested myself in, and that I am now trying to educate myself on, but what better place to get excellent information than college?

Richard: Take courses and or internships in a specific field to balance the generalist nature of their degrees.

Stephanie: Develop specialty skills. Do not be a jack of all trades but master of none. Be a jack of all trades and master of quite a few.

Who is in the best position to offer an English graduate help with his or her resume and cover letter?

John: I think it helps to have someone who works in the field you're trying to get a job in to look over your resume, because that person will have some insight into what it is that will impress an employer.

Lilith: If your college's career center extends their services to alumni, you should definitely take advantage of that. If you get involved with a temping, staffing, or a job-search firm, they will often help you with your resume and cover letter. They want you to get hired because it makes them look good.

Maryelien: I think it helps to have anybody read and edit both resumes and cover letters (and everything else written for that matter). Career Services would be a good bet because they are people who know exactly what to look for and what pitfalls to avoid.

Richard: A person who is already affiliated with a specific industry or function is the best person to ask.

Stephanie: Someone involved with either the company or field you are applying to. They will know what is most important to hit—enthusiasm, skill sets, professional and to the point, etc.

What pitfalls should English graduates avoid when applying to and interviewing for positions?

John: Never downplay the importance of the physical interview. Once you're in that room, you're on stage, and you need to make the best impression impossible, because chances are you're only getting one shot. An employer might not remember one word of your resume, but he or she will probably remember your awesome conversation skills.

Lilith: Many English majors are more articulate on paper than they are in person. If interviewing makes you feel nervous, you can bring in a sheet of paper with the points you want to make written on it or do practice interviews with a friend.

Maryelien: English graduates should not sell themselves short. I can't emphasize enough the fact that the English major prepares its graduates for any career choice they choose to make, and it's important to highlight all the benefits of a strong liberal arts background. (And what employer isn't looking for an employee with superb oral and written communication skills?) One downfall of my own liberal arts experience is that I never took the initiative to learn about interviewing, selling myself, etc. That is one area where business majors definitely have the advantage, at least in my case.

Richard: Avoid clichés about your degree being a reflection of the fact that you are a "people person" or are "flexible." More affirmative language regarding your degree, such as "an English degree gives you the ability to think critically," and "it helps one apply a broader perspective to a specific issue," will get you further.

Stephanie: Being too open. Know what you want and go get it.

Q & A WITH FORMER COMMUNICATIONS MAJORS

The following professionals dedicated their time to answering our questions:

Ben Miller is a self-employed photographer who will be entering the Foreign Service in 2007.

Ramatu Bangura is a graduate student in international educational development and has worked as an outreach and educational services director for various non-profits, most recently for an organization that provides services to sexually exploited and trafficked youth.

Ryan Reczek works for the American Cancer Society in sales and educational services.

Seth Burleigh is a direct marketing assistant for the marketing and communications department of the UCLA Extension School.

Todd Evans is currently in graduate school. Prior to school, he was the manager of public relations and investor relations at a small cap-software company.

Why did you major in communications?

Ben: I chose it because it was the closest thing to a photography major that UC—Berkeley offered.

Ramatu: I chose a communications degree because I didn't know what I wanted to do at the time. I did know that whatever I did I would need to learn how to write well. I preferred journalistic writing to literary writing.

Ryan: I originally majored in communications because I thought I was going to go into the field of advertising. Like so many college students, that changed, but I gained a deep respect [for] and interest in rhetoric and media theory along the way. Business courses probably would have made more sense once I decided I wasn't going into advertising, but I enjoyed my communications classes too much to change majors.

Seth: I really didn't know what I wanted to do, and the media always interested me, so I decided to study it.

Todd: I was interested in mass communications.

What skills or information learned in college do you find yourself making the most use of?

Ben: I learned how the mass media and advertising works, which has allowed me to be successful in planning advertising campaigns for my own business.

Ramatu: The ability to write and think critically.

Ryan: I get the most use out of what I learned in my public speaking courses. I find what I studied in those classes not only influenced my public speaking skills, but also made an impact on my daily interpersonal communication abilities.

Seth: Working with others (specifically adults), computer skills learned from doing course work and other related projects, time-management skills, Spanish skills, being able to link current events/issues with sociological history or reasoning.

Todd: Ability to write clearly and quickly.

What skills or information learned in college do you find yourself not using at all?

Ben: A lot of the academic papers and high-level theory often does not prove as useful as practical experience.

Ramatu: I can't think of any skill or information that I don't use. Or, maybe I've already forgotten the information I don't use. My interests are so varied that it's always good to know a little about everything. It's a good idea to really take a multi-disciplinary approach to a liberal arts education.

Ryan: In regard to communications, I don't often talk about the history of mass media. While that is an area that I'm glad I know about, it is not an area that I find particularly useful in my day-to-day life.

Seth: All the theoretical information that doesn't really apply to everyday use, unless one is in academia. Sociological research methods.

Todd: Foreign languages.

Which internships or extracurricular activities that you pursued in college have been most valuable to you personally and professionally? Why?

Ben: I was a senior editor of the newspaper. It gave me valuable leadership experience that looks very impressive on my resume and taught me real lessons on how to work with others and motivate people. I also had a great time doing it, and I made some extra money.

Ramatu: Going to school in the DC area, I took advantage of the many internship opportunities available. My most valuable internship experience was at an organization called Share Our Strength, a national anti-hunger organization. I was able to work on a silent auction benefit dinner. Because the staff was small I was given lots of responsibility. I was able to see how an actual workplace functioned, learn etiquette for an office environment, and become familiar with the nonprofit industry.

Ryan: The job I have today was the direct result of my internship with St. Jude Children's Research Hospital. Had I not interned with St. Jude (an internship I found because of an extracurricular organization) I would have never realized my passion for nonprofit work, especially in the health charity realm.

Seth: I interned at a start-up marketing and promotions company and learned a lot about the challenges of a start-up and the effects it has on the entire staff. I was unpaid, the company had little money, and thus they didn't have much leverage, resources, or a large staff. I also learned about the value of working hard and being loyal. I eventually became paid and know that they would hire me back in a heartbeat because of the work I did for them and the value I added to the company. Today I use that experience knowing that if I work hard and produce quality work it will get noticed and appreciated. I was also president of the ultimate Frisbee team and handled all the logistical aspects of the team (and played on it). I actually learned how to better use Excel as a result of it—which helps me today. It also helped me organize things and learn basic budgeting and time management skills.

Todd: Work at a public relations firm helped introduce me to an office environment.

How did you decide which field, either in academia or the real world, to go into?

Ben: I chose to pursue photography, simply because I love it. I did not know how I would make money, but I knew I would work it out.

Ramatu: Through internships I learned that I enjoyed nonprofit work. Through more nonprofit work and starting my own organization, I learned that I wanted to work for nonprofits that focused on issues of gender and feminism.

Ryan: Working in the nonprofit cancer-related world was a direct result of an internship I had in school. I spent two and a half years after college with the organization that I interned with, and today I work for the American Cancer Society spreading preventive health information to worksites throughout the Philadelphia area.

Seth: I knew I wanted to go into business, but not the number-crunching side (I don't like math), so basically the thinking side of business, which is marketing (among other areas).

Todd: Combination of skills and interesting work and location.

Did you have a mentor when you entered the workforce/graduate school?

Ben: My first boss served as my mentor in a way. We had a good personal relationship, and he taught me a lot about the business. He definitely sped up the learning curve a lot.

Ramatu: Yes. My mentor was a professor whom I had in my junior year of college. He has been a great resource and friend.

Ryan: My first boss played the biggest role in my professional development. After hiring me, he took me under his wing and showed me the ins and outs of fund-raising for a major nonprofit. He truly fostered my nonprofit business savvy, and I find that I continue to learn new elements of this field each day because of what he showed me.

Seth: No.

Todd: Yes.

What is the number-one bit of advice you wish you were given before you entered the job market?

Ben: Only go for jobs that you really want. If you go for jobs you don't want, the employers will see it written on your face, and you will not get them anyways. Even if you do get them, you will not be happy. So do what you love.

Ramatu: Before getting into the job market, look to get experience any way that you can (i.e., volunteer, intern, start your own [business]). Also, interview your prospective employers just as they are interviewing you. You will spend most of your waking hours there. Make sure it's where you want to be.

Ryan: Be patient. Sometimes the hiring process can take months, especially at larger companies.

Seth: It will take longer than you think—and even though you will get discouraged, something will come along.

Todd: You have to put up with 18–36 months of crap before you really get some autonomy.

What were your job-related expectations when you were still in school, and how did they match up with your experience of the "real world?"

Ben: I was pretty idealistic in school. Once I did some internships, I realized that I hated the day-to-day reality of my planned career choice. In the real world, economics is everything. So, you have to find a way to do what you love *and* make good money doing it.

Ramatu: I expected to get the job I wanted right out of school. Your ideal job often doesn't come until at least five years after you graduate because you have to pay dues. Often, your first job is grunt work. Don't get discouraged. The learning doesn't end when you graduate college.

Ryan: I expected to find a professional position that allowed me to continue to grow and develop my skills and knowledge base. That's exactly what I've found in my two jobs since graduating.

Seth: I expected there to be lots of marketing jobs available—the ones where you sit in meetings and think of new ways to market a product or brand. I found out that most marketing jobs aren't really like that, and thus, not too many exist. I also learned that some marketing jobs, in fact many marketing jobs, are also sales jobs. I also expected that I would be making more than I am.

Todd: I thought I would have more responsibility sooner than I did, but once I got there, it was great.

What was your first job out of college? How did you find that job?

Ben: I was a freelance photographer, and had a part-time job at a photo studio. The pay was not high, and I worked a ton, but I learned a lot about the business, and I had a lot of fun.

Ramatu: When I was a senior in college I started a girls' organization in DC and ran that program for two years after college. I eventually partnered with a campus organization that incubated my organization for a year. In exchange, I did some work for them.

Ryan: My immediate first job was a temporary position working as the interim marketing manager at a boutique hotel. I was recommended to the owner of the hotel by his brother whom I interviewed with at another company. I took that position for a few months while I waited to hear back from St. Jude, where I ultimately went to work for two and a half years after school.

Seth: The one I am at now, a direct marketing assistant at UCLA Extension School. I found it via Craig's List.

Todd: I was an account executive at a public relations agency; I had interned there for 18 months prior to graduation.

If you went straight into the workforce after receiving your bachelor's degree, do you wish you had attended graduate school first? If you went on to grad school, do you wish you had worked first? In either case, why?

Ben: I am glad I went straight in with my BA. I want to get a MA someday, but I want to be really serious when I go back. I think that anyone who goes straight for their master's may be missing a lot of real-world experience, and may end up in a career that doesn't actually suit them well.

Ramatu: I believe very strongly that no one (with a few exceptions like law and medical school) should go on to graduate school immediately after receiving a BA. You do yourself such a disservice. There is often a stark contrast between the "real world" and academia that you can't know how your degree will translate in the work force. Adding more debt and a graduate degree on top of something you may find out later you don't want to do can be very limiting and discouraging. Had I gone to graduate school immediately after earning a BA, my career would have gone down a completely different path, and I may not have been happy with the result.

Ryan: I went straight into the work force, and I wouldn't change that for anything. I wanted to make sure my field was for me by getting professional hands-on experience before I attended grad school.

Seth: I don't wish I attended graduate school, because if I do go back to school it will be for my MBA, and I need to get some work experience before that.

Todd: I am in grad school now, and I worked for six years before I went back. People should definitely work before they go back; it's a waste of money and time to go back and have no reference for the real world (unless you want to be in academia forever).

What is the best piece of advice you've received from a colleague?

Ben: Always conduct yourself with absolute, unbending integrity. It is the only thing we have.

Ramatu: Think about your title. The pay is important, but the titles on your resume tell a story about your career and can mean better pay in the immediate future. If you have to take less money, you may be able to negotiate a title that you can leverage for more money in your next job.

Ryan: Be friendly, and be sure to impress your boss' boss with your work ethic at least once a quarter.

Seth: It's all about relationships so get to know people—you never know when it will help you. Be persistent.

Todd: Think twice, and speak once.

What is the smartest move you've made since receiving your bachelor's degree?

Ben: Realizing when my current job was starting to become stale, and making the decision to move on. My new job as a U.S. diplomat will be even more challenging and rewarding.

Ramatu: Learning Spanish as a Peace Corps Volunteer. Second smartest: Waiting to attend graduate school.

Ryan: Being flexible about where I lived. In my first professional position I was asked to move to Memphis, Tennessee. I was a kid from the Northeast who knew absolutely no one in Memphis. But I learned a lot about myself and put myself in a position to move back home after a year and a half to open a new office for my company. Opening an office for a major national organization is not a skill many 23-year-olds can say they have. I find that it definitely sets me apart from many of my peers.

Seth: Getting a job at the UCLA Extension School.

Todd: When I was unhappy in a job, I made a proactive move quickly rather than waiting too long to languish.

Describe your current job and its major responsibilities.

Ben: Until my new job starts in 6 months or so, I am a self-employed photographer. I am responsible for every aspect of my one-man business, including marketing, client relations, information archiving, and product delivery.

Ramatu: Currently, I am a graduate student in international educational development at Teachers College Columbia University. Prior to that, I ran the Training and Outreach department for an organization that advocates and provided services to sexually exploited and trafficked youth.

Ryan: In my current job I work for the American Cancer Society as a Preventive Health Specialist. My position is one part wellness program salesman and one part health information advocate. There is no typical day, but most of what I do revolves around working with companies to initiate wellness and chronic-disease-prevention programs at their places of business.

Seth: I am the direct marketing assistant for the marketing and communications department of the UCLA Extension School. My job entails many things; in essence I have a hand in a little of everything (except for the creative aspect): e-blasts, direct mailings, market research, and market list research.

Todd: Prior to graduate school, I was the manager of public relations and investor relations at a small cap-software company. I was responsible for executing investor relations strategy, which included serving as company spokesperson to sell-side analysts and investors, press, industry analysts and employees. I conducted competitive financial analyses and evaluation of investor models. I provided guidance to senior management and board of directors on investor sentiment. I managed crisis communication dealing with FTC and SEC investigations, audit committee investigation of foreign accounting procedures, and delisting from the NYSE. I established and implemented industry analyst and employee relations programs. Finally, I was responsible for speechwriting and presentations for executive staff.

What experience was required for your current role?

Ben: I took photos for four years in college.

Ramatu: Adult education training, supervisory experience, grant-writing experience, and experience seeking funding.

Ryan: My background in the nonprofit world and my ability to present information in a clear, concise manner. People dread public-speaking classes, but a person can truly turn them into a career.

Seth: Dealing with other people, problem-solving skills, computer skills, Microsoft Office, common sense, [and] basic research skills.

Todd: Public relations and corporate communications experience.

To what extent has your communications degree helped you in your current role?

Ben: It has mainly helped me understand how different forms of advertising and mass media work. Aside from that, it taught me how to think critically, which is crucial in life in general.

Ramatu: I do a lot of writing. Also, I have to figure out ways to adapt the message of my organization to several different audiences.

Ryan: Well, beyond the obvious "it was required to get the job," my BA really helped sharpen my critical thinking skills and my ability to write.

Seth: It really hasn't. The things I learned for my degree were, on the whole, very theoretical, and not practical.

Todd: A good springboard for the writing and research skills.

What do you like most about your current role?

Ben: I have absolute power and flexibility. If I want to go on a vacation for two months, I need only ask myself. The money is pretty good as well.

Ramatu: I love being a student again. I also feel passionate about issues of gender-based violence and love that my work allows me to fight the good fight everyday.

Ryan: N/R.

Seth: The laid-back academic environment—not tight and corporate. I'm learning about different things each day. (Example: I did extensive research on a new search engine for the website and new e-mail campaign software.) I receive free training in computer applications like Microsoft Access.

Todd: Being a resource and spokesperson.

What aspect(s) of your current role do you not like?

Ben: I am often working alone at home, which can be a bit alienating at times. Also, since I am the only employee, there is nobody else I can give work to if I don't want to do it.

Ramatu: Office politics.

Ryan: N/R.

Seth: It can be repetitive. Sometimes I have very little to do, and it's boring (could be a by-product of my being fairly new to the job).

Todd: Being the first line of defense in bad times is tough.

What skills have you had to acquire that your communications degree did not help you cultivate?

Ben: I have had to develop my people skills, specifically interacting with people from widely varying backgrounds. I also had to learn all the practical aspects of the business, as my degree was mostly grounded in theory.

Ramatu: Curriculum development/instruction, design training, and adult learning.

Ryan: A bachelor's degree doesn't give you the know-how to get hired. While I had a great Career Services department at my alma mater, no class ever taught me how to interview.

Seth: Access skills (I received training though). I haven't really had to acquire any new skills, but rather learned new things that pertained to the job that no degree would have really taught.

Todd: Financial analysis and understanding of the public markets.

What suggestions would you have for those still in college? Are there any "optional" elements of the undergraduate experience that you would recommend they explore?

Ben: Take your time in college. It really is one of the best times of your life. I graduated in three and a half years, but would have taken longer if I could do it again. Also, get to know your professors; they are really smart people, and one hour a week with each one can start friendships that will be beneficial to you in the future.

Ramatu: Internships, internships, internships. Use internships to explore your professional interests. You can save a lot of time if you can get some sense of where you would like to be professionally before you graduate.

Ryan: I always recommend taking a leadership role in a major student organization. Having leadership experience before you leave college will help improve your odds of getting a job befitting of your desires and skills.

Seth: I recommend learning another language—the learning process in college is completely different than in high school. If I practiced more I would be very good in Spanish because of what I learned in college. Do extracurricular activities—whatever floats your boat—it allows you to meet people and do things you wouldn't otherwise do. Explore the area your school is in; you may find it's pretty interesting and that life isn't just confined in the few streets around the school.

Todd: Take as many classes as you can.

Do you have any tips for those entering the workforce/graduate school now?

Ben: Theory is important, but so is practice. If you are sure you are interested in one field, look for internships or other ways to get involved, and get some practical experience under your belt.

Ramatu: Take advantage of the multidisciplinary nature of liberal arts degrees to learn a little bit about everything. Graduate schools and employers are looking for more skills than they put in the job description. You never know when your extra knowledge may come in handy.

Ryan: Find the job you want and go after it with gusto. Be proactive without being pushy. You are the only one looking out for your best interests when it comes to your career, so show potential employers why you are better than all the other candidates.

Seth: Be persistent when looking for a job. It may be easy, but it may also take a while.

Todd: Try to get a consulting job or another job where you can get a good broad exposure to lots of different businesses.

What is the best way to get a job in your field?

Ben: Write a business plan, have a solid knowledge of your equipment and your competition. Make a lot of calls and do a ton of advertising.

Ramatu: Start in small organizations where you can get a lot of experience very quickly. Keep an eye out for new opportunities.

Ryan: Volunteer for the nonprofit that you want to work for. If you impress the staff member you work with there, you have an automatic advocate on the inside.

Seth: I think that I'm beginning to realize that in my field it's all about the connections you have and who knows whom. If you can get recommendations, it's always easier than a cold application.

Todd: Get a job at a big consulting or services firm.

What mistake do communications grads often make?

Ben: Thinking that their degree is worth anything. Most employers know it is a very easy major, so you need to have other experience to show that you actually can do the job for them.

Ramatu: Not paying attention to what story their resume tells. When you take a job or leave a job, make sure that the title and your tenure at the organization say what you want it to say. Moving around too much makes you look unreliable. Staying too long in the same position makes you look unambitious and limited in your skills.

Ryan: As a person who hires employees, the biggest mistake I see is when a communications major doesn't specify what exactly they studied. Communications is an incredibly broad field, and you need to be able to tell a potential employer, "I studied public relations and public communication" or "I focused my efforts in the area of marketing and media studies." They need to know your skill set in order to make the best match.

Seth: I can't speak for all grads, but I know that I underestimated the job market and the ability to find a job.

Todd: Not having any quantitative skills, even if you don't have a financial or quantitative job, it helps to understand finance and the markets.

What is something that you think more communications grads should do to advance their careers?

Ben: Read industry magazines to spot current trends. Know the main players in the industry and the roles that they play. Always network, network, network.

Ramatu: If you work in nonprofits you'll need to be familiar with grant-writing. I hate it, but there is no way around it, and it's a great selling point for employers.

Ryan: Take advantage of internship opportunities. Communications is such a broad field of study that there are many types of internships available no matter where the school is located or how big the student population.

Seth: Learn about the field and get some kind of experience in the field. The experience will set candidates apart. And show that you are eager to learn new things.

Todd: Get in every day 30 or 60 minutes early and *read*. To get ahead, it helps to be the most knowledgeable.

Who is in the best position to offer a communications graduate help with his or her resume and cover letter?

Ben: Someone who has already been in the workforce for at least five years—ideally in the industry you want to get into.

Ramatu: This is where having a mentor in your field is very useful. Every field has its own conventions for resumes. You'll need to learn what is expected for your field. Also, I have asked interviewers for feedback on my interview and resume at the end of an interview. This isn't always appropriate, so use your best judgment.

Ryan: That's tough. I think it really depends on what subfield of communications you choose to go into. Communications is an expansive field of study that ultimately encompasses hundreds of different concentrations. I would suggest asking someone who works in the area you wish to get involved in to take a look at your resume.

Seth: Career counselors. Oftentimes your parents or family know people who are in the fields you are looking to go into whom you had no idea even existed; have them look at your resume and cover letters and let them give you advice. Sometimes they are/have been in a position where they actually do hiring and know what to look for and what they would look for.

Todd: Friends.

What pitfalls should graduates avoid when applying to and interviewing for positions?

Ben: Don't "play to the crowd." Be yourself and let it show. Know who you are, and let them know what you stand for and what you can do. Don't under-dress for interviews. Don't send out shotgun applications; personalize each one as much as possible.

Ramatu: Avoid not tailoring your cover letter to the position. Grammar and spelling mistakes.

Ryan: Remember that communications is a fairly new field of study and what is studied at each school is different. It's not like better-established fields such as biology or psychology. People have heard of communications, but I think many would be hard-pressed to give you a solid definition of the field. Define it for them to ensure that a potential employer knows your academic background.

Seth: Giving up. Keep going until you get a "no"—even if it's with more than one company. Apply to anything that looks like it may be interesting—you never know what will happen. The job I have now I almost didn't follow-up on. Granted they may have still gotten back to me, but my persistence may have paid off.

Todd: Don't just look for the trophy jobs at big firms, look around and be willing to work at smaller firms where you can get better experience.

GOOD LUCK!

Jobs and Internship Resources

ALTERNATIVE TEACHING CREDENTIALING PROGRAMS

NYC Teaching Fellows

If you have not been certified to teach and hold a bachelor's degree, you have the opportunity to become a teaching fellow for a variety of schools located in New York City.

www.nyctf.org/prospective/mayteach.html

Project Pipeline

A two-year program designed to prepare college grads to teach in the classroom. Different programs for elementary and secondary teachers available.

www.projectpipeline.org

Public Allies

Opportunity to become a Public Allies Fellow or to apply for the alternative licensure program, which will give you a three-year provisional license.

www.publicallies.org

Teach For America

Teachers will be provided with a paid salary plus education reward. A two-year teaching commitment is required.

www.teachforamerica.org

EDUCATION JOB LISTING SITES

Agent K–12 jobs for teachers and administrators

www.agentk-12.org

EdWeek Job Postings

http://edweek.org/ew

Jobs in Higher Education

www.academic360.com

LAW JOB LISTING SITES

Findlaw

A website providing resources on the Internet for legal professionals and students, including job listings.

http://careers.findlaw.com

Law Employment Center

www.lawjobs.com

Lawyers Weekly Jobs.com

Paralegal positions searchable by state and by legal specialties.

www.lawyersweeklyjobs.com

MEDIA AND COMMUNICATIONS JOB LISTING SITES

American Copy Editors Society's Job Bank

www.copydesk.org/jobbank.htm

Bookjobs.com

Jobs within the book publishing industry.

www.bookjobs.com

Creative Hotlist

www.creativehotlist.com

Detroit Free Press

Links to journalism job banks and job-hunting advice for those interested in newspaper careers.

www.freep.com

Job Link

Print and broadcast listings including reporting/writing/editing, research, photography and design.

http://newslink.org/joblink.html

Journalism Jobs

TV, radio, and newspaper jobs and internships.

www.journalismjobs.com

The Write Jobs

Writing jobs including journalism, editing, staff writing positions, technical writing, freelance.

www.writejobs.com

NONPROFIT JOB LISTING SITES

Foundation for Sustainable Development

www.fsdinternational.org

Idealist.org

A project of Action without Borders, Idealist offers a global clearinghouse of nonprofit resources, including jobs, internships, mailing lists, and nonprofit resources by state and country.

www.idealist.org

InterAction

Coalition of U.S.-based international development and humanitarian ongovernmental organizations.

www.interaction.org

Opportunity Knocks

www.opportunitynocs.org

Union Jobs Clearinghouse

Staffing and trades positions in organized labor searchable by state and by union name.

www.unionjobs.com/staff.html

Fellowships, Scholarships, and Loans

Amy Lowell Poetry Traveling Scholarship Fund

Amount: $47,000

Overview: The scholarship is awarded to a poet of American birth who is prepared to spend one year outside of the continent of North America in a place that the recipient determines will advance his or her poetry. Open to college students, graduate students, and postgraduates.

F. Davis Dassouri, Esq.

Choate, Hall & Stewart

Two International Place

Boston, MA 02110

E-mail: amylowell@choate.com

Tel: Cathleen S. Croft, Trust Administrator   617-248-4855

Website: www.amylowell.org

National Endowment for the Arts Literature Fellowships: Creative Writing

Amount: $20,000

Overview: These fellowships are for published authors of prose (fiction or creative nonfiction) or poetry who show exceptional talent. The sum of the fellowship allows the author time to research, write, and travel.

1100 Pennsylvania Avenue Northwest

Washington, DC 20506

E-mail: webmgr@arts.endow.gov

Tel: 202-682-5400

Website: www.nea.gov/grants/apply/Lit/index.html

Film and Fiction Scholarship

Amount: $10,000

Overview: This scholarship is open to students who intend to pursue an MFA in film or creative writing and who will embrace liberal ideas and their role in contemporary society.

Institute for Humane Studies George Mason University

3401 North Fairfax Drive, Suite 440

Arlington, VA 22201-4432

Tel: 800-697-8799

Website: www.theihs.org/scholarships/id.783/default.asp

JOURNALISM

American Prospect Writing Fellows Program

Amount: $20,000

Overview: This program offers young journalists two full years of employ-ment at the American Prospect, during which time they are expected to pro-duce three to four full-length articles as well as some short pieces. They are also expected to provide general editorial support. Fellows also receive a stipend for living expenses.

Writing Fellows Program

The American Prospect

2000 L Street Northwest, Suite 717

Washington, DC 20036

E-mail: epressley@prospect.org

Tel: 888-MUST-READ

Website: www.prospect.org/web/page.ww?section=root&name=Writing +Fellowships

Asian American Journalists Association Scholarships

Amount: $2,000–$25,000

Overview: These scholarships are awarded on the basis of financial need, and the student's demonstrated commitment to journalism as well as sensi-tivity to the issues of Asian American and Pacific Islanders. There are a wide variety of scholarships available.

1182 Market Street, Suite 320

San Francisco, CA 94102

Tel: Kimberly A. Mizuhara, Student Programs Coordinator 415-346-2051 ext. 102

E-mail: programs@aaja.org

Website: www.aaja.org/programs/for_students/scholarships

Associated Press Television Radio Association Journalism Scholarships

Amount: $1,500

Overview: These scholarships are for currently enrolled California, Nevada, or Hawaii college students who are pursuing careers in broadcast journalism.

Roberta Gonzales

CBS 5 TV

855 Battery Street

San Francisco, CA 94111

Tel: 408-297-8780

Website: www.aptra.org

Felix Morley Journalism Competition

Amount: $250–$2,500

Overview: Awards are given to young writers who enter the best published newspaper or magazine articles inspired by the theme of liberty.

Institute for Humane Studies George Mason University

3301 North Fairfax Drive, Suite 440

Arlington, VA 22201-4432

Tel: 800-697-8799

Website: www.theihs.org/grants_and_contest/id.70/default.asp

International Radio and Television Society Foundation Summer Fellowship Program

Overview: Fellows participate in a nine-week all-expenses-paid program during which they are exposed to various forms of media, take related field trips, and attend industry events. Career-planning advice is also included.

IRTS Foundation, Inc.

420 Lexington Avenue, Suite 1601

New York, NY 10170

Tel: 212-867-6650

Website: www.irts.org/programs/sfp/sfp.html

Inter-American Press Association Scholarship

Amount: $20,000

> Overview: This scholarship supports young journalists or journalism school graduates (ages 21–35) who are interested in studying and reporting abroad in Latin America or the Caribbean. Applicants must have an excellent grasp of the language in which they plan to report.
>
> IAPA Scholarship Fund
>
> 1801 Southwest Third Avenue
>
> Miami, FL 33129
>
> Tel: 305-376-3522
>
> Website: www.sipiapa.com/otheractivities/scholarships.cfm

National Association of Black Journalists Scholarship

Amount: $2,500

> Overview: Scholarships for students interested in pursuing a career in journalism. Each year, NABJ awards more than $30,000 in NABJ scholarships. Open to any foreign or American-born student currently attending an accredited 4-year college/university in the United States or those who are candidates for graduate school.
>
> 8701-A Adelphi Road
>
> Adelphi, MD 20783
>
> E-mail: iwashington@nabj.org
>
> Tel: Irving Washington, Program Coordinator 301-445-7100 ext. 108
>
> Website: www.nabj.org/programs/scholarships/index.html

National Iranian-American Council Public Service and Journalism Fellowship Program

Amount: $1,500

Overview: Eligible college juniors, seniors, and graduate students who are U.S. citizens or legal permanent residents of Iranian descent are eligible to apply. Fellows will attend committee hearings; work on special projects; research legislation; and engage in other activities that promote firsthand knowledge of the American legislative process.

NIAC c/o OAI

2801 M Street Northwest

Washington, DC 20007

E-mail: Trita Parsi, tparsi@niacouncil.org

Tel: 207-719-8071

Website: www.niacouncil.org/index.php?option=com_content&task=view &id=328&Itemid=2

Pulliam Journalism Fellowship

Amount: $6,500

Overview: Fellowships are for college juniors, seniors, and graduate students enrolled in a related degree program. Previous newspaper internships and/or experience on a college newspaper are preferred. Applicants must demonstrate that they are committed to a career in newspaper journalism. Pulliam Fellows earn $650/week for the 10-week program and also get to participate in writing workshops.

Pulliam Fellowship Director

The Indianapolis Star

PO Box 145

Indianapolis, IN 46206-0145

Tel: 317-444-6001

Website: www2.indystar.com/help/jobs/pjf/experience.html or www2.indystar.com/pjf/

LAW

ABA Legal Opportunity Scholarship Fund

Amount: $5,000–$15,000

Overview: Scholarships for ethnic minority students consisting of $5,000 of financial assistance awarded annually to each scholarship recipient attending an ABA-accredited law school.

Office of the President

American Bar Association

321 North Clark Street

Chicago, IL 60610-4714

Tel: 312-788-5137

Website: www.abanet.org/fje/losfpage.html

ABA Minority Fellowships in Environmental Law

Amount: $5,000

Overview: The ABA Minority Fellowships in Environmental Law program is designed for minority law students who wish to study and pursue careers in environmental law. The fellowships are open to first and second-year law students and third-year night students.

American Bar Association

321 North Clark Street

Chicago, IL 60610

Tel: 312-988-5602

E-mail: environ@abanet.org

Website: www.abanet.org/environ/committees/lawstudents

Skadden Fellowship Foundation

Amount: $46,000

Overview: These fellowships are geared toward graduating law students who wish to devote their professional lives to providing legal services to the poor, elderly, homeless, disabled, and those deprived of their civil or human rights. The fellowships are designed to give fellows the time to pursue their own projects at public interest organizations.

Susan Butler Plum, Director

Skadden, Arps, Slate, Meagher & Flom

Four Times Square, Room 29-218

New York, NY 10036

Tel: 212-735-2956

Fax: 212-795-2000

Website: www.skaddenfellowships.org

Janet D. Steiger Fellowship Project

Amount: $5,000

Overview: An eight-week summer fellowship program open to all first- and second-year law students throughout the United States. The project is intended to provide unique training opportunities to law students who may wish to consider public service as a profession.

ABA Section of Antitrust Law

321 North Clark,

Chicago, IL 60611

E-mail: douglasd@staff.abanet.org

Tel: 312-988-5606

Fax: 312-988-5637

Website: www.abanet.org/antitrust

NATIONAL FELLOWSHIPS

The Harry S. Truman Scholarship Foundation
712 Jackson Place, NW
Washington, DC 20006
E-mail: office@truman.gov
Tel: 202-395-4831
Fax: 202-395-6995
Website: www.truman.gov

The John D. and Catherine T. MacArthur Foundation
140 South Dearborn Street
Chicago, IL 60603-5285
E-mail: 4answers@macfound.org
Tel: 312-726-8000
Website: www.macfound.org

Office of the American Secretary, The Rhodes Trust
Elliot F. Gerson
8229 Boone Boulevard, Suite 240
Vienna, VA 22182
E-mail: amsec@rhodesscholar.org
Website: www.rhodesscholar.org

LOAN SOURCES FOR GRADUATE AND PROFESSIONAL STUDENTS

Stafford Loan (Federal):

This is a type of federal loan with a maximum debt limit of $138,000 dollars. The amount you can borrow is based on your year in school and your status as a student (for example, independent students can qualify for bigger loans, as they are solely absorbing the cost of living expenses and tuition). Also, a student must be enrolled at least half-time in a graduate program. A subsidized version of this loan is available for those with financial need, meaning that you will not be charged interest until the time of repayment. Unsubsidized loans, which are available to all eligible students, require interest payments from the time that the loan is disbursed until it has been repaid. For more information, visit StaffordLoan.com.

Graduate Plus Loan (Federal):

A new federal loan program, the GradPLUS Loan, is a low-interest, federally backed student loan guaranteed by the U.S. Government. Like its undergraduate counterpart, the Grad PLUS Loan can be used to pay for the total cost of education less any aid you've already been awarded. Also, like the undergraduate version, eligibility for the Graduate PLUS Loan is largely dependent on the borrower's credit rating and history, as opposed to the purely financial need-based Stafford Loan Program.

Federal Work-Study:

This program provides funding for students to work part-time during the school year and full-time during the summers. Most students work directly on campus, but some also work for nonprofit agencies. Not all graduate schools participate in this program (this is mainly due to the fact that many schools require that students are enrolled full-time). To find out which schools participate in the work-study program, visit each school's financial aid website, and read more about FWS at the Federal Work-Study website: Ed.gov/programs/fws/index.html.

APPENDIX III

Useful Web Resources

CREATIVE WRITING

The Association of Writer's and Writing Programs

George Mason University, MS 1E3

Fairfax, VA 22030-4444

Tel: 703-993-4301

Website: www.awpwriter.org

This organization has an excellent website with information on writing conferences, a career center with academic position postings, an organization magazine, a bookstore from which you can purchase the AWP's official guide to writing programs, forums, and contests.

The Academy of American Poets

584 Broadway, Suite 604

New York, NY 10012-5243

Tel: 212-274-0343

Website: www.poets.org

This website has a terrific search tool that allows you to find the work of many poets. Excellent information for those who plan on teaching poetry (information on lesson plans, good poems to teach to students of different ages).You can also keep track of your favorite poets as they tour the country and attend their next reading. You can join a discussion forum and read tips on writing and publishing.

The Asian American Writer's Workshop

16 West Thirty-second Street, Suite 10A

New York, NY 10001

Tel: 212-494-0061

Fax: 212-494-0062

Website: www.aaww.org

For a very reasonable student membership fee, you'll receive discounts to AAWW workshops, free or cheap admission to events, discounts on books, the ability to access special organization fellowships, and a copy of their literary journal.

The Hurston/Wright Foundation

6525 Belcrest Road, Suite 531

Hyattsville, MD 20721

Tel: 301-683-2134

Fax: 301-277-1262

E-mail: info@hurstonwright.org

Website: www.hurston-wright.org

This organization is dedicated to discovering, cultivating, and honoring black writers. HWF offers workshops about finding editors and literary agents, managing timelines, and turning fear into motivation. As a member, you'll also have access to special events featuring illustrious black authors as well as emerging talent. The organization also offers numerous awards.

The MFA Weblog

http://creative-writing-mfa-handbook.blogspot.com

This blog is run by Tom Kealey, a graduate of the University of Massachusetts at Amherst's creative writing program, and author of numerous short stories. He is also the author of *The Creative Writing MFA Handbook*. It provides tons of valuable advice, including information on funding for different programs and letters of recommendation.

COMMUNICATIONS, PUBLIC RELATIONS, MARKETING, AND ADVERTISING

The American Marketing Association

311 South Wacker Drive, Suite 5800

Chicago, IL 60606

Tel: 800-AMA-1150

Fax: 312-542-9001

Website: www.marketingpower.com

This professional association offers resources for undergraduate and graduate marketing students including information about the marketing PhD and the academic job search, an excellent "Who Went Where" section on the placement of new assistant professors in marketing, as well as PhD grants and awards and information on international marketing careers.

National Communications Association

1765 N Street, Northwest

Washington, DC 20036

Tel: 202-464-4622

Fax: 202-464-4600

Website: www.natcom.org

Offers a communications doctoral program database where you can search by state and specialization (interpersonal communication, public relations, health communication). There's also a section on graduate degree statistics and trends and a doctoral programs reputational study.

JOURNALISM

News Reporting Simulation from Columbia University

http://ccnmtl.columbia.edu/projects/newssim/introduction.html

The Center for New Media at the Columbia University School of Journalism offers this very useful reporting simulation. You'll be able to play the role of a reporter who is assigned to cover a local fire, facing the typical challenges associated with news reporting assignments. In the end you are able to write and file your own news story.

The Project for Excellence in Journalism and the Committee of Concerned Journalists

1615 L Street, Northwest, Suite 700

Washington, DC 20036

Tel: 202-419-3650

Fax: 202-419-3699

E-mail: mail@journalism.org

Website: www.journalism.org

This organization is devoted to providing research, resources and ideas to improve journalism. The tools for students include a list of all accredited journalism schools by state as well as numerous articles on how to interact with media professionals, understanding the media, and a job links section.

The Society of Professional Journalists

Eugene S. Pulliam National Journalism Center

3909 North Meridian Street

Indianapolis, IN 46208

Tel: 317-927-8000

Fax: 317-920-4789

Website: www.spj.org

An organization devoted to the free practice of journalism and promoting high standards of ethical behavior. The comprehensive website includes detailed information for graduate students about internships, fellowships, and scholarships. There's also a small but excellent repository of articles for those who are considering attending journalism school.

LAW

American Bar Association

321 North Clark Street

Chicago, IL 60610

Tel: 800-285-2221

Website: www.abanet.org

Although most of the information on the ABA website is geared toward practicing attorneys, pre-law students can benefit from staying up to date on the latest trends in the profession. The website includes information about every kind of law specialization, and discusses hot topics in law, such as promoting diversity and ethical standards. There are also links to a variety of other useful sites. There's also a list of ABA-approved schools and information on the bar examination.

Law School Admission Council

www.lsac.org

This megasite is a comprehensive hub for all pre-law hopefuls. Download registration materials for the LSDAS and the LSAT and browse information about financial aid and opportunities for underrepresented students.

National Association for Legal Career Professionals
1025 Connecticut Avenue Northwest, Suite 1110

Washington, DC 20036

Tel: 202-835-1001

Fax: 202-835-1112

E-mail: info@nalp.org

Website: www.nalp.org

This website has useful articles about the job market for new graduates, a directory of legal employers, and up-to-date information about law career fairs. There is also an excellent contact list for GLBT students including national and student organizations.

Internet Legal Research Group
www.ilrg.com

This website offers links to hundreds of other law-related websites including an archive of law school course outlines, legal form sources, and legal associations.

Law School Discussion
www.lawschooldiscussion.org/prelaw

Students can post their questions on everything from issues for underrepresented applicants, to taking the LSAT, to choosing schools. This site also connects students to with some of the most useful pre-law blogs on the Internet.

MEDICAL SCHOOL

The American Association of Medical Colleges
2450 N Street, Northwest

Washington, DC 20037-1126

Tel: 202-828-0400

Fax: 202-828-1125

Website: www.aamc.org

Megasite with links to the MCAT and AMCAS. The site has information on how to register for tests and download guidelines for your application, and it features a job center, a "focus on issues" section which discusses hot topics in medicine (very useful information for medical school interviews), a link to medical school admissions requirements and general information about applying to medical schools. The section on "Considering a Career in Medicine" walks you through some of the realities of practicing medicine. Those who are interested in a postbaccalaureate program will find the list of programs and specializations useful. There's also a hotline for applicants who need advice on sticky application-related questions.

The American Medical Association
515 North State Street

Chicago, IL 60610

Tel: 800-621-8335

Website: www.ama-assn.org

The website provides information on the climate of medicine, the career outlook for medical practitioners, and future trends in medicine.

The Student Doctor Network
www.studentdoctor.net

Not just for medical students, this nonprofit charitable organization is dedicated to providing an information forum for premed students. There are med school blogs, an MCAT forum, and interview feedback. There are also plenty of links to other helpful premed websites.

Medical School Ready
www.medschoolready.com

A partner site of the Student Doctor Network, Medical School Ready walks you through the application basics, and it also connects you with current medical students via blogs and chat rooms. You can read medical student profiles that include interviews about how each student got into medical school and get their take on the application process.

FINDING THE FUNDS

What you should know about paying for your graduate school education

Furthering your education is an investment in your future. Laying down $120,000 — probably more — in exchange for a top-notch graduate school education requires just as much research and planning as deciding which school you'll hand that money over to.

The good news is that you still have a little time before you have to really worry about signing on the dotted line for any type of financial assistance. That gives you some time to research options, to properly calculate the actual costs of going to graduate school beyond just the sticker price, and to create a plan so that your potential future earnings cover your costs of living when you're out of school and using that degree you will have worked so hard for.

You're going to be responsible for the choices you make. Cutting your ancillary expenses for the next few years and building up an out-of-pocket school fund before you ever register for that first class might save you thousands of dollars in interest payments down the road. But how will you know if you don't come up with a plan?

No doubt you've accumulated some sort of credit history, most likely through undergrad student loans and/or some high-interest credit card debt, so you might think you have it all figured out when it comes to paying for graduate school. While you might understand the basics about how federal loans work and how scholarships, grants, and fellowships can help to cut down the final bill, there are lesser-known and fairly new options out there that can make your postgraduate life a little easier to enjoy.

OTHER PEOPLE'S MONEY

Scholarships and Grants

These are the best form of financial aid because they don't have to be paid back. Remember, though, that most scholarships require a minimum GPA and that some grants are good for only one year. When evaluating your payment options, make sure there is a reasonable expectation that the financial aid package being offered will be available for the full term of the degree requirement or that you have a way of managing funds if they are not enough.

Fellowships and Stipends

Fellowships come in many different forms. Sometimes partial tuition scholarships are called fellowships. These university-sponsored fellowships consist of a cash award that is promptly subtracted from your tuition bill. You can earn the amount of the award by teaching for a department or by completing research for a faculty member. The percentage of students who receive this type of fellowship and the amount paid to each will vary depending on the intended degree and field, enrollment status (full- or part-time), and years of enrollment.

It is important to note that survival on a fellowship alone is unlikely. Fellowships are taxable income—federal, state, county, and city—and you may be expected to pay for school fees, supplies, and books out of your fellowship, as well as tuition. If the fellowship doesn't cover the full cost of your attendance, you'll have to explore other financing options.

Employer-financed Opportunities

Some employers will offer a tuition reimbursement or a limited financial sum for employees to attend graduate school part time. Employers expect the advanced degree to enhance your performance on the job or to make you eligible for a different job within the company. Be sure you understand all aspects of your employer's tuition reimbursement program before you sign on and be prepared to meet any commitments expected of you.

LOANS

When scholarships, grants, and fellowships don't cover the full cost of attendance, many students take out loans to help out with the rest.

The government only lends money directly to you under the Federal Direct Loan Program. Lenders provide loans guaranteed by the federal government in the Federal Family Education Loan Program.

Avoid loans if you can. A loan can best be described as renting money. There's a cost and it may not be an easy cost to bear.

Here's an interesting anecdote. Many students graduate without knowing what types of loans they received, who the lender was and how much they owe. The first time many students become aware of the scope of their obligation is when they receive their first bill—six months after graduation.

This is often because students are passive participants in the financial aid process and do not educate themselves or ask questions. Most students receive a list of "preferred lenders" from their financial aid office and simply go with the lender recommended to them. Over the course of the previous year, relationships between financial aid offices and lenders have been called into question by State Attorneys General, the Department of Education, and regulators. Financial aid offices in certain cases received revenue from lenders in exchange for being placed on the "preferred lender list." Some schools have even rented out their name and logo for use on loan applications. These practices occur without disclosure to parents and students.

It is important to know that the "preferred lenders" may not offer the best deals on your loan options. While your financial aid office may be very helpful with scholarships and grants, and is legally required to perform certain duties with regard to federal loans, many do not have staff researching the lowest cost options at the time you are borrowing.

Remember that your tuition payment equals revenue for the school. When borrowing to pay tuition, you can choose to borrow from any lender. That means you can shop for the lowest rate. Keep reading. This will tell you how.

TYPES OF LOANS

The federal government and private commercial lenders offer educational loans to students. Federal loans are usually the "first resort" for borrowers because many are subsidized by the federal government and offer lower interest rates. Private loans have the advantage of fewer restrictions on borrowing limits, but may have higher interest rates and more stringent qualification criteria.

Federal Loans

There are three federal loan programs. The Federal Perkins Loan Program where your school lends you money made available by government funds, the Federal Direct Loan Program (FDLP) where the government lends its money directly to students, and the Federal Family Education Loan Program (FFELP) where financial institutions such as MyRichUncle lend their own money but the government guarantees them. While most schools participate in the Federal Perkins Program, institutions choose whether they will participate in either the FFELP or FDLP. You will borrow from FFELP or FDLP depending on which program your school has elected to participate in.

The Federal Perkins Loan is a low-interest (5%) loan for students with exceptional need. Many students who do not qualify or who may need more funds can borrow FFELP or FDLP student loans. Under both programs, the Stafford loan is the typical place to start. The Stafford loan program features a fixed interest rate and yearly caps on the maximum amount a student can borrow. Stafford loans can either be subsidized (the government pays the interest while the student is in school) or unsubsidized (the student is responsible for the interest that accrues while in school). Starting July 1, 2007, the maximum amount a student can borrow for graduate school is $20,500.

It is often assumed that the government sets the rate on student loans. The government does not set the rate of interest. It merely indicates the maximum rate lenders can charge. These lenders are free to charge less than the specified maximum rate of 6.8% for Stafford loans. There is also a maximum origination fee of up to 2% dropping to 1.5% on July 1, 2007. In some cases you may also be charged up to a 1% guarantee fee. Any fees will be taken out of your disbursement.

Historically lenders have hovered at the maximum rate because most loans were distributed via the financial aid office whereby a few lenders received most of the loans. The end result was limited competition. At 1,239 institutions, one lender received more than 90% of the number of Stafford loans in 2006.

The GradPLUS loan is a federal loan that is another option for graduate and professional students. GradPLUS loans can be used to cover the full cost of attendance and have a fixed interest rate. The maximum rate a lender can charge for a GradPLUS loan is 8.5%. GradPLUS loans also have an origination fee of up to 3%, and a guarantee fee of up to 1%. Any fees will be taken out of your disbursement. Getting approved for one might be easier than getting approved for a private loan, so long as you don't have an adverse credit history.

For either program, the borrower submits a federal application known as the Free Application for Federal Student Aid (FAFSA). The application is available online at www.fafsa.ed.gov.

Certain lenders offer rate reductions, also known as borrower benefits, conditioned on the borrower making a certain number of on-time payments. Unfortunately, it is estimated that 90% of borrowers never qualify for these reductions.

Last year, MyRichUncle challenged this process by launching a price war. The company cut interest rates on Stafford loans and Graduate PLUS loans and introduced widespread price competition. These interest rate cuts are effective when students enter repayment and do not have any further qualification requirements. In addition, students only lose the rate reduction if they default.

Your financial aid office is legally required to certify for lenders that you are enrolled and based on your financial aid package, the amount in Federal loans you are eligible to borrow. You are free to choose any lender even if the lender is not on your financial aid office's preferred lender list.

To shop for low cost Federal loans, call a number of lenders before applying to determine their rates and fees. This is an effective approach because your application will not impact the price. Once you are comfortable that you have the lowest cost option, apply and submit

the Master Promissory Note to your lender of choice.

Private Loans

Private student loans can make it possible to cover the costs of higher education when other sources of funding have been exhausted. Additionally, when you apply for federal loans, you can borrow up to what your institution has pre-defined as the annual cost of attendance. If your anticipated expenses are above and beyond this predefined cost because of your unique needs, it will take a series of appeals before your institution will allow you to borrow more federal loans. Private loans help you meet your true expectation of what you will need financially. Private loans can pay expenses that federal loans can't, such as application and testing fees and the cost of transportation.

When you apply for a private loan, the lending institution will check your credit history including your credit score and determine your capacity to pay back the money you borrow. For individuals whose credit history is less than positive, lenders may require a co-borrower: a credit-worthy individual who also agrees to be accountable to the terms of the loan. While private loans do not have annual borrowing limits, they often have higher interest rates, and interest rate caps are higher than those set by Federal loans. Generally, the loans are variable rate loans, so the interest rate may go up or down, changing the cost.

To shop for a private loan, after you've researched several options, apply to as many of them as you feel comfortable. Once you are approved, compare rates. Pick the lowest cost option.

EXTRA LESSONS

Borrow the minimum

Just because someone is offering to lend you thousands upon thousands of dollars doesn't mean you should necessarily take them up on that offer. At some point, you'll have to repay the debt and you'll have to do it responsibly. Wouldn't it be better to use your money for something more worthwhile to you?

Know your rights

Currently, student lending is an industry that is under heavy scrutiny. It is important, now more than ever, for parents and students to have an active voice and to make educational and financial choices that are right for them.

Some schools work with "preferred lenders" when offering federal and private loans. You are not required to choose a loan from one of these lenders if you can find a better offer. With respect to federal loans, the financial aid office has a legislated role which is to certify for the lending institution that you the borrower are indeed enrolled and the amount you are eligible for. They are not legally empowered to dictate your choice of lender and must certify your loan from the lender of your choice. You have the right to shop for and to secure the best rates possible for your loans. Don't get bullied into choosing a different lender simply because it is preferred by an institution. Instead, do your homework and make sure you understand all of your options.

Know what you want

When it's all said and done, you will have to take a variety of factors into account in order to choose the best school for you and for your future. You shouldn't have to mortgage your future to follow a dream, but you also shouldn't downgrade this opportunity just to save a few bucks.

Call us:
1-800-926-5320

or learn more online:
MYRICHUNCLE.COM/ENGLISH

MYRICHUNCLE

Who we are:

MyRichUncle is a national student loan company offering federal (Stafford, PLUS and GradPLUS) and private loans to undergraduate, graduate, and professional students. MyRichUncle knows that getting a student loan can be a complicated and intimidating process, so we changed it. We believe students are credit-worthy borrowers, and that student loan debt should be taken seriously by borrowers and lenders alike. We propose changes in the student loan industry that will better serve parents, schools, and most importantly, students.

Why it matters:

Your student loan will be your responsibility. When you enter into a loan agreement, you're entering into a long-term relationship with your lender—15 years, on average. The right student loan with the right lender can help you avoid years of unnecessary fees and payments.

What we do:

MyRichUncle pays close attention to the obstacles students face. Removing these obstacles drives everything we do. MyRichUncle discounts federal loan rates at repayment rather than requiring years of continuous payments to earn the discount, which saves you money right from the start. We help you plan ahead, so you can choose the best loans and save.

Our credentials:

MyRichUncle is a NASDAQ listed company. Our symbol is UNCL. In 2006, MyRichUncle was featured in FastCompany Magazine's Fast 50 and in Businessweek's Top Tech Entrepreneurs. MyRichUncle and its parent company, MRU Holdings, are financed by a number of leading investment banks and venture capitalists, including subsidiaries of Merrill Lynch, Lehman Brothers, Battery Ventures and Nomura Holdings.

More expert advice from The Princeton Review

Also available:

WHEN *God* *Hurt* AND *When* HE *Heals*

WHEN *You* *Hurt* AND *When* HE *Heals*

EXPERIENCING the SURPRISING
POWER OF PRAYER

JENNIFER KENNEDY DEAN

MOODY PUBLISHERS
CHICAGO

© 2004 by
JENNIFER KENNEDY DEAN

Library of Congress Cataloging-in-Publication Data

Dean, Jennifer Kennedy.
  When you hurt and when he heals: experiencing the surprising power of prayer / Jennifer Kennedy Dean.
    p. cm.
  Includes bibliographical references.
  ISBN 0-8024-4600-0
  1. Prayer—Christianity. I. Title
  BV215.D344 2004
  248.3'2—dc22

                                    2004012475

1 3 5 7 9 10 8 6 4 2
Printed in the United States of America

To my sons:
Brantley, Kennedy, and Stinson

*"And this is my prayer: that your love may abound more and more
in knowledge and depth of insight, so that you may be able to
discern what is best and may be pure and blameless until the day
of Christ, filled with the fruit of righteousness that comes through
Jesus Christ — to the glory and praise of God" (Phil. 1:9–11).*

CONTENTS

⌒⌒

INTRODUCTION

I am convinced of this: God wants us to bring our hurts to Him in prayer. This little book consists of a series of meditations meant to encourage and challenge you to put yourself in God's hands and allow Him to begin healing you from the inside out.

I'm making no attempt to write a theological treatise on healing or argue any doctrinal position. And I want to say from the outset that I'm not writing so much for the person who has experienced deep emotional trauma. If you have wounds like these, you most likely will need deeper counsel than I can provide here. Prayer will surely be a vital part of your healing too, but God will probably put you on the way to wholeness with the help of a counselor He has gifted with wisdom for your needs.

The people I am mainly writing for are those who carry around everyday human pain, those who are stuck in limiting habits and patterns of thought and want to be set free. Maybe you find fear and anxiety ruling your emotions. Perhaps you have seen relationship after relationship poisoned by your need to control. Maybe you sense a barrier between you and others erected by your sense of inadequacy. We are all riddled with soul wounds, and if they're left to fester, their noxious impact oozes into our personalities, our relationships, our emotions, and our thought patterns. Whatever it is that holds you back and diminishes your life, I want to tell you that God desires to set you free!

My hope is that this book will nudge you into a journey on which you will open yourself to the healing balm of the Spirit of God, allowing the Healer Himself to detoxify your soul. He can speak His Word into the recesses of your heart, rooting out lies and replacing them with truth.

Through this journey, I'll have you focus your attention more on the Healer than on your hurts. Your hurtful memories and experiences will be the platform for God's power and the context for His healing work. You will examine how He can heal memories and relationships and how He can teach you to walk in wholeness.

I am neither a counselor nor a psychologist. I am a prayerful intercessor, and it's from this point of view that I wrote this book. I have seen the power of prayer accomplish what nothing else could. I started writing these meditations originally for the women for whom I was praying. I realized quickly that in praying for either physical or emotional healing, God was working at many levels. I have seen firsthand that the concepts in this little book lead people into an experience of healing power and open them to the deep work of the Spirit of God. As those for whom I was praying began to work through these meditations on a daily (or at least regular) basis, our times of prayer became much more fruitful.

These short meditations deal with healing of memories,

emotions, and relationships. But I know from experience that when the healing you need is physical, the healing of your inner person supports and activates the healing of your outer person. Scripture affirms this: "A heart at peace gives life to the body" (Prov. 14:30). I am not suggesting that all illness and disease is the result of sin or of inner wounds. I just want to say that the inner peace God has available for every one of His children will enhance the health and vitality of the body. Neither am I suggesting that inner healing of emotions and memories will automatically result in the healing of your body. But your inner wholeness will allow for a new supply of energy to be available.

For example, you may have witnessed a person who is dealing with depression or discouragement. That person is likely to be physically tired and mentally distracted. As Solomon observed, "An anxious heart weighs a man down" (Prov. 12:25). When the depression is lifted, the whole body is energized again, and thinking becomes more focused. People who have found relief for their inner pain will have a body more able to function at its optimum, fighting disease more efficiently.

Sandra D. Wilson explains in her book *Hurt People Hurt People*:

> An accumulating body of research demonstrates that our bodies and emotions are inextricably bound together in a miraculous

merger, which, of course, we know has been designed by God. This means that we wound our bodies when we wound our emotions.[1]

Another thought I want you to consider as you begin this healing journey is about how God can use the difficulties in your life if you allow Him to exercise all His power in the midst of your pain. Your hurt can be the opening for leading you into a deeper relationship with the Father. Even Job, whose suffering was never fully explained, found at the end a fuller understanding of who God is. At the end of his ordeal, we meet a new Job. Job has himself in perspective now, because he has experienced the presence of God as never before. "My ears had heard of you," he tells the Lord, "but now my eyes have seen you" (Job 42:6). Job gained something precious and irreplaceable through his ordeal. He was not diminished by his pain, but instead was enriched through his experience.

Whatever circumstances you find yourself in, and for whatever reason, I want you to feel confident that God can bring healing and maturity to you.

I don't want to imply that healing is easy and instantaneous. It's not. And it will come in the form that God chooses, which may not exactly match what you've envisioned. But I have seen healing come in response to concentrated, prolonged, persevering prayer. Praying for healing is not smooth and easy. Rarely—in my experience, never—is prayer for healing a one-time event. It takes committed prayers who don't give up when circumstances contradict their confidence.

This is what I would say to you if you and I could sit down face-to-face. This is what I have learned and pieced together over the years about how God restores from the ground up.

As you walk through this journey toward healing, I want you to keep two things in mind. First, fix your eyes more on the Healer than on your need. He is everything. He is your healing. Second, put yourself in the patient's role. That's what you are—the patient, not the doctor. Don't work hard to heal. Don't strain to recall memories. Don't try to evaluate and grade your progress. Just let God, who is truth, work in you (John 14:6; 1 John 5:6).

◇—HOW TO USE THIS BOOK

I have divided this book into four sections. The first section lays the foundation for healing. It challenges you to fix your eyes on your Healer. It encourages you to be open to whatever He wants to do in you. The second section deals with healing of memories or personal healing. You will find that most other layers of woundedness have their roots in hurtful memories that have laid a false foundation for understanding yourself, love, and relationships. The third section deals with healing of relationships, and the fourth section gives guidance for living in wholeness and freedom. Each section has short meditations and includes reflective questions.

The arrangement of the book lends itself easily to a small group experience as well as individual reflection. You may want to spend more than one day on each meditation. Please use it any way that best meets your needs.

If you use this book with a prayer partner or a prayer group, I think you will find that these concepts will redefine your prayer experience together and give you a deep focus for your group praying. The elements of healing that begin to unfold in your life may be strengthened and furthered as you work through them with a group of like-minded believers.

Finally, as you read this book, I will be praying that the Spirit of truth will disclose to you the power of your Healer.

1. Sandra D. Wilson, *Hurt People Hurt People* (Uhrichsville, Ohio: Discovery House Publishers, 2001), 111.

The Healer

PRAYER'S POWER

May God himself, the God of peace, sanctify you through and through. May your whole spirit, soul and body be kept blameless at the coming of our Lord Jesus Christ. The one who calls you is faithful and he will do it (1 Thess. 5:23–24).

Prayer is a conduit through which the power of God flows. Prayer brings the power of heaven into the circumstances of earth. God has designed prayer to be the avenue by which the power promised in Scripture becomes available to His people.

If we take God at His Word, then nothing on earth is beyond the reach of His astounding power. "Ah, Sovereign LORD, you have made the heavens and the earth by your great power and outstretched arm. Nothing is too hard for you" (Jer. 32:17).

Am I overusing the word *power?* My writer's instincts tell me I am. But there is no other word to take its place. Power is the essence of prayer. James 5:16 states: "The prayer of a righteous man is powerful and effective." Prayer is not a benign, feel-good, stress-relieving exercise. Prayer releases the power of God to change the circumstances of earth.

In this book, we will consider specifically the power of prayer to bring healing. As we examine what the Word of God tells us about this topic, keep in mind that prayer is not convincing God or even bringing your need to His attention. He knows what you will need before you need it; He yearns to supply your need and is awakening in you the inclination to seek Him and His provision. Prayer is simply opening your life to receive what He has to give.

Ole Hallesby, one of Norway's leading Christian teachers, wrote, "To pray is nothing more involved than to let Jesus into our needs. To pray is to give Jesus permission to employ His powers in the alleviation of our distress. . . . To pray is nothing more involved than to open the door, giving Jesus access to our needs and permitting Him to exercise His own power in dealing with them."[2] And E. Stanley Jones writes in *Abundant Living*, "Prayer is . . . the opening of a channel from your emptiness to God's fullness."[3]

Whatever form of healing you need, God is able to do it. God cares about every aspect of your being. He created you to be a multidimensional creature, one layer interacting with and affecting another layer. In 1 Thessalonians 5:23, Paul prays that "your whole spirit, soul and body be kept blameless." John writes to his friend Gaius, "Beloved, I pray that in all respects you may prosper and be in good health, just as your soul prospers" (3 John 2 NASB). "*In all respects,*" he says. And he uses the word prosper, a Greek word that means "to be led down a good path" or "succeed."[4] Every part of you—your spirit, your soul, and your body—matter to God. He created all of you.

Your Creator does not disregard any part of you. You may begin these days with one agenda for healing, only to discover that the need extends to another level. You may begin with a felt need for healing a relationship, only to discover that first you need a healing in your memories.

My friend Anna wanted prayer because she had done all she could do to repair her failing marriage. Her husband seemed oblivious to the fact that she was miserable. She felt continually angry with him, and that anger seemed to grow with each new offense. And the offenses seemed to come daily.

As we prayed regularly together, I asked Anna to concentrate on taking her focus off of what her husband did to hurt her and instead to observe what these hurtful incidents made her feel—other than angry. She found that as she monitored her emotional responses, a pattern emerged. At the bottom of most of her hurt feelings was a sense of having failed. She knew that her mother had regularly communicated to her that nothing she did was ever good enough. In subtle ways her mother caused Anna to feel as if her decisions were wrong and her actions never measured up to her mother's expectations.

Anna began to realize that she read into her husband's words what she was used to hearing from her mother. This realization led her to deeper inner healing as she came to a compassionate understanding of her mother. Anna also recognized that she believed that she was a failure and expected to hear it from others. Her need for healing in a relationship was the impetus for a deeper healing.

So be open to how the Spirit directs your thoughts, and

trust Him. Know that He can and will guide you into all truth. "The lamp of the LORD searches the spirit of a man; it searches out his inmost being" (Prov. 20:27). "You will know the truth, and the truth will set you free" (John 8:32).

Are you willing right now to open your entire life to His healing presence? Even knowing that His power may interrupt cherished sin-patterns or challenge comfortable beliefs? Do you want *all of Him* more than you want any other thing? You can have as much of Him that you make room for.

ᴖ—REFLECT

As you begin this healing journey, what is motivating you to seek the Healer? List your symptoms as you perceive them right now.

Do you have any anxiety about putting yourself in the hands of the Healer and holding nothing back? Are there areas of your life that you would like to keep off-limits from Him? Remember, you can be fearlessly honest. He knows your heart inside and out. Write out today's date, and give a brief description of the circumstances of your life right now. This will be a reference point for you for years to come.

ᴖ—PRAYER

Lord, I am opening myself fully to You. I release all of my needs to You. I invite You to search out the hidden toxins in my soul. *I want to cooperate with You in the healing You will bring. Let the rushing, mighty wind of Your Spirit blow through my life. Even now I thank You for the mighty and powerful work of healing You have already begun and will complete. I claim it now as my own. Amen.*

HEAR HIS HEART

"Being confident of this, that he who began a good work in you will carry it on to completion until the day of Christ Jesus" (Phil. 1:6).

GOD'S COMPASSION

Filled with compassion, Jesus reached out his hand and touched the man. "I am willing," he said. "Be clean!" (Mark 1:41).

God is full of compassion. The word compassion actually means "to suffer with" (com, "with"; pati, "to suffer, bear"). To say that God has compassion on you means that your pain, your need, touches His heart as if it were His own.

Are there people in your life whom you love so deeply and with whom you are so intimately connected that their pain hurts you more than your own? Truthfully, I have more difficulty recovering from my children's hurts than from my own. Their pain is more painful to me than it is to them sometimes. But hurting with them and for them is usually all I can do. My compassion for them does not heal them. So it is wonderful to know that God also has compassion on them.

God's compassion compels Him to exercise His power on our behalf. The Lord defines His compassion this way: "Can a mother forget the baby at her breast and have no compassion on the child she has borne? Though she may forget, I will not forget you! See, I have engraved you on the palms of my hands" (Isa. 49:15–16).

In this word-picture, Isaiah is setting up a highly unlikely, almost impossible scenario: *Could a mother forget her nursing child?* He used the same device in a later chapter: "'Though the mountains be shaken and the hills be removed, yet my unfailing love for you will not be shaken nor my covenant of peace be removed,' says the LORD, who has compassion on you" (54:10). Here's the logic: As impossible as this scenario is, what God is proclaiming is *even more* impossible. Even if a mother could forget her nursing child, God says that He would never, never forget you.

Why is it so impossible for a mother to forget her nursing child? When a nursing baby cries, the mother's body is suddenly flooded with what the baby needs. It is an amazing physiological phenomenon that the cry of need releases the supply. When a woman's body is full of the baby's provision, the mother is in pain until the baby nurses—takes what she has ready to give. The cry of hunger is met with an answering cry of compassion. She cannot forget her nursing child because her body reminds her.

Like the nursing mother, God is completely sufficient to provide what you need, and He has the supreme power to deliver it.

Even more wonderful than that, your pain echoes in His heart. And He is so full of provision that He aches for you to receive it from Him. He knows about the need before you do, and the supply is ready and waiting for you. He hears your cry before it escapes your lips—while it is still an inarticulate groaning to which you have not attached words. Never at any moment is your pain or your need silent before Him. Even when you are not consciously thinking of it or feeling it, He sees it and knows it. As the psalmist wrote, "All my longings lie open before you, O Lord; my sighing is not hidden from you" (Ps. 38:9).

It is not the cry of the lips but the cry of the heart that God hears. "Before they call I will answer; while they are still speaking I will hear" (Isa. 65:24).

ᴑ—REFLECT

Describe compassion as you have felt it for another person. Often an element in human compassion is the sense of helplessness. Was that part of your experience? Describe how that felt.

Write a statement about the confidence you have in God, even if you cannot define what you need.

ᴑ—PRAYER

Lord Almighty—El Shaddai—I believe that You Yourself are the answer to my heart's cry. I need You because You are full and overflowing with the power to heal me. I am coming to You now, receiving Your compassion. Let your power flow over me, through me, in me. Amen.

HEAR HIS HEART

"Let your face shine on your servant; save me in your unfailing love" (Ps. 31:16).

A Platform for His Power

All things are yours, whether Paul or Apollos or Cephas or the
world or life or death or the present or the future—all are yours,
and you are of Christ, and Christ is of God (1 Cor. 3:21–23).

To know firsthand God's compassion, to receive into your experience His life-giving power, all you need to do is turn your need toward Him. Let your need for healing—whether it be a need for emotional healing, healing of memories, healing of a relationship, or physical healing—be the platform for His power.

Do you doubt that He could be full of compassion for you? Have you believed that you are not valuable enough to Him that He should long to care for your needs? Do you rehearse your failures and your shortcomings and convince yourself that He could not possibly yearn over you and ache to give you every good thing? Do you see Him as maintaining distance between Himself and you—as if He holds Himself aloof and shuns you?

Look at the end of God's very own definition of His compassion: "See, I have engraved you on the palms of my hands" (Isa. 49:16). Just as His people write on their hands "The Lord's" as a sign of their belonging to and reverence for Him (44:5), so God Himself carves on His hands His belonging and eternal attentiveness to His people.

What else does an engraving or carving on God's palms

remind you of? Yes, the nail-scarred hands of Jesus. Do you see? The stakes that were meant for your hands pierced His instead. The whip that was meant for your back fell on His instead. The scorn meant for you He took. The unimaginably savage death you deserved He bore for you. All for you! All for you! His compassion for you is no sentimental, imaginary feeling. It caused Him to step into your place and let your punishment be inflicted upon Him (see Isa. 52:13–53:12).

My dear friend, would He pay the full price for you and then withhold from you any good thing? The remedy to every pain or grief or difficulty that comes into your life was provided for in His death and resurrection. Does He not want you to have everything He paid so high a price to obtain? Paul assures us that "He who did not spare his own Son, but gave him up for us all—how will he not also, along with him, graciously give us all things?" (Rom. 8:32).

Imagine that someone purchased an appliance for you and also paid for a warranty to take care of any repairs. Imagine that at some point the appliance breaks down and is in need of repair. You don't know about the warranty, so you forgo the use of your appliance because you can't afford the repair. Then imagine the giver's despair when she discovers that you have not accessed the provision she had already paid for. Think of her sorrow at knowing that you have scraped by when she had already paid the price that would guarantee you exactly what you needed.

God, too, has paid for your healing. He has paid for your wholeness. He wants you to have the fullness of everything that is already yours in Him. Paul writes in 1 Corinthians 3:21 that "all things are yours." Why? Because you belong to Christ, and Christ belongs to God. You belong to Christ because He has purchased you. Now everything He has is yours, and He has everything because He is God's.

He is so determined that you should have everything He paid for that He put His life in you as a guarantee (Eph. 1:13–14). His love for you is so intense that it compels Him to come near. He desires intimacy with you to such an extent that He has made His home with you (John 14:23). He is not a faraway, arms-length, distant deity. Turn to Him, and you will find rest for your soul.

Take to heart the words of Major Ian Thomas:

If you are to know the fulness of life in Christ, you are to appropriate the efficacy of what He is. . . . Relate everything, moment by moment as it arises, to the adequacy of what He is in you, and assume that His adequacy will be operative. . . . Simply expose by faith every situation as it arises, to the all-sufficiency of the One who indwells you by His life. Can any situation possibly arise, in any circumstances, for which He is not adequate? Any pressure, promise, problem, responsibility or temptation for which the Lord Jesus Himself is not adequate? If He be truly God, there cannot be a single one![5]

ᕲ—REFLECT

Do you think there is anything—any problem, any hurt, any illness—for which Christ is inadequate? Is He lacking anything?

In his tender poem to love, Solomon has the bride declare to her bridegroom, "My beloved is mine, and I am his" (Song 2:16 NASB). As the bride of Christ, you belong to Jesus, and Jesus belongs to you. Everything He is belongs to you, and everything you are belongs to Him. What does that mean to you?

ᕲ—PRAYER

Lord, I do want all that You have provided for me. I do not want to miss out on Your abundance. I choose to believe Your Word—that You love me with an everlasting love, that nothing will keep the full force of Your love from me. I welcome Your love into my life and my circumstances. You love me. You love me. You love me. Amen, and amen.

HEAR HIS HEART

Who shall separate us from the love of Christ? Shall trouble or hardship or persecution or famine or nakedness or danger or sword? . . . No, in all these things we are more than conquerors through him who loved us. For I am convinced that neither death nor

*life, neither angels nor demons, neither the present
nor the future, nor any powers, neither height nor
depth, nor anything else in all creation, will be able
to separate us from the love of God that is in Christ
Jesus our Lord (Rom. 8:35, 37–39).*

PEACE LIKE A RIVER

"If only you had paid attention to my commands, your peace would have been like a river" (Isa. 48:18).

The salvation for which Christ died is a complete salvation. The word translated "salvation" (the root is the Greek word *sozo*) also has as one of its meanings "to heal." Jesus is interested in your mind, in your emotions, in your relationships, in your memories, in your body, in everything about you. Whatever hurts you matters to Him.

He cares about your wholeness. Once you begin to open your life to His power and provision, He will leave no part of you unchanged. Real prayer leaves nothing untouched. He will push through the barriers you have erected and penetrate areas you want to leave alone. All because He loves you. All because He is not willing to compromise your wholeness.

Do you hear His voice right now speaking in your heart— "Would you be made whole?" What is your response? Perhaps you need to consider what it means to be made whole before you can respond honestly.

You are made up of many arenas. You have the faculty to think and reason, to feel, to remember, to love. All of who you are is packaged in a body. Your body is your vehicle for relating to the material realm—the physical environment in which you live. God's goal for you is that all your parts would work together as one integrated whole. His desire for you is that all of you would be in tandem, operating in unity.

Sin brought disunity, not only between God and humans, but also within each human. In our fallen state, each of us is in conflict with ourselves. The human experience became this: "I do not understand what I do. For what I want to do I do not do, but what I hate I do" (Rom. 7:15).

Do you experience conflict with yourself? Do you believe one way and act another? Do your emotions rule your thoughts even when they contradict what your mind believes? Is your spirit willing but your flesh weak (Matt. 26:41)? Do you long for the conflict to end? Do you want the peace that wholeness brings?

At the moment of salvation, God in all His fullness comes to indwell your spirit. Your spirit is justified, freed, made right with God. As Paul wrote to the Corinthian church, "He who unites himself with the Lord is one with him in spirit" (1 Cor. 6:17). From that moment, He is in the process of restoring your soul (mind, will, and emotions—your human nature) to its intended purpose—to be the place where He communes with you and displays His glory.

God comes into your life and begins to make Himself known as Jehovah Rapha, "the Lord Your Healing." The Hebrew word *rapha* has as one of its meanings "to mend by stitching; to make whole." So think of the Lord as "stitching" together the various aspects of your nature, making them parts of one whole, lining up your personality and your body to work in harmony with His Life in your spirit.

As that occurs—as you begin to respond to His life in you—you find that peace flows through you. The layers of your nature are working together productively instead of sabotaging each other. His peace reigns in you, guarding and watching over your heart. "And the peace of God, which transcends all understanding, will guard your hearts and your minds in Christ Jesus" (Phil. 4:7). Jesus promises you His peace. Not peace as the world knows it, not peace that is determined by outward circumstances, but peace within (see John 14:27).

No layer is isolated from the others. All are intertwined. You may experience your need for healing, for example, in a relationship. This may be what you come to the Healer for. As you respond to Him in obedience, His peace and His healing power begin to flow through you like a river. You will find it working in your emotions, in your memories, in your physical being. His power takes its own path. Will you follow Him on that path?

ᕀ—REFLECT

In what ways do you experience conflict between the different aspects of your nature? How does this inner conflict spill out to those around you, causing conflict in your experience?

✑—PRAYER

Jehovah Rapha, I celebrate Your healing presence in me. I know that You can still the turmoil within me. I know that You can bring wholeness to my mind, will, and emotions. I know that You, gentle Healer, love me and have only my welfare in mind. I trust You. Let the river flow. Amen.

HEAR HIS HEART

"Peace I leave with you; my peace I give you. I do not give to you as the world gives. Do not let your hearts be troubled and do not be afraid" (John 14:27).

YOUR HEALER IS YOUR HEALING

"On that day a fountain will be opened to the house of David and the inhabitants of Jerusalem, to cleanse them from sin and impurity" (Zech. 13:1).

Once Jesus Christ has become Lord of your life and has come to indwell your spirit, you're made forever whole. He is your healing. Now begins the process of entering into your salvation more fully, with every part of your being.

As you set out now to experience His healing and His wholeness, get this fixed in your mind: your healing is within you. God is your healing, and His Spirit is in you. F. B. Meyer called Him "the living Fountain rising up in the well of our personality."[6] By cooperating with His healing power, you are surrendering yourself in deeper and more meaningful ways to His lordship. Opening your life to His presence is opening your life to His healing. His healing does not come separately from Himself.

His healing presence begins to permeate your mind, your will, and your emotions. The wholeness of your spirit will then spread, infusing your personality with His power—a process similar to the yeast that leavens the whole loaf. Or to use another image, the healing that rises up as a fountain in you spills over even in the very cells of your body. Healing rejuvenates your mind, your memories, your instinctive responses, your emotions, your perceptions, and your body.

The healing God pours out in you will go deep. It will soak into your soul and saturate your mind. In the book of Hebrews we read,

> *For the word of God is living and active. Sharper than any double-edged sword, it penetrates even to dividing soul and spirit, joints and marrow; it judges the thoughts and attitudes of the heart. Nothing in all creation is hidden from God's sight. Everything is uncovered and laid bare before the eyes of him to whom we must give account (Heb. 4:12–13).*

This might have called to mind for the writer's Jewish audience the role of the priest in examining animals to determine their fitness as sacrifices, since the sacrifice had to be pure, spotless, and without blemish. The priest would examine the skin, then the muscle layer, then the organs, and finally the bones and the bone marrow, each layer laid open by the priest's double-edged knife. Even if everything else looked spotless, there might be something in the bone marrow. Something that had not yet manifested itself in any other portion of the body but would eventually find its way from the bone marrow into the bloodstream and into the organs of the body. Do you see how deep the examination went?

You, my friend, are not being examined to see if you are presentable. Your sacrifice—the precious Lamb of God—has already been examined, and no fault or blemish has been found in Him. But the word of God is penetrating with its life and energy into the marrow of your soul to bring healing at the deepest levels—even finding and healing the festering memories of which you have no conscious recollection.

David Seamands, in his book *Redeeming the Past,* explains:

Many of us have hurtful memories which we try to push out of our minds. Such memories cannot be healed by the mere passage of time any more than an infected wound could be. The infection turns inward and actually worsens because it spreads to other areas, affecting and infecting them. So it is with certain painful experiences, especially those that happened during the important years of early childhood and teenage development.[7]

Nothing can hide from God's healing power. All of it is laid bare before Him. Even hurts that lie so deeply buried that you cannot state them in words. These, too, are open before Him. "Before a word is on my tongue you know it completely, O LORD" (Ps. 139:4). "All my longings lie open before you, O LORD; my sighing is not hidden from you" (Ps. 38:9).

This healing is not something you have to "get." Healing is yours. The Holy Spirit is a fountain of healing in you. He is the Word of God spoken into the depths of your soul, bringing order and light.

Paul prays that you will "be kept blameless," in your "spirit, soul and body" (1 Thess. 5:23). Wholeness is when your whole being is functioning as an integrated whole. So bring all of yourself to God. Abandon yourself completely to His power-filled presence. Let Him well up in you, filling and saturating you with all of Himself.

ᴏ—REFLECT

Think about the accounts in the Gospels of Jesus healing people. Choose a story. Close your eyes and use your sanctified imagination to put yourself into the role of the person Jesus healed. Imagine with all your senses.

Is Jesus any less able to heal you?

Is Jesus any less willing to heal you?

Isn't it true that Jesus is even nearer to you than He was to the person in the Gospel account? He was with *them, but He is* in *you.*

ᴏ—PRAYER

Healing Jesus, well up in me. Leave no part of me unchanged. Do everything that needs to be done. Be healing in me. Amen.

HEAR HIS HEART

"The LORD will guide you always;
he will satisfy your needs in a sun-scorched land
and will strengthen your frame.
You will be like a well-watered garden,
like a spring whose waters never fail" *(Isa. 58:11).*

CHRIST IN YOU AND CHRIST THROUGH YOU

*"Now that I, your Lord and Teacher, have washed your feet,
you also should wash one another's feet" (John 13:14).*

Is it selfish or self-centered to desire wholeness for yourself? Would your time and effort not be better spent reaching out to others? Isn't it a sign of spiritual immaturity to focus on your own needs?

Dear friend, please reject the sense of insignificance that tells you that you should ignore your needs and that you are only valuable for what you can do for others. That is entirely false.

I want you to relax. You will find that as healing flows through you, it also flows *from* you. As Christ restores you, you will become a vessel for His healing, carrying it into the lives of others. True healing will not make you self-absorbed. Instead it will free you to be a willing, eager servant to those in need around you.

Remember Jesus' words? "Now that I, your Lord and Teacher, have washed your feet, you also should wash one another's feet. I have set you an example that you should do as I have done for you" (John 13:14–15). You cannot wash the feet of others until He has washed your feet. Once you have personally experienced His love for you, then you are called to show that very same love to those around you.

Often the serving we do is out of our own neediness instead

of our wholeness. It is possible to serve others in order to control them, attempting to manage our environment and try to make it meet our need to feel whole. When we are wounded inside, we tend to look for peace and happiness outside. External circumstances become the focus. If we can keep our circumstances under control, if we can surround ourselves with possessions and relationships and situations that make us feel significant, then maybe happiness is possible. If we can take care of other people and solve their problems for them, we can ensure that they value us. The problem is that the externals will not stay in order. You will be caught in a trap. Your work will never be done. It will wear you out.

Your wounds, your anxieties, your bitterness compel you to respond to others in certain ways. Some of these responses are disguised as loving, and you mean them to be loving. Others are blatantly harsh or unkind, and you seem unable consistently to rein them in. In either case, your responses are originating in the wounded areas of your soul rather than from the wholeness of your spirit, the indwelling life of Christ. Your healing and wholeness is the key to ministering to others. It is from the places where you have been wounded and have experienced—or are experiencing—the healing that only Christ can bring that His life flows like a river of living water. Allowing Christ to well up in you, bringing His healing to you, is one of the most loving and serving actions you can take for those around you.

Christ in you wants to flow through you unhindered, dispensing His life to all with whom you come into contact. Let Him wash your feet, then you wash the feet of those around you. Let Him meet your needs, then you will be free to meet the needs of others. Once your wounds have experienced His healing touch, they will be the strength from which you serve others.

᧬—REFLECT

Do you see any responses emanating from your own hurts and insecurities that masquerade as service to others? Might you be serving others from a desire for their approval rather than out of your personal encounter with Jesus?

How do you feel about the idea that as you experience marrow-deep healing, the shape of those responses might change?

Are you willing to let them go?

᧬—PRAYER

My Lord, I release all my external circumstances to You. I commit to You that I will stop manipulating situations. I will stop trying to control people. I will trust You with all the outer trappings and I will fix my eyes on You in me. Live fully in me, Jesus. Draw me to You. Fasten my heart on You. Amen.

HEAR HIS HEART

"Praise be to the God and Father of our Lord Jesus Christ, the Father of compassion and the God of all comfort, who comforts us in all our troubles, so that we can comfort those in any trouble with the comfort we ourselves have received from God" (2 Cor. 1:3–4).

HEALING REST

"Be still, and know that I am God" (Ps. 46:10).

What kind of healing do you need? No matter the kind, God is as able to heal your memories as He is to heal your body. He is as able to heal your sin-patterns as He is to heal your relationships. He is not at all overwhelmed by your need for healing. It is all within His scope and well within His ability. He knows exactly how to diagnose your illness and precisely how to treat it. He has established a protocol for healing that He designed just for you, targeting your need and working within the framework of your personality and experiences.

You belong to Him. He has called you by name. Before you were born, He marked out a path for you. He knit you together in your mother's womb. He has your days written in His book. He knows you inside and out. He knows your thoughts before you speak them. He understands your sighs. There is nothing about you He does not fully know and understand (Ps. 139). Whatever you need to know, He can tell you. "He reveals deep and hidden things; he knows what lies in darkness, and light dwells with him" (Dan. 2:22).

If you will, please turn your thoughts to a woman we meet in Mark 5:25–34. Her body had become her enemy. For twelve years her body had been bleeding, and no one could make it stop. "She had suffered a great deal under the care of many doctors and had spent all she had, yet instead of getting better she grew worse" (v. 26). No one could diagnose her. No one understood her ailment.

As her body was damaged by disease, her soul was damaged by rejection and shame. The wounds that had been inflicted on her emotions were the most devastating of all. The nature of her illness, a twelve-year-long menstrual flow, marked her as "unclean." Anyone who bumped up against her became ritually defiled and had to perform the rites of cleansing. Can you imagine how many times in the course of her illness she had been demeaned and humiliated as her inconvenient presence interrupted someone's day?

Then, one day, she touched Jesus. Just the hem of His outer robe—not a bold enough touch to be noticed, she thought. She could get by with just touching His garment. "She came up behind him in the crowd and touched his cloak" (v. 27). And the most astounding thing happened. The life in Him flowed into her. The life in Him overcame the death in her. "Immediately her bleeding stopped and she felt in her body that she was freed from her suffering" (v. 29). But her elation turned to fear when He asked, "Who touched my clothes?"

She had learned the skill of being invisible. She found safety in hiding. She had so carefully planned her approach— she would sneak up behind Him in the crowd and just touch His clothes, not His person. But here He was, calling her front and center. She tried to disappear into the crowd, but she found that she could not hide from Him. "Jesus kept looking around to see who had done it. Then the woman, knowing what had happened to her, came and fell at his feet and, trembling with fear, told him the whole truth" (vv. 32–33).

She braced herself for the scorn she knew was coming. Yet she found instead that Jesus looked her in the eyes and called her by a new name: "*Daughter*, your faith has healed you. Go in peace and be freed from your suffering" (v. 34, emphasis added).

You see, He was not satisfied just to heal her body. He wanted to heal her soul. When the healing flooded her body, she had what she desired from Him. But He did not have what He desired from her. He longed to bring her into His presence where He could shower her with love. He wanted to make her whole.

She did not need another diagnosis. She did not need another name for her disease. She did not need another explanation of her symptoms. She needed to touch Jesus. And we need to touch Him too.

Not only does Jesus fully know and understand you, He also knows and fully understands that what ails you—whether emotional or physical. He knows your wounded emotions and your painful memories better than you do.

Are your doctors stymied by your symptoms? Are you mystified by the source of your emotional pain? Are you out of ideas for how to help your wounded relationships?

Turn to Jesus—reach out and touch Him. He knows all that you need.

Let it rest with Him. You can safely leave it all in His hands. He will not fail you. Enter into the soul-sabbath that absolute faith in Him makes possible. Rest.

"None ever sought Me in vain. I wait, wait, with a hungry longing to be called upon; and I, who have already seen your hearts' needs before you cried upon Me, perhaps before you were conscious of those needs yourself, I am already preparing the answer."[8]

ᷗ—REFLECT

List the things that puzzle you or cause you to feel anxious and uncertain. As you list each thing, let it be an act of placing it on the altar and leaving it in His hands.

ᷗ—PRAYER

Lord, please heal me. I trust You. I look to You. You are the artist and I am Your masterpiece. Create of me what You will. I am Yours. Amen.

∽∾

HEAR HIS HEART

"I went down to the potter's house, and I saw him working at the wheel. But the pot he was shaping from the clay was marred in his hands; so the potter formed it into another pot, shaping it as seemed best to him" (Jer. 18:3–4).

2. O. Hallesby, *Prayer* (Minneapolis: Augsburg Publishing House, 1931), 12.

3. E. Stanley Jones, *Abundant Living* (Nashville: Abingdon Press, 1942), 16.

4. Andrew E. Hill, "Prosper; Prosperous," in *The International Standard Bible Encyclopedia*, rev. ed. (Grand Rapids: William B. Eerdmans Publishing Co., 1986), vol. 3, 1012.

5. Major Ian Thomas, *The Saving Life* (Grand Rapids: Zondervan, 1961), 18.

6. F. B. Meyer, *Our Daily Walk* (Grand Rapids: Zondervan 1989), 169.

7. David A Seamands, *Redeeming the Past* (Colorado Springs, Colo.: Victor Books, 2002), 37.

8. A. J. Russell, ed., *God Calling*, by Two Listeners (New York: Jove Books, 1993), 28.

. . . .

SECTION TWO

Healing Your Memories

THE WELLSPRING OF LIFE

Above all else, guard your heart, for it is the wellspring of life
(Prov. 4:23).

The Hebrew word translated *heart* could accurately be rendered "mind." It is the center of thought, reasoning, and emotion. So your mind is the wellspring of life. A wellspring is "a source of continual supply."[9] All of your reactions, responses, and emotions flow from your heart and mind. If the source, the wellspring, is contaminated, everything that flows from it will be too. As Jesus said, "The good man brings good things out of the good stored up in him, and the evil man brings evil things out of the evil stored up in him" (Matt. 12:35).

Your mind organizes information and experiences and assigns meaning to them. It files them for you and gives them labels. It also compares new input and experiences to existing files and cross-references them so that old thoughts, feelings, beliefs, and experiences help define new ones. In this way, new experiences are automatically linked to old ones.

Because of the way your mind works, something that enters your experience today will very likely evoke emotions associated with experiences from the past. This is so ingrained that the process goes unnoticed. It feels to you like a response to the present moment, but it is really a cumulative response from cross-referenced experiences throughout your life.

If, for example, early in your life you had numerous experiences that your mind labeled "rejection," those files are filled with self-loathing. The meaning your mind assigned was "I'm unlovable. I'm not good enough. I'm incompetent." Later, as new files were added, you began to have files labeled "anger," "defensiveness," "need to prove my worth," "need to be right." Keep in mind that all these files are linked and cross-referenced. Every new experience and interaction is defined by the beliefs already on file.

So you interpret most experiences as rejection, either overt or subtle. That activates the self-loathing file, which activates the defensiveness file, which activates the anger file, which activates the need to be right file. On a computer, when you open one file, all the files linked to it automatically open. And so it is with your mind's filing system. You can't open one file without all linked files opening with it.

A friend of mine grew up in squalid poverty. Her early days were filled with shame and embarrassment. She was looked down on and scorned. Today she is a beautiful and accomplished woman. She was, however, extremely defensive when anyone tried to correct her or even make a suggestion to her. She read criticism into many comments that were not even slightly critical. She felt compelled to cover over any small mistake she might make by lying about it.

Before she began to seek inner healing through prolonged prayer, her reactions seemed justified to her. But gradually she realized she was assuming that anyone who knew the "real her" would look down on her and reject her. She feared that any slipping of her façade would show that little, barefoot, dirty girl she once was.

As she healed, she became aware of her reactions. "When I felt all those defensive and shame files opening, I'd step back from the moment mentally and spiritually. I asked the Spirit to show me truth. I intentionally lined my reactions up with truth. After years of practice, the truth is now my truth."

The power of the living God can refile and redefine your past experiences, bringing healing to memories that have been coloring your present experiences. He will not change the past, but He will allow you to see the past through His eyes. You can revisit those old, hurtful experiences, and with the Holy Spirit as your loving guide, you can "extract the precious from the worthless" (Jer. 15:19, NASB). For example, you can see the things that have added wisdom or compassion or dependence on God that could have come in no other way. You can see the ways that God was present, protecting you from the full force of your experience.

Norman Wright explains in his book *Making Peace with Your Past:* "A painful memory can become a healed gift instead of a searing reminder. How does this healing occur? By facing your memories, remembering them, letting them out of their closet."[10]

In that old memory, you might also recognize a lie that you embraced about yourself or about God. When you identify those lies that have worked themselves into the fabric of your life and have poisoned your wellspring, you then have the freedom to deliberately and willfully reject them. You can start the process of replacing them with the truth that sets you free.

ᴖ—REFLECT

I want to remind you again: Do not work and strain to recall memories. Instead let the Holy Spirit bring to me surface what is necessary. Why do I feel so strongly about this? Because the memories that occur to you might not be in the distant past. They might be recent memories. What I believe the Holy Spirit will guide you to are those events in your life that still cause you pain when you remember them. And please know that you don't have to complete this process in a day. In fact, you can't. You will go through this process again and again throughout your life.

Recognize that Jesus is going to be in you and with you as you remember. With a strong awareness of His presence, let the memory surface. See it unfold as you rest safely in the protective and loving embrace of Jesus.

Let Him point out to you the lie you believed about yourself. Let Him tell you the truth.

Let Him point out to you any lies you might have believed about the person who hurt you. Let Him tell you the truth.

Let Him tell you the productive things that were added to you through this experience, even though it was hurtful. Let Him tell you the truth.

Eventually you'll be able to listen to Him as He tells you that He forgives your offender and has already died for that sin. And when that time comes, you can let Him forgive through you.

⌒PRAYER

Master, Savior, Healer, renew the spirit of my mind. Put Your thoughts in me. I give You every past hurt. You know each one better than I do. Bring light and freedom to my mind. Clean all the untruth out of my memory files. I look to You. Amen.

HEAR HIS HEART

"Test me, O LORD, and try me, examine my heart and my mind; for your love is ever before me, and I walk continually in your truth" (Ps. 26:2–3).

HIDDEN THINGS

"He reveals deep and hidden things;
he knows what lies in darkness,
and light dwells with him" (Dan. 2:22).

Many of the experiences that color your present may not be things that you consciously recall. Several things can account for this. Let's examine one today and another in our next reflection.

Your mind, at its subconscious level, is like a magnet. Everything sticks to it. Every impression, every experience, every emotion is banked in your subconscious mind. These stored memories and impressions actively shape your perceptions in the present. Every experience you have today will be filtered through a paradigm that your subconscious mind has constructed over your lifetime. You will respond to today in light of all your yesterdays, dating back to impressions made even in the womb.

Recent research strongly suggests that babies in the womb respond to sounds and emotions and retain memories. So you are unaware of many of the occurrences that dictate your reactions and perceptions today. Some of these impressions became embedded in your emotional memory from the time when the universe of your mind consisted only of sensation and imagery. You had no logic or ability to evaluate or reason. Yet they are part of you forever.

The part of your brain that activates factual memory—memory of events—is called the hippocampus. The part that activates emotional memory—the stored emotion from an event—is called the amygdala. The hippocampus is not fully developed before the age of three, but the amygdala is present from the time you are a fetus. Therefore, your brain may have stored an emotional memory, but your brain has no factual memory to go with it. [11]

Many of your memories are recorded only as impressions and emotions. You don't consciously remember the event. This gives the impressions more power, because to you it's something you "just know." It doesn't seem to have come from a skewed view of an event, because you don't remember the event. Only the emotion lives in your mind.

But the Father, who knit you together in your mother's womb, knows. You can ask Him to bring healing into your earliest, precognitive memories. You can invite Him into your emotional memory to do a deep work that He alone can do. He can remove the toxins from those memories and leave them powerless. Remember you don't have to consciously remember an event to ask the Spirit, who searches the deep and hidden things, to heal.

David Seamands writes of his experience with this:

Again and again I have been amazed at the power which painful memories from infancy seem to have in adult experience.

Years ago when I first began the ministry of inner healing, I was very skeptical of these early memories. Slowly but surely, I have been forced to abandon my skepticism and in several instances have had to pray for the healing of memories which could only have begun before birth.[12]

Your role in this healing is to keep your attention on God. Worship Him. Adore Him. Follow Him. All the while, He is performing a sort of spiritual chemotherapy in you. He is directing healing power to cancerous memories and emotions, destroying their power to continue hurting you. He is bringing truth to your inner parts. As the psalmist reminds us, "Surely you desire truth in the inner parts; you teach me wisdom in the inmost place" (Ps. 51:6). Let Him do His work.

᠀—REFLECT

Prayerfully read through these verses from Psalm 139.

For you created my inmost being;
you knit me together in my mother's womb.
I praise you because I am fearfully and wonderfully made;
your works are wonderful,
I know that full well.
My frame was not hidden from you
when I was made in the secret place.

When I was woven together in the depths of the earth,
your eyes saw my unformed body.
All the days ordained for me
were written in your book
before one of them came to be (vv. 13–16).

Write out what the Holy Spirit is speaking to you from this passage.

Spend time worshiping the Lord, focusing on His presence, knowing that He is performing a healing at depths you cannot know.

ᕣ—PRAYER

Creator, Sustainer. Move over the surface of my mind. Search out the hidden memories. Command them to release their toxins. Let the cleansing power of Your life in me scrub my memories clean of all their poisonous and hurtful power. Amen.

HEAR HIS HEART

Search me, O God, and know my heart;
test me and know my anxious thoughts.
See if there is any offensive way in me,
and lead me in the way everlasting (Ps. 139:23–24).

HIS WORK IN YOU

"I know that you can do all things;
no plan of yours can be thwarted" (Job 42:2).

Your unawareness of experiences that color your present-day perceptions and reactions might also be caused by the conscious mind's ability to bury painful memories. Sometimes events or circumstances are too much for you to deal with at the time, so as a protective defense, your mind sets the memories aside. Perhaps you can cope with it better later, or perhaps your subconscious will try to push it down forever. When a memory pathway goes unused for a period of time, your brain prunes it and puts it into something like deep storage.

David Seamands explains what happens when memories are left repressed:

Such repressed and fixated memories can never be forgotten. . . . The harder we try to keep bad memories out of conscious recall, the more powerful they become. Since they are not allowed to enter the door of our minds directly, they come into our personalities . . . in disguised and destructive ways. These denied problems go underwater and later reappear as certain kinds of physical illnesses, unhappy marital situations, and recurring cycles of spiritual defeat.[13]

To some extent, the mind's ability to repress is a safety

hatch, protecting you from being forced to deal with events that are too overwhelming for you at the moment. But if you want to be released from their grip, you will have to let the Father's healing power into them.

Buried memories are not forgotten. They are on file in your subconscious mind. Because they are not recognized, they are able to wreak havoc in your emotions undetected. The memories are actually surfacing through your responses such as fear, anxiety, anger, worry, insecurity, jealousy, and the like. However, because you don't consciously recognize them, you're not aware of what they are doing.

Remember these memories need not be of monumentally traumatic events. They can be things that were just difficult for you to process at that point of your development.

Let me insert a clarification here. I approach this idea of buried memories with caution. I know that many innocent people have been hurt by others' claims of repressed memories. It is not only very easy to manipulate this phenomenon but also easy for others, even with the most sincere motives, to implant false memories.

Here's what I mean by that. If you imagine something in detail, your brain does not know the difference between something you have imagined and something you have remembered. So if a trusted person suggests memories to a person who is honestly seeking the truth, it's possible to imagine a scene and mistake it for a memory. This is why I have told you several times and will repeat again, do not strain to recall memories. Let them surface naturally under the Holy Spirit's guidance. As you pray, ask the Spirit to stand guard over your mind and let only the truth emerge. Trust His ability to do that.

I strongly considered not even talking about this aspect of healing, because there is so much room for misunderstanding and misuse. But I could not avoid it because of how many times I have seen a real breakthrough in healing as buried memories surface. Most of the time a person is not claiming to have never previously remembered the event but is saying instead that she has not thought about it or remembered it in many years.

So I want you to ask the Father to reveal to you any buried memories that color your perceptions and create reactions that are out of proportion to the present situation. Don't strain for them or work to remember. Simply stay open to the Spirit's healing work, and when old, painful memories assert themselves, recognize them as a step in your healing. Do not fear them. Let the Father walk you through them, giving them new meaning and releasing you from their power. He won't recreate the past, but He will redefine it. He will replace lies with truth. He will break the power the past has over you.

Brain surgeons know that if they touch a particular place in the brain, it will activate memories as if they were happening at the very moment. Even sounds and smells will come flooding back. You can be absolutely certain that if a brain surgeon can touch your brain and activate memory, the Creator of your brain can do so too. Let Him do the work. You are the patient, not the surgeon. Put yourself in His hands.

Sometimes these memories will surface in dreams. You may not dream the actual event, but you will dream an event that evokes the same emotions or impressions. When these dreams are God's healing process, the impression from the dream will stay with you strongly for some time—maybe even days. Let the Spirit lead you in examining what He is bringing to you. What emotion did you feel in the dream? Now relax in Him and see if a memory of an event in which you felt that very emotion surfaces. You may dream the same emotion for many nights before the event comes to your conscious memory.

One woman, over a few weeks' time, had two distinct dreams. In one she was running away from something chasing her and knew that safety was on the other side of a body of water. Most of the dream consisted of her trying to run through waist-deep water and the frustration that she could not seem to make progress. In the other dream, she was in a car and arriving at a party of some sort. She could hardly wait for the car to come to a stop so she could join the party. The rest of the dream consisted of her trying to get her seat belt unhooked.

The emotions from both of these dreams lingered. Although the dreams were different, she gradually identified the same emotion she often felt as a teenager when her very strict father restricted her freedom to pursue some of her interests. She identified several memories of incidents that had evoked those emotions. She remembered that she felt both angry with her father and guilty about her feelings. By remembering these things, the Lord was able to help her forgive her father and herself. She was able to see the incidents in a new light and identify the good that had come out of them.

Let me emphasize that in most cases, these buried memories are not seismic events. When they happened, they seemed hurtful or traumatic at the moment. Their power lies in how you felt them or interpreted them in that moment. Many times, when you go back to these memories as an adult, the Lord will help you reinterpret them and place them into their true context.

For example, a friend who was going through an extended time of prayer for healing struggled with anger toward her mother. At some point, she remembered a time when, as a little girl, she fell out of a tree. She clearly remembered her panic. Her mother rushed out and, seeing that her daughter was not hurt, began to scold her and even spanked her. My friend has a clear emotional memory of how hurt she was by her mother's response. Emotional memory is the strongest kind of memory. In remembering events, your brain will nearly always give precedence to emotion.

Now having recalled that event and identified many of her present feelings with the same emotion she felt then, she could go back to that memory as an adult. She could view it through the eyes of a mother, having raised three boys herself. She could understand how her mother's fear at seeing her daughter fall and her relief at finding her unharmed was expressed inadequately and came across as anger. She could have compassion on her mother. The door was open to more healing.

ᔐ—REFLECT

Do you have any painful memories that try to surface, but you push them down again each time because they cause too much discomfort?

Would you be willing to bring them into the light and look at them?

If you are willing, will you just place them into Jesus' hands and say to Him, "Do with this as You will. Use this in my life to accomplish Your will. Please release me from the hold of this memory."

ᔐ—PRAYER

Lord, I surrender to Your compassion. I surrender to Your healing. I surrender to Your wisdom. Because I fully trust Your love for me, I cast all my burdens on You. You can do all things, and Your plans for me will come to pass. Amen.

HEAR HIS HEART

"Send forth your light and your truth,
let them guide me" (Ps. 43:3).

UPROOT BITTERNESS

See to it that no one misses the grace of God and that no bitter root grows up to cause trouble and defile many (Heb. 12:15).

Your memories of childhood may be primarily happy. You may remember your parents as loving and supportive. But your parents were not perfect. The hurtful things they did or said that were stored in your memory and filed away for future use may not have been intentional. They may not even have been wrong. Their power lies only in how you perceived them at the moment. And, being human, no doubt your parents did or said things out of frustration or weariness or momentary anger that hurt you.

Before the age of eight or so, your universe was too narrow for you to be able to factor into an experience such things as the other person's emotional state or even another person's unique way of expressing himself or herself. So if a child's mother has a moment of impatience, the child cannot reason, "My mother is having a bad day." The child will interpret the situation as, "I'm bad. My mother doesn't like me." Your mind's filing system is filled with such impressions, and they are real to you. They live in your memory.

Maybe, on the other hand, your childhood memories are not pleasant. Maybe you remember your parents or the significant adults in your life as selfish or cruel. You will need to revisit some of those memories and the perceptions formed from an adult perspective. Your parents might have been doing the best they could, however inadequate or twisted that was. It will help you to remember that whatever they did came from their own wounded state. Anger expressed at you might have been anger they felt at themselves. Like you, for them every new event was linked to a series of files filled with lies. So they have passed on their filed memories and the accompanying emotions that will poison you too. In a way, you have inherited their old files.

Sandra D. Wilson makes these observations:

As children, we believed that the image of ourselves that we saw mirrored in our parents' faces and in their behaviors toward us accurately reflected our true identities. . . . Young children lack the reasoning skills to figure out that what they were in their parents' faces and hear in their voices reflects and echoes who the parent is, not who the child is. Children have no way of knowing that even the most loving parents are marred mirrors. . . . All parents are wounded to some degree by their own hurting and hurtful parents. As a result, parents may unintentionally send confusing and distressing messages to their children.[14]

As you pray, ask the Father to clean out those files. You may not need to consciously remember an event in order to surrender the emotion to the Father. Simply ask Him to "move over the surface of the deep" of your memories, deleting files that are skewing your current perceptions. As David Seamands explains, "Often we are not able to pinpoint particular experiences or happenings. Instead . . . it can be an aggregate of surrounding influences, an all-pervasive atmosphere which encompasses us with a whole set of generalized memories which require healing."[15]

There were experiences in childhood with others besides your parents. Your siblings, your friends, your peers, and your teachers all had great impact on you. You have memories that probably caused some root of bitterness to take hold, and now that bitterness grows fruit in your relationships.

Here's how those kinds of memories often surface. The more emotion that is attached to an event, the more memory cues you will associate with it. When a very hurtful episode occurs that causes great anger, hurt, or resentment in you, your brain will store it as episodic memory. Episodic memory means that in storing the event in your memory, you have memorized many physical details. You can recall the room, the arrangement of the furniture, the stance and tone and facial expression of the other person, sounds and smells that were present, and other physical aspects. You can recreate the scene in your mind with much detail. Because of this, you often stumble across triggers that bring that memory out of storage.

Now the very nature of memory is that it is making the past present. As Eugene Peterson says, "Memory . . . is vigorously present tense, selecting out of the storehouse of the past, retrieving and arranging images and insights, and then hammering them together for use in the present moment."[16] So at a moment's notice, a memory with strong emotional content can rush at you, and the anger or hurt can be as sharp as it was when the event first occurred. Most people have developed very good reflexes for pushing that memory down quickly, but the emotion it engaged cannot be so easily dismissed. The emotion sits just under the surface and will have to be expressed somewhere. It may be turned outward at others, or it may be turned inward against yourself.

Simply living in contact with other people affords many opportunities for being hurt or angered or disappointed. Your memory bank is filled with them. But another thing to understand about episodic memory is that you will remember it as it *seemed* to you. It is a subjective memory. For example, a person might remember her childhood home as very large, only to visit it as an adult and discover it is really quite small. In the same way, you have hurtful memories stored from your viewpoint. Many people have found that as they allow those memories to surface freely and look at them from an adult perspective, they can get a very different viewpoint.

I had a memory that used to surface often. I was very young. I can remember a particular piece of furniture, the certain way the light fell on my mother's face, the very way my parents were seated on the sofa, the stairway to my right. I told my parents something that was very important to me, and they laughed. I remember the absolute horror and shame I felt, because I thought I had said something that they thought was stupid and laughable.

Of course, now I know that I probably told my story in some cute childish way, and they were laughing because they thought it was cute. But that feeling or the fear of that feeling was a big part of my personality that I had to overcome. When I finally hit upon that memory and let it play all the way out and recognized that feeling as very familiar to me, I was able to identify the source of my fear of making mistakes and up-root the bitterness that memory had planted in me. Do you see that it's not what anyone else would identify as an important moment, but it was so important to me that my mind stored every detail about it? For a child with a personality different from mine, it may not have made any impact at all. My parents certainly did not intend harm to me in that incident.

So I encourage you to let those memories surface. Look at them from your adult perspective. Let the Holy Spirit over-write the old memory with the adult view. Little by little, you will find roots of bitterness being destroyed and new fruit growing in your life.

◈—REFLECT

Consider the words of Psalm 119:45: "I will walk about in freedom, for I have sought out your precepts." What is the Holy Spirit saying to you?

What memories is the Holy Spirit prompting that you need to let Jesus clean out, erasing the bitterness that has taken root?

ᴐ—PRAYER

I see now, Jesus, what You mean when You say, "If the Son sets you free, you will be free indeed" (John 8:36). I confess that my flesh is a tangled and chaotic web of lies and false impressions that are too complex and overwhelming for anyone but You to set right. Only You can set me free. Jesus, set me free. Amen.

HEAR HIS HEART

Praise be to the LORD,
for he showed his wonderful love to me
when I was in a besieged city (Ps. 31:21).

ᘒᘒ

SCAR TISSUE

We take captive every thought to make it
obedient to Christ (2 Cor. 10:5).

The way our minds deal with the perceptions and memories of the past is to create defense mechanisms. "Because a lot
of specifics are protected by our defense mechanisms and hidden in our buried memories, we cannot find emotional and
spiritual relief from their onslaughts,"[17] this according to
David Seamands. Defense mechanisms are behavior patterns
that protect us from unpleasant feelings.

Some people lash out in anger out of proportion to the circumstance. Some make jokes about themselves or others.
Some people criticize. Others blame those around them and
refuse to take responsibility. Some people are overly defensive
and sensitive to any perceived criticism. The list is endless.

Our minds have developed patterns of behavior that we
exhibit automatically, without conscious thought. You might
think of them as *flesh-patterns*. They are the ways your flesh—
(the part of your inner self not fully surrendered to Christ's
indwelling life; the places where you are still acting on your
own power)—has learned to react to situations.

Defense mechanisms act like scar tissue, which develops
over a wound to make it less sensitive. The defense mechanisms are not the main problem. It's the wound beneath them

73

that needs healing. But the scar tissue has to be removed first so the wound can come to light. As long as we don't recognize our flesh-patterns, as long as we see our reactions as justified, we can continue to hide from the wound.

I have a dear friend whose flesh-pattern was to explode in anger at the tiniest offense (or imagined offense). Her ability to be utterly cruel and vicious was astounding, but she was always sorry later. As she began to experience deep emotional healing, she said to me, "I realized that the anger I spewed all over everyone around me is the hatred I feel for myself. I had to turn it outward to give myself some relief from the horrible feelings I carry around." Little by little, over a period of years, she began to lose her hostility toward herself, and her temper tantrums tapered off. Now she is free of them completely.

How did this work? First, she had to recognize the truth. Then she had to walk in the truth. At the start, she had more failures than victories. Yet each failure taught her something else about how her flesh-pattern was activated. When you are "walking out" a process of healing—consciously and deliberately choosing to walk in the light and the truth—even failures can become steps forward.

My friend continued to look to Jesus and away from herself, counting on His truth to overcome her lie. She began to take her thoughts to Him, making them His captives. Are you "convinced that he is able to guard what [you] have entrusted to him for that day" (2 Tim. 1:12)? My friend learned that Jesus is trustworthy and that He will honor your desire to surrender your thoughts to Him.

Ask the Holy Spirit to lead you into all truth on the matter of the flesh-patterns that act as scar tissue for you. Remember that you have had these patterns for most of your life and they seem instinctual to you. You don't think about them and decide to act in your flesh-pattern. Rather the action has overtaken you before you have time to think. This is about to change. The Holy Spirit will separate truth from lies for you as you allow Him to be your Teacher. His promise to you is this: "I will instruct you and teach you in the way you should go; I will counsel you and watch over you" (Ps. 32:8).

What is your flesh-pattern? What do you struggle with over and over again? What behaviors or attitudes do you use to protect yourself? Do you play the victim, mentally listing your offender's many faults and telling yourself how unfair and uncalled for such actions are? Or do you immediately accept all the blame and rehearse your own failings and feel that you deserve any hurt inflicted on you? Do you argue and defend yourself until you have had the final word? Do you take your anger out on someone else, watching for the next opportunity to explode? Do you eat, shop, or gossip?

Ask the Father to show you your flesh-patterns and what those defense mechanisms are protecting. Only when you recognize and define those patterns and stop using them to avoid the pain can you begin the discovery of the wound they are protecting.

ᖌᐧREFLECT

Write out Psalm 25:4-5, praying it phrase by phrase as you write it.

Keeping in mind that your flesh-patterns will be revealed completely to you over time, which ones do you immediately recognize? Write down what you are thinking. Ask the Spirit, by His laserlike power, to remove scar tissue so your wounds can be healed.

ᖌᐧPRAYER

Light of the World—Light that darkness cannot overcome—enlighten the eyes of my heart. Show me anything I need to see. I confess to You that my behaviors and ways of thinking are so familiar to me that it will be impossible for me to see them as they are unless You reveal them. Would You? I bring my thoughts into captivity to You. Amen.

HEAR HIS HEART

Praise the LORD, O my soul;
all my inmost being, praise his holy name.
Praise the LORD, O my soul,
and forget not all his benefits—
who forgives all your sins

and heals all your diseases,
who redeems your life from the pit
and crowns you with love and compassion,
who satisfies your desires with good things
so that your youth is renewed like the eagle's
(Ps. 103:1–5).

HEALING THE ROOT

They saw the fig tree withered from the roots. Peter remembered and said to Jesus, "Rabbi, look! The fig tree you cursed has withered!" (Mark 11:20–21).

Please don't think of this process of inner healing as mystical. I don't want to leave you with that impression. Don't imagine that it will require you to dredge up past hurts or scour your memory bank for offenses. Simply be aware of the probability that you have memories stored and cross-referenced in your subconscious that influence the way you think and respond to situations today. And remember that the healing power of the Father that flows through prayer is more than sufficient to strip those memories of their power over you.

As you let the Healer recreate the landscape of your subconscious mind, your job is simply to be still. You will become more aware of behaviors that once came instinctively and spontaneously. You will find yourself progressively more able to think about the behavior before acting it out.

Don't be discouraged if at first you only recognize a flesh-pattern when you are already finished with an episode. Recognizing it for what it is will be the first step to allowing God to dismantle it. Be patient with yourself. It is God who is at work in you to bring about the changes. Learn from Beth Moore's experience:

You may be wondering, "But what about the sins of our pasts?" Beloved, one of the times when Satan pounced on me most ferociously and used my past sins against me, I had already repented of those sins. They could no longer be used as sins against me. But here's the catch: They were still weaknesses! Why? Because I had asked God to forgive me, but I had never asked God to heal me completely, redeem my past, restore my life, sanctify me entirely, and help me forgive myself.[18]

God has already forgiven you. Now He is healing you. Put yourself in His hands. If you need to specifically and consciously remember an event, then the Spirit of God will bring it to your memory. If long-buried memories emerge, don't fear or resist them. Just be responsive to the powerful presence of Jesus with you, engaging memory only in order to heal.

When and if memories emerge, remember that the important thing is not what happened but how you *interpreted* what happened. As you remember, think about how it made you feel. What did it make you think? Can you connect that feeling from back then to feelings in the present? Let God begin to dismantle your flesh-patterns from their foundation. Let the tree wither from its roots.

Ask the Father to make you progressively new, old things passing away, new things coming.

REFLECT

Pray slowly, reflectively and deliberately through Psalm 143:10:

> *Teach me to do your will,*
> *for you are my God;*
> *may your good Spirit*
> *lead me on level ground.*

Let an awareness of His presence settle on you and fill you. Let your mind see the reality of Him being fully with you. Let Him encourage you and speak to you about His love for you. Write out the things He impresses on your heart.

PRAYER

Here I am, Lord. Speak. Your servant is listening. Amen.

HEAR HIS HEART

> *He does not treat us as our sins deserve*
> *or repay us according to our iniquities.*
> *For as high as the heavens are above the earth,*
> *so great is his love for those who fear him;*
> *as far as the east is from the west,*
> *so far has he removed our transgressions from us.*

As a father has compassion on his children,
so the LORD has compassion on those who fear him;
for he knows how we are formed,
he remembers that we are dust (Ps. 103:10–14).

9. Merriam-Webster's Collegiate Dictionary, 11th ed., see "wellspring."

10. H. Norman Wright, *Making Peace with Your Past* (Grand Rapids: Baker Book House, 1997), 41.

11. Marilee Sprenger, *Learning and Memory: The Brain in Action* (Alexandria, Va.: Association for Supervision and Curriculum Development, 1999), 37, 56.

12. Seamands, *Redeeming the Past*, 14–15.

13. Seamands, *Redeeming the Past*, 37.

14. Wilson, *Hurt People Hurt People*, 41.

15. Seamands, *Redeeming the Past*, 38.

16. Eugene H. Peterson, *Answering God* (San Francisco: HarperSanFrancisco, 1989), 117.

17. Seamands, *Redeeming the Past*, 70

18. Beth Moore, *When Godly People Do Ungodly Things* (Nashville: Broadman and Holman, 2002), 73.

Healing Your Relationships

❧

HEALING FRUIT

"I am the vine; you are the branches. If a man remains in me and I in him, he will bear much fruit; apart from me you can do nothing" (John 15:5).

As you begin letting the healing power of the Father flow through your memories and your flesh-patterns, you'll discover that inner healing is being expressed in your relationships. When your inner healing starts to take hold, the way you relate to those around you will change. However, those people are used to the old you. They are conditioned to respond to you in a certain way, and it takes them some time to "relearn" you. Be patient.

Sometimes your inner healing can disrupt a relationship and throw it into crisis. Don't let that scare you. This probably means that the relationship has had underlying problems that have needed to be dealt with. For example, a friend of mine, through consistent prayer, experienced a powerful healing that allowed her not to feel unworthy of love. Before she had been very subservient and afraid ever to voice an opinion. She always felt intimidated, as though she had no right to her own thoughts.

When she began walking out her healing, she became less servile and compliant. Please understand, she didn't become aggressive or rebellious. She simply became a person. This was new to her husband and her children, and they had a hard time with it at first. She went through quite a time of testing, but God was so real to her and her healing had been so powerful that she eventually recreated her relationships with her family so that they were healthy. She learned that God is as able to heal her relationships as He is able to heal her memories.

The flesh-patterns in which you have operated are not new to you. They have been in place basically for all your life. Everyone who knows you, knows you to some extent by your flesh-patterns. Interestingly, the people closest to you often enable and engage your flesh-patterns. And your flesh-patterns encourage and activate their flesh-patterns in turn.

Why does this happen? Well, your family has formed your flesh-patterns, and you're usually drawn to those who keep engaging them because it's what you know. And even if it gets painful, you probably prefer the familiar to the unknown. Most of us do.

God, however, wants to set you free. He wants to dismantle your flesh-patterns from their foundation. For this to happen, the symptoms of your soul-wounds need to manifest themselves, driving you into God's arms. I wrote a book called *He Restores My Soul: A Forty-Day Journey Toward Personal Renewal,* which is about how to die to your flesh-patterns and receive the power of resurrection in their place. I explained it this way:

Does it seem to you that certain situations repeatedly bring out the same reactions in you? Do you often find yourself repeating destructive behavior patterns? Do you find that numerous situations arouse in you familiar emotions like anger, fear, envy, or shame?

When we react in the flesh, it is the tendency of our human nature to blame circumstances or to blame people around us. You may be able to pinpoint an outside cause, but that outside cause is not the ultimate source. God is always in the process of breaking the patterns established by your flesh. He allows you to be confronted with the same weaknesses over and over again. See these incidents for what they are: crucifixion moments.

At a crucifixion moment you are offered two choices: to react in the old way of your human nature or to react in the new way of the Spirit. When you choose to place blame on others, or feel martyred by circumstances beyond your control, you resuscitate your self-life. When, on the other hand, you choose to look away from the outside cause and accept the crucifying work of the Spirit, you begin, little by little, to let the old nature die and the new nature emerge.[19]

It's not unusual to find, for example, an overly sensitive woman married to an overly critical man. Or a person who resents authority continually finding herself under the authority of an overly controlling person. Do you see why the very arrangement of your circumstances and relationships, even those that seem to add to your problems, is the context in which healing will occur?

Your healing also has the potential to trigger healing in those around you. When your flesh-patterns are replaced by new Spirit-created responses, the Spirit flowing through you can touch a chord in others. It is He, not you, reaching out to those around you. His touch has power in it—power to draw, power to transform, power to bring truth.

ᢙ—REFLECT

Do you see that those whom God has placed around you often activate your flesh-patterns? List specifics as you now see them.

Thank God specifically for every person and every circumstance that forces your flesh-patterns into the open. Release any past efforts to force people or circumstances into a form that would not challenge your flesh-patterns.

ᢙ—PRAYER

Holy Spirit, let me be the vessel that contains Your life. Let Your healing flow through me. Teach me how to be the branch that abides in You, bearing Your fruit. Amen.

HEAR HIS HEART

"Let your light shine before men, that they may see your good deeds and praise your Father in heaven"
(Matt. 5:16).

INVITATION TO WHOLENESS

"Forgive us our debts, as we also have forgiven our debtors"
(Matt. 6:12).

Healing is a lifelong process of growing into wholeness. It is not a one-time event. As you learn the ways of the Healer and the power of His healing, you enter into a cooperative interaction with Him. He is always healing. You are always receiving His healing. A healing of one flesh-pattern and its source opens the way for another healing. An uninterrupted undercurrent of prayer is operative in you all the time. This is the reality of Christ in you.

Central to the healing journey is forgiveness: forgiving those who have wronged you and receiving forgiveness for the offenses you have committed. Forgiving others is one of the most freeing, most healing, actions you will ever take. But let's save that for another day. First, before you can forgive others, you must acknowledge your own sins, admit your own guilt.

Not only do buried memories of hurt quietly poison your life, so does unconfessed sin. David put it this way: "My guilt has overwhelmed me like a burden too heavy to bear" (Ps. 38:4). In coming to a place of acknowledging your own sin, you will be more able to forgive others.

As you pray, let the Spirit bring to the surface the attitudes and behaviors you have been justifying and rationalizing. Will you right now name them "sins"? As you let the Spirit spotlight sins, remember that you have likely assigned to each sin an outside cause—something that justifies the sin in your mind. The outside cause may indeed be wrong, but it does not have to cause you to sin. Today you must not coddle that sin inside you. Face the truth and name it. Quit assigning blame elsewhere. As Solomon observed, "The wisdom of the prudent is to give thought to their ways, but the folly of fools is deception" (Prov. 14:8).

So let the Spirit do the searching. As He brings a thought to mind, surrender to Him. He is not chastising you. He is offering you wholeness and healing. Admit to yourself that you have hurt others, just as others have hurt you. When appropriate, go to the person you have hurt and ask for his or her forgiveness.

You have now recognized that you have hurts and wounds that were inflicted on you by others, even if unintentionally. The people who hurt you were probably acting out of their own woundedness and the lies they believe about themselves and others. It's possible that they don't even know they've hurt you. Doesn't it make sense that, in some cases, you are the one hurting someone else for the same reasons?

Now this is not the time to beat up on yourself. That's not my goal in teaching this at all. The purpose is to bring everything out into the light and leave nothing hidden in the darkness. When you boldly recognize that you have caused pain to others, you will be much more willing to forgive those who have caused you pain. You will begin to have compassion on them, as the Lord has compassion on you (see Eph. 4:32).

I want you to fully receive into your experience the forgiveness that has always been yours. God did not wait for you to make the first move—He took the initiative to bridge the gap that sin created. He forgave you at the Cross. He "forgave it forward." But hanging on to a sin and covering it over and making room for it keeps you from the full experience of His forgiveness. It keeps you bound to and operating according to a lie. So please repent—change the direction of your thoughts. Reorient your mind to the truth.

ᴄ—REFLECT

Consider Psalm 119:32: "I run in the path of your commands, for you have set my heart free." Write out what these words are saying to you right now.

Let the Spirit bring to mind those sins of which He is convicting you. He is not scolding you or condemning you. He is setting you free. Let His conviction of sin be a reminder of His love for you. He is not willing to see your life compromised by sin. Read these words from Hebrews 12:5-11:

  "My son, do not make light of the Lord's discipline,
  and do not lose heart when he rebukes you,

because the Lord disciplines those he loves,
and he punishes everyone he accepts as a son."

Endure hardship as discipline; God is treating you as sons. For what son is not disciplined by his father? If you are not disciplined (and everyone undergoes discipline), then you are illegitimate children and not true sons. Moreover, we have all had human fathers who disciplined us and we respected them for it. How much more should we submit to the Father of our spirits and live! Our fathers disciplined us for a little while as they thought best; but God disciplines us for our good, that we may share in his holiness. No discipline seems pleasant at the time, but painful. Later on, however, it produces a harvest of righteousness and peace for those who have been trained by it.

Write down the things He is impressing on you.

ᕀ—PRAYER

Lord, I surrender to Your love, calling me to break my ties with sin. Because I so completely trust Your love for me, Your grace toward me, and Your plan for me, I choose to face my own sins and let Your healing forgiveness flow through me, in me, to me. I receive Your love. Amen.

HEAR HIS HEART

Keep your servant also from willful sins;
may they not rule over me.
Then will I be blameless,
innocent of great transgression.
May the words of my mouth
and the meditation of my heart
be pleasing in your sight,
O LORD, my Rock and my Redeemer
(Ps. 19:13–14).

YOUR FREEDOM

But where sin increased, grace increased all the more
(Rom. 5:20).

God is not convicting you of sin to condemn you but to free you. He is not surprised at your sin—He has already made a way for that sin to be separated from you and stricken from your record. He wants you to experience the forgiveness He has for you, and that requires your acknowledgment and repentance.

It's very likely that as your memories are being cleansed and healed, you will discover the sins those inner wounds have given birth to. You must honestly acknowledge that the sins you have committed have been harmful to others, just as the sins others have committed against you have brought you harm. The very same spiritual and emotional dynamics that caused you to sin against others are what have caused others to sin against you.

This realization will allow you to replace condemnation and anger with grace. The greater the offender's sin, the greater spiritual and emotional void and toxicity it reveals. Let the bitterness be replaced with compassion. Would you allow the Spirit to make you able to forgive others as God, in Christ, forgave you? (Eph. 4:32).

The processes in your brain that create memory are fascinating. Your brain divides its work into highly specialized functions. One area analyzes and files smell, another area handles visual input, yet another deals with auditory input, and so on. One area deals with factual information and another with emotion. Even within these specialized areas, the breakdown is even more detailed. For example, in the occipital lobe, where visual information is translated, labeled, and filed, a certain area deals with color, another with shape, still another with movement. Then there's size and depth. And the list goes on.

When your brain encodes a memory, neurons from all these different areas create a bond, a pathway, called an *engram*. The physical structure of your brain actually changes and is different than it was before you stored that memory. Therefore, some cue that activates one aspect of a given memory will then automatically activate the whole engram. I just find that fascinating.

The more you relive a given engram, dwelling on it and focusing on all the emotions, the stronger the neural connections—the memory pathways—become. As you surrender to the Healer's work, He will help you find the balance between remembering for the purpose of healing and reliving painful, hurtful memories for the purpose of keeping them alive.

You can deal with a painful memory one of two ways. You can let your flesh be master. In that case, the memory will activate anger and resentment. You can feel the anger as if the incident had just happened. As you rehearse the memory, you actually strengthen the emotions connected to it. You get angrier every time you go over it again. When you relive the incident in depth, the details become more fixed in your factual memory, which also brings into play your emotional memory. You can keep the incident alive until the end of your life if you so choose. If you choose this path, remembering an incident that had been buried will be destructive rather than healing.

A woman came to me asking for long-term prayer for emotional healing. She had debilitating anger at her family, including her ex-husband and her children. She, however, did not call it anger. She insisted she had forgiven them. Yet she actually brought with her a journal detailing every painful memory she could dredge up. Her agenda was to have me listen to her read her journal and then join her in her self-pitying outrage.

When, instead, I challenged her to rethink these painful memories from another perspective, she was offended and certain that I could not understand all the pain that had been inflicted upon her. She could not find relief from her pain because she chose to remember in order to feed her anger rather than to let her anger go.

In contrast, the second way to deal with painful memories is to let the Spirit have control. You can allow Him to lead you into the truth. You can give Him your heart so He can shape and mold it to conform to Jesus' prayer: "Father, forgive them, for they do not know what they are doing" (Luke 23:34). The person or persons who hurt you may not have known how much harm they were doing. They were probably acting from their own misguided, sin-clouded wounds and needs, thinking of the moment, not of future ramifications. In many situations, the people who hurt you had no idea how you would interpret their words or actions.

Can you let it go? It may take you time to do so, and you will need the Spirit's help. But it really will set you free.

Let me suggest something, based on the understanding of how memories are stored in your brain as engrams. Do you see that it is actually a physical arrangement of the components of your brain, which is a physical organ? What if, after having dealt in healing ways with the memory, we just ask the Creator to dismantle and weaken those neural connections that make up the storage place of that memory? He won't change the past, and the ramifications of the event remembered are intricately woven throughout your personality. But why could He not simply weaken an engram's connections and render it powerless? I think that sometimes He might do just that.

⌒—REFLECT

Are there any hurtful memories that you have been rehearsing and keeping on life support? Will you let them go now? Write down a word or phrase that will name the memory for you, and let the act of writing it down be your act of surrender.

⌒—PRAYER

Spirit of Truth, show me the truth about those whom I need to forgive. Pour Your love for them into my heart. I release them to You. I choose Your freedom over the tyranny of anger and bitterness. I will forgive others as fully and freely as You have forgiven me. Amen.

HEAR HIS HEART

*If you, O LORD, kept a record of sins,
O Lord, who could stand?
But with you there is forgiveness;
therefore you are feared (Ps. 130:3–4).*

LEAVE THE PAST BEHIND

"If the Son sets you free, you will be free indeed
(John 8:36).

Your own confession and repentance is working hand-in-hand with your progress in forgiving others. You are entering into the freedom of letting go of bitterness.

Think of anger and bitterness as tethers that keep you tied to a past event. As long as you hold on to the resentment, you are a prisoner to the wrong done you. It keeps pulling you back, making you live in the past. As you forgive your offender, imagine Jesus cutting those tethers. With your mind's eye, look closely at the severed ends now hanging loose from your waist. Affirm the truth—say it out loud: "I am no longer a prisoner to (name the offense). Jesus Himself has broken its hold over me. I'm leaving the past behind and moving forward to what lies ahead."

Don't be discouraged if some of the old anger or the old flesh-patterns still surface. Corrie ten Boom had a wonderful explanation for this in her book *Tramp for the Lord*. She referred to it as "the ding-dong effect." Satan no longer has hold of the bell's rope. He is no longer ringing the bell, but there are a few last ding-dongs as the bell gradually becomes still.

Forgiving is usually a process. Even when a person seems to be able to completely forgive in a single act, that act is likely to be the culmination of a process. Once you have entered into the process of forgiving your offender, you begin to become free. That freedom will gradually manifest itself in your life and experience if you continue in the process no matter what directions your emotions take at any given moment.

When the old anger asserts itself in your emotions, tell yourself the truth. "I have forgiven (name your offender). This anger and bitterness no longer has the power to tie me to the past. These emotions are not my truth. I choose to die to this flesh-based anger and live in the power of the resurrection. The life of Jesus flowing through me is cleansing me of all anger. I refuse the anger. I embrace the life of Christ in me."

Marsha's parents had been neglectful and irresponsible. Marsha and her brothers and sisters were taken from their parents time and again to be placed in a variety of foster homes, none of which was a positive experience. As an adult, the anger and resentment Marsha had toward her parents had taken its toll. Her feelings were so intense that she had to develop a range of defense mechanisms to protect herself and keep her memories at bay.

Through prolonged prayer for inner healing, she came to terms with the fact that her parents were deeply wounded people who did the best they were capable of doing. Gradually, the Holy Spirit dismantled her anger from the ground up, withered it from the root. Marsha was able to forgive her parents, free herself from the past to which she had been bound, and progressively learn new ways of living. It was a painful, difficult process, but not nearly as painful and difficult as remaining a slave to her bitterness. Even now, she sometimes has a flash of the old anger. But she does not accept it as her truth. Forgiveness is an act of her will, empowered and carried to fruition by the Spirit of God.

REFLECT

What tethers to the past have been broken? Write them down. Celebrate your freedom.

PRAYER

Jesus, when You make me free, then I will be free indeed. I want to be free. I refuse to be bound to the past. I am letting go of what lies behind and reaching out for what lies ahead. I am taking hold of that for which You took hold of me. Amen.

HEAR HIS HEART

"Forgetting what is behind and straining toward what is ahead, I press on toward the goal to win the prize for which God has called me heavenward in Christ Jesus" (Phil. 3:13–14).

❦

COME INTO THE LIGHT

*"But whoever lives by the truth comes into the light,
so that it may be seen plainly that what he has
done has been done through God" (John 3:21).*

As you become more sure-footed in negotiating the territory of healing and wholeness, as you learn to live in the prayer interaction always going on between you and Christ dwelling within you, your desire for healing at every level will grow deeper. You won't be satisfied with relationships that are not whole. Your confidence in the power of God for every need will give you the courage to begin praying for the healing of a broken or damaged relationship.

This healing for which you long involves the will and mind-set of another person—a person over whom you have no control. How can you confidently expect healing in a relationship if the other person involved is not responsive? You are about to learn one of the most wonderful prayer secrets!

The power of God that flows into situations through prayer has no limitations. None. As you pray with tenacious faith, faith that is stouthearted and doesn't fold in the heat of battle, the very same God who knows exactly how to get your attention also knows how to get the attention of the person for whom you are praying. You can surrender all control to the One who knows the secrets of every person's heart and who knows how to break through any barrier and tear down any stronghold.

So pray for God to move in the innermost being of that person to bring wholeness and teach truth that will eventually work itself out in a healed relationship. Just as God reached out to you, moving you to seek healing, so He will reach out to those for whom you pray. Be as patient with that person as God has been with you.

ᕲ—REFLECT

Name the relationships that you are surrendering to God for His healing power.

ᕲ—PRAYER

Lord, I lay this relationship on Your altar. It is Yours. Do in it and through it what You desire. I will be a living offering to You. Use me however You want to initiate healing in this relationship. I relinquish all my machinations, all my anxiety, all my manipulations. You do all the work. I focus my energies on seeking Your kingdom and Your righteousness. Amen.

HEAR HIS HEART

"But seek first his kingdom and his righteousness, and all these things will be given to you as well.

Therefore do not worry about tomorrow, for tomorrow will worry about itself. Each day has enough trouble of its own" (Matt. 6:33–34).

WATER IN THE WILDERNESS

Water will gush forth in the wilderness
and streams in the desert.
The burning sand will become a pool,
the thirsty ground bubbling springs.
In the haunts where jackals once lay,
grass and reeds and papyrus will grow (Isa. 35:6–7).

Do you fear that there is no hope? Do you feel that this relationship is ruined and there is no way to reconstruct it? Then it's time for you to think about the One to whom you are bringing this wasteland.

He makes dry bones live again (Ezek. 37:1–14). He causes streams to flow in the desert (Isa. 35:6). He makes a root to grow out of dry ground (53:2). He turns a mountain into a way (40:4). He makes water gush from a rock (Exod. 17:5–6). He causes a dead and barren womb to give birth to a nation (Gen. 21:1–7). Because of Him, a crucifixion becomes a prelude to a resurrection. Bringing life out of death is His way.

Do you bring Him a relationship that is barren desert land? That is prime ground for the healing power of Jehovah Rapha. Wrap it in prayer. "What Your will is in heaven for this relationship, let it be so on earth. Let Your kingdom come in this relationship."

Prayer is birthing the will of God out of the spiritual realm and onto the earth. As you look at this situation and it seems overwhelming to you, spiritually take the birthing position. Recognize that labor pains are part of the process, and every labor pain is bringing the end that much closer. As you move into the final stages of the process, the labor pains increase both in intensity and duration. Do not be discouraged.

You are like Paul, who told the Galatians, "My dear children, for whom I am again in the pains of childbirth until Christ is formed in you" (Gal. 4:19). Paul was specifically talking about his praying for others to be conformed to Christ. We, too, are involved with God through prayer in the final outcome.

There is no guarantee that when the relationship is made whole it will be as you expected it to be. But it will be right, and you will be satisfied. So let God do His work in His way. Keep your focus on Him, not on your expectations. My son Brantley wrote this prayer: "God, knowing You is my concern. Everything else is Your concern." Make that your prayer as well.

In this relationship, you are acting and responding from a different motivation than before. You don't have to protect your wounded places anymore. You are a new person. Gradually, the other person will change in response to you. It won't be immediate. And it may not be the change you envisioned. But don't get discouraged. Just be the new you, letting Jesus flow through you in every situation. Jesus will know how to handle it.

As you look back, do you see that Jesus was always wooing you? That He was always whispering a promise of healing to you? Even at your most discouraged, something in you kept seeking wholeness. Remember? It is the same with the person for whom you are praying. The very same Jesus is working in that person's heart and life. Let Jesus do what only Jesus can do.

ᓂ—REFLECT

Write out your personal statement of surrender.

PRAYER

Lord, I know You are able to accomplish anything that concerns me. In Your sovereignty, You knew that this relationship and this situation would be in my life right now. You have a plan in place for how to bring healing, and I trust Your plans for me. Out of this death, You will bring life. I believe. Amen.

HEAR HIS HEART

"I am the resurrection and the life" (John 11:25).

19. Jennifer Kennedy Dean, *He Restores My Soul: A Forty-Day Journey Toward Personal Renewal* (Nashville: Broadman and Holman, 1999), 32–33.

· ·

SECTION FOUR

Living in Wholeness

PROGRESSING IN WHOLENESS

The path of the righteous is like the first gleam of dawn,
shining ever brighter till the full light of day (Prov. 4:18).

The journey toward wholeness continues your whole life long; the path, like the light of dawn, growing clearer and brighter with each step. The more healing you experience, the more you will recognize your further need for healing. As you discover for yourself the power of God to heal, the process will become less intimidating and overwhelming. You know that if you rest in God, He will bring everything into focus. So even though this healing will be a lifetime journey, don't think of it as a lifetime struggle.

As your healing progresses, you will also become more aware of the reality of the spiritual realm. You will learn that all of life has a spiritual dimension, and that spiritual aspect is the driving force and purpose. Paul says, "Set your minds on things above, not on earthly things" (Col. 3:2). Elsewhere he tells us to "fix our eyes not on what is seen, but on what is unseen. For what is seen is temporary, but what is unseen is eternal" (2 Cor. 4:18). In other words, the invisible aspects of a situation are not fleeting or momentary, but the visible aspects are. Wherever you are, look for the kingdom.

Susan had an unreasonable boss. He piled more work on her than she could possibly do within the deadlines he imposed. That's what she could see, and as she focused there she became stressed and angry. One day she decided to take her eyes off the situation as it looked from earth and put her eyes on the kingdom. What flesh-pattern was coming to the surface because of her situation? She began to ask the Lord to show her what He was doing and why He had her in this stressful situation.

She soon realized that she feared addressing the situation with her boss because she thought he would fire her. That led her to understand that her faith was misplaced—she was trusting her boss's power over her rather than God's power for her. When she addressed the situation with her boss, he was amazed to find out that he was being unreasonable. Because she never said anything about it, he assumed she was just fine with the way things were. When Susan began to look for the kingdom, recognizing the spiritual dynamics of her situation, God was able to use it to further mature her and move her toward wholeness.

As you recognize the spiritual dynamics of each situation that comes into your life, train yourself to focus on growing through it. What emotions and responses are brought to the surface by a situation? Could it be that your responses are revealing hidden toxins, and the Healer is drawing them out in order to rid you of them? God could be allowing certain circumstances in your life to further your healing. They can act as a spiritual poultice, drawing out infection.

ᖇ—REFLECT

What situation right now is God using as a spiritual poultice?

Will you ask Him to help you replace any anxiety or anger you have in this situation with thanksgiving for the further healing God wants to use it for? Focus on each word of this verse:

"Do not be anxious about anything, but in everything, by prayer and petition, with thanksgiving, present your requests to God. And the peace of God, which transcends all understanding, will guard your hearts and your minds in Christ Jesus"
(Phil. 4:6–7).

ᖇ—PRAYER

Thank You, Lord, for every situation that is bringing out the flesh-patterns in me. I acknowledge that this is part of the healing I have asked You for. You are answering my heart's cry for wholeness. I place myself in Your healing hands and gratefully walk the path You have laid out. Amen.

HEAR HIS HEART

"Consider it pure joy, my brothers, whenever you face trials of many kinds, because you know that the testing of your faith develops perseverance. Perseverance

must finish its work so that you may be mature and complete, not lacking anything" (James 1:2–4).

THE FINISHING TOUCH

Do not conform any longer to the pattern of this world,
but be transformed by the renewing of your mind. Then
you will be able to test and approve what God's will is
—his good, pleasing and perfect will (Rom. 12:2).

As you learn to live in wholeness, you'll become more and more familiar with the reality of having to let go. Another word for that is *relinquishment*. It means "leave behind; give up; release; to give over possession or control of." [20] When you find the secret of relinquishment, you have come upon one of the most powerful weapons in the healing arsenal. I call this a weapon because many people mistakenly think of it as a weak or passive word. In its spiritual context, it is an aggressive and strong word.

The ability to relinquish is rooted in a full and total confidence in God. Your ability to relinquish grows with your experience of God's faithfulness. When you have relied on Him and seen how trustworthy He is, you'll find that relinquishing your control comes more easily. "Your promises have been thoroughly tested, and your servant loves them" (Ps. 119:140). At first, relinquishment will be difficult and feel risky, but with practice it will become your way of living. You will feel at home in it.

God has placed in your mind a hope and an expectation of healing and wholeness. This comes from Him. If "the whole creation has been groaning" to be renewed and restored, how much more have we who have been made in God's image (Rom. 8:22–23)! The Lord Himself has awakened this yearning in you. It is the vision He has given you, so hold on to it. But beware of the flesh-based tendency to decide that it is your job to bring the vision into being. It's God's vision—relinquish! Leave it to Him.

What is it you need, right now, to relinquish? A relationship? A person's behavior? A circumstance in your life? A need or desire? A past hurt or disappointment? Here is the central question: Do you believe that God is fully able to manage every detail of any situation? Do you believe that He has a plan that He will work out in His own way and in His own time? Do you believe that God's will is "good, pleasing, and perfect" (Rom. 12:2)? Then let healing flow through relinquishment.

Haley loved her teenage daughter and wanted only the best for her. And Haley knew what was best. She was sure of it. If her daughter would lose weight, Haley thought, then she would be happier with herself. If she were happier with herself, she would be more motivated in school. If she were more motivated in school, she would make better grades, get into a better college, have a better career, make more money, find a wonderful husband, and have perfect children.

You see where this is going. It all hinged on her daughter losing weight. This was the focus of Haley's existence—or so it seemed to her friends. She did everything she could think of and made her daughter's life miserable. In desperation, she came to me and said, "Would you pray with me that my daughter will lose weight?" So began Haley's journey toward learning the power of relinquishment.

As we talked, she identified one of her motivations for wanting her daughter to lose weight. Secretly, she feared that it reflected badly on her. She was embarrassed that her daughter was so heavy. She needed to relinquish her flesh-pattern of worrying about what others would think of her. So each time she began to feel angry or stressed about her daughter's weight, she confessed her pride and chose to die to it. She embraced the opportunity to have her flesh-pattern brought out into the open where she could recognize it and turn away from it.

She found that she also wanted her daughter to lose weight because she wanted her to be happy and to feel confident. I asked her if she believed that God wanted her daughter to be happy. She agreed that He did. I asked her if God knew exactly what would bring her daughter happiness. We agreed that a trusting walk with Him would be the key to her daughter's happiness, not her weight. And that's what we began to pray for her daughter. The tension in their house gradually dissipated, and the relationship improved. Haley quit trying to control her daughter's eating habits. Her daughter has not lost weight, but she is involved in a small group Bible study and is growing spiritually. Her countenance, once dour, has become cheerful and happy. It is only the beginning.

Haley has been freed of a burden. She felt that it was up to her to make her daughter happy. Now she knows that it is God's work in her daughter that will bring happiness, and Haley can just enjoy the relationship. She has learned that when she allows her thoughts to be transformed and brought into alignment with God's, she finds His will to be good, pleasing, and perfect.

REFLECT

Where do you need to relinquish control in your relationships in order to see healing flow? As you write down what comes to mind, make your writing an act of relinquishment in itself.

PRAYER

Sovereign Father, I will let You be fully in control. I will not try to impose my will or my expectations on those around me or on my relationships. You are the Potter, I am the clay. You are the Shepherd, I am a sheep of Your pasture. I am Yours. Amen.

HEAR HIS HEART

"Peter turned and saw that the disciple whom Jesus loved was following them. . . . When Peter saw him,

he asked, "Lord, what about him?" Jesus answered, "If I want him to remain alive until I return, what is that to you? You must follow me" (John 21:20–22).

A LIVING OFFERING

Therefore, I urge you, brothers, in view of God's mercy, to offer your bodies as living sacrifices, holy and pleasing to God—this is your spiritual act of worship (Rom. 12:1).

How does full relinquishment express itself? Like everything else in this journey, as you learn its power, it becomes more than something you do only at certain times. It becomes a way of life—a living surrender, a living sacrifice.

My son Brantley recently taught this about surrender: "Let your every prayer become, 'God, all I want is what You want. Whatever You want to do, let it flow through me.'" Do you realize that when God flows through you, His healing power is flowing? Because He Himself is our healing—not just our Healer, but our healing.

Christ in you begins to flow through you like rivers of living water. Wherever a river flows, it changes the landscape. Nothing in the river's path remains the same. In the same way, Jesus rearranges the landscape of your mind, your will, and your emotions. They become the reflection of Him. They become the conduits through which He expresses Himself. Like Him, you will learn to say, "I have come . . . not to do my will but to do the will of him who sent me" (John 6:38). Over the course of your life, your will and your desires are being shaped to match His. He is using everything in your life to shape you into what He has destined you for (Rom. 8:29).

His healing power flows through you and from you. As you lay aside your old patterns of behavior and ways of thinking, your growing wholeness will impact those around you. Why? Because you are navigating new territory, walking a new path. When the Israelites crossed over the Jordan River into the land of Canaan, they were told to keep their eyes on the ark of the covenant, the symbol of God's presence. You, too, must keep your eyes on the Lord, and "then you will know which way to go, since you have never been this way before" (Josh. 3:4). What an adventure you embarked on!

I want to encourage you to walk in the wholeness and healing that unfolds more every day. The old ways don't work anymore. Learn the new ways.

As you walk with the Healer, you will have a different perspective on all situations. Every situation that God allows in your life has the potential to bring deeper healing and greater growth and maturity. When you respond to situations from this perspective, the whole texture of your life changes. Events, circumstances, and personalities will not define your days. You will be defining your life more purposefully, based on your values and beliefs. You'll be impacted by your reactions, of course, but you won't be a slave to them anymore. This is our freedom in Christ.

A friend of mine wrote this to me: "It used to be that when anyone around me was in a bad mood, I immediately thought it was directed at me. So I became angry and defensive. If someone else was in a bad mood, then I was forced to be in a bad mood. But I'm a new woman now. I'll decide my own mood, thank you!"

If the Son makes you free, you are free indeed.

ᴓ—REFLECT

How can relinquishment make more room for healing in your life?

ᴓ—PRAYER

Father, all I want is what You want. Amen.

HEAR HIS HEART

"It is for freedom that Christ has set us free. Stand firm, then, and do not let yourselves be burdened again by a yoke of slavery" (Gal. 5:1).

❧

GOD'S WORKMANSHIP

But I trust in you, O LORD;
I say, "You are my God."
My times are in your hands (Ps. 31:14–15).

You are a person of destiny. Before you were born, God had assigned you a purpose—a reason for being. You do not exist by chance. Nothing about you is random. He has been bringing you into that destiny from the moment of your conception—in fact, even before that. In the circumstances that led up to your birth, in the generations of your ancestors, and that which was passed from one generation to the next, in the time assigned you in history—all were laying the foundation for your destiny.

The process of healing is part of your progress toward your destiny. Your wounds have set the stage for God to move in your life and form you into "that for which Christ Jesus took hold of" you (Phil. 3:12). What has been formed in you on your journey from woundedness to wholeness has made your life richer than it would have been if you had never been wounded. I know that may be hard to accept, but I believe with all my heart that it's true. The beautifully designed, intricately woven, brilliantly created masterpiece that you are becoming owes its depth and beauty to the method of the Master who is forming you. Your wounds can become beautiful in His hands. Just think of Jesus' wounds.

The body of His resurrection was perfect and eternal. It is the very body in which He ascended from earth to take His place at the right hand of the Father. This perfect, resurrected body retained its scars.

How often our pride, or our mistaken sense that we need to present a perfect front to those in our care, causes us to think of our wounds and our scars as something to hide; something ugly; something demeaning; something that lessens our value. But look at Jesus. Look at what Jesus thought of His wounds. "Here, Thomas. Look at My wounds. Touch My scars. These are the proof of My resurrection. I bear the marks of death, but I am alive!" Jesus knew His wounds were beautiful.

Thomas said, "Unless I see the nail marks in his hands and put my finger where the nails were, and put my hand into his side, I will not believe it" (John 20:25). My friend, hurting people are doubting the life of Christ in us, you and me. "Unless I see your wounds, I will not believe it. Unless I see your scars I cannot trust your message of hope and resurrection."

. . . At the places where I am broken, the power of Christ is authenticated in me for others. Where I have submitted to the crucifixion, the resurrection is put on display. I can say, "Look at my wounds. Touch my scars. I have death-wounds, but I am alive." I can wear my wounds without shame. They tell a resurrection story.[21]

Do you feel angry with God about your wounds? You can admit that anger to Him. He already knows about it. Express all of it to Him, and you will find His healing flowing even more. Move to a moment when you can, even without feeling it, thank Him for what He is creating out of the chaos and the hurts in your life. Praise does not change your circumstances, but it alters your viewpoint.

Who are you that you would not have been unless you had experienced the hurts in your life? What do you know that you could not have known apart from the disappointments you have suffered? What can you do that you learned in the crucible of your pain?

ᔐ—REFLECT

Can you see how your scars are the very instruments of healing for those around you? Spend some time thinking about and describing the beauty of your wounds.

ᔐ—PRAYER

My Lord, thank You for accepting my feelings as they are. Thank You for loving me enough to let me express myself honestly to You. My heart is safe when it rests in You. Amen.

HEAR HIS HEART

But we have this treasure in jars of clay to show that this all-surpassing power is from God and not from us. We are hard pressed on every side, but not crushed; perplexed, but not in despair; persecuted, but not abandoned; struck down, but not destroyed. We always carry around in our body the death of Jesus, so that the life of Jesus may also be revealed in our body (2 Cor. 4:7–10).

THE SURGEON'S SCALPEL

*Before a word is on my tongue
you know it completely, O LORD (Ps. 139:4).*

As you deal with your emotions and your memories, be completely honest with God. You don't need to have acceptable feelings or use cautious words. You won't shock the Almighty. Before a word is even on your tongue, He knows all about it. Before a thought has taken the shape of words, while it is still unformed and raw, He knows it completely.

Look at Simon Peter's experience.

"Simon, Simon, Satan has asked to sift you as wheat. But I have prayed for you, Simon, that your faith may not fail. And when you have turned back, strengthen your brothers" (Luke 22:31–32).

Jesus is telling Simon that Satan himself has asked permission to put him to the test. Obviously if Satan asked permission, God could have denied him that permission. No doubt, God had denied him numerous times before. But this time Satan was given permission to tempt Simon.

Why? God knew before the event that Peter would be defeated by the test. However, the Father also knew that he would repent and turn back again. So the Lord's plan was to use Peter's failure and subsequent repentance and restoration to strengthen believers. Peter's failure and Jesus' response to him would mark Peter for the rest of his life. But through Simon Peter's failure, God would be able to accomplish and teach things that He could not have if Peter had never fallen.

Have you ever thought of your failures in this light? It changes your point of view, doesn't it? I'm not saying that God is pleased when we fail, but I am saying that we don't need to give in to despair over it. We shouldn't give up, because God doesn't give up on us. As the psalmist wrote,

> *As far as the east is from the west,*
> *so far has he removed our transgressions from us.*
> *As a father has compassion on his children,*
> *so the LORD has compassion on those who fear him;*
> *for he knows how we are formed,*
> *he remembers that we are dust (Ps. 103:12–14).*

Deep down, when you've failed or been hurt by others' failings, you may have had the same feeling as Gideon: "'If the Lord is with us, why has all this happened to us?'" (Judg. 6:13). When a thought like this has begun to worm its way into your consciousness, have you pushed it back down? Did you think it was sinful or disrespectful? Did you fear that God would be angry with you? Take courage; He knows we are fragile, and He has compassion on us. Speak your true and honest feelings to Him. Do you feel angry with Him? Trust

His love enough to tell Him all about your feelings just as they are.

Think of it as surgery. You are opening yourself, exposing all the hidden hurt and anger. You've kept it hidden because it seemed wrong to you to let yourself be angry with God. But now you are laying your inner self open and letting Him reach in and pull all the anger out. It may hurt while it is happening, and you may be sore for a while afterward, but this is a healing wound.

ᴑ—REFLECT

How do you feel about the details of your past being the seeds of your future welfare?

ᴑ—PRAYER

Lord, here I am. I bring You my confusion and my anger. Thank You for remembering my fragile frame and for wanting honesty more than right-sounding words. Amen.

HEAR HIS HEART

Therefore, since we have a great high priest who has gone through the heavens, Jesus the Son of God, let us hold firmly to the faith we profess. For we do not have a high priest who is unable to sympathize with our weaknesses, but we have one who has been tempted in every way, just as we are—yet was without sin. Let us then approach the throne of grace with confidence, so that we may receive mercy and find grace to help us in our time of need (Heb. 4:14–16).

A NEW THING

"See, I am doing a new thing!
Now it springs up; do you not perceive it?
I am making a way in the desert
and streams in the wasteland" (Isa. 43:19).

I hardly know who I am anymore. I don't recognize my-self. I've forgotten how it feels to be pain-free," wrote a friend who had been progressively healed of fibromyalgia, a disease that causes muscle and joint pain. She went on to describe the spiritual and emotional crisis she experienced because now she had to completely redefine herself and learn a new way to live. Amazing, isn't it? She had suffered so much pain for years that she wasn't sure how to live without it.

It is the same for our emotional pain. We make a truce with it. We learn to live with it. We let it define our lives. It is so much a part of us that we don't even notice it. When it is gone, or when it begins to lessen, we get disoriented. All the behaviors and all the flesh-patterns that I have thought of as "me" are no longer effective. I'm someone altogether new.

When Moses led the Israelites out of Egypt, they knew nothing but slavery. Although they were free, they still cringed in fear when the unexpected happened. And when the conditions of their freedom got a little rough, they longed for the predictable, familiar "security" of their life in Egypt. They grumbled to Moses, "If only we had died by the LORD's hand

131

in Egypt! There we sat around pots of meat and ate all the food we wanted, but you have brought us out into this desert to starve this entire assembly to death" (Exod. 16:3). They had twisted their journey to life into a death march!

You, too, are being freed from bondage to hurt, unconfessed sin, and painful memories. The journey you're taking may get pretty scary sometimes. But learn from the Israelites, and don't yearn to return to what enslaved you. Don't take the pain of new birth and life and distort it into a picture of death. It's time now to learn the new way of the Spirit, leaving behind the old way of the flesh. Let go of the old and take hold of the new with both hands. God is doing a new thing in you. Now it springs up all around you. Look for it. Expect it. Say yes to it!

ᐤ—REFLECT

Look around you. What new things is God doing? How do they make you feel? What seems more bearable to you: the old familiar pain or the pain of new birth? What are you risking if you turn back?

ᐤ—PRAYER

Healer, Restorer, Lord, teach me Your way. Guide me in Your truth. Show me what You are doing. I am an entirely new creation. Amen.

HEAR HIS HEART

*Therefore, if anyone is in Christ, he is a new creation;
the old has gone, the new has come! All this is from
God, who reconciled us to himself through Christ and
gave us the ministry of reconciliation: that God was
reconciling the world to himself in Christ, not counting men's sins against them. And he has committed to
us the message of reconciliation (2 Cor. 5:17–19).*

SPIRITUAL ANTIOXIDANTS

Let me live that I may praise you,
and may your laws sustain me (Ps. 119:175).

Wellness is a word that has become part of our vocabulary in recent years. It relates to maintaining health rather than treating illness. It refers to actions and lifestyles that lead to the prevention of illness. In the healing that God is doing in you, wellness will eventually become the focus.

Nothing is more powerful in your spiritual wellness program than praise. It sets the stage for God. "He who sacrifices thank offerings honors me, and he prepares the way so that I may show him the salvation of God" (Ps. 50:23). Remember that *salvation* is a saving, healing, and delivering of every part of you. Every time you choose to praise God rather than dwell on the negative in any given situation, you lay the groundwork for His healing to flow.

Praise is not pretense. Praise is based on the solid truth of who God is. He is bringing healing out of every single circumstance. He has a loving purpose for everything He allows in your life. He has a master plan, and each situation fits perfectly into it.

Praise is a powerful spiritual antioxidant, if you'll allow me to use that image. It destroys spiritual toxins before they have a chance to do damage. Praise changes your focus, fixing your eyes on the Supplier more than on the need. Just try to remain discouraged or hurt in the midst of genuine praise. You can't do it!

Try this experiment. At the first hint of stress, anger, or hurt, start looking at the situation for every positive aspect you can find. Then thank God for whatever He is bringing out of it that you can't see right now. Do this as the situation is in progress, not later in review. You will find that you respond differently to the situation. And the other person may very well respond differently to your response. When praise defines the moment instead of anger or hurt, spiritual toxins find nowhere to attach.

Erin and Josh Shaffer are young parents who recently left Kansas City to follow God's call to be missionaries in Jamaica. I saved one of their newsletters from December 2003 because in it Erin wrote the most honest account of moving from disappointment to praise. Let me share her words with you.

"God is so good," I heard myself saying time and again. And then on one occasion I paused. "That's odd," I thought to myself. "Am I only saying that because things are going the way I want them to go?" Our house had sold in only 50 days, and not only that, we had the privilege of choosing between TWO contracts. Our close friends had had their home on the market for a year before it sold. I found myself wondering if I'd still be exalting God and his "perfect plan" in 11 months if my house was still sitting with no offers. A reason for pause.

And then I went to Jamaica, where the majority of people you talk to, despite the fact that they have no idea how they'll put food on the table tomorrow, praise God anyway and truly believe that He's good. Despite the hunger. Despite the lack of medical aid. Despite the fact that seven of them share a one-room house and sleep together in a queen-size bed. It seemed to me that in Jamaica God is good not because of the circumstances surrounding us, but because He IS. A question of character mostly.

And so as I ponder this reality, the phone beeps. A message from our realtor. Bad news: the buyers want out. THEY WHAT!? What kind of person gives us such a short amount of time to get out, pesters us to leave one of our shelves for them, counters the offer THREE times to negotiate a possession time and date, and then says, "Oh you know what—never mind." I was steaming. We had turned down a perfectly good offer from another couple because this was the more promising of the two. I had spent $600 to change our Christmas tickets because we wouldn't be flying out of Kansas City anymore. I wanted to scream and throw something.

And then it all came together. God is good, not because of our circumstances. God is good because that's WHO HE IS. Not because things are happy for me. Not because we have material things or health or children or jobs. It wasn't really a settling fact immediately. I used the words "freaks" and "jerks" more times than I'd like to admit in the following days. But gradually I began to realize that if I held to the idea that God is good BECAUSE I FEEL GOOD, then the oppo-site would mean that God is not good if I'm suffering in some way. And that's just not true. God is good all the time.

And so I've been mulling over this fact as it relates to many aspects of my life and recalling verses like, "God is light; in Him there is no darkness at all." And thinking about how shallow I can be, and how my emotions so often rule my thoughts. Our house is NOT sold. Our house has NO current offers. We're moving on the 14th anyway. And God is good.

Got it? *God is good!*

So ask the Father to create a heart of worship and praise in you. Invite Him to fill your mouth with His praise so that your lips overflow with it (see Ps. 71:8; 119:171).

ᕤ—REFLECT

Spend time praising God right now. Ask the Spirit to call your heart back to praise all day so that a steady sound of praise and worship ascends from your heart today.

ᕤ—PRAYER

Lord, make me a praise to You in the earth. Let praise rise from me spontaneously, as my first response to anything that comes my way. All my springs of joy are in You. My praise is the proof of my confidence in You. Amen.

HEAR HIS HEART

For you have been my hope, O Sovereign LORD,
my confidence since my youth.
From birth I have relied on you;
you brought me forth from my mother's womb.
I will ever praise you (Ps. 71:5–6).

WHOLENESS

Do not be wise in your own eyes;
fear the LORD and shun evil.
This will bring health to your body
and nourishment to your bones (Prov. 3:7–8).

You can maintain your spiritual, emotional, mental, and relational health by the daily practice of the spiritual disciplines. Even your physical health can be promoted and enhanced by opening your life to the power and provision of God through these disciplines. Knowing God at progressively deeper and more intimate levels, the Bible says, will add fullness to your days, years to your life, healing to your body, and refreshment to your bones (see Prov. 3:1–8; 4:20–22).

This is not to suggest that physical illness is a punishment or that it indicates a lack of faith. Not at all. But it does state in strong and clear terms that keeping your life open to God results in a flow of power that fills your soul and even affects your body.

What are the spiritual disciplines? Traditionally, they are these five:

- Consistent intake of the Word, digesting it and allowing it to bring life and light into your inner self.

- Living a praying life—a life engaged in ongoing and habitual give-and-take with the Father.

- Fellowship with other believers.

- Fasting as the Lord leads, centering your heart on the sustenance you receive from the spiritual realm.

- Tithing and generosity, a sweet-smelling aroma to God.

Ask the Lord to help you develop a spiritually disciplined life, which is essentially a life made open to God's presence and power and love. It is a life to which God has full access and can move and work in all His healing power to bring wholeness at levels too deep for words. He can strip memories of their power to hurt; He can drain off all the sin-infection. As you engage in the disciplines, He will do the work that He alone can do.

ᵔ—REFLECT

What would you identify as the most life-changing truth God has taught you through this experience with healing prayer? How have you changed as a result of healing prayer?

ᵔ—PRAYER

Almighty God, Creator of heaven and earth, Sustainer of all matter and substance, I believe that Your power works in my

mortal body. I believe that the very Spirit that raised Jesus
from the dead lives in me. I embrace You and all of Your plan
for me. Amen.

Hear His Heart

*"Those who live in accordance with the Spirit
have their minds set on what the Spirit
desires. The mind . . . controlled by the
Spirit is life and peace"* (Rom. 8:5–6).

CONCLUSION

For this reason, ever since I heard about your faith in the Lord Jesus and your love for all the saints, I have not stopped giving thanks for you, remembering you in my prayers. I keep asking that the God of our Lord Jesus Christ, the glorious Father, may give you the Spirit of wisdom and revelation, so that you may know him better. I pray also that the eyes of your heart may be enlightened in order that you may know the hope to which he has called you, the riches of his glorious inheritance in the saints, and his incomparably great power for us who believe. That power is like the working of his mighty strength, which he exerted in Christ when he raised him from the dead and seated him at his right hand in the heavenly realms, far above all rule and authority, power and dominion, and every title that can be given, not only in the present age but also in the one to come. And God placed all things under his feet and appointed him to be head over everything for the church, which is his body, the fullness of him who fills everything in every way (Eph. 1:15–23).

I have been praying for you, and Ephesians 1:15–23 has been my prayer. I want you to focus with me for a moment on this phrase: "his incomparably great power for us who believe" (v. 19). His power is *for* you. Always for you, never against you. The Spirit of God will have to enlighten the eyes of your heart in order that you may know—know from firsthand experience—this power.

Look at how Paul describes this power that is for you. "That power is like the working of his mighty strength, which he exerted in Christ when he raised him from the dead and seated him at his right hand in the heavenly realms, far above all rule and authority, power and dominion, and every title that can be given, not only in the present age but also in the one to come" (vv. 19–21).

It is the power that overpowers every other power. Nothing can stand against it. And the Lord works on your behalf.

Let me encourage you to keep your heart focused on Him and not be distracted by circumstances around you. When you look at your hurts and your wounds, look at them in the context of His power. Don't feel that you have to force healing. Just let healing come.

May God himself, the God of peace, sanctify you through and through. May your whole spirit, soul and body be kept blameless at the coming of our Lord Jesus Christ. The one who calls you is faithful and he will do it (1 Thess. 5:23–24).

20. Merriam-Webster's Collegiate Dictionary, 11th ed., see "relinquish."

21. Dean, *He Restores My Soul*, 140.

WHEN YOU HURT AND WHEN HE HEALS TEAM

ACQUIRING EDITOR
Elsa Mazon

COPY EDITOR
Wendy Peterson

BACK COVER COPY
Elizabeth Cody Newenhuyse

COVER DESIGN
UDG DesignWorks, Inc.

COVER PHOTO
Steve Gardner/pixelworksstudio.net and Digital Vision

INTERIOR DESIGN
Ragont Design

PRINTING AND BINDING
Versa Press, Inc.

*The typeface for the text of this book is
Fournier MT*